A GRAYWOLF REDISCOVERY

The Graywolf Rediscovery Series aims to give new life
in paperback to previously out-of-print literary favorites.
We are pleased to bring these books back to a
wider readership and are grateful to all those who
have brought the titles to our attention.

A SONG OF
LOVE
AND DEATH

The Meaning of Opera

PETER CONRAD

GRAYWOLF PRESS

Publication of this volume is made possible in part by a grant provided by the
Minnesota State Arts Board through an appropriation by the Minnesota State
Legislature, and by a grant from the National Endowment for the Arts. Significant
additional support has been provided by the Andrew W. Mellon Foundation, the
Lila Wallace–Reader's Digest Fund, the McKnight Foundation, and other generous
contributions from foundations, corporations, and individuals. Graywolf Press is a
member agency of United Arts, Saint Paul. To these organizations and individuals
who make our work possible, we offer heartfelt thanks.

Published by Graywolf Press
2402 University Avenue, Suite 203
Saint Paul, Minnesota 55114
All rights reserved.

Printed in the United States of America

ISBN 1-55597-241-1

2 4 6 8 9 7 5 3 1
First Graywolf Printing, 1996

Library of Congress Catalog Card Number: 96-75707

Series and cover design by Foos Rowntree and Stanton Publication Services, Inc.
Cover Photo credit: Wayne Easter
Courtesy Asolo Center for the Performing Arts

Acknowledgments

Describing specific productions and performances, this book draws extracts from essays and reviews I have contributed since 1978 to the *Times Literary Supplement*, *The Observer*, *The New Statesman*, *Harper's and Queen*, *Tatler* and *Vanity Fair*, as well as *Opera News* (published by the Metropolitan Opera Guild), *About the House* (published by the Friends of Covent Garden), and various programs for the Royal Opera.

The quotations from Peter Brook, Peter Stein, Jean-Pierre Ponnelle, Peter Hall, John Schlesinger, Michael Hampe and Robert Lloyd in chapters 5 and 6 of part III derive from interviews conducted between 1983 and 1985 for a documentary on directing opera, broadcast by BBC Radio 3; the producer was Brian Barfield.

I am grateful to Katharine Wilkinson of the Royal Opera, Helen O'Neill of Glyndebourne Festival Opera, Shelagh Nelson of Welsh National Opera, Maggie Sedwards of English National Opera; and, especially, to my friend Johanna Fiedler of the Metropolitan Opera.

My four largest debts I discharge last. Glenys McGregor of Christ Church, Oxford, doubled—while typing the manuscript—as an encouraging and eagle-eyed reader. I have profited from the friendly advice and moral support of my American agent, Gloria Loomis. The book owes its existence to Elaine Pfefferblit; she has been its good angel as well as its tireless editor. It is dedicated to Jorge Calado, who first taught me to love opera.

New York
September 1986

Contents

PREFACE   11

I: RITE   17

1. Orpheus   19
2. Dionysus   30
3. Eros   42
4. Mephistopheles   55
5. Dagon   66

II. REPERTORY   79

1. Classical Opera   81
2. Mozart   93
3. Romantic Opera   109
4. Beethoven and Political Opera   123
5. Berlioz and Historical Opera   133
6. Verdi   147
7. Wagner   167
8. Realism and Puccini   186
9. Wagnerism and Strauss   202
10. Past and Present   215

CONTENTS

III: PERFORMANCE

III: PERFORMANCE 233

1. Phantoms of the Opera 235
2. The Met and the Metropolis 246
3. Opera in a Garden 259
4. New Theaters 265
5. Drama Against Music 278
6. After the Revolution, and Before 292
7. Beating Time 308
8. A Black Goddess 318
9. Archetypes 330
10. The Ecstasy and Agony of Song 347

IV. AFTERWORD 361

INDEX 383

Preface

OPERA is a mystery. This cumbrous, expensive relic of the past, so absurd in its conventional demand that people should sing when offering each other a whiskey or lamenting that they have dropped their door key, refuses to fade away. Instead it acquires new converts every year; and converts is what it demands, for like a religion it changes the lives of those it wins over, transforming them into acolytes and partisans who will queue all night in a blizzard to buy tickets or cross continents for a performance—who think, talk, read and dream about the art that is their avocation.

Opera has this potency because it is itself mysterious. Like the rites of initiation in pagan religion, where neophytes were ushered into a secret and sensual knowledge, opera treats aspects of experience no other art has the boldness to address. It is the song of our irrationality, of the instinctual savagery which our jobs and routines and our nonsinging voices belie, of the music our bodies make. It is an art devoted to love and death (and especially to the cryptic alliance between them); to the definition and the interchangeability of the sexes; to madness and devilment; to drink when Don Giovanni sings his so-called champagne aria, to eating when Carmen invites Don José to gobble up everything in the tavern; and to blasphemy against a Christian religion that reproves this bodily glory and chastens the organism in which the voice is warmly housed.

The characters of opera obey neither moral nor social law. They are women like Isolde with her erotic medicine chest or Carmen with her intoxicating flower, men like the overworked phallic symbol Don Giovanni or Gounod's Faust who, rather than bothering with good works for mankind (to which the hero of Goethe's play commits himself), licks his lips and asks the devil to supply him with pleasures and young mistresses. Music buoys up and bears along these clamorous creatures. What rises in and overflows from the orchestra pit is the geyser of their desires: they give voice to the promptings of the underground unconsciousness.

These people sing what they feel, rather than tamely speaking (like the rest of us) what they think they ought to say. Love and hate tend to reduce us to speechlessness—to embarrassed stammering, or to expletives. Who, without the aid of music, could make love seem so compelling or true as the heroine of Ponchielli's *La Gioconda* does when, musing on her affection for Enzo, she spins out a thread of pianissimo sound as tenuous as her hopes yet as durable? Who has ever sworn as eloquently as Santuzza in *Cavalleria Rusticana* when she wishes Turridu, in a voice which should scar him, an unlucky Easter? Who, without the chromatic ambiguities of music, is able to suggest the rankling hate in Gioconda's love or the desperate love in Santuzza's hate? Words are always failing us when we need them most. To remain articulate in states of extreme emotional intensity almost convicts you of insincerity. Love poetry often apologizes for its linguistic fluency, afraid it will seem specious. But when words give up, music takes over.

Operatic characters can dispense with words altogether, and reveal their natures in passages of vocalizing—melodic doodles with no verbal content, like Carmen's teasing "Tra la la la," the delighted, explosive "Pa pa pa" of Papageno and his bird-bride in *Die Zauberflöte*, Lucia di Lammermoor's crazed conversation with a flute, or Alberich's sneezing and sputtering in the river in *Das Rheingold*. The stabbing B-flats with which Isolde curses Tristan, and the instant high Cs—each one a premature climax—with which she embraces him, say it all.

Living subliminally, people in opera are proud to be amoral. Their whim or will is an authoritarian edict. Nerone in Monteverdi's *L'Incoronazione di Poppea*, infuriated when Seneca contradicts him, rages "voglio, voglio, voglio il voler mio"—I will, will, will have my way—and shouts down opposition. When Arsamene in Handel's *Serse* is denied Romilda by the Persian monarch, he sings defiantly "Sì, la voglio e la otterò"—I want her, and intend to have her—and flaunts his stubbornness by decorating the vowels. Rodrigo in Rossini's *La Donna del Lago*, celebrating his military victory, sings fanfares on the same word "voglio." Norina in Donizetti's *Don Pasquale* deletes it from her henpecked husband's vocabulary: "voglio," she legislates, "lo dico io sola"—the word is to belong exclusively to her. Nerone, the first of these willful beings, is a tyrant, and opera is an empire of irresistible, coercive impulse.

There is no question of such people learning from experience or reforming themselves, as characters in drama (and moral agents in life) are supposed to do. Some of opera's most psychologically thrilling moments are refusals to repent. Don Giovanni won't amend his ways when menaced by the statue, Carmen won't return to Don José when he unsheathes his knife, Brünnhilde in *Götterdämmerung* won't surrender the ring even though by doing so she could preserve Wotan's world order. Salome insists that she must have the Baptist's head, and spurns the alternatives offered by Herod. Calàf in Puccini's *Turandot* announces this operatic willfulness at its most ruthless. The world can end, he cries, so long as he has the woman he desires. Id in opera never learns to fear the superego; libido never acknowledges the repressive rule of society. This is a realm of emotional atavism. Morally, of course, these characters are a reprehensible crew. Music bypasses the rational quibbles of language to plead on their behalf, and persuades us to envy such lack of inhibition and such maniacal consistency.

Often operatic characters enunciate the grumblings of our lowlier natures. They are a race of justified malefactors. Wagner's King Marke, who begins by condemning the sexual transgression of Tristan and Isolde, ends by blessing them. But these holy sinners also minister to our better selves. They are capable of a sacrificially generous love which the daily ego, sticking up for its rights, would never countenance. Violetta in *La Traviata*, renouncing Alfredo in deference to his family, or Gilda in *Rigoletto*, volunteering to die to save the philanderer who abuses and discards her, both possess this gratuitous goodness. Drama can't explain their actions, which is why the original plays by Alexandre Dumas and Victor Hugo have been so triumphantly superseded by Verdi's setting of them; music, abstracted from the actual, can understand their idealism.

Opera therefore is drama *about* music, not just accompanied by it. The earliest definitive operatic hero, Monteverdi's Orfeo, is a singer. Later on, it is Tosca's profession too, while both Don Giovanni and Carmen are skilled at serenading or musically bewitching their victims. As well as glorifying the voice, opera celebrates, sometimes fearfully, the musical force which wells up in the orchestra. The subject of *Tristan und Isolde* is the oceanic life which unites us all, and that shared existence—into which the characters are merged when they die—flows through Wagner's tidal score.

In German opera, the pit housing this eruptive sound is often a hell: the shrill, demon-infested declevity of the Wolf's Glen in Weber's *Der Freischütz*; the mines with their pounding anvils where Alberich reigns in *Das Rheingold*; the hollowly resounding dungeon in *Fidelio*, or the hole in the ground where the Baptist is beheaded in *Salome*. Music, for the German romantics, seems an infectious madness, a state of perdition. The orchestra sulfurously boils like a caldron, or seethes like Don Giovanni's retributive fire.

For the Italians, music is more usually a vital joy, the human animal's spirited frisking and romping: a tonal laughter like that of Rossini's Figaro with his offstage "Tra la la la"; the delight which is frenetic when Violetta brittlely instructs herself "Gioir!" in *La Traviata* or is lamely derided when the tragic jester Rigoletto mopes on muttering his heavy, humorless "Tra la la la." If *Don Giovanni* is considered a German opera, its hero is tragically driven by music, which speeds up his life and anticipates his death; if it's considered Italian, he's a blithe hedonist, enjoying music's capacity to transcribe his sensations, living in the tuneful present tense without thought of tomorrow.

In French opera, music has neither the German violence nor the Italian ebullience: it inclines to the condition of lucid speech, and French operatic characters can read letters like Charlotte in Massenet's *Werther* or recite poems like Werther himself, can scribble farewell notes in song like Massenet's Manon when she deserts Des Grieux or even talk on the telephone like Elle in Poulenc's *La Voix Humaine*. Marguerite in Gounod's *Faust* pauses between the verses of her Gothic ballad to ponder the proposition of the handsome stranger. A French opera has no problem conceiving of itself as conversation, like Poulenc's *Dialogues des Carmélites*.

At first, music in opera is a supernatural power. It vanquishes death when Orfeo sings, it tames the wilderness when Mozart's Tamino plays his magic flute and makes the beasts dance. Later, music relinquishes this control over nature. In romantic opera, it has retired inside the head, and is the character's overheard monologue. The mad pyrotechnics of the flute in *Lucia di Lammermoor* happen within the heroine's mind, and enforce no external covenant like the same instrument played by Tamino. At the end of Strauss's *Elektra*, a choral cacophony rejoices in Orest's execution of his mother. Chrysothemis asks Elektra if she hears those voices. Elektra proudly replies that the music they make floods out of her. It is as if her exultant, electric body had burst into song.

Though music has disappeared into the consciousness, opera keeps its Orphic promise. The legendary Orpheus could sway trees and soothe threatening animals; the operatic Orpheus can do better than that, enabling those trees and animals to sing. One of opera's blessings is its gift of a tongue to dumb things—to the woodbird in *Siegfried*, the fox in Janáček's *Cunning Little Vixen*, or the laurel with its melodic fronds in Strauss's *Daphne*. Ravel's *L'Enfant et les Sortilèges*, in which the nursery furniture and the garden shrubbery conspire to punish the spoiled child of Colette's story, invents a musical language for elemental or vegetable nature: sparky coloratura for the expiring fire, a rumbling brassy lament for the tree trunk wounded by the boy's knife. The teacups garrulously chatter and clink, while the garden moans like a wild beast. Britten too in his operatic version of *A Midsummer Night's Dream* hears the earth snoring as it clumsily turns over in its sleep.

The climax of Ravel's tender elegy for those who have been deprived of voices is the syllabic mimicry practiced by the animals. They learn articulacy from the child's panic, and in their concluding chorale pronounce the word he has uttered, the first we form after our melismatic wailing begins to give way to language—the primal "Ma-ma." Operatic music also confers eloquence on men who can't enunciate their feelings or elaborate their thoughts. The orchestral interludes in Berg's *Wozzeck* wordlessly grieve or rage for a poor and humiliated hero who daren't raise his own voice in protest.

The composer Gustav Holst, perhaps remembering the Orphic bounty, said that music was "identical with heaven": a shower of light from the sky. In Monteverdi's *Orfeo* its patron is the sun-god Apollo, and in Renaissance diagrams of the music made by the spheres, each planet contributes a note to the octave, with Apollo situated in the center emitting the sound called "sol," which also means sun. The Orfeo of Gluck finds his way back to that harmonic heaven when he arrives in the Elysian fields and hears the gracious, placid music which is the spirit of the place. In other, later operas, that heaven is established on earth by a human and musical initiative—by the Countess's calming pardon in the nocturnal garden of Mozart's *Le Nozze di Figaro*, by Leonore's unshackling of Florestan in *Fidelio*, by Falstaff's fugal anthem to folly in the forest at the end of Verdi's opera. A sonic mirage of shimmering violins in the prelude to Wagner's *Lohengrin* describes the descent of grace and the Grail from the upper air to mortal nature.

Alternatively, opera can prefer hell to heaven. Don Giovanni makes that choice when he refuses to repent, and in E. T. A. Hoffmann's story the chaste Donna Anna follows him, electing to share his damnation rather than suffer respectable married life with Ottavio. They are given courage by music: by its sensual fervency and fever. So is Tannhäuser during the song contest, when the Wagnerian orchestra fumes in recollection of the Venusberg and its prohibited revels. In Britten's operas too, music is an irrational, often venereal infection, which words are helpless to placate: the thwarted love for a boy in *Peter Grimes*, for a fairy or an ass in *A Midsummer Night's Dream*, for a devil in *The Turn of the Screw*. Plague spreads from the orchestra in *Death in Venice*.

One of opera's gospels is gluttony. It delights in Don Giovanni's gorging last supper and in the gobbled repasts of Puccini's bohemians. Isabella in Rossini's *L'Italiana in Algeri* manages Mustafà by sentencing him to a regime of full-time eating and stupefied sleep. The fat man Falstaff has an operatic bulk. Opera also irrigates the well-fed body, and abounds in the praise of drinking, from the inebriated romp of the emperor and the poet in *L'Incoronazione di Poppea* to Herod's inventory of his wine cellar in *Salome*. But this physiological art—about bodily satiation just as ballet is about the body's ascetic training—is at the same time metaphysical, redefining the boundaries between earth and heaven, sanctity and profanation, love and death; and that is the greatest mystery of all.

This book begins by identifying the gods of opera, the subjects of its rite. The first is Orpheus, awarded the power of song by Apollo. After him come Apollo's antithesis Dionysus, then Eros and the Christian devil's henchman Mephistopheles; the rest are represented by Dagon, the idol of the Philistines in the biblical story of Samson and Dalila. The first section diagonally crosses the history of the form; the second section follows the course of that history to show how opera in one period after another makes drama out of music. The works surveyed constitute the repertory, and they depend, to stay alive, on institutions and interpreters: the third section of the book salutes the performers who are responsible for the current rebirth of opera.

I

_____

RITE

ONE

Orpheus

OPERA begins with a mystery: the revival of pagan worship, in seditious opposition to Christianity, during the Italian Renaissance. For the classically learned intellectuals of the Florentine association known as the Camerata, opera was an esoteric matter, to be investigated in camera. These initiates saw it as a resurrection of Greek tragedy: a drama ritualized by music. Its symbolic hero therefore, in the musical fable *Orfeo* by Monteverdi performed at Mantua in 1607, was a singer who was also an ancient mystagogue. Orpheus is opera's founder, and he presides over it throughout its subsequent history.

The classical Orpheus left behind him a set of abstruse hymns, much venerated by Renaissance mythographers like Pico della Mirandola because of the theological secrets their obscure diction concealed. These poems were the means of entry to a religious mystery; they call love a bitter sweetness and couple it with death, which the small expiry of the orgasm imitates. Orpheus took it upon himself to test that analogy by following his dead beloved Eurydice into the underworld. In this, according to Pico della Mirandola, he resembles another fearless operatic character: Alceste, who in Gluck's opera volunteers to die to reprieve her moribund consort Admète. Yet in the end Orpheus lacks the courage of Alceste. Rather than dying, he seeks to wheedle death into releasing Eurydice by employing his musical charms. And this, in Plato's judgment, is why he failed. He couldn't attain true felicity because he wouldn't consummate love in death, and he lost his Eurydice all over again; he held back from that transfiguring operatic mystery celebrated by Wagner's Tristan when he tears off his bandages and by Isolde when she so effortlessly extinguishes her own life—the liebestod.

Though Plato criticized Orpheus for singing rather than dying, the mystery in which he participates is made possible by music. For music is a song both of the senses and the spirit, and its genius for modulation and metamorphosis empowers it to represent a passage from one existence to the next. The first words in the first great opera, Monteverdi's *Orfeo*, are therefore declaimed by the embodiment of the art, La Musica, introduced by triumphal fanfares. The bards of the Camerata had willed the pagan gods to return (which is what the Renaissance meant). La Musica arrives as proof of that arcane restoration, announcing her descent from Parnassus. She extols the esoteric emotional force which is music, able—she says—to calm or agitate human beings at will, and hints at its otherworldly source: it's an echo of a heavenly lyre, playing among the spheres.

In Arcadia, where Orfeo is married to Euridice among the shepherds, music is also an enforcement of order. The attuning of the lute's strings, sings Silvia, betokens a concord in society. Orfeo's first song describes the creation of the world by music and by that light—Sol, or Apollo—which is itself a sound. His harp seems to traverse the sky, like the rainbow bridge to Walhall in *Das Rheingold*. He attunes Euridice to himself, for song means that they breathe in unison: at his sigh, Orfeo says, she also sighed. The shepherds attribute their happiness to heaven, from which music also rained down. But as exercised by men, music is a magical prescription for giving life to the earth. The nymphs sing to the earth, encouraging it to bring back spring. The idyll is almost intolerably serene and sweet, with its soothing chitarones and rustling pipes. How can such beauty dare to exist? One of the shepherds describes the woods and meadows laughing: laughter is the most liquidly gracious music of all.

When Euridice's death is reported, Silvia (who brings the news) curses her own tongue. Language with its disagreeably meaning-ridden words is an enemy to musical joy. For Orfeo, the loss is not the desolating human pain felt by Gluck's Orfeo a century and a half later, but a cryptic metaphysical challenge. It goads him to try out the effectiveness of his song to carrying it with him to the lower depths (as he vows to do so, that abyss is opened by the sound of the organ); and it inducts him into an enlightenment available solely in darkness—the eyes of Euridice, he tells the figure of Speranza (Hope) who guides him, are the only sunrise he acknowledges. Orfeo's journey from nature to the underworld is a voyage up and down the chain of being, and that chain is also a musical scale, surmounted by the countertenor Speranza, grounded by the rumbling basses who sing Charon and Plutone.

He will win, Speranza tells him, if his "bel canto" remains serenely unperturbed. Whereas Gluck's Orfeo wails helplessly or sings a rondo which returns him to his unassuageable grief, Monteverdi's character is immaculately self-possessed, and cows Charon by his virtuosity, in the fluting rhetorical flourishes of his vocal line. Gluck's Orfeo argues with the Furies; Monteverdi's sets out to impress rather than dispute, and Charon after applauding his aria conveniently falls asleep and lets him pass. His success is acclaimed as well, according to the chorus of spirits, by "memoria," which loosens its tongue to praise him: music with its untroubled repetitiousness has reorganized time to decree the past's perpetual return, or its total recall. The reclamation of Euridice is only Orfeo's alibi for a higher ambition: reclamation, by music, of his own godly power. Therefore the loss of her a second time, when he disobeys the warning and looks at her, isn't the tragic crisis which Gluck makes of it but a hasty accident—he is startled by a noise behind the curtain, and turns round—and a blessing in disguise. He is easily consoled for that loss when his disconsolate duet with himself, in which an echo hollowly repeats his cries, turns into a glorified duet with his alter ego and divine self-image Apollo, the origin of his music.

Rather than berating the indifferent gods like his counterpart in Gluck, Orfeo addresses Apollo as patron and (replacing Euridice) muse: my lyre and my song are sacred, he says, to you. Apollo consequently withdraws him from earthly felicity and invites him to become immortal. Orfeo asks after Euridice, but she has already been abstracted into a symbol of his music-making. Apollo says he will reencounter her likeness "nel sole e nelle stelle." That sun, however, is by now the musical note which the planetary Apollo emits. Proserpina is grateful for the day when Plutone, ravishing her away to his dark realm, caused her to forfeit "il sole"; Orfeo is equally unregretful, because he has regained that sun as musical sound in Apollo. Gluck ends with a trio in which Orfeo and Euridice thank Amore, their savior. Monteverdi concludes with a duet in which Orfeo and Apollo, colleagues and equals, rise singing to heaven: the first opera sanctifies the form.

Monteverdi's Orfeo is deified; Gluck's in *Orfeo ed Euridice* (1762) tumbles from heaven—the "Eliso" or Elysium of paradisial love with

Euridice—to a bereft earth. Music in Monteverdi is a divine grace, handed down to men; in Gluck, it's a human capacity straining upward to a god who may not exist. Orfeo's cries of "Euridice" are answered only by an echo. His sad consolation is what the romantics called the pathetic fallacy: he's convinced that the lachrymose brooks weep with him. In contrast with Monteverdi's theater, which comprises an entire world, hell and heaven in Gluck exist inside Orfeo's mind. He tells the Furies that he carries an inferno within him; recovering Euridice means regaining that private "Eliso." Music, no longer a transcendent bounty, is this single creature's emission, hoping for reciprocation. That's why he appeals to the "dolce, lusinghiera armonia" of nature in the realm of the blessed spirits. At its frailest, music is the palpitation of a live, dying body: the expiring respiration of Euridice, who refers to her heavy breathing and then weakens into gasps as she collapses.

Gluck's Orfeo must work without benefit of clergy. He is the romantic artist, striving to replace an absent god with his own ordaining imagination. This is why Euridice's agnosticism is so cruel. Asking "E sara ver?" she is questioning the miracle he has wrought; his aria when he loses her, "Che farò senza Euridice?" is the artist's complaint when deprived of the muse or instrument which served him in lieu of the inspiring god. His triumphs, depending as they do on his energy and ardor alone, are never automatic. His lyre can't appease the growling Furies: his voice eventually does. But he does not display it like the superb divo who is Monteverdi's Orfeo: he pleads and remonstrates discreetly, quietly. And the Furies know his vulnerability because they say that no one can survive their baying unless he is a god ("se un Dio non è")—which Orfeo is not. They wonder at his temerity in following the path of Hercules into their realm, yet Orfeo lacks the superhuman might of that ruffian, who vanquishes death for Gluck's heroine in *Alceste*.

Though Orfeo trusts in art as a surrogate theology, there's a difference between its glib transformations and the immitigable realities of human suffering and desire. Euridice when revived irritatingly insists that this is some arty contrivance: "Io vivo? Come! Ma con qual arte?" The dialogue with the echo asks whether the romantic is a self-made god, or whether he may just be deceived by the sound of his own voice. Gluck's opera is a work of nagging, frustrated interrogation: Orfeo's "Ombra cara, ove sei?" or "Che farò?"; his anxious cross-questioning of Amore: "Ah, come? Ah, quando? E possibil sarà?"; the querulous demands of Euridice. Ignoring the human need to be sustained by reason and explanation,

Amore issues edicts enforcing silence within this lyrical work, so that Euridice can lament "L'idol del mio cor / Non mi risponde." The plaintive singing voice, unaided, can make nothing happen. For the most part, *Orfeo ed Euridice* is the hero's disconsolate monologue. The deity who presides over opera has already failed the form.

A happy ending is improvised, rather too easily, by Amore. The next stage in the evolution of Orpheus and of opera recognizes that such lucky escapes aren't plausible. Opera's subject is to be the tragic pride of romantic imagination, as the human voice claims that power to utter the world into being once exercised by God. Haydn's *Orfeo ed Euridice* in 1791 anticipates this apostasy. Gluck's temperate Greece has been invaded by an elemental savagery. Orfeo is here no classical calmer of nature but a romantic consumed by nature's violence. Haydn's hero ends torn apart by marauding Bacchantes, who in turn are overwhelmed by the tempests Pluto angrily arouses. He can no longer rely, as Monteverdi's character did, on protection by Apollo; he falls victim to that god's opponent Dionysus—or rather to his Thracian acolytes, who punish him in their frenzy because he forswears all women once he loses Euridice. Apollo has been mysteriously reinterpreted. Pico della Mirandola, writing about Bacchic religious practices, proposes that those whom Apollo inspires must undergo the fate of Osiris or Orpheus, which is dismemberment. The artist creates out of a schismatic, schizophrenic division of himself. Haydn's Orfeo is wrenched in contrary directions by irreconcilable forces. Wooed by the Bacchantes with lustful promises, he rejects sensual pleasure and volunteers to die; like Faust, he must choose between heavenly philosophy—in which he's instructed by the sibylline Genio who guides him through Hades—and a carnal hell. He is already in the self-destroying creative predicament of Wagner's singer Tannhäuser, that patron sinner of opera.

Tannhäuser is Wagner's demonic Orpheus, made vocally eloquent by his season in the hell of the Venusberg. His chaster counterpart is Walther in *Die Meistersinger von Nürnberg*, who wins the song contest by retrieving the paradise which Gluck's Orfeo has lost. Walther is an Adam who declares a suburban garden to be his Eden and sets there, in his prize song, an Eve who is his adored Ev'chen. The two heroes represent alternatives for opera: song as obsequious worship, or (when the surging chromaticism of the Venusberg infuses Tannhäuser's aria at the Wartburg) as a vital, welling aphrodisia. The only Verdian hero who is a professional singer, the troubadour Manrico in *Il Trovatore*, retains some of the Orphic power, now employed by a vagabond to flout society and its official religion. As arrogantly self-assured as Monteverdi's Orfeo, Manrico claims privileges which are the due of his lyrical authority. A troubadour, he sings, is greater than any king, and he has transcended the twin regions of heaven and hell which constrain his prototypes in Monteverdi, Gluck and Haydn: when he steps down as if from heaven to rescue Leonora, the Count treats him as a revenant from the underworld, amazed that the dead can rise from their graves unannounced; but Manrico denies that either heaven or hell had any power to hold him. This Orpheus, impenitently disbelieving in the gods, has all the same made himself one of them by the compulsiveness of his singing.

Opera's Orphic faith in itself is derided soon enough by operetta. In *Orphée aux Enfers* (1858), Offenbach unsettles the Apollonian dispensation of Monteverdi. The Theban pastoral where the operetta begins is a stuffy small town, its shepherds ceremoniously ruled by pompous municipal elders. The music played there isn't a divine harmony but an interminable, trivial droning: Orphée boasts that his next violin concerto lasts an hour and a quarter; Eurydice is aghast at the prospect of having to listen to it, and squeals her protest in caterwauling high notes. Because this earthly heaven is so boring, Eurydice, when she has the good fortune to die, opts to remain in hell, where the entertainments are spicier. The Olympian gods who arrive in a deputation to rescue her behave with courtly decorum down below, dancing a stately minuet. The devils introduce them to infernal enjoyments, and to demonstrate dance a furious galop (or, in most productions of the work, a cancan). Orphée, required despite his better judgment to retrieve Eurydice, is tricked into looking behind him by an electric uproar. Jupiter creates the diversion, because he wants to keep Eurydice for himself. Orphée's glance back at her is no fraught moral decision, as in Gluck: "un mouvement involontaire" is how he explains it— like a sneeze, or an orgasm. Eurydice passes contentedly from the cult of Apollo to that of Dionysus, and doesn't need to suffer, as Haydn's Orfeo does, in the process. Her ambition, she announces, is to become a Bacchante, and the operetta ends with her induction into these infidel holy orders: "Reçois ta prêtresse" she tells the god of drunken revelry, promising that her voice will sing the praise of inebriation and irrationality forever.

In Offenbach's hypocritical moral universe, the Furies have been replaced by a social superego: the vigilant bourgeois bogey of Public Opinion, scandalized by the hero's delight when he loses the querulous

Eurydice. Arriving on Olympus, the operetta desecrates the decrepit gods, and they collaborate in their own shame, for Pluton, making off with Eurydice, suggests "abusons de notre divinité." The classical gods revived by opera in the seventeenth century are not so much dead as dozy. The Olympians are discovered asleep, off-duty. Perhaps the only one who retains the creative potency Orpheus shared in is Mercure, who calls himself the god of eloquence. However, his is not the divine rhapsody of the singing Orpheus; it's the gabbling talent of the shyster, and he acknowledges lawyers—not poets or musicians—as his offspring. Here there is no need for a humanly inspired Götterdämmerung to unseat these hierarchs. They foment a rebellion of their own, to the sound of the "Marseillaise," because they're fed up with the diet of nectar and ambrosia served on Olympus.

The occult scholars of the Camerata believed they were restoring Greek tragedy when they invented opera. Offenbach questions the analogy between the ancient religious rite and its modern social imitation. His figure of Public Opinion introduces herself by citing her Greek lineage. She corresponds, she explains, to the chorus of the antique theater, or perhaps to the deus ex machina flown in to sort out the disputes of mortals. But as her name implies, she has altered that choral function, which Nietzsche believed had been assumed by the voluminous orchestra of Wagner's operas: she's a force of communal persecution, harrying offenders—which all operatic characters are—against her precious moral laws. To mark her disapproval of musical abandon, she speaks rather than singing.

In hell, however, the operatic cult can be reconstituted. The sole god worthy of veneration is the one celebrated in a brassy, frantic infernal chorus, and in the hymn of Eurydice: "le Dieu Bacchus" she calls him, and she persuades the toppled Olympians to praise his coronation—"Bacchus est roi!" He's the god of musical and alcoholic fervor, and his singing is a euphemism for sexual conquest. Eurydice in her guise of a Bacchante describes him teaching his tricks to satyrs and nymphs, who—as she put it— "répétaient ses chansons!"

The joke suits the operetta's critique of opera. How can music pretend to be so mystic a gift, Offenbach demands, when it has been turned instead into an industry? The virtuosity of Monteverdi's Orfeo changes in the case of Orphée to pedantry. He directs the Theban orphéon (a choral society), and gives violin lessons. When he brags of his artistry to Eurydice, he's merely fatuous. The truth is that the music serves him as an excuse for other, grubbier inclinations. He fiddles passionately to impress a nymph he fancies, and only remembers the choral rehearsal he must conduct because it will delay his journey to the underworld in pursuit of the unloved Eurydice. The tunes he dispenses are already clichés. When he quotes Gluck's "Che farò," the Olympians join him in a jeering singalong. The offstage Furies who anathematize him have a merely technical interest to this bored professional: he's impressed by the acoustic phenomenon. Other characters have lost that conviction of music's power to raise words skyward which emboldens and justifies opera. Public Opinion delivers her sermon as speech not song; Pluton is assigned an aria in prose.

The singer no longer possesses, as Orfeo did, the moral right to music. Offenbach's *Les Contes d'Hoffmann* anatomizes the uses and abuses of song. The doll Olympia is a clockwork nightingale. The coloratura of the aria she delivers at Spalanzani's reception is the machine's demonstration of its oiled and calibrated technique, her pitch losses the winding down of her engine. Compliantly chirping "Oui," she is at the same time a docile creation of sexual cybernetics, a toy manipulated by the man who desires her. While she symbolizes the automation of sex and of song, for the consumptive Antonia—killed because she strains herself singing in obedience to what Dr. Miracle calls the demon of music—both sex and song are maladies, modes of self-expenditure. Her artistic gift renders the integrity of her emotion suspect, leading her eventually to curse her voice. Hoffmann is jealous of her music: she loves it too much, more perhaps than she does him. When they try out a reprise of their old love song, she vows to show him she has not forgotten her talent. She is destroyed by opera, with Miracle as the evil entrepreneur urging her on by describing the bravos of an imaginary crowd. She dies of a high note, and expires on a trill. Olympia has no emotions, and in response to Hoffmann's ardor can only squeak her consent. Antonia's emotions are too violent for the body they agitate and the musical instrument which expresses them. For the third heroine, Giulietta the courtesan, emotion (and therefore song) is no more than fulsome social compliment or formulaic dissimulation. Hoffmann's lyrical muses incapacitate rather than inspire him.

What fate remains for a modern Orpheus but, in shame and remorse, to lose his voice? Opera in this century often finds itself unable to justify the singing which is the occupation and existence of its characters. Words brutally mar the emotional appeasement of music when, at the end of Berg's *Wozzeck*, a child tells Marie's son that his mother is dead. Thereafter the resumption of music, when the boy returns to his melodic hopping game, can only stand for an incapacity to feel. Britten's Peter Grimes raves as lyrically as Lucia in his madness on the foggy beach, but the prosaic matter of arranging for him to kill himself has to be dealt with in tuneless speech. Balstrode curtly tells him to sail his boat out, and sink it. The compact of Orpheus with Apollo has broken down.

The words of modern opera are increasingly alienated from the music. The society the works describe has vulgarized music as Muzak. A maudlin, overpedaled piano wallpapers the saloon with sentiment in Kurt Weill's *Aufstieg und Fall der Stadt Mahagonny*. As it thuds through a battery of false notes, Jake enthuses that this is eternal art. Only an oaf would be so deceived. Weill's librettist Brecht, in the novel written after their collaboration on the *Dreigroschenoper*, further impoverishes music. His beggars hire barrel organs and trumpets from Mr. Peachum's shop to soften up almsgivers in the streets, though they soon find the Orphic spell failing: the citizens, aware that they're being exploited, harden their hearts all over again. From these orchestral beginnings, Peachum moves on to the manufacture and sale of maimed or prosthetic limbs, with which the mendicants have more success. Music has use only as a crutch.

Brecht and Weill introduce opera to a modern society where tunes are merchandise. The Orphic covenant belongs to a more innocent condition of being—to Monteverdi's pastoral idyll, or to Eden where before men fell there was no fractious speech, only prayerful, grateful song. Opera returns there in Gershwin's *Porgy and Bess*. Du Bose Heyward set his novel about Porgy in a state coeval with the Arcady of *Orfeo*. It takes place, he says, in "the Golden Age . . . when men, not yet old, were boys in an ancient, beautiful city that time had forgotten." Because his blacks still inhabit a world where song is the natural medium of communication, Heyward's novel often seems to anticipate and prescribe Gershwin's scoring of it. He specifies that the soprano voice which laments over the grave of Robbins should keen in its highest register, then collapse into an agonized minor key; one of his baritonal laborers hums "Ain't it hahd tuh be a nigger" and rouses a chorus of "low, close harmonies." Porgy himself, Heyward notes, sings in his "rich baritone" to sustain morale during the hurricane. Tribal rites are musically choreographed. A strophic dirge is kept up while the contributions are raised to bury Robbins; the picnic parade on the way to Kittiwah Island explores the raucous atonality of jazz, with what Heyward describes as its "wild, barbaric chord" and its "daring . . . excursions into the realm of sound."

Gershwin makes lyricism the full-time job of residents in Catfish Row. Among his bountiful nothings Porgy includes "my song," and when he tallies the activities of his day with Bess, he describes the routine of Adam and Eve in Eden, or Orfeo and Euridice in Elysium: when they're not eating and sleeping, they spend their time singing and praying. His neighbors hear him and Bess singing all day long in their hut. Porgy doesn't mention work among his daily activities, because it's a penalty of the Fall. When the people of Catfish Row do work, they conduct their business musically, which charms labor into pleasure. They cry their wares—honey, crabs, strawberries—to lilting refrains with yodeled cadenzas. Gershwin denies music only to the invading white officials. The detective, policeman, lawyer and coroner are agents of rationality, who long since forfeited their membership in the communal, melodic garden.

Failing the primitivism of Gershwin, Orpheus has been presented with two further options in modern opera: to go mad in self-defense, or to take off for that outer space from where his Apollonian music is broadcast. The first alternative is that adopted by Tom Rakewell in *The Rake's Progress*. Stravinsky's opera, first performed in Venice in 1951, recollects the form's origins in Monteverdi. The heraldic fanfares with which it begins imitate those of *Orfeo*; Tom by the end, incarcerated in Bedlam, believes himself to be Orpheus. In between, Monteverdi's otherworldly locations have been grounded on a map of Hogarthian England: Elysium is here a rural arbor, the Styx the Thames across which the bankrupt are ferried to prison. With a kiss, Tom and Anne hope to "restore the Age of Gold," that musical realm wherein Heyward sets *Porgy*. The asylum, as it happens, vouchsafes Tom the same bliss of dulcet self-deception. This is why he calls himself Orpheus, and why the madmen believe Anne's lament is a "sacred music of the spheres." Tom commands Orpheus to take up his lyre in "a swan-like music," which may die but will rise again. That resurrection is the ascent of Gershwin's child in "Summertime," who rises up singing and reaches for the sky. The season of the lullaby is the Eden of infancy, where time is suspended and, as Clara assures her baby, nothing can harm you. She and Tom are both reiterating the promise of Orpheus, restoring losses and prohibiting sorrow.

For Karlheinz Stockhausen, the sky the baby longs for with its spherical harmonies can be regained only by an astronaut. Monteverdi's Orfeo was a harpist; Stockhausen's Michael, in the opera *Donnerstag* from the cycle *Licht*, is a trumpeter, touring the world inside a rotating globe from which he steps down, like Monteverdi's Apollo, to disseminate musical rejoicing. With the aid of science—that global spaceship, and the prepared tapes which supplement his instrumental playing and make audible the electronic vibrations and coruscations of the upper air—this Orpheus can trespass on Apollo's domain. Michael explains that his ambition is to "invent . . . sounds which . . . can *still* move the souls of angels." Introducing his work at Covent Garden in 1985, Stockhausen counseled his audience, as Wagner had done at Bayreuth in 1876, to look with its ears: "music," he said, "is the most sublime language, and if we were higher beings, we would only need to listen, and then we would see." Though Apollo now arrives in the guise of an extraterrestrial, Stockhausen adheres to the ancient gospel of Orpheus, which is the faith of opera.

TWO

Dionysus

DESPITE the benevolence of those higher beings who from Monteverdi to Stockhausen are opera's elect, there is another theory of the form's origin and another interpretation of its history. Monteverdi chooses for the first operatic hero a peaceable, worshipful shepherd. Nietzsche, however, in his account of the classical tragedy which the Camerata attempted to revive, argues differently. For him, the first operatic hero is a satyr—a demon of sensuality, whose rabid ecstasy is expressed by music. The god of the art for Monteverdi is Apollo, serene, lucid, brilliant. Nietzsche chooses as opera's instigator the god who challenges and darkens sunny Apollo: Dionysus, whose mysteries beget a contagious madness.

Nietzsche's *Birth of Tragedy* (1872) is actually about Greek tragedy's rebirth as opera. That rebirth extends from the experimental research of the Camerata to the sacrifices staged in Gluck's operas about Iphigénie. Agamemnon offers his daughter on the altar in *Iphigénie en Aulide*; her brother Oreste is sentenced in *Iphigénie en Tauride*. Wagner said Bellini's *Norma* reached "the heights of Greek tragedy" when its heroine ascends the pyre; after Wagner the revival continues with the adaptation of Sophocles by Strauss and Hofmannsthal in *Elektra*. In *The Bassarids* of Henze, written by W. H. Auden and Chester Kallman, Nietzsche's Dionysus appears as the genie of European romanticism, responsible both for the natural religion of the nineteenth century and the revolution inside or beneath consciousness of the twentieth century. Strauss's Bacchus brings erotic deliverance to Ariadne on Naxos; Henze's Dionysus slyly assaults moral normality when he entices Pentheus to dress as a woman to spy on his revels. Thomas Mann suspected that even Siegfried, the fair-headed Teuton, was one of Dionysus's many manifestations. When Gunther in *Götterdämmerung* calls Hagen the cursed wild boar who slew the hero, Mann remembers a pantheon of sacrificed, seasonally regenerated gods who are the protagonists of myth—"Tammuz and Adonis, slain by the boar, Osiris and Dionysus, torn asunder to come again as the Crucified One." For Mann, Wagner himself was "the Dionysian actor": able to migrate in and out of human bodies at will (Wagner with fiendish versatility played all the parts in the *Ring* during rehearsals at Bayreuth in 1876), able to quit humanity altogether, taking on the character and the musical voice of storm clouds, tempestuous seas, walls of flame or surging rivers.

The enlivening, deranging spirit of both tragedy and opera is, for Nietzsche, that of music: the enchantment he calls dithyrambic, a wild exhilaration vented in song and dance, as man feels in himself the impulsive life of nature. The demon rises "from unfathomable depths"—within the earth, or within the body where the singer guards the voice; within the covered, darkened orchestra pit of Wagner's Bayreuth. As opposed to this lyric frenzy, the "ethical deity"—Monteverdi's Apollo—must make do with prosy words. In opera, according to Nietzsche, the two gods meet and continue their warfare. Apollo rationally utters the words, but the music of Dionysus belies them. Isolde's narrative in Wagner's opera says that she hates Tristan. The orchestra meanwhile intimates that she loves him. Music confesses what can't or couldn't or shouldn't be spoken, as in that languishing phrase which begins the prelude to *Tristan* and fuses the yearning of love with a lapse into death.

Apollo psalmodized, Nietzsche says, with his phantasmal harp (as he does in Monteverdi's *Orfeo*); Dionysus raves. Nietzsche admits the dangers of the powers his favorite unleashes: his jubilees are orgies. Dionysus blends sensuality and cruelty. But—in Norma's attempted slaughter of her children and of all the other people she loves, Scarpia's adoring assault on Tosca, or Salome's lust for the Baptist's head—does not opera do the same? Nietzsche understands and applauds the profanation which is the first motive of all artists (who rob creative authority from the god who created them) and which becomes the agenda of opera, forever desecrating oratorio: he declares that "the best and highest possession mankind can acquire is obtained by sacrilege." Operatic characters hold nothing sacred. Don Giovanni mocks heaven when his laughter sounds through the graveyard. Siegmund in *Die Walküre* rejects Brünnhilde's offer of heaven, preferring the company of his incestuous bride; Brünnhilde herself in *Götterdämmerung* sabotages that heaven. Every Wagnerian hero is, like Tannhäuser, an apostate. Elektra has no need to abolish the gods as Brünnhilde does; she has herself, she tells Chrysothemis, become one of them.

Nietzsche's theory explains the grand generality of opera. Its characters never seem to be single beings; they embody huge human potentialities. Shakespeare's Othello is a professional soldier and an ethnic outsider, unsure of everything but his own military craft, which is irrelevant in private affairs—a recognizable being, sympathetic in his particularity and his imperfection. Verdi's Otello, soaring in on the whirlwind, is not a man but a force of nature. Between the drama and the opera an absolute change has intervened. When Othello speaks in his alluring, exotic, singsong manner, he sounds specious; when Otello sings, it is as the trumpet tone of an unchallengeable authority.

Dionysus accounts for this massive emotional scale. Apollo, Nietzsche says, is the god of individuality. His acolytes learn precisely who they are, and how small they are. But in opera the self is aggrandized, not whittled away. "Son io" insists Norma, ecstatically accusing herself of a crime which is of course sacrilegious. Nietzsche argues that this impersonal egomania is the bequest of Dionysus. In his "mystical triumphant cry . . . the spell of individuation is broken." The way lies open to the one life in which all beings are enmeshed and married: that oceanic volume of sound from which Otello emerges or into which Senta, diving from the cliff after the Dutchman's ship, hurls herself.

Expanding beyond a merely personal life, the people in opera merge with multitudes. This too in Nietzsche's view derives from Dionysus, whose worshipers hunted in packs. The chorus in tragedy—and, by implication, in opera—possesses this collective excitement: the tragic protagonist has transfused his emotion into this crowd, and transformed himself into each and every one of them. We hear that process at work when Hagen in *Götterdämmerung* infects the Gibichung vassals with his warwhooping good humor, or when Chrysothemis in *Elektra* radiantly joins her voice with the invisible masses who are intoning the name of Orest. The "community of unconscious actors who consider themselves and one another transformed" exists as well in Italian opera. Rossini's ensembles describe such concerted madness as a comic state. The society of *L'Italiana in Algeri* erupts in a cacophony of animal noises and mechanical eructations.

Wine is one Dionysian prescription for creating this state of frenzy. Drinking songs are synonymous with opera. The convention establishes itself at once, when Nerone and the poet Lucano carouse and join in a tipsy madrigal in Monteverdi's *L'Incoronazione di Poppea*. The purpose is Dionysian: to celebrate the death of the reproving moralist Seneca, who stood between Nerone and his instincts. The characters of Shakespearean tragedy—generally too preoccupied with introspective worries to care for such joviality—are acclimatized to opera by being given drinking songs, which declare their new Dionysian faith in inebriation. In Shakespeare's *Macbeth*, drunkenness is strictly functional, emboldening Lady Macbeth for her share of the murders. In Verdi's operatic setting, though, she sings a brindisi to distract the guests during Macbeth's delirium, and its lurching ungainly coloratura and dizzy trills suggest a new characterization of her. She sounds like a maenad, a colleague for the witches whose brew Nietzsche used as an image of the Dionysia, delighting in violence with winy glee. Likewise a drunkenness which Iago in *Othello* merely uses to disgrace Cassio becomes the first definitive account of his character in *Otello*. In contrast with Otello's heroic declamation, Iago accents the drinking song with licentious scoops and gulps. He even sings in this scene, as Nietzsche would have wished, of the reeling dithyramb. It's appropriate that his praise of drink should happen around a bonfire: fire and liquor are man-made hells. After this hymn to wine, Iago in the next scene logically dedicates himself to an infernal deity as cruel as Dionysus.

The libations of the god arouse Hamlet from his melancholy meditation. In Shakespeare's play he despises the drinking bouts of his uncle's court, and his promise that he'll teach Rosencrantz and Guildenstern to drink deep emptily remembers a long-gone student past. Once translated to opera, in Ambroise Thomas's *Hamlet* in 1868, this abstinent character has a change of heart, and welcomes the players with goblets and an enthusiastic drinking song. He aligns himself with the ideology of Dionysus, calling for wine to relieve his sadness: he wants to live, he says, in a drunken dream, laughing with the ribaldry of Silenus; he calls for the enchanting liquor to intoxicate him. Marcellus and Horatio comment while he sings that he has found oblivion in his cups. The operatic Hamlet has no need of the tragic character's self-slaughter or his metaphysical disquiets. He decides that, in a dismal life, the boozing fool is the only wise man.

Pedrillo stultifies the harem-keeper Osmin with wine in Mozart's *Die Entführung aus dem Serail*; the drinkers sing in praise of opera's patron, "Vivat Bacchus!" Mozart's sweltering, sensual Orient, where Konstanze luxuriates in the pleasure of pain, is close after all to the Nietzschean god's

33

homeland. The same refrain recurs in Massenet's *Werther*. Johann and Schmidt, burghers of Wetzlar, spend Sunday morning quietly tippling, though they do so in decorous Latin—"Vivat Bacchus, semper vivat"—and balance that mild addiction with an admiration for "divin Klopstock," the eighteenth-century poet who celebrated a very different god: the Christian Messiah, about whom he wrote a scriptural epic. Don Giovanni's brief act of self-definition is an invitation to his party, known, although it doesn't specify the wine he's serving, as the champagne aria. The title refers to the effervescence of his singing, and of the yeasty life-force in him. His vinous zest is parodied in *Les Contes d'Hoffmann*. Offenbach sets his work in a tavern next to an opera house where *Don Giovanni* is being performed, with Hoffmann's current love Stella among the singers. Hoffmann is an unsuccessful Giovanni, whose decline from the exhilaration of Mozart's hero is marked by his lugubrious drunkenness: he is, as Lindorf sneers, "un ivrogne." Instead of Giovanni's bubbling delight, Offenbach's first scene transcribes the glummer state of Hoffmann when the beer barrels belch a chorus of glug-glugs.

Opera generally contents itself with raising glasses, like Alfredo in the "Libiamo" from *La Traviata*. The Duke demands a room and some wine in *Rigoletto*; supplied with them, he sings his sardonic toast to all his sexual victims in "La donna è mobile." Operetta is fond of showing what happens afterward. Apart from Hoffmann's depressive stupor, Offenbach depicts a heroine's unrepentant tipsiness in *La Périchole*: she staggers on, relishing the aftertaste of her supper and the "vin extraordinaire" on which she has overdosed; her speech is slurred, her walk zigzaggy, and Offenbach takes a mischievous glee in encouraging her to deviate from the musical measure. Johann Strauss's Orlofsky, at the party in *Die Fledermaus*, sings a hymn to the king of wines, champagne. He takes his metaphor literally and celebrates champagne's coronation: its imperial majesty commands allegiance throughout the world, and it sponsors a boozy communion between all men. After Orlofsky's toast, Falke proposes a swooning reconciliation between the characters who, glasses in hands, are "Brüderlein und Schwesterlein." The saturnalia is meant to inaugurate a United Nations. But instead it reels into a drunk and disorderly farce, and the revelers end in a prison where they are ordered about by the dipsomaniac jailer Frosch.

Rossini's characters inherit the appetite of Don Giovanni, though in them it's a more glad and innocent hunger, not a maddening addiction. Raimbaud in Rossini's *Le Comte Ory* rejoices over some rare wine he discovers in the castle cellars. Donizetti too converts a Dionysian tragedy of

34

inebriation into harmless comedy in *L'Elisir d'Amore*. As the opera begins, Adina is sitting in the fields reading a romance about Tristan and Isolde. It's a rather different version than the one later authorized by Wagner. Here only Tristano drinks the elixir, which is enough to make Isotta love him. Adina giggles at the improbability of it: Isotta didn't drink, so she must have felt that way all along; the elixir was just a helper of nature. Nemorino, wanting to make Adina love him, buys an elixir from the itinerant doctor Dulcamara, but it's only a flask of rough Bordeaux wine. Despite his quackery, Dulcamara is wise in the comic ways of Dionysus. He claims to have emptied hospitals with his cure-all medicines, and indeed he does dispense an infallible pair of tonics, comedy and music. The comic spirit, here as for Verdi's Falstaff, alcoholically alleviates cares; and Dulcamara during his sales pitch also calls for music, at which a jaunty trumpet starts up.

According to opera, music is the true elixir of love, the gratifier of desires, the creator of happiness. Thus the potion, when Nemorino swigs it, invites him to blithely meaningless song—"La la la" he says, or, more infectiously, "Tra-la rà la rà la rà!" wordlessly caroling like a bird as he taunts Adina.

Donizetti's *Lucrezia Borgia*—first performed in 1833, the year after *L'Elisir*—treats the bewitching potion more fatally. Lucrezia shares opera's Dionysian propensity to orgy. Her enemies hack the initial letter from the name BORGIA outside her palace in Ferrara, leaving the legend ORGIA, with which she's synonymous. The philters she prescribes aren't love drafts but poisons, poured from a gold chalice. Lucrezia possesses the art, like Dulcamara, of chemically undoing tragedy and changing it to comedy: the first time Gennaro (her son) drinks poison, she slips him a phial containing an antidote, which saves him; the second time, to spite her, he refuses.

The opera's source is a play by Victor Hugo, who described his Lucrèce as a psychological conundrum, her moral ugliness encased within an irresistible physical beauty. This ambivalence serves as a formula for opera: the profane and the sacred, lust and love, are mingled in Lucrèce, just as enjoyment and derangement, piety and lasciviousness are joined in the worship of Dionysus. In Donizetti's second act, Astolfo and Rustighello, henchmen of the Borgias, arrive independently to fetch Gennaro. One has been dispatched by the Duchess to summon him to a rendezvous, the other by the jealous Duke Alfonso to entice him into a trap. One of them offers the jollity of a fiesta, the other promises death.

Opera's carnivals always entwine such opposites, for music can couple emotional extremes: as the crowd cheers with bloodthirsty glee inside the bullring, Carmen is murdered; Siegfried's wedding procession in *Götterdämmerung* raucously interrupts the trio which is conspiring his slaughter. Therefore the conclusion of *Lucrezia Borgia*, like that of *Don Giovanni*, is a lethal festivity. At the Princess Negroni's party, the roisterers celebrate the wines of Madeira, Cyprus, Syracuse and the Rhine; they are enthusing over the poison which soon after kills them all. To one of them, Orsini, drink is an inspiration. The wine is credited with making every man a poet, and Orsini in his cups extemporizes a song which sums up the ideology of the operatic Dionysus: life, he says, is a drunken scherzo, and should be raced through with no care for the future. The giddy lurching coloratura of the piece transcribes this recklessness, as he suicidally carouses. If Rossinian characters like Raimbaud or the supposedly drunk Almaviva in *Il Barbiere di Siviglia* are guileless Don Giovannis, saved from self-destruction by comedy, Donizetti depicts a heedlessly tragic Giovanni, toasting his own extinction; and as in Mozart's opera, the sensual riot is interrupted by a supernatural remonstrance, when between Orsini's verses a bell tolls and sepulchral voices condemn the joys of the ungodly.

Falstaff too is changed by music from the fat, shabby, conniving intriguer of Shakespeare's *Merry Wives of Windsor* to a reverent Dionysian, the heir to both Don Giovanni and Wagner's Tristan. Boito's libretto set out to repatriate the character from puritanical England to sensual Italy: Falstaff's "clear Tuscan source," he argues, is in Boccaccio. Pursuing all women indiscriminately and deriving his energy from drink—he cares less about the grosser business of eating—Verdi's Falstaff has, in more cumbrous and elderly form, the grace and vigor of Mozart's hero. He is a Don Giovanni slightly over the hill, spared perdition because he is able, like Thomas Mann's Dionysian actor, to disappear into nature: he dresses as a stag (an English satyr) for the tryst in the nocturnal forest. Drink revives him after his dunking in the Thames, but the Wagnerian potion has undergone a change. The morbidly passionate Tristan denounces sensuality; Falstaff relaxes into the pleasure of inhabiting a human body. The treacherous chromatic shifts of Wagner's score become in Verdi a mercurial pursuit of momentary musical pleasures, no sooner savored than they have gone.

The mystic ferment of Dionysian wine persists in the harsher world of operatic verismo, though for the new realists it has a sleazy emotional purpose. Turiddu's drinking song in Mascagni's *Cavalleria Rusticana* is his credo, and the clue to his moral squalor. He sings of wine in the traditional way, acclaiming it like Orsini or Orlofsky for banishing black humors and exciting joy. He also calls it "sincero," and it provokes an unwonted sincerity in him: this heartless hedonist is made maudlin by drink, and the wine is his opportunity both for confessing his emotional weakness and excusing his misdeeds. The wine is "generoso" as he's unable to be, so he is right to tell Mamma Lucia that when he begged her blessing it was the wine talking. It's characteristic too that the drink should send him toward his mother, again disclosing an unsuspected truth about him: he's a mother's boy, callously disgusted by his sexual conquests but weepily devoted to Lucia, to whom at last he consigns the rejected Santuzza.

Puccini's characters need the encouragement of drink, to justify the casual violence of their existences. Scarpia offers Tosca some Spanish wine to put her in the mood for his assault on her, just as Herod in Strauss's opera tries to tempt Salome with the rare vintage Caesar has sent to him. Pinkerton's offer of "Milk-punch, o Wisky?" to the consul Sharpless in *Madama Butterfly* seals a contract, and bluffly challenges Sharpless to approve Pinkerton's sexual double-dealing. It lowers the moral issue to the level of the saloon bar. Having secured the grudging consent of his government's envoy, he proposes a toast to the grand, rapacious national enterprise in which they're colleagues—"America forever"—since whether on his gunboat or purchasing a temporary Japanese bride, Pinkerton is, like Sharpless, an emissary of American imperialism.

Equally unconventional in its use of the conventional brindisi is *Il Tabarro*, one of the three operas which make up Puccini's triptych, the *Trittico*. Its characters are Zolaesque bargemen and stevedores, laboring on the murky Seine. Work makes their lives a misery, and drink is a merciful oblivion. Tinca is an alcoholic who's grateful to the bottle for quelling his thoughts of revolt. He who drinks, he says, doesn't think; he who thinks doesn't laugh. His brief song erupts into cracked mirth. The Dionysian musical ecstasy is here a disease.

Isolde is not alone in brewing enchantment: Carmen goes to Lillas Pastia's tavern to drink Manzanilla. Among Lulu's clients, when she's degraded to a London prostitute in Berg's third act, is a Negro who has hearty tastes: "Immer trink ich Schnaps," he tells her, "Schnaps ist gut." Lulu, coercing others to hunger and thirst for her but herself almost seraphically immune to such cravings, never expresses an appetite; however, the Dionysian theory of opera is indirectly relevant to her. During the time he was working on *Lulu*, Berg composed a concert aria, "Das Wein" (1929), in the musical idiom of the opera. It sets Stefan George's translation of three Baudelaire poems, which amount to a gospel for Dionysus. In the first, wine boasts of its solace to careworn men, creating fraternity like Falke's toast in *Die Fledermaus*; in the second, it's an incentive to love; in the third, it's the inspiration of a Hoffmannesque poet, exalting him to equality with the gods. Flooding down the throat into the warm chest, as Baudelaire puts it, liquor irrigates the cavity which produces resonant song, and Berg's chromatic scale (so close to that which defines Lulu in her lied) sounds like a plinking of liquid droplets, each separately savored. The poems are treated to a slightly woozy blues: Baudelaire's angelic lovers are given a snatched tango to dance, and a saxophone wails raunchily at the mention of a gambling den; a barroom piano like that in *Mahagonny* hammers out a cheery refrain. If only so easily forgetful a way out had been available to Lulu!

At his festival, the operatic god dispenses cakes as well as ale. Jean the juggler, who is Massenet's *Jongleur de Notre-Dame*, sings a hallelujah in praise of wine and confesses to the monks of medieval Cluny that, though he has a Christian heart, his stomach remains pagan. He joins their order only because of the meals prepared by the abbey's cook Boniface. Don Giovanni lays on a repast with prosciutto and chocolate to divert Masetto while he seduces Zerlina, and invites the statue to supper; Leporello marvels at the gigantic mouthfuls he gobbles. Carmen too takes care to satisfy Don José's greed, summoning Pastia to supply them with all the food he has on the premises. José comments that she guzzles the bonbons like a six-year-old. Isabella, Rossini's Italian girl shipwrecked in Algiers, prescribes stupefaction for the gluttonous Bey who wants to detain her in his harem. She offers to induct him into the sacred order of the Pappataci, named after the verbs for feeding (pappare) and for keeping quiet (tacere). The Pappataci's responsibility is to eat and shut up. While Mustafà occupies herself with the edibles (and gets ready to go to sleep, which is also required), Isabella escapes with her lover.

Rossini himself was a legendary gourmand, as famous for tournedos as for operas; the novelist Stendhal delighted in his music on the Dionysian principle that it is "un-reason . . . perfected," and traced that irrationality to its alcoholic and culinary sources. Stendhal described music as a physical intoxication, or as a pleasure for the taste buds: Italian melody was a luscious fruit, a ripe peach; German harmony was sauerkraut, curry or kirschwasser, a spicier stimulus to more jaded palates.

The Dionysia were a rampant madness, and opera specializes in scenes of insane rapture. Donizetti's Lucia dizzily restages her wedding to a husband she has just slaughtered; Bellini's Elvira in *I Puritani* drifts in and out of madness, singing of love and invoking death (according to Giorgio's report) in that ancient operatic compound of ecstasy and anguish. Madness for these heroines is lyrical free-association. Dionysus teaches them to parody Orpheus. Anna Bolena, deliriously advancing to her execution in Donizetti's 1830 opera, recalls the Orphic imagery and asks the page Smeton—who has betrayed her—why he doesn't tune his harp. Its strings have been torn, he says. She continues to sing serenely, as if the harp accompanied her, but only because the musical spirit in her is by now blithely distracted from the excruciation of the drama. Operatic madness is a trial of music's power over drama, and beauty's power over a repellent ugliness. Like the maenads, it couples marriage with carnage in a maimed or polluted rite which is almost a definition of opera: as Lucia solemnly recapitulates her wedding, so the rejected Elvira crazily invites Giorgio to her wedding with Arturo, and Anna Bolena believes the block where she'll be beheaded is the flowery altar where she'll be married.

Opera co-opts the archetype of such heroines, Shakespeare's Ophelia, to its new style of mellifluous mania. In the play, Ophelia's madness is an embarrassment to those who witness it, as she brokenly voices snatches of smutty and unmusical ballads. The Ophélie of Ambroise Thomas has taken off, like the lark she describes, into wheeling flight, sketching arabesques of dazzling sound in the air; she has also retired into a deathly underground, singing—in verses which replace Ophelia's wistful bawdry—of the Willis or water sprites who lure untrue lovers into the lake and drown them. Her vocalizing is the heartless laughter of the Bacchante. In the play, Ophelia's death is only reported; here she subsides as we watch, borne away uncomplaining. For Shakespeare, she remains a dramatic problem even after death—a corpse to be buried, and to be quarreled over. For Thomas, there can be no thought of such a practical postmortem, because she expired in a self-justifying joy.

Opera's obsessions are continuous throughout its history, so that these crazed revels last beyond romanticism into the twentieth century: Elektra's murderous hilarity, Stravinsky's rake in Bedlam. Britten's first operatic hero, Peter Grimes, secretly subscribes to the Dionysian creed. In earnest of this faith, he's first given a drinking song, then a mad scene. Invading the inn, Grimes the moral renegade takes over the tepid chantey the customers are singing in unison and turns it into a furious monologue, delighting in his alienation from this staid society. The Peter Grimes of George Crabbe's narrative poem sickens and dies of moroseness in his outlawry; Britten's Grimes, like a bel canto heroine, enjoys the harmonizing recourse of madness. An old-fashioned operatic convention enables Britten to tell disconcerting new truths about the character as he wanders babbling through the fog. Grimes's has been a forbidden love, expressed in his violent treatment of his boy apprentices, consummated only in death. Like Lucia, he begs for Ellen Orford's hand, then angrily spurns it; like Anna Bolena, who asks to be led back to the castle where she spent her childhood and sings a pastiche of "Home, sweet home," he dreams of a peaceful home which social prohibition denies him. Gabbling his name in defiance of the chorus's punitive nomination of him, he's insisting on his right to invent and to be himself. He reviews and regurgitates themes and tags from all the previous scenes of the opera, exploiting the charmed repetitiousness of music to undo and reverse the accusing past—to "turn the skies back and begin again." Music liberates and licenses the raging demon in him. The sou'westered East Anglian fisherman, worrying over a love whose name he dare not speak, is one more legatee of Dionysus.

So, more timorously and guiltily, is the hero of a subsequent Britten work, *Albert Herring*. In a country village, the local dowager organizes a pageant of purity to celebrate the spring. Since the farm girls are all hussies, her chaste festival honors a May King—Albert Herring, whose tyrannical Mum keeps a grocery shop. Albert's friends take pity on his innocence and corrupt him with a dose of naval rum. Freed from maternal constraints, he spends the night carousing in the countryside.

Albert Herring is Britten's nervously jocular parody of *Tristan und Isolde*. The liquor which leads Albert astray is Wagner's love potion, and some bars from *Tristan* are abstemiously quoted on piano and violin as the rum slurps into Albert's lemonade glass. The homage is a repressed yearning: he doesn't dare to be Tristan. The swelling compulsiveness of the Wagnerian orchestra is censured at once by pealing bells from the churchyard; and to disinfect the elixir, the Mayor boasts that his administration has sanitized the town's water supply by laying a new pipe along Balaclava Avenue and equipping it with filters. When Albert drains his glass and gets the hiccups, Britten blearily adapts the wrenching coitus interruptus at the end of Wagner's love duet. Tristan in the third act curses the drink. Albert, in another of the brief Wagner parodies, remembers the taste of the lemonade and wonders how it was made. Tristan screams in anguish; Albert's voice quavers deliciously, as if salivating. Since his rapture was so short-lived and so mild-mannered, he needn't expiate it at the cost of his life. *Albert Herring* recognizes music's Dionysian force, yet submits it to a parsonical discipline: Miss Wordsworth, the village schoolmarm, polices the dropped aitches of her choir, calls for open throats and controls the rowdy youngsters with blasts on her pitch pipe. The satyr has been tamed.

THREE

Eros

AMONG opera's pagan motive forces, none is more powerful or ever-present than the god (or goddess) of love. Operatic characters blame all their infractions on Eros. The perky, resourceful Amore rescues Monteverdi's Poppea, pardons her crimes and resolves to make her empress. Basilio in *Le Nozze di Figaro* sees the page Cherubino as a conniving androgynous Cupid, and in Berlioz's *Les Troyens*, Ascagne, the son of Enée who is in his turn the son of Venus, seems to Anna to have metamorphosed into Cupid as he slips the wedding ring from Didon's finger, easing her surrender to his father. Venus presides in *Tannhäuser*, alternately a persuasive siren and a spiteful termagant; Isolde personifies her as a sister and a colleague, whom she entitles Frau Minne. Later, her religion is institutionalized as whoring. When the Christian ideologue Athanaël converts the courtesan in Massenet's *Thaïs*, he has to shatter the statuette of Eros which she wants to keep as a souvenir of her harlotry. In her carpeted and perfumed den, she had practiced her trade beneath a votive idol of Venus. Mother Goose in *The Rake's Progress* and Leokadia Begbick in *Mahagonny* are raddled Venuses who keep brothels, while Lulu scavenges a living in London as a prostitute.

The two most dangerous and scandalous operatic characters are a pair for whom existence is an erotic career—Don Giovanni and Carmen. Don Giovanni is dedicated to pursuit and research, the imperial and universal adventure of sensuous experience. Carmen's more feminine concern is evasion, escape from the monopolistic men who presume to own her. Though Don Giovanni pretends when it suits him to love Zerlina, just as Carmen pledges that she loves Escamillo, neither of them is interested in love as an emotional unison. The erotic imperative dismisses such stability. They must remain in motion forever—pursuing in Giovanni's case, maneuvering free in Carmen's—and can be satiated only in death. They are complementary, though as eternal antagonists not marital partners: Giovanni seeks to know all the women in the world, which means to enumerate and then briskly forget them; Carmen seeks to keep all the men in the world from knowing her, and she does so by being unguessable, unpredictable, perpetually contradictory.

Don Giovanni's antecedents are in the drama—in Tirso de Molina's monastic morality play of 1630, where he's punitively fed on scorpions and gall; in Molière's version of 1655, where he's a rational man, an encyclopedist who conducts his affairs arithmetically. Carmen derives from the novel—from the ethnographic investigations of Mérimée's narrator in 1845, who studies her as an interesting specimen of Andalusian folkways.

But for both of them the operatic adaptation is definitive, because song is their natural medium. They are indeed made from music, and thus stand as embodiments of opera. Don Giovanni must have an orchestra to accompany his supper, and masticates tunes from operas—*Una Cosa Rara, I Litiganti*, even *Le Nozze di Figaro*. Enticing Elvira's maid, he's a professional serenader. Carmen too, told not to speak by Don José, sings instead. The same musical impulse goads her to dance, cavorting to entertain Zuniga and smashing a plate into improvised castanets when she performs her teasing cabaret in honor of José. Surprised by Masetto as he's sneaking off with Zerlina, Giovanni summons music to his aid. Some instrumentalists tune up in the distance, as if cued by him; hearing them, he invites Masetto and Zerlina to the party. Incidental noise is also commandeered by Carmen as an accompaniment. When the bugles bray for retreat and order José back to the barracks, Carmen welcomes their intrusion. It's woeful, she says, to dance without an orchestra, and she salutes the music which (like Apollo's hymn in *Orfeo*) is showered down freely from heaven.

Why should opera have such an interest in vindicating the libertine and the promiscuous gypsy? One answer is Søren Kierkegaard's, in *Either/Or*. Kierkegaard's ironic, ambiguous treatise, published in 1843, investigates the morality of romanticism. It sets an aesthetic hedonism against a starchier ethical rectitude, identifying its twin personae as A and B. A the philanderer explains his personal code by an exposition of *Don*

Giovanni. He declares Mozart's hero to be a "sensuous genius," whose vital urgency and animal exuberance can be expressed only by music. Giovanni is musical because he impatiently demands immediate satisfaction. Only music, abolishing the reflective equivocations of language, can grant him that, making his storm of desire voluble without ever forcing it to be self-conscious. "Music is the demonic," Kierkegaard says; it's therefore averse to an abstinent Christian spirituality. Giovanni's fatal enemy is a dead man, the statuesque Commendatore who utters remonstrances from beyond the grave with the baleful aid of trombones, hitherto reserved for ecclesiastical music.

Mozart perjures this musical genius when he makes it sanctimonious, or even respectable: Kierkegaard deplores *Die Zauberflöte* because its dialogue marks music's defeat by verbal reason. It has also reneged, he believes, on the erotic ebullience of Giovanni. It celebrates weddings and procreation, and Kierkegaard comments that while marriage may have many advantages, there's one thing it is definitely not, and that is musical. Opera does seem able to tolerate every erotic vagary and unhallowed relationship except connubial bliss. "Isolde," Wieland Wagner once cautioned, "is not the kind of woman one marries."

The musical impetuosity of desire hastens Giovanni onward. He is always either chasing or (as the women hound him) being chased. Escape from an impasse is as easy as a modulation: hence his unexplained evasion of his accusers at the end of the first act. He dines on culinary operas, and lays on an international array of dances—a minuet, a folia and an allemande. True to his driving genius, he never pauses for self-assessment or retrospection. He doesn't even keep his own list of conquests; that archival responsibility devolves on Leporello, who is anxious to know whether Donna Anna's name should be registered. He does without a sense of himself altogether. This is what differentiates him from the Count in *Nozze di Figaro:* Almaviva is jealously proprietorial, and resents any slight to his rank because it irritates his self-esteem; but when Giovanni brags of his gentlemanliness to Zerlina, it's only another ruse. He's so unmindful of his social position that he relishes the chance to turn into Leporello, whereas it's impossible to imagine a similar exchange of identities between the Count and Figaro. Kierkegaard calls him an idea, not an individual—a process, being formed as we watch and listen yet never reaching completion. The catalog rests at a thousand and three victims in Spain because the number is absurd and arbitrary, rejecting any hint of termination.

Giovanni's champagne aria is his tribute to this musical dynamism.

Carmen's corresponding statement is the gypsy song at Pastia's, with which she begins the second act. Though Mérimée's Carmen doesn't sing, this incident is carefully set up in the story. José, demoted after his term in prison, is on sentry duty outside the colonel's residence; Carmen arrives with two colleagues, carrying her Basque tambourine, followed by a guitarist. She has been engaged to entertain at the colonel's party by doing her national dance, the romalis. José suspects that she will be called on to perform other services as well, and he listens in jealous frustration to the noise of the castanets and the laughter inside the house and catches occasional glimpses of Carmen through the wrought-iron gate, vaulting with her tambourine. All this preparation Bizet omits (though Carmen does later, in conversation, taunt José by saying that Zuniga made her dance for him). The gypsy song comes from nowhere, for no reason—and its very gratuitousness is what makes it such a revelation about Carmen. For it is a song about music, and about what Kierkegaard calls its demonism.

It begins faintly, distantly, languidly, as a mere rhythmic tattoo. But even in this understated, muffled way, it acts as an enchantment and an exhortation, stirring Carmen to a frenzy. This, like Iago's song at the pyre, is her dithyramb. One possible meaning of that mysterious Greek word is "twice-born": after the incineration of his mother Semele (dramatized in Handel's opera), Dionysus was secreted in Zeus's thigh, and later hatched a second time. Carmen accordingly, like Giovanni, in "Fin ch'han dal vino," is describing her own birth from the spirit of music. The song's instrumentation is cued and imitated by her. Its first sound is that of the sistrum jangling metallically. (The sistrum was an Egyptian device of shaking rods associated with the worship of Isis, the goddess of fertility, who has a long line of operatic adherents: Sarastro and his masons in *Die Zauberflöte*, Amneris in *Aida*, Glass's Akhnaten.) Then come the clattering tambourines, and the vibrant guitars. The musical cacophony begets a whirling motion, as the bodies of the gypsy girls silently sing: "la danse au chant se mariait," says Carmen. She compares the crowd's frenzy to a whirlwind, which is one of Kierkegaard's analogies for Giovanni; in terms of the Dionysia, it is a fever or an intoxication. At its most intense, it passes beyond articulacy. Its climax is Carmen's triumphant, shouted "Tra-la-la-la."

Giovanni uses words, but does so gabblingly, torrentially, without concern for their meaning. Perhaps the only word whose sense he really values is that boldly iterated "No!" he hurls at the statue when it demands that he repent. The sound most truly characteristic of him is not verbal at all: it is the atheistic laughter which echoes through the graveyard, or later the shriek he emits as the fiends seize him. Carmen too is at her most eloquent when doodling with sound, paraphrasing words she doesn't need to speak. Before her stamping, climactic "Tra-la-la-la" in the gypsy song, there are the suggestively hummed repetitions of "tralalalalalalala" with which she avoids Zuniga's interrogation: a purely instrumental employment of the voice, since she can make those nonsensical syllables sound—depending on her whim—obliquely absentminded, chestily sultry or as defiant and enraged as a paragraph of curses. Later in the second act she has more occasions for onomatopoeia, in the wayward "la-la-la-la" of her dance for José, or the braying "Ta ra ta ta" which mocks the bugler.

The secret Carmen says she guards is voicelessly stated by the orchestra beneath José's song about the flower she threw at him. There is no definable tune, only a tantalizingly endless and elusive melody, coiling and winding, never the same from one phrase to the next. Carmen's enigma is this musical mutability. In the same way, Mozart's overture is his completest characterization of Giovanni, and of the contrast between Eros and Thanatos, love and death. That initial, paralyzing chord, announcing Giovanni's end before he has even begun, is what provokes the heedless jollity which ensues (though the chase is stalled from time to time by new retributive thunderclaps). Giovanni's sexual career is his desperate attempt to outrace his own imminent demise.

For both Giovanni and Carmen, music states the terms of a moral and mortal predicament. It is their comic livelihood; yet it also passes a tragic judgment on them.

The vital speed and elation of Giovanni only bring his end nearer. At their marriage, Zerlina and Masetto sing of time's swift passing. She urges the girls not to let their season of youth elapse without enjoying it; he says that the joys of life have hardly begun for him, while for his friends they have already been used up. Music enforces a terrifying abbreviation. *Don Giovanni* abounds in agitated episodes whose accelerated musical pulse gets them nowhere: the first raging trio, in which Anna detains Giovanni while Leporello grumbles; the ensemble accusing him at his party, which for all its righteous indignation and hurtling anger has no power to arraign him; the sextet upbraiding Leporello in the second act, which the culprit wriggles out of.

Music moves through time, and tempo is one of Giovanni's anguished preoccupations. He wants to live, with the nonchalant forgetfulness implied by Kierkegaard's "sensuous immediacy," in a time without tenses—the perpetual present of desire and its instant, spontaneous gratification. He is menaced by Elvira, because she emerges from a past whose existence he doesn't wish to recognize, since to possess a past makes you accountable for your actions. Anna too dedicates herself to cherishing a memory, the "rimembranza amara" (as Ottavio calls it) of her loss. At last, desperate to save him, Elvira offers to become as amnesiac as Giovanni: interrupting his supper, she says that she will no longer remember the harm he has done her. José, in his last attempt to regain Carmen, is similarly baffled by her refusal to acknowledge a time past. "Carmen, il est temps encore," he uselessly pleads. He first proposes, like Elvira, to forget their past and begin a new life; when she declares that to be impossible, he begs "souviens-toi du passé."

The other tense which threatens Giovanni's present with extinction is the future, symbolized by the Commendatore's afterlife. Giovanni declines to believe in that future until the Commendatore tells him he has run out of moments. Carmen is more fatalistic about a future ordained by the cards, but this predestination in practice frees her to behave as willfully or whimsically as she pleases. She knows what the end will be: José will kill her. Why then shouldn't she do whatever she likes on her way to that end? Her preview of tragedy is responsible for her risky, feckless comic gaiety. *Don Giovanni* has a similar resilience. Music irrepressibly fends off the last dying cadence. Deaths are followed by resurrections, more or less at once—Giovanni's recovery after the first bars of the overture, Anna's revival when she faints or again when she tells Ottavio (having guessed her attacker's identity) "son morta!", the Commendatore's marmoreal return from the grave, the recuperation of the opera itself when Mozart added that last bouncy, dauntless sextet for the survivors.

The time Giovanni flees from eventually forecloses. He tells the Commendatore to be off; when the old man won't go, Giovanni says he can stay if he wants to die. Stand still for a moment and death will catch you up. As the Commendatore expires, the trio drags and ebbs, losing energy and unable any longer to argue against the end. The present is peremptory: "Vengo! vengo!" growls Masetto as Leporello drags him away; "Vieni," Giovanni implores as he tugs at Zerlina. The agent of his undoing materializes in the form of musical tempo, prompt as that fell sergeant death who comes, in Hamlet's phrase, to arrest us. "Io sono a tempo," Elvira declares as she prevents him from abducting Zerlina. During the second act, with a fatal conclusion impending, the characters busy themselves inventing postponements, buying more time and a further lease of life, prolonging the music which keeps Giovanni alive. Elvira, groping through the darkness with Leporello, feels that death is near. Anna tells Ottavio that only death can relieve her suffering. But Elvira in her aria "Mi tradì" tries to retard the judgment she sees overtaking Giovanni, and Anna in "Non mi dir" bargains for a deferment of her alliance with Ottavio. Meanwhile Ottavio, though promising a speedy resolution, keeps the other characters indefinitely on hold, asking them to shut themselves for a few hours in Anna's house and delivering an aria, "Il mio tesoro," which exists in order to be interminable. Leporello can't get through the message he's made to relay to the statue: "non posso terminar." Only Giovanni seems now eager for the end: "Finiscila," he orders Leporello. He wants to hear "com'è finito" the prank played on Elvira; he's intrepidly ready to follow the statue into the undiscovered country, and says "verò." Goethe's Faust forfeits his life because he wants the moment to last forever. Giovanni is destroyed because the moment, disregarding him, moves on of its own implacable accord. Not even music's charmed, repetitious ordering of time can prevent the sentence from winding down to a full stop.

Tempo also warns of destiny in *Carmen.* This is why the heroine plays fast and loose with it. Music marks time, with the strict regularity of the trumpet announcing the change of guard or the bell signaling a break from work in the tobacco factory; Carmen's time is idle, syncopated, unprosodic. She sings the habanera casually, its considered slowness mocking the urgency of the men who pant for her favors. She dashes off the seguidilla skittishly, canceling it with a flourish. Her delivery with its slithering inflections and its rhythmic levity protects her freedom of maneuver and secures her temporary immunity from time. Maybe she will love the men in the crowd tomorrow, maybe never; she doesn't mind, so long as she doesn't have to do so today. But is such question-begging a concession to time rather than a victory over it? Carmen suffers, as she admits in the seguidilla, from boredom. Perhaps she sings to pass the time and to kill it, or to hasten the moment of truth when it will kill her—as Moralès or the factory girls smoke "pour tuer le temps." The motif in the overture which denotes her fate is ominous because of its authoritarian finality. Its quivering chords and thumping period mark a dead end, after which the score is hard put to recover.

For the opera's other characters, who lack the inventive opportunism of Carmen, music betokens an enslavement to time. The work is full of praise for metrical punctuality. Moralès assures Micaëla that José will be along just when he's needed—"tout à l'heure il y sera"—and, on the dot, he is. The children who mimic the parading soldiers are pedantic about their timekeeping and enumerate the steps they take, "marquant sans faire de faute." José's song about the dragon d'Alcala is proud of the soldier's undeviating tread: he is "exact et fidèle."

Carmen herself exhilaratingly uses the moment as a chance for revising herself and confounding expectation, as when she refuses to join in the smuggling escapade because (she claims) she's in love. Giovanni has the same talent for plucking motives and extenuations out of the air, as when he explains Elvira to Anna and Ottavio as a harmless madwoman or when he accuses Leporello of his own assault on Zerlina. Both Carmen and Giovanni live playfully and inconsequentially, which means unaccountably. José has no such temporal liberty. Anxious to mortgage the future by extorting futile promises from Carmen, he is as well the helpless creation of his own past—of the crime he committed in Navarre, and of the mother whose deputy is Micaëla. His music is all reverie, revisiting that lost past. In the duet with Micaëla, he goes back to his native village; in the flower song he reexperiences his imprisonment. Micaëla is forever retiring to that past while announcing that she'll emerge from it again later. "Je reviendrai" might almost be her motto. José's direst threat to Carmen is his assurance that the future will be another installment of their past. "Nous nous reverrons" he warns her as he disappears to visit that apocryphal mother.

The games Carmen and Don Giovanni delight in are existential caprices. The most thrilling erotic sensation of all, for them, is to risk everything on a dare or a jest or a practical joke. Don Giovanni can act in no other way. This is why he invades Anna's house, then later hints at his identity when he meets her with Ottavio; above all, it is why he accepts the Commendatore's challenge in the graveyard. Carmen behaves in the same way when she exchanges insults with Manuelita in the factory, and furthers her sarcastic advantage with a knife, or when she issues her ultimatum to José: kill me now, or else let me pass. Escamillo is an inevitable partner for her, because the bullring is the arena for just such a suicidal gambling. He exhibits this disdainful theatrical valor, relishing risk, when he fights with José. He warns his opponent of his disadvantage; winning the first round, he spares José's life because to take it wouldn't accord with the stylish etiquette which governs the rules of his game. It's ignominious to be the victor if you have never been seriously imperiled.

Such courting of danger is the energy of theatrical performance, which toreadors share with opera singers driven to produce exorbitant high

notes. Escamillo relies, to keep his courage up, on musical stimulation—
the "apostrophes, cres et tapage" of the crowd, with which his aria resounds. Great acting and singing are a leap into the unknown, a gladiato-
rial defiance of death. Giovanni tells the statue he won't be afraid. Carmen
awaits her rendezvous with José despite the counsel of her friends, and
taunts him with her love for Escamillo until he has no alternative but to
kill her. At such moments, their sensual music acquires its highest value: it
is the noisy protest of the life-force, decrying extinction.

Yet the music on which Giovanni and Carmen rely proves tragically
inflexible. Theatrically they can set their own tempo, but they must sing as
the measure dictates. The score has predestined them. Opera is a live performance, where things can change and be made new on the inspiration of
the instant; but it is also a book, foreknown and unalterable. The stage
may seem comically free, but the text is tragically fixed and fated. Hence
the punctiliousness in *Carmen*, which limits the heroine's liberty. In the
fourth act, the procession must happen in just the order the chorus prescribes—first the quadrille, then the alguacil, next the chulos, the ban-
derilleros and the picadors, after these the matador, and last of all the
alcalde. Giovanni suspects a devilish determinism is at work against his
pleasant adventuring ("miei piacevoli progressi"), since every time he initiates a scheme it is interrupted or frustrated. Carmen lives chancily and
arbitrarily, yet the dice she hurls into space—the flower she throws, at random, at José; the card she turns over in the mountains—can figure forth a
destiny by which she must abide. José rages to persuade her that, like the
rest of us, she is conditioned, forcing her to "subir la destinée."

In both operas, that tragic dispensation resides in a book. In *Don
Giovanni* it is the catalog, in *Carmen* the book on high she speaks of during the game of cards, where everyone has a page whose redoubtable words
(as she calls them) constitute your lot.

Leporello's catalog, by computing Giovanni's successes, renders him
finite. He encourages the numerical exponentiation of lust which is Giovanni's madness, arguing that it's necessary—for the sake of the scientific
method—to make love to every woman in the world. Giovanni has already
consoled eighteen hundred in this way, mutters Leporello as he advances
on Elvira. In his tour through the catalog, he tells her that Giovanni seduces crones for the arithmetical pleasure of adding them to the list. Giovanni himself anticipates that his party will yield him a dozen new entries.
The more accessions there are, the sooner Leporello can close the book on
an exhausted Giovanni, as he does in the epilogue when he sets out for the

inn to recruit a new master. The tally symbolizes accountancy, and thus the exaction of penalties. It is Leporello's cruelest joke to treat Elvira's passionate tirade as mere bookmaking. "Pare un libro stampato!" he says—she talks like a printed book. For him, print is an indictment. To write something down is to impugn it, to falsify it, or to kill it.

Carmen is equally superstitious about the sacred book which pre-empts her. Life, she believes, is scored. The cards are pitiless, and so is the musical text which she must obey. Mercédès and Frasquita read in the cards only what they want to find there: prophecies of love and money. Carmen interprets them more strictly, and resigns herself to their agenda for her. As she does so, the orchestra solemnly slows into a premature funeral march. Interestingly, there is no such scene in Mérimée. Carmen's fortune-telling belongs to Bizet's musical and fatally metrical conception of her. But Mérimée's story does end with her reduction to a book—indeed, with her cataloging. Its last chapter is a learned disquisition on the dialect of the gypsies, and their numerical system. Carmen has been long since dispensed with; she matters to Mérimée's taxonomist only as a footnote to his Romany studies.

Of course the tragedies of Giovanni and Carmen are not final. As gods, they die only to be reborn in other guises. As archetypes, they generate a prolific offspring in later operas. E. T. A. Hoffmann called *Don Giovanni* "the opera of operas," and is himself portrayed by Offenbach as a dejected Giovanni. Rossini, asked which of his operas he liked best, replied *"Don Giovanni!"* He had good reason for saying so. *Il Barbiere di Siviglia* is his epilogue to *Don Giovanni* rather than to *Le Nozze di Figaro* because its subject is the avidity of appetite, the ravenous sensuousness which quickens romanticism. The manic compulsiveness of Giovanni gives way to the frisky hedonism of Rossini's young people. When, at the end of the first act, the stunned Don Bartolo appears to have turned into a statue, Rossini parodies and thus reverses the tragic petrification which chills the flesh of Giovanni. The stultification is only temporary; Bartolo recovers, and the irrepressible comedy revives.

Verdi has his Giovannis too. The Duke in *Rigoletto*, conceding that even princes are the abject slaves of love, is one of them. Falstaff is another, though overripe, and more interested in keeping warm and well-fed than in the sexual chase. Thanks to this reformation, Falstaff is a Giovanni who survives to participate in—or rather to lead—the final ensemble of self-mockery. In *Un Ballo in Maschera*, Verdi winningly humanizes the Mozartean demon. Riccardo is an unpredatory Giovanni, content to be a flirt. Like Giovanni, he gives a party as a cover for assignations; and just as Kierkegaard nominates Cherubino as a junior Giovanni, a guileless adolescent libertine, so Riccardo has as his shadow, his emissary and his young self the mischievous and disrespectful page Oscar. Like Carmen, Riccardo is confronted by a prophecy when the sorceress foretells his assassination. But his response is Giovanni's in the graveyard: he laughs it off.

Opera's women continue to reincarnate Carmen. Wagner differentiated the operatic music of the Italians from that of the French by contrasting two variants of female immorality. Italian music, he thought, was a whore, brazen and lurid; French music was a coldly smiling coquette. The difference is that between Puccini's *Manon Lescaut* and Massenet's *Manon*—a savage, grasping ardor which parches and dies in the desert of its own obsession, against a more courtly frippery and a giggling wantonness. If these twin women are spirits of music, they are both aspects of the musical sensuality in Carmen. Her tragic ferocity is handed on to Puccini, her comic flouncing to Massenet.

In German opera, the fatal woman turns literally homicidal: Salome, Lulu. Dissected, Carmen reappears as the two sisters of Weill and Brecht in their sung ballet about the seven deadly sins of the bourgeoisie, *Die sieben Todsünden der Kleinbürger* (1933). Anna I is the singer, Anna II the dancer. Carmen could perform both functions, like Salome with her veils or Lulu in her cabaret act: when these characters start into motion, the body speaks. The two Annas, however, are segregated by their mercenary society. The singer is a vigilant objective commentator, the dancer a mute and wayward subject. The operatic truce between the arts breaks down. Anna II is the amoral heedlessness of music and dance, Anna I is the repressive superintendence of words. While the ballerina unguardedly gives herself to all comers, the singer stands back and worries about economic survival.

Giovanni's eroticism challenges death, Carmen's thrillingly embraces it. This reunion of opposites—of loving liveliness and extinction—is opera's perpetual subject, and perhaps its profoundest mystery, starting from the journey of Orpheus through the underworld. Necrophilia is endemic in opera because music and mysticism are natural allies. The singing voice, inordinate in its power and somehow miraculous as the production of a single human body, infuses the world with the vibrancy of its emotion; it makes audible the pantheistic collective life, unifying us all, which Jung called the oceanic sense. Love is one occasion when such self-enlargement occurs in human experience. In their duet, Tristan declares that he has become Isolde, and Isolde names herself Tristan. In love, the lonely self is obliterated by another; in death, that self is obliterated by all other things, or rather is absorbed into them.

Shaw's Giovanni, the evolutionary socialist Jack Tanner in *Man and Superman*, therefore laughingly proposes a suicide pact to Ann, his Donna Anna. He imagines clasping her on the edge of a precipice, then jumping off. The Mozartean hero has grown into self-destructive Tristan, and the music of desire has undergone a morbid alteration. In *Tristan und Isolde*, music has given up that vital hilarity which surges through Giovanni's champagne aria or Carmen's invitation to Lillas Pastia's. In Wagner's prelude, the unresolved chord is a nervous excruciation: a desire which longs for its own anesthesia, attained only—after many hours—when Isolde voluntarily dies. The orchestra with its wavily endless, ebbing melody is the undifferentiated oblivion in which the characters drown.

Carmen hears music descending from the sky. In *Tristan*, its source is inside the characters, or in the subconscious well underneath the stage. The bugler in *Carmen* or the fiddlers onstage for the parties in *Don Giovanni* are social suppliers of music. But there is no society left in *Tristan*, where the mind has consumed the world. The steersman high up the mast on Tristan's ship, the jeering sailors on the deck, the hunters sounding their horns at night, and the shepherd keeping watch with his doleful pipe on the headland at Kareol are all invisible, because their refrains are a psychological eavesdropping. Isolde draws the ocean into herself when she orders it to swamp the ship, and in her liebestod sinks into that same fluency, whose tides pour from her body. The chromaticism of Wagner's score, forever mutating motifs, won't rest until it has transformed and canceled everything, like Frau Minne who has—as Isolde tells Brangäne—changed death into love only to change it back again, at Tristan's bidding, into death. The duty of the characters is to sit still and wait for the music to extinguish them. Isolde allows herself to be delivered to Marke, and stays with him when Tristan is wounded. Tristan draws his sword on Melot, then allows himself to be run through. Music enjoins a suffering dramatic passivity: Tristan and Isolde are patients not agents.

They lack words to translate their experiences. Tristan tells Isolde he's a votary of "des Schweiges Herrin," the lady of silence. Their secrets are imparted by music: by the hiatus after Tristan enters Isolde's cabin, or after they drink the potion. Tristan ponders the shepherd's plaint on the cor anglais, that "alte Weise" which is crudely primitive yet at the same time anticipates a modern music at the end of its tonal tether—bleak, tuneless, intolerably repetitious. He remembers it as his earliest experience of the world; still he can't determine what it means. In the liebestod, Isolde attempts in vain to describe for the others the music which floods from the dead Tristan. "Höre ich nur diese Weise?" she asks—do I alone hear this song? Both words and music have been silenced. Desire attains its annihilation.

FOUR

Mephistopheles

DON GIOVANNI is claimed at last by the devil; José, tormented by Carmen in the smugglers' camp, says she is herself the devil, and she reminds him that she has already told him so. Opera's demons are proud of their infernal patron. Satan, as Gounod's Méphistophélès cries at the riotous Kermesse, directs the dance. Classically, the source of music is heaven, into which Monteverdi's Orfeo soars. Romanticism amends the myth: music is more likely to bubble out of a sensual hell. Opera has its birthplace in the underworld.

This devilment is the subject of Weber's opera about romantic nature, *Der Freischütz* (1821). In the spooky forest, Max the disgraced hunter angrily demands "lebt kein Gott?"—is there no God? The benign Christian overseer seems in abeyance, until the hermit belatedly appears as his representative; but an operatic devil is on hand to fill the place left vacant. Kaspar the free-shooter, in league with hell, tempts Max in a ribald drinking song, addressed to "Gott Bacchus." His hideout is a woodland inferno, the Wolf's Glen, where he arranges a circle of stones with a skull in the middle for the conjuring of spirits. The demons he raises materialize in Weber's orchestra—cawing birds, baying hounds, or a snarling boar. Opera is on the edge of impiety because it raises its voice in protest or imprecation against heaven, in Max's atheistic question (which leaves a somber, empty silence behind it), in Kaspar's shouted countdown as he casts the bullets, or in the growling speech of the monstrous Samiel.

Even indoors, there are bogeys and devilish portents. The cheery Aennchen tries to laugh Agathe out of her dismay by explaining away a nightmare. She calls herself "ein geschikte Traumdeuterin," a clever dream-interpreter. Yet this is a Freudian talent, which confirms the residence of ghosts and ogres inside the mind. Aennchen goes on to prove the point by interpreting another dream. Her cousin imagined that a moaning fiery-eyed beast with clanking chains had invaded her bed; she awoke and found it was Nero the watchdog. Does the banal explanation really appease the erotic terror of the fantasy? Agathe prays, in her aria "Leise, leise," to pacify the nature which Kaspar rouses to stormy fury, but it demands a sacrifice. Kuno at the beginning of the opera tells the story of a wrongdoer punished by being fettered to a stag, which was then hunted; in Weber's source, the Gothic anthology called the *Gespensterbuch*, Agathe herself was the target, shot by the marksman Max, who ended in a lunatic asylum. That conclusion is averted in the opera, but only just, and improbably. Agathe's successors will have to complete the ritual by espousing the demon: Senta bewitched by the Dutchman, Renata inflamed by her infernal lover in Prokofiev's *The Fiery Angel*, the nuns maddened by hysterical desire in Penderecki's *The Devils of Loudon*.

The paroxysms of Prokofiev's Renata are wished upon her by Mephistopheles, who happens to be traveling through sixteenth-century Germany with Faust, cannibalizing tardy waiters and playing other devilish tricks on humanity. This is the latest of his apparitions in opera; ever since Goethe, Mephistopheles has been one of the form's most irresistible agents.

Goethe's *Faust*, which occupied him from the 1790s to 1832, redeems both the apostate and the devil who misleads him. For the sixteenth century, the necromancer Faust, selling his soul to Mephistopheles in exchange for prohibited knowledge, led a "damnable life" and had a "deserved death." Goethe's hero is no sinner. His quest to understand the mysteries of existence is justified, and Mephistopheles, encouraging this ambition, is the unwitting instrument of goodness. Because its drama is metaphysical, *Faust* needs music, which Goethe called "the mediator of the ineffable." He likened it to *Don Giovanni* and *Die Zauberflöte*, and wished Mozart had lived long enough to compose a score for it. Beginning as tragedy, *Faust* advances into opera—for Helen of Troy in the second part, Goethe wanted an actress to mime while an opera singer intoned his poetry—and ends as oratorio: in 1844 Schumann set Goethe's final scene, representing the ascent of Faust's soul, and in 1906 Mahler made the same choral episode the conclusion of his Eighth Symphony.

Faust the scholar, at the beginning of Goethe's play, despairingly rejects his dusty books. Opening his Bible, he reads that "in the beginning was the Word." He can't believe that creation is verbal; he wants it to be tonal, and the rationality of language is overruled by the life-force which resounds in music—the choir at Easter, the trumpeting song of the soldiers, the serenades of Mephistopheles. When Faust is wedded to his muse Helen, he derives music from her. He gives her a lesson in rhyming: language aspires to lyricism, and attains it. Hofmannsthal declared in an introduction to a volume of Goethe's opera texts that the dramatic poet's abounding joy directed him toward an art of incantation. Nature for Goethe is a sequence of festivals, and opera is the most festive of forms; *Faust*, which as Hofmannsthal puts it "postulates music at every step," is therefore the archetypal opera.

Nevertheless, the first musical setting of Goethe's drama—*La Damnation de Faust*, begun by Berlioz in 1828, first performed in 1846—can't call itself an opera. Berlioz subtitled it a "dramatic legend." It lies between song and narrative, or between symphony and drama. It is not an opera because Faust is so disengaged from it, self-exiled from a choral, communal life which disgusts him—the rowdy peasants enjoying "la musique et la danse," the students searching the nocturnal town for girls, the bestial mob in the tavern. His position is always that of an ironic, remorseful detachment. Gounod's Faust spots Marguerite in the marketplace, and exchanges a glance and some flirtatious words. Berlioz's hero dreams of her, and she in turn recognizes him as a figure of reverie. This Faust can imagine the world but not participate in it. He belongs in the solitude of landscape—promenading morosely on the plains, testing the echo of his own voice on the mountaintop, plunging to sublime annihilation in the abyss.

The penalty of such isolation is boredom. Faust complains throughout of ennui, the most unoperatic emotion. To divert him, Berlioz keeps him constantly and arbitrarily on the move. The ground plan of *La Damnation de Faust* is a map of the discontented, whimsical, digressing romantic mind, traversing an entire continent in the hope of escaping from itself. Berlioz worked on it during a concert tour of eastern Europe in post chaises, trains and steamboats. Its sections mark the stages of his itinerary, like the moping pilgrimage of the Byronic hero in his *Harold en Italie*. Music relieves Faust's depression because of its ease at free association. For the orchestra, movement is as quick as modulation; a few bars can cover a thousand miles, like the headlong gallop of Vortex and Giaour toward the sulfurous lake at the end of the work. Those horses, Méphistophélès says, are swift as thought. *La Damnation* takes its form from this mental impatience. This is why it begins in Hungary, never visited by Goethe's hero. Berlioz explained that he wanted to make use of the Rákóczi March, and decreed the detour so he could include it—"and I would have taken Faust to any other place on earth had I had the smallest musical reason for doing so." He is Méphistophélès to his own Faust, prescribing (as the devil does when he ejects the scholar from his study) a change of air.

The Méphistophélès of Berlioz does indeed function as a supplier of musical diversions, barking out the song of the flea or conducting the will-o'-the-wisps. He constructs illusory theaters to give play to Faust's stifled desires: hence the aerial ballet of sylphs chased by lustful gnomes. He must churn out music on demand. Before his jeering serenade he mimics a man grinding at a hurdy-gurdy. He calls for the assistance of fiddlers from hell, and commands the fireflies "au nom du diable, en danse!" He identifies himself to Faust as the spirit of life, and if Faust's domain is the verbal intellect, Méphistophélès rules over the musical body, feeding its appetites with sensation and delirious sounds. He debauches language, and when Faust tumbles into the pit the devils rejoice in a jargon of nonsensical grunts and yells—"Diff! diff! merondor, merondor aysko! Has! has!" Berlioz on another occasion invented a language to match the savagery of music, when the Nubian slaves dancing for Didon in *Les Troyens* chant in their own nonsensical tongue: "Ha! Ha! Amaloué! Midonaé!" Here his Pandaemonium is music's unleashing as barbarous noise, which mangles words or engulfs them. This infernal hullabaloo romantically rescinds the contract between Apollo and Monteverdi's Orfeo.

When Goethe's Faust demands the immediate seduction of Gretchen, Mephistopheles sneers that he's talking just like a Frenchman. The character's acclimatization to France and to grand opera happens thanks to Gounod, whose *Faust* was first performed in 1859. Gounod's hero has dispensed with the moody mental disquiet of his predecessor in Berlioz. His ambition is sexual adventure; he is operatic because orgiastic—"A moi les plaisirs des jeunes maîtresses!" he cries. The girls he overhears sing of the mad lyricism of the birds in the fields: all of nature is infected by his hedonism. When he resolves on suicide, he lifts the goblet of poison in a cheery brindisi. He has a devil to suit his cravings. As Faust longs for youth, so Méphistophélès here flatters himself on being fashionably up-to-date, dressed like a gentleman. No enemy of God, he is Faust's colleague in rakery. Gounod's fiend, like romantic music, swamps the anxious reason. Méphistophélès appears when Faust curses science, faith, and the patience of delayed gratification. At first he tempts his new client with the vulgar gains and glories of bourgeois man—gold, fame, power. Only when he offers youth does Faust respond, as skittish as a rejuvenated Don Pasquale, exhilarated by "l'energie des instincts puissants, et la folle orgie du coeur et des sens!" He signs away his soul after Méphistophélès teases him with the preview of Marguerite. Their relation is already clear: the devil is to be his panderer. Méphistophélès finds time for an erotic conquest of his own, answering the unvoiced prayer of Marguerite's friend Marthe by telling her that her husband is dead, then courting her himself and alluring her with tales of his travels. She is, he smirks, only too itchily eager to wed the devil. Gounod makes Faust a small-town Don Giovanni, with Méphistophélès his gloating Leporello.

The Faust of Berlioz shunned the guzzling in the Leipzig wine vaults. Gounod's Faust, however, is at home with the swilling students, adepts of the barrel as Wagner calls them, and the Kermesse is a festival commemorating the Dionysian birth of opera. As the glasses clink and Gounod's instrumentation jingles, Wagner supplements the ideology of Faust: he wants to go on drinking forever. Méphistophélès challenges Bacchus to open his personal cellar, and in a diabolical miracle causes the wine to pour forth unchecked. His song of the golden calf is another defiant apology for opera: an anthem to material splendor and carnal passion, pounded out to insult heaven like the brazen idol (which Méphistophélès calls "vainqueur des dieux"), and exciting the crowd to a fury of song and dance. Revved up by Méphistophélès, the earth gyrates, and at the end of the scene a giddy compulsive waltz sweeps Marguerite away.

Expensive and ostentatious, opera is the art of Mammon. It's this aspect of the form which Gounod's *Faust* celebrates. Its lushest melodies swell with the pride of possession: Faust surveying Marguerite's "demeure chaste et pure," Valentin congratulating himself on having defended the native soil of his ancestors. Its tenderest dreams are of unearned wealth: the devil's wine, which no one has to pay for, or the jewel casket deposited in the garden. Its worst curse is the reversal of this Midas touch, with which Méphistophélès afflicts Faust's rival Siébel. When he picks up the posy of flowers, it withers; he automatically devalues everything. Marguerite's fantasies are of wealth. Her song about the King of Thule dwells on the gold cup, invested with so many charms. She wonders if he's a nobleman (and in this opera, God is at the summit of a social hierarchy, saluted by Valentin as "Seigneur et Roi des cieux"); when he complimented her as a fine lady, she denied that she was one, but the jewel box encourages her to dress up as if she were a king's daughter, and her voice takes on the spangly glitter of the ornaments she wears.

Gounod the church organist and student of Palestrina's music was himself a spoiled priest, aware of the blasphemy inherent in opera. Therefore the church in *Faust* is the last refuge of a smug sanctimoniousness. When the guilty Marguerite goes to pray, the devil is her confessor, and Méphistophélès also leads the priggish congregation in condemning her. Immediately afterward, the soldiers troop home, full of the same pious rectitude which bolsters up the churchgoers. Their pompous, jaunty march is the sound of the bourgeoisie on strutting parade. Valentin, supported by this conformism, tells Marguerite that though God may forgive her, society never will.

When Siébel resents the innuendo of his chuckling serenade to Marguerite, Méphistophélès sneers "Vous n'aimez pas donc la musique?" Music and lecherous devilry, it seems, are synonymous. So are dance and harlotry. The first ballet in French grand opera is that of the corrupt nuns in Meyerbeer's *Robert le Diable* (1831); for the Paris performances of *Tannhäuser* in 1861, Wagner composed an orgasmic Bacchanal to be danced by the inmates of the Venusberg; when *Faust* was revived at the Opéra in 1869, Gounod added a balletic riot—the voluptuous cabaret of Walpurgis Night, choreographed by Méphistophélès.

Since *Robert le Diable*, opera had been a school of delicious perdition. Meyerbeer's Bertram promises the soul of his Faust, Robert, to a congress of fiends who shriek and howl in a cavern. Though he warns Alice that she has trespassed on a mystery forbidden to humans, hell sounds no worse than a shrill, rowdy party. The defiled nuns—raised by Bertram from their unhallowed graves to entice Robert—are another of opera's profanations: harlots in religious habits. During the Walpurgis entertainments, Gounod's Méphistophélès serves Faust a potion to extinguish his remorse, and the chorus proposes a toast to the ancient gods—the pagan patrons of opera, whose recipe for human suffering is drunkenness and sexual indulgence. Faust, drugged, asks where they are. Méphistophélès answers "Dans mon empire," and he could mean the Paris Opéra as well as the Brocken, for at his bidding the Hartz Mountains part to disclose a banqueting hall where the ballet is performed by a lineup of notorious courtesans, among them Hélène (whose face launched the thousand ships to Troy), a bumping and grinding Cléopâtre, and Phryné. Faust watches titillated, like a salacious clubman in his box at the Opéra or a customer reviewing candidates in the salon of a brothel; he selects Phryné.

Goethe's metaphysical quest, adapted to music, has become an erotic escapade. The *Mefistofele* composed by Verdi's librettist Arrigo Boito—first performed in 1868, revised in 1875—is more conscientiously faithful to Goethe; yet in its own way it warps the source, to wrest from it a Faustian justification of opera. Where Gounod's *Faust* is worldly, mercenary and luxurious, Boito's *Mefistofele* respects the spirituality of Goethe's drama. It retains the prologue in heaven, where Mefistofele taunts the nebulous angelic hosts and takes up God's challenge to ensnare Faust. Though Gounod's Marguerite is concerned about the social pedigree of her suitor, Boito's Margherita has theological scruples, and solemnly asks whether he believes in her religion. He replies that he has his own (which is opera's as well): he believes in instinct and ecstasy.

Boito knows that there is more to *Faust* than the hero's dalliance with Gretchen. He includes excerpts from Goethe's second part, with the dying Faust's summation of his humanitarian endeavors and his pilgrimage to the civilizing source of Greece—a classical Sabbath to match the Gothic witches' Sabbath on the Brocken. Gretchen was merely a sexual conquest; Faust's muse and goddess is Helen of Troy. Boito's Margherita is discomfited by Faust's rapturously unorthodox hymn to "Natura! Amor! Mistero! Vita! Dio!" Outgrowing her, he goes on to share this operatic faith in erotic mystery with Elena, in her Arcadian paradise. Goethe sent Faust to Helen—against the urging of Mephistopheles, who prefers the somber north—in the hope of reuniting European culture: the romantic hero weds the classical heroine, Germany is fused with Greece. Boito's opera proposes a different merger: that of Germany with Italy. A northern artist observing the Walpurgis Night in the first part of *Faust* announces his plan to make a tour of Italy, which Goethe himself had done in 1786. The match between Faust and Elena in *Mefistofele* is less an accord between Germanic and Grecian souls than the marriage of words and music, Teutonic philosophy and Latin melody. From their embrace, Boito said, the pair generated "an ideal poetry, eclectic, new, powerful"—the operatic amalgam of all the arts.

In practice, there are difficulties. Boito was preoccupied by dualisms, and in an 1863 ode described man as a compound of seraph and demon, butterfly and grub. Opera is equally dualistic, with rational words yoked to passionate music. Faust's pupil Wagner intellectually scorns the jubilation of the Kermesse: words are superior to the vulgar romping and yodeling of music. Faust too begins as the student of holy words, meditating on his Gospel and academically insisting that Mefistofele should speak clearly ("parla chiaro") when explaining the terms of their pact. But the more nimbly these characters use words, the less truth they possess. Mefistofele mocks Faust for asking his name, because he knows his victim has lost faith in verbal proofs ("gli argomenti . . . del Verbo"). The devil is himself a witty casuist, who remarks that it's pleasant to exchange chitchat with God; he plays on words to rob them of meaning. One word only, a minimal monosyllable, is essential to him, since it's his means of nullifying and negating everything: the refrain of his aria "Son lo Spirito che nega" is a rumbling, guttural "No." Mefistofele's campaign against the lyricism of harmonious heaven and the rationality of human intellect employs an idiom which is neither musical nor verbal—the hissing he invites during the prologue, his howling in Faust's study, the derisive whistles which are the cadenza to "Son lo Spirito," the explosion of mirthless hilarity at the end of the aria "Ecco il mondo." At the witches' Sabbath, he is an inverted Orpheus, commanding nature to erupt in untuned tumult rather than subduing it to the serene rule of music.

Therefore Mefistofele's antagonist in the opera is not God but the songstress Elena. Helen is a recurring character in opera, one of the form's disreputable deities. She appears in Gounod's ballet as a legendary immoralist; this is her meaning for Offenbach, in whose operetta *La Belle Hélène* (1864) she's a bored wife itching for an affair. Offenbach's Greeks believe the gods have deserted them. Hélène complains that Vénus has extinguished desire. The arrival of Pâris to abduct her, disguised as the priestly envoy of Vénus, proves her wrong. The operetta restores a licentious faith, and Oreste gratefully sings a toast to Vénus and Bacchus. Anatole France's novel *Thaïs*, laughing at the asceticism of Christianity, suggested an alternative to our official redeemer: a benevolent corrupter, like Helen of Troy. This female Christ, devoted to pleasure, is reincarnated as the Alexandrian courtesan Thaïs. Bewitched by her, the monk Athanaël flogs himself in Massenet's *Thaïs* (1894), but he's still perturbed by the same harlots who dance for Gounod's Faust—Hélène, Phryné, Vénus Astarté. They are the resident good-time girls of opera.

Strauss returned to the mystery of Helen in *Die Ägyptische Helena* (1928) and challenged Hofmannsthal "to find a definite moral solution" to the problem of her infidelity. He did so by splitting his Helena in half: a sorceress saves her from the rage of her husband Menelas by persuading him that the gods kept the real Helena safe in Egypt, while Paris abducted and enjoyed a phantom; Helena, assuming responsibility for her guilt, rejects the deceit and is accepted by Menelas in all her ambiguity, as loyal wife and as fickle adulteress. The solution works "in terms of music," as Strauss said, because music is moodily unstable, allowing its characters to be many different people at once. Menelas must learn to accept that Helena is composed of opposites, which are twined together in her like the dissonant chords and unresolved tonalities of the Wagnerian or Straussian orchestra.

The myth of Helen, in all these instances, serves as an apology for music. For Boito too, her significance is lyrical: she's an operatic siren, first heard in a barcarole where she and her companion Pantalis alternately direct each other to sing—"Canta"—while Faust, in the distance, melodiously repeats her name. Mefistofele comments on the scene in his grotesque, stammering patter. Faust, abandoning the words Mefistofele twists and tortures, extols Elena as the spirit of music: he delights, he says, in her fluid, songlike idiom. The language he praises is supposed to be Greek; of course in actuality it's Italian, where the lilt and liquidity of speech swell naturally into song. In Goethe's play, Faust teaches Helen how to rhyme. In the opera, he doesn't need to, because they are conversing not in German but in Italian, where everything rhymes with everything else already. He admires her song, and she admires his speech: "Parla, parla!" she says, and begs him to teach her his loquacity. Their union is a sexual symbol for opera, coupling the female unconsciousness of music with the upright male articulacy of drama. Faust, who appears in this classical landscape dressed as a Renaissance knight, brings about Elena's rebirth. At first she is remorsefully preoccupied with memories of Troy; he draws her out of her despair, uplifts her and restores her to vitality. In the course of their duet, Greek tragedy is reborn as Italian opera.

The chorus acclaims their union as "Poesia libera." Music has freed poetry from its bondage to words. Expiring, Boito's Faust sees his career a sacred poem. Though he's referring to his scheme for the betterment of mankind, this "santa poesia" is in fact the compound of different arts and cultures he has experienced with Elena and the merger of sacred and profane, angel and demon, which he learned from Mefistofele: he can die content because his life's achievement is to have invented opera.

The tradition terminates with Ferruccio Busoni, whose *Doktor Faust* was first performed posthumously in 1925. Helena appears in it as a veiled, mute chimera whom Faust cannot seize—no romantic muse, merely a scenic illusion, briefly irradiating the tavern in Wittenberg. Busoni's Faust deals in such unrealities, which are the insubstantial stuff of music. At the court of Parma, he stages a silent operatic pageant of shadows, with Dalila embracing Samson and Salome condemning the Baptist. These women are not projections of his desire, like Gounod's courtesans; they're the obsequious marionettes directed by his magic. Nor is Faust a damned soul craving absolution. For Busoni he's simply a man of the musical theater, conjuring sounds into sight.

Busoni objected to realism in opera because he thought music had no business trying to present things. Wagner's themes, supposedly depicting swords or rings or dragons, are an elaborate hoax. Strauss, even more credulous, thought the day would soon arrive when music could compose a dinner table, enabling you to hear the difference between the spoons and the forks. Busoni dispensed with this mimicry of painting. He also disapproved of opera's adjustment to so-called real life: the smugglers of Bizet, the peasants of Mascagni. Because the terrain of music is invisible, the subjects of opera should be supernatural. When Busoni's Faust arrives at Parma to mount his eerie spectacle, the courtiers whisper that he brings with him the unseen world. Before settling on Faust, Busoni considered an opera about another magus, Merlin; he was attracted as well to the subject of Don Giovanni, whose obsession is elusive and impalpable—not the actual women itemized on the list but some ideal, unattainable creature, like the Helena envisaged by Faust.

As Busoni's opera begins, Faust is studying an experimental process in his alchemical laboratory. The orchestra seethes like his phials and tubes, uncannily transforming matter. The temptation he's offered is cabalistic rather than sensual: a volume of conjuring formulae, both mystical and musical. From it he learns a theatrical sorcery. Describing a circle on the ground, into which he steps to invoke Lucifer, he is demarcating the stage as a precinct where a rite can be performed. At Parma he effortlessly switches off the daylight before he begins his demonstration. He exults in the dangerous power of the theater and its cruel realization of fantasies, taunting the Duke with a caricature of himself and ordering Mephistopheles to murder the creditors who besiege him. Since this is a musical drama, his grandest endeavor is to make sonic ghosts take on material form. His infernal counselors are six tongues of flame, hovering in the room as aerial voices chant. Here Busoni hints at the arcane power of opera: to sing is to speak in tongues. When the sixth flame calls itself Mephistopheles, Faust issues a theatrical challenge. He dares it to show itself in its true form and substance; the devil promptly appears.

Busoni was reluctant to take Goethe as his source. Romantic metaphysics no longer mattered to him. His Faust is a showman, so Busoni borrowed him from the ancient German puppet play. Faust is free to disbelieve both in heaven and hell, and when he dies both God and devil—as he says—expire with him. While Catholics and Protestants squabble in the tavern, he enumerates his own articles of faith: wine, women, and the surest consolation of all, which he calls "heilige Tonkunst," the holy art of music. Busoni believed that "music was born free," and that its destiny lay in asserting this freedom by casting off the reality of earth and taking to the sky, where it enjoys an "untrammeled immateriality." Faust, the master of "sounding air," has himself been liberated by music. For the free man, opera is the only plausible religion.

FIVE

Dagon

AN ORATORIO is a room for prayer. It is also a sacred alternative to opera, and throughout its history it has existed in competition with the secular form. Could opera be defined as oratorio profaned? During the hurricane in *Porgy and Bess*, the God-fearing inhabitants of Catfish Row huddle indoors intoning a babble of prayers. Into their congregation bursts the outlaw Crown, who turns their pious oratory into a randy operatic party with his song about the redheaded woman. Sportin' Life enunciates opera's attitude to biblical writ when he argues that "It ain't necessarily so." Certainly the characters of opera worship strange gods—a heterodox pantheon including Poppea's Amore and Isolde's Frau Minne; Sarastro's Isis or Osiris and Akhnaten's Aten; the Fthà of the priestess in *Aida* and the Irminsul of the Druids in *Norma*; Dourga, Ganeça and Siva, the Oriental deities tended by Lakmé in the opera by Delibes; and Dagon, with whom the Israelites taunt the Philistines in Handel's *Samson* and Saint-Saëns's *Samson et Dalila*.

The earliest of oratorios, Emilio de Cavalieri's *Rappresentatione di Anima, e di Corpo*—a debate between soul and body, written for the carnival season in Rome in 1600—already defines the opposition between its own devotional form and the unbridled passion play of opera. Cavalieri's aspiring Soul is the rhetorical crusader of oratorio, like Handel's soloists prophesying vengeance or purveying comfort in the *Messiah*. Beefy, contented Body is the carnal genius of opera: Don Giovanni gorging at his last supper, Falstaff igniting himself with his beaker of wine, Isolde with her potion. Though Soul may win the debate, music is a bodily joy, and the argument concludes with an anthology of jubilant dances, each of the chorus's stanzas performed to a different step.

In the eighteenth century, opera and oratorio remained inimical, obliging Handel to make a choice between them. Exhausted by egomaniac singers and disgusted by the frippery of opera, Handel in 1741 abandoned it. Thereafter his dramatic works were officially oratorios, but they continue to discriminate between sacred and secular passion. *Samson* in 1743 is oratorio's reproof to the heathenism of opera; *Semele* the next year questions that judgment, and operatically extols pleasure rather than faith, the concern of Samson and of oratorio. Samson is the chosen one of the God of Israel, who tests him by breaking him and endows him with moral strength; Semele is the erotic favorite of a different god, the philandering adulterous Jupiter.

Semele's world is that of classical myth, licentious and fantastic. Yet Handel also derived the Christian forbearance of Samson from a classical source: Milton's *Samson Agonistes*, a version of Greek tragedy. The exchanges in Milton's drama between the hero and a chorus which is his conscience suggested to Handel the solemn moral inquisitions of oratorio. Wagner and Nietzsche proposed opera as a rebirth of Greek tragedy—a theater devoted to the musical revelry of Dionysus. Handel returns to the same origins, but sees the tragedy's rebirth in oratorio not opera.

The agony of Handel's Samson is that he must abide the performance of an opera. The oratorio is set on the feast of Dagon, when Samson is allowed a day's respite from the mill: "Their superstition yields / This rest." The Philistines treat the holiday as a rite, a "joyful sacred festival," but they mean that it's an opera, and they chirp that "To song and dance we give the day." The purposes of song are immoral. Dalila uses her voice to wheedle and seduce, the ogre Harapha with his "rougher tongue" uses it to boast, blowing his own trumpet in "Honour and arms." In her aria about the turtledove, Dalila's companion describes an erotic and luxurious vocal music of "plaintive notes and am'rous moan"; Dalila converts her followers to a warbling exhibition of what she calls "the voice of love." Samson, dismissing her, mutes her: "I'll hear no more / The charmer's voice." Harapha appraises Samson as a colleague in vocal gigantism, and says he has come "to see if thy appearance answers *loud* report." For Samson, it's a rule of opera that empty vessels resonate the most impressively, and he dismisses Harapha as "Thou bulk, of spirit void!"

The Philistines scheme to lure Samson back into the theater. Harapha describes the "triumph, pomp, and games" with which they sacrifice to Dagon, and wants to exhibit Samson at "this solemn feast." Samson scorns their vaudeville, "prostituting holy things to idols," and declares that his Hebrew law "forbids / My presence at their vain religious rites"; he will not "be their fool, / And play before their God." Abstaining from anything which might be mistaken for operatic showing-off, Samson won't even dramatize his feelings. He explains that his torments aren't physical but oppress "the very inmost mind," and only consents to attend the feast when prompted by "some inward motions"; he's not seen pulling down the temple. The Philistines "shout and sing," but his judgment is to reduce their brassy music to confused noise when the pillars fall. His funeral enjoins a muffling of music. Manoah orders that he should be attended to his tomb "with *silent* obsequies, and fun'ral train."

Once Samson has iconoclastically ruined opera, music can be redeemed and restored to men. Manoah wishes his "great acts enroll'd / In verse heroic, or sweet lyric song." Priority is given to poetry, written to be read in respectful silence; the lyricism which is at last released in the Israelite Woman's address to the bright seraphim is the sound of the retuned, harmonized sky, rather than a music made by men. She hears loud, uplifted trumpets blow, but the players are angels, and when the chorus commands

> Let their celestial concerts all unite,
> Ever to sound his praise in endless blaze of light

it is light not a voice which is imagined to be singing, and doing so soundlessly.

The creed of oratorio is a self-denial like Samson's: refraining from drama, hushing music. However, as soon as Handel propounded his gospel he went on to outrage it, in a work which is opera camouflaged as oratorio. Dalila pleads that Samson should "let other senses taste delight"; *Semele* is about the titillation of those senses. Samson is God's abject prophet. Semele, though, is ambitious to be made a goddess. Jupiter promises that she need only utter her desire and he will empower her to obtain it. She demands immortality, and Juno advises her to have Jupiter appear before her in the form of the Thunderer, as when he embraces Saturnia to pay "the nuptial rites." Coition with a god, Semele thinks, will deify her; instead she is scorched by his incandescence, and destroyed. Denied divinity, she decides, like one of those preening opera singers whose antics infuriated Handel, to worship herself as a diva. "Myself I shall adore," she vows; dazzled by her reflection in the mirror, she shakes off small galaxies of vocal ornament and elasticizes the word "pleasing"—which is how she finds her image—so that it lasts forever. Jupiter's amorous technique depends on that hedonism which is the ideology of opera. "I must with speed amuse her," he says when she grows bored and irritable.

Samson's asceticism has been vanquished by pleasure. The rite changes to a social observance. *Semele* begins with a sacrifice to Juno on the flaming altar, but the goddess when she appears in person is a vengeful termagant, only too human, and Jove's thunderbolts express sexual pique not moral outrage. Somnus the god of drowsy stupor is no unmoved mover: rather he is too lazy to move. Cadmus, rebuking Ino, demands in the quartet "Why dost thou . . . all our solemn rites profane?" and when thunder extinguishes the altar flame the priests suspect a blackening of their Mass: "Some god averse our holy rites controls." They advise the betrothed to "fly this holy place with speed!" The spirit of opera is glad to quit a prim and pious sanctuary. Samson's moral vigilance—sternly wakeful during his "total eclipse," as oratorio demands—relaxes into a delicious slumber. Juno applies to Somnus for a spell to make the insomniac dragons guarding Semele nod off: opera emerges from the sleep of reason. Semele lolls in a coma, and complains that she must wake up and lose her "visionary joys." "Oh sleep, again deceive me," she begs, "to my arms restore my wand'ring love!" and she induces that deception in her self-hypnotizing elongation of "wand'ring." Music suspends time, indulging the idling vagrancy of the voice.

Semele has its own operatic answer to oratorio's celestial concert. During the entertainments in the Arcadian fields, Ino comments that the planetary spheres thrill with music, "and silence now is drown'd / In ecstasy of sound!" She and Semele instruct the "immortal choir" and bid "each sacred minstrel tune his lyre." Yet the ecstasy they purvey is terrestrial and carnal, and their chorus, while garlanding earth with heavenly lays, seeks only to make "all appear divine."

Opera debauches oratorio again in a later work dealing with Handel's hero: the *Samson et Dalila* of Saint-Saëns in 1877. Saint-Saëns first planned the work as oratorio, and never completely adapted it to opera. A conflict remains between the God of Israel worshiped by oratorio and the festive Dagon who is the patron of opera—between moral uplift and sensual subversion; between the declamatory, sermonizing idiom of Samson and the slithery, chromatic style of Dalila.

Samson, as in oratorio, emerges from and conducts the choir of his acolytes, rousing the populace from despair to indignation outside the temple of Dagon. His followers treat this outburst as divine ventriloquism, not lyric effusion: the breath of the Lord has inspired him, they say. Like the oratorio singer, he is a high-minded lecturer. The fanatically stolid, steady march of Samson's "Nous avons vu . . ." contrasts with the sly maneuverings of Dalila's dance; the hymn of the aged Hebrew men gives way to the seditious entreaties of the Philistine women, who invoke the pagan, seasonal god of earth when they sing of spring, not a Christian deliverer above this world. The first of these ensembles is reverently quiet, the second suggestively whispered; the men are an orderly regiment, underpinned by the bass who is their leader and mentor, the women more rhythmically wayward, liable to little syncopated detours, and encouraged by a lavish orchestra—swooning violins, a tinkling triangle. Operatically, Dalila counterfeits emotion. For the tryst with Samson she has, she says, prepared her tears, and her erotic appeal—"Mon coeur s'ouvre à ta voix"—is a calculated show.

Opera and oratorio proceed in parallel. Dalila is melodically languorous, while Samson berates her in the rough-hewn lumpish lines of "Esclave de mon Dieu . . .": instinct confronts law. In the first act, Samson upbraids the pusillanimous chorus whose conscience he is; in the third act, he is upbraided by a chorus which is unseen because it's now within him, as his accusing conscience—and to ensure their safety from the sensuous contagion of music, the offstage voices at the mill are unaccompanied by the orchestra. This chorus, a moral jury, is at once contrasted with an operatic mob, in the yawning aubade of the Philistines. Theirs is the collective voice of desire and satiation. The final scene is the clash of two irreconcilable musical cultures. It is set in the temple of Dagon, but the worship of this spurious god is a Bacchanal. Though the libations are supposedly sacred, Dalila takes the occasion for a drinking song, and her flourishes sound almost like hiccups. The Philistines romp through an infectiously hilarious laughing chorus. Religion in opera must be an orgy: the dance round the golden calf in *Faust* or in Schönberg's *Moses und Aron*. Samson's only recourse is vocal abstinence. His utterances in the final scene are asides, directed away from the indecent rite. Asked by the Philistines to repeat his love song, he delivers himself of a desperate prayer; when he destroys the infidel theater which poses as a temple, oratorio renders its last judgment on opera.

Oratorio venerates a single, true god: Samson's "seul Dieu d'Israel."

Opera is happy with an eclectic polytheism, and the Philistines, fleeing from Samson, mutter that they'll abandon their houses, their wives, and—in the plural—their gods. When Dalila speaks in the singular of "un dieu plus puissant que le tien," she means an urge not a deity.

Throughout the nineteenth century, opera is an alternative religion, and its characters profess to be recondite pagan gods, or else their priests and priestesses. In the Babylon of Rossini's *Semiramide*, they are devotees of Baal or else, like Assur, his descendants. Though Semiramide is hailed as a goddess on her entrance, she's among the sinners pledged to false gods who are lodged in hell by Dante. Her incestuous love for her son Arsace is one of those violations of taboo which opera relishes and encourages.

In 1863, forty years after *Semiramide*, Rossini composed a *Petite Messe Solenelle* in which four singers carol and trill the Latin text of the Mass in epicurean jollity, accompanied by two pianos and a wheezing harmonium. He underlined this comic sacrilege in impishly begging God's forgiveness for it. He called it "the last mortal sin of my old age" and wondered "is it really holy music that I wrote or in the end music of the devil?"

Meyerbeer's operas go further than Rossini's teasing: they declare religion a fraud. *Les Huguenots* (1836), dealing with the massacre of Protestants by French Catholics on St. Bartholomew's Day in 1572, wishes a plague on both bigoted camps. The Huguenots are as vengeful as the Carlists, who call on their friars to sanctify a mass murder. The old retainer Marcel interrupts a Catholic party to sing a thundering Lutheran chorale, which he follows with a military scherzo rebuking papistry and the infernal sex, hellish temples and sinful Dalilas. All are blown away by his snorting cannonades of derision: "Piff, paff, piff!"

In *Le Prophète* (1849), Meyerbeer exposes another Protestant fanatic—John of Leyden, who established a Zionist theocracy at Münster in 1534—as an astute faker. The holy ministry of the Anabaptists, whose savior Meyerbeer's Jean pretends to be, conceals their operatic bedevilment. Jean's mother Fidès aptly defines them as priests of Baal. The Anabaptists condemn the lecherous feudal lord Oberthal to lead a pure life, as a sample of which they embark on the boozy communion of a brindisi; Jean's last gesture as their leader, at the party which celebrates their conquest of the cathedral, is another drinking song, saluting the intoxication and delirium which are his and opera's equivalents to religious experience. The goblet he wields contains, instead of Christ's blood, a "nectar brûlant." Jean's prayers are political oratory, exploiting the superstitious dread of his followers and attributing his military ambitions to the harping angels who (he claims) urge him on. The opera abounds in accusations of sacrilege—Fidès arraigns her son for his crime, and is herself called a blasphemer when she curses the spurious savior—but the boldest sacrilege is opera's own: Meyerbeer is, as Fidès calls Jean, a "faussaire" or faker, theatrically transforming a Mass into a circus.

Verdi doesn't so much deride the morality and theology of oratorio as advance beyond it, supplying opera with its own spiritual code. He denounces a religion which exacts penalties—in the auto-da-fé of *Don Carlos*, or when Amneris abuses the priests in *Aïda*—and pardons those whose crime is love, like Violetta or Gilda. These revisions of the moral law meant that his work was censured for its profanations. *Stiffelio*—about an Ahasuerian preacher who forgives his wife's adultery with a quote from Scripture—incurred disapproval in 1850 because it represented a church onstage, and the censors demanded removal of the altar and pulpit. Opera has secularized the temple, and made earthly love into a heavenly bounty. Stiffelio is both Lina's husband and her confessor, so when, speaking from "il santo libro," he forgives the adulteress, she falls at his feet exclaiming "Perdonata," treating her spouse as if he were the all-high judge. Is religion only a cover for eroticism? The guilty Raffaele, hiding a love letter, pretends to be looking for "la Messiade di Klopstock"—the religious epic considered divine by the provincial fogies in Massenet's *Werther*. In 1857, to circumvent pious objections, Verdi rewrote *Stiffelio* as *Aroldo*, transforming the priest into a Palestinian crusader; yet the new version is if anything more unorthodox than the old, for it retains the gestures of expiation and absolution even though there's no longer any doctrinal excuse for them. The heroine, now called Mina, submits herself to Aroldo as judge, "come fosse a Dio presente"—as if she were before God, although Aroldo is only, as Briano reminds him, "crociato e cavaliero." Aroldo too continues to use Stiffelio's words, and in reproof asserts "Di Dio / Ora parlo nel nome." The opera singer takes it upon himself to be the messenger of God: this is the divinity of the divo.

Italian opera vindicates those whom the church condemns. The chorus at Easter in *Cavalleria Rusticana* is dominated by Santuzza, who has been excommunicated for her sexual frailty yet who all the same takes vocal control of the rejoicing ensemble. German opera appropriates Christianity and makes of it a self-glorifying aesthetic cult. The temple in *Parsifal* is Wagner's theater at Bayreuth, the Grail the sanctified artwork he unveiled there in an operatic festival modeled on a religious pilgrimage. French opera, more slyly nonchalant about the gap between religion and sensual delectation, deserts Christianity for Oriental theologies which are less severe and abstemious.

In the Ceylon of Bizet's *Les Pêcheurs de Perles* (1863), Nadir and Zurga remember Leïla lifting her veil in the temple. The priestess of Brahma is herself a goddess, obligingly incarnated for them to pursue. Massenet's *Le Roi de Lahore* (1877) happens during a holy war between Hindus and Muslims, while conducting its own operatic war against holiness. Scindia accuses Sità—whom he wants for himself—of defiling the temple by using her evening prayer to call to a lover. She admits she has done so, though she's unsure whether her visionary visitor Alim is human or divine. As it turns out, he manages to be both. Killed in battle, he ascends to heaven where he petitions the god Indra for the right to rejoin Sità on earth; claiming his sexual prize, he announces that "l'esprit divin m'éclaire," and Timour adds "c'est un dieu qui l'inspire." The paradise which hovers in the sky above Massenet's Lahore is a place of gaudy luxury—opera's self-image; a Palais Garnier in the clouds, replete with "les délices du ciel! . . . d'eternelles voluptés!" and reached across bridges of harps beneath which swirl glinting clouds of strings. Two divertissements are staged there for the sybaritic angels: a ballet introduced by a coiling, snaky flute, then a saxophone waltz. The heroine of Massenet's *Esclarmonde* (1889) appears from the iconostasis in the basilica at Byzantium. She inhabits the altar in a fume of incense, but her divinity is a power of wish-fulfillment. Her "science profonde" can magically summon lovers at will, and transport them to a floating island where she enjoys them.

Delibes's *Lakmé* (1883) concerns another of these dubious priestesses. Her vocation is the service of Dourga, Ganeça and Siva, and she is defamed when Gérald, an officer of the British Raj, presumes to woo her. They retire together to a haven in the forest, where she proposes to reeducate him in her theology, teaching him "l'histoire de nos dieux." He is nervously aware, as he listens to the enchantments of her coloratura, that her divinity may be a vocal illusion, and Lakmé's bell song asks the same question of itself. It describes the god Vishnu's ravishment of the Pariah's daughter, hustled off by him to heaven; the agile display with which it decks out the story is "la clochette des charmeurs." Is the voice the gift of a god, or just a scintillating technical skill? The doubt nags during the ballet in the marketplace. The temple girls who dance are employed to pleasure the priests of Brahma; priggish Mistress Bentson assumes them to be "les vestales," but Frédéric says they're certainly not virgins.

Deity is either sensually imitated in these operas, or else brazenly defied. The god who has been supplanted is challenged to manifest itself, and can't do so. In the Middle Ages of Edouard Lalo's *Le Roi d'Ys* (1888), Margared curses her sister and defies St. Corentin to quit his tomb and punish her. She repeats her dare and the Bishop of Cornouaille—Lalo's Cornwall—has to sneak into the shrine and boom a reproof on the enfeebled saint's behalf.

During the godless age of romantic revolution the theater supersedes the church. This happens to Sant'Andrea della Valle, where *Tosca* begins. Tosca is a pious believer in the deity from whom, as an opera singer, she takes over when onstage; the church she visits is itself a repertory theater, mounting sacramental extravaganzas like the Te Deum every day. Sanctity is camouflage, mere propped-up scenery. What Scarpia the police chief refers to as the "santissimo governo" relies on the infliction of pain—an irreligious inquisition—for its efficacy. The church is a formal cover for profane intrigues: the nave and chapel are a place of flirtatious rendezvous for Marquesa Attavanti (or so Mario believes), a refuge of political conspiracy for her brother Angelotti, a lunchroom for the greedy Sacristan, a workshop for the choir (who rejoice that they'll receive double pay for overtime at the gala), and a stage for Tosca when she commandingly flounces on. The imposture compromises the portrait of Mary Magdalen which Mario has been commissioned to paint in the church. Is it a religious icon or—since the painter is an infidel—a mere secular pinup? Praying to the Madonna, Tosca addresses the mother of Christ as an intimate and an equal ("E tanto buona!"). Is she divine, as Scarpia calls her, or no more than a self-dramatizing diva? Might she even be a fallen angel? Scarpia, who begins by blessing her, finally blames her for causing him to forget God. His religion is in turn a pretense. Though his manner is pharisaical, Mario calls him a pagan satyr, and the Sacristan shuns him as a devil from whom—muttering "Libera me, Domine!"—he hopes to wriggle away.

Tosca, wise in the morality of opera, secures sacred remission for profane lapses. She first prays, then arranges a nocturnal meeting with her lover. Mario notes that she spends much time with her confessor, though that institution is revealed to be bogus when Scarpia, calling for "pronta confessione," models his interrogatory techniques on it. She prises compliments from Mario in a wily catechism. When he replies distractedly to her question about their plans for the evening, she makes him repeat the phrase in penance. Mario adopts her logic in the third act. The jailer offers him the services of a priest before his execution; he refuses, and writes to

Tosca instead. The letter is the invocation of a personal and—as he describes his unveiling of her in "E lucevan le stelle"—flagrant goddess. Tosca in "Vissi d'arte" had prayed ineffectually to the God who, she complains, has let her down; Mario prays to Tosca, and his yearning plea is at once answered when she appears before him. These characters revise religious usages to suit themselves. Tosca has her own flamboyantly theatrical sense of what constitutes a sin: she calls it a "peccata" when Mario musses her hair.

Puccini's opera contains, offstage, the aborted performance of an oratorio—the cantata at the Palazzo Farnese, in which Tosca is obliged to perform. The text of the cantata proposes a morally conventional reply to Puccini's erotic, operatic music, extorted from his characters as their cry of ecstasy or of agony on the rack. It describes the human voice hymnally raised to the King of Kings. However, the religious protestation is patently hypocritical. The monarchy the cantata flatters isn't the one on high, but a political imposition—the Kingdom of the Two Sicilies, reestablished when Angelotti's Roman republic was overthrown, and the iniquitous dynasty of the Neapolitan Bourbons; the occasion honors Queen Charlotte, sister of Marie Antoinette, and is planned to fete the defeat of Napoleon's revolutionary army. As well as providing an alibi for political propaganda, the cantata professes a false humility. The choir praises "l'uman cantico" which beseeches its maker; the voice the composition exists to show off is, however, Tosca's. While the chorus sings of a regimental "Iddio della vittoria," the god who always sides with the big battalions, she celebrates a small, vainglorious victory of her own: the operatic glory of the single voice outsoaring the massed community. Scarpia cancels her triumph by slamming shut the window. She won't permit him the last word, and in her duet with Mario at the Castel Sant'Angelo she adapts and alters the cantata's text. Now, instead of sending forth their voices to appeal to God, they esteem themselves gods of the operatic kind, joined in the "celesti sfere" and inundating the world with "armonie di canti"—the rapturous music of their love.

Opera continued to experiment with and to be prosecuted for blasphemy. Debussy's *Martyre de Saint Sébastien* in 1911 called itself a sacred mystery play, but the hero of d'Annunzio's text is a pagan voluptuary, enjoying the arrows which puncture him; despite denials that the intention was sacrilegious, the opera was officially placed on the Index of works banned by the Catholic Church. Strauss's *Salome* incited a similar scandal. It describes the attempted seduction and vengeful execution of the

Baptist who announced Christ's coming: was it a work of indecent dei-
cide? Moral outrage forced the Metropolitan Opera to drop the work after
a single performance in 1907. When Thomas Beecham proposed staging it
in London three years later, the Lord Chamberlain (in charge of theatrical
censorship) demanded changes to the text. "The passion of the precocious
princess," Beecham recalled, "was refined into a desire for spiritual guidance." But the music had its way, and consumed the puritanical words. In
the course of the performance, the singers gradually reverted to the forbidden original. The censor, incorruptibly ignorant, didn't notice, and
thanked Beecham for his consideration.

Stravinsky revived oratorio in what an early critic called the "Handelian pastiche" of Oedipus Rex (1927). But for Stravinsky, opera and oratorio are formal alternatives not moral opposites, and he temporizes between
them by describing his Latin digest of Sophocles as an "opera oratorio."
For him, there is no question of sanctity. He liked the idea of moving
backward from a "secular" to a "sacred" language, which is why he had
Jean Cocteau's text translated into Ciceronian Latin. However, by "sacred" he meant, he explained, no more than "antique." Oratorio suited his
desire to petrify the urgency and activism of Wagner's music drama: he
wanted a "still life," he told Cocteau. The stiff posture of oratorio was his
prescription for a new kind of opera. Lecturing at Harvard in 1939–40,
Stravinsky argued that the "Dionysian" imagination of the creator can't
flow free into the rivery vagueness of Wagner but must accept limits, be
fitted to neat shapes. "Apollo," he said, "demands it." The Dionysia remained, though repressed. Stravinsky quoted André Gide's remark that
"classical works are beautiful only by virtue of their subjugated romanticism." So it is with Oedipus: oratorio serves to discipline and formalize
opera. Despite its classical language and the undramatic rigidity of the action, the characters—the dangerously arrogant Oedipus and the babbling
Jocasta—are demon-infested romantics. Oratorio as written by Stravinsky
is opera in a straitjacket.

The doubts which afflict Handel and Saint-Saëns in their treatments
of Samson perplex Schönberg in his Moses und Aron, a work initially intended to be oratorio, then revalued by the composer (as he told Berg in a
letter in 1930) as opera. The stammering Moses quarrels with his brother
Aron who is too glibly lyrical, too fickly effusive. The holy word Moses
venerates and which he says he lacks is best preserved in silence; speech
and music both traduce it. Schönberg, as if in agreement with the tacitur-
nity of Moses and of Handel's Samson before him, left the third act un-

composed. Its text exists to be read, not performed. The work's integrity is saved by a precaution which ensures that it's unstageable.

Rossini had dealt with Schönberg's prophet in 1819, cheerfully ignoring any ethical dispute between oratorio and opera. He called his *Mosè in Egitto* an "azione tragico-sacra," but it is unabashedly operatic. It begins in a minor-key darkness which terrifies the benighted Egyptians. Mosè appeals to God, waves his wand, and the gloom is vanquished by light: he is a cosmic magician, a colleague of the infernal Basilio brewing calumnies in *Il Barbiere di Siviglia*. God stages scenic marvels, like the lightning which fells Osiride. Mosè and Aronne, not at odds as in Schönberg, join in acclaiming his stunts; Aronne notes that it's a trifling matter for this deity to cleave the waters of the Red Sea, and a choral prayer suffices to bring it about.

The wizardry of Mosè cheekily sanctifies the theater's box of tricks, while Aronne orders jubilee from "i sacri timpani." *Moses und Aron*, however, is on guard against the seductions of music. Its god sounds invisibly from the burning bush in a dodecaphonic humming: six voices placed in the orchestra wordlessly intone the row of twelve notes which hint at the deity's presence. Schönberg's Moses can only lamely paraphrase his prophetic meaning. He speaks while Aron sings. The two components of opera divide into recriminating opposites: Moses mutters, against Aron's mellifluous falsetto; Moses strictly enumerates the one god's qualities, while Aron translates theology into flattering musical politics and reminds the Israelites that they have been complimented by being made the chosen people; Moses upholds the written text of the tablets he brings from the mountain, though Aron's delight is in taking the line on the page and warping, inflecting and decorating it, as in his modulatory exposition of the miracle. The rod Moses wields turns to a supple reptilian twister in Aron's hands. When music claims a word, its moral import is overwhelmed. A priest spells out in toneless declamation the rules against blasphemy; the chorus meanwhile croons and warbles about a barbaric sacrifice, "Blutopfer!" Disbelieving in Moses, the people call for a new god and a new sacrifice: "Ein neuer Gott: Neue Opfer!"

The sacrifice Schönberg prescribes is of opera itself, for the quarrel between the brothers undoes the pact built into music drama. Moses the composer or conductor, haltingly deficient in vocal powers, needs Aron the ingratiating, accomplished performer. But the performance misrepresents his prophecy, and rather than tolerate that, like Handel quitting the theater, Moses forbids it to take place.

Only in his absence can *Moses und Aron* indulge its desire to be an opera. It does so in the orgy, a choral symphony honoring the golden calf. Its most frenzied passage is inaugurated by the gurgling throaty trill of the four virgins who, crying "Ah!", are killed for the idol's pleasure. This is an operatic Dionysia, all music and balletic movement. Schönberg's directions specify a "wild inebriation," like that of Nietzsche's crazed cultists, and his orchestra, no longer responsible to sacred texts, reverts to the uproar of Saint-Saëns's Bacchanal—a bright cacophony, with snorting brass, thumping drums and a rhythm which reels or pounds the earth in a galloping mayhem.

Handel forswore the theater; Bach, a Lutheran, never wrote for it. Yet opera, in a new installment of its ancient rivalry with oratorio, has had its revenge on those who deny it, enticing their sacred works back into the profane arena of the theater. In 1985 Achim Freyer staged the *Messiah* in Berlin, and Yuri Lyubimov dramatized the *St. Matthew Passion* in Milan. For the atheist Freyer, the religious ceremony is only a play: his *Messiah* was a Shakespearean comedy, with a mute fool impersonating Christ and exhibiting the gashes in his stomach. Seiji Ozawa conducted a staged version of the *St. Matthew Passion* at Tanglewood in 1985, with a barefoot Christ on trial before choral groups in jury boxes. Meanwhile that same summer, in his Vienna production of *Faust*, Ken Russell unsuccessfully begged his Méphistophélès, Ruggero Raimondi, to blaspheme onstage, urinating in the font of holy water and stabbing the crucified Christ to provoke a gusher of blood. Where opera pretends to sacredness, it must be mockingly desecrated—shown to be a black Mass, reveling in that music which an inmate of Shaw's hell calls "the brandy of the damned."

II

REPERTORY

ONE

Classical Opera

THE FIRST operatic characters are gods, or else monsters. It amounts to much the same thing. Beginning as a revival of ancient religious drama, opera is impatient with middling secular reality. It has divinity within its gift, thanks to the ennobling powers of music. Apollo deifies Monteverdi's Orfeo, and in Cavalli's *La Calisto* (first performed in 1651) a chorus of heavenly spirits calls for the translation of the nymph Calisto to the skies. She owes her immortality to the favoritism of Giove, who seduces her. On earth, these divine caprices are mimicked by monsters who imagine themselves to be gods; mythology is replaced by politics when the emperor Nerone, in Monteverdi's last opera, enthrones his adored and unscrupulous mistress Poppea.

Flaubert called Nero, who killed his own mother, the culminating man of the antique world. The rabid tyrant believes he has created himself and thus exterminates the source of his being; he is man running mad in a godless void. The same mania which places Nero at the decadent end of classical culture also locates him, in Monteverdi's version of his reign, at the outset of a modern history to be chronicled by opera, with its defiant romantic sacrilege. Between *Orfeo* in 1607 and *L'Incoronazione di Poppea* in 1642, opera's subsequent development is foretold. The ideal landscape of nymphs and shepherds turns into the actual, imperfect city, its streets crowded with assassins, eavesdroppers and the lookers-on whom Poppea's nurse Arnalta hopes to impress after her employer's promotion.

Orfeo seduced an intractable world by singing. Nerone cows all opponents by shouting, bellowing when Seneca tries to disagree with him and sending a curt message that he should kill himself. The Orphic legacy is abused: the more beautifully Nerone and Poppea sing in their final duet "Pur ti miro, pur ti godo," serenely rejoicing in the reward of their rapacity, the more disturbed we are by their lack of conscience and by the music's indifference to anything but sensual delight. Opera began as a showering of grace from above, when Apollo tuned the spheres. It is now already a human problem, lavishing music on characters who are, to say the least, morally dubious.

Opera is a vertical theater. In it, men can be hauled aloft into the galaxy, like Calisto transformed into Ursa Minor or Wotan in *Das Rheingold* leading his relatives across a rainbow bridge into Walhall. They can also descend into or be engulfed by the nature beneath the fragile platform of the stage. In Monteverdi's *Il Ritorno d'Ulisse in Patria* (1641), Giove swoops from the air brandishing thunderbolts while Nettuno emerges from the sea. Such transcendent feats were made possible by the technology of the court masque, whose machines launched performers into orbit. Giove in *Calisto* speaks of his divinity mechanistically: he tells Calisto he is "il tuo motore"—her motor and motive, her prime mover. Long after these theatrical flying circuses were obsolete, opera continues to be the scene of man's levitation or descent into nature. Wagner's *Ring* begins and ends beneath the Rhine. Tosca hurls herself from the battlements of a Roman fortress, Fenella in Auber's *La Muette de Portici* jumps into the crater of Vesuvius; less violently, the nymph in Strauss's *Daphne*, a latter-day Calisto, effloresces into a laurel. Sometimes opera's characters are gods, sometimes beasts (the outraged Diana in *Calisto*, when the satyrs are torturing Endimione, calls them vile plebeian gods, who have learned their manners from the animals in their caves); they are always forces of nature.

Orfeo optimistically maps a universe which is to remain the scenic world of opera. Earth hangs between the ether and the inferno—between the clouds from which Donner concocts the thunder in *Das Rheingold* and the subterranean mines where Alberich's workers toil. The prologue to *La Calisto* takes place in the mountaintop cave which is the home of Eternity. The operas of the seventeenth century see human affairs from far above, under the aspect of this eternity. *Poppea* is introduced by a debate in midair between Fortuna, Virtù and Amore, who have rival claims to preside over earthly destinies; *Il Ritorno* opens with an argumentative trial between Fortuna, Amore and two more contenders, Tempo and L'Humana Fragilità.

Il Ritorno, taking up Homer's narrative of man's long journey through the world in quest of his home, is about characters desperate to ground themselves in this vertiginous theater, and to reassure themselves of nature's orderly design. Ulisse, awakening, situates himself at once at the midpoint between heaven and earth: what air do I breathe, he asks, and what terrain do I tread on? Minerva helpfully identifies the place for him as Ithaca, but it's merely a stage—any stage, the floating plank man rides between the infinite spaces above and the abyss or the welter below. It could as well be Tristan's ship, or the house of the dyer Barak in *Die Frau ohne Schatten*, a collapsible hovel visited by haughty shadowless spirits from the heaven of Keikobad, and overwhelmed by a flood which sends its inhabitants whirling into limbo. Monteverdi's Eumete trusts in the security of this earth, and lovingly addresses the meadow grasses and the flowers he tends; but it soon gapes open and swallows up Ulisse, snatching him away from his son Telemaco, then disgorging him again.

Penelope, awaiting the return of Ulisse, practices a patient equilibrium which is for her a rule of nature, guaranteed by the metronomic regularity of music. The suitors appeal to her using metaphors from the vegetative world—the vine, the ivy, the cedar—where all things entwine and embrace. But Penelope, who calls herself a piece of iron stabilized between two magnets, must preserve her stasis, because she sees balance as the principle of nature, which tempers and pacifies the contentious elements. She likens her emotional state to a calmed ocean, and expects the return of Ulisse as an elemental inevitability. Every parting, she says, awaits the desired reunion. Her immutability is praised by Minerva as the constancy of nature. The world turns, and music too is fluctuant, forever changing and evolving; but Penelope is its eternal return, the "ritorno" which Vico's cosmology called the "ricorso"—in musical terms, its refrain. She understands her predicament by universalizing herself, which is always opera's way. Man, she says, is soul and body. The soul returns to heaven, the body to earth, after the short time of life—that incarnation which is but a stage, a passage across the human scene from one eternity to another—is over. Therefore, her husband's arrival is in the nature of things. When he does reach her, her relief expresses itself in a discreet musical joining of love and death, like Isolde's expiring reunion with Tristan. She has spoken of the soul's resort to heaven; its exhalation is song, making music as it is breathed out into the air. At the end Ulisse tells her to unleash her voice in joy, and Penelope issues an instruction to the atmosphere which now, after her long-suffering muteness, she vocally stirs— "Aure, gioite!" The breezes must rejoice with her.

For all Penelope's resignation, *Il Ritorno* does anticipate that rivalry between men and gods which is to be the abiding concern of opera. Leonore and Florestan in *Fidelio* beseech a god who is indifferent; Beethoven finds a man-made substitute for religion by orchestrating the choral fervor of humanity. *Götterdämmerung* is an accusation and execution of the gods: man now sentences them to death. Nettuno, disagreeing with Penelope's worldview, interprets the return of Ulisse as an offense against nature, because it misuses his own private element, the ocean. Ulisse disputes Giove's superintendence, claiming that even the law of chance is fairer than divine dispensation. Penelope begs the gods to satisfy her desires, though only she—by cunning and quiet force of will—can accomplish that.

Poppea begins with a quarrel in heaven. Fortuna laughs at Virtù as a god without a temple, a goddess without acolytes or altar. Many such disgraced deities will follow in opera: Nettuno, so tempestuously angry in *Il Ritorno*, is dissuaded from vengeance in Mozart's *Idomeneo*; in *Lohengrin*, Ortrud rails on behalf of her outlawed gods Wotan and Freia, banished by Christianity, but in *Götterdämmerung* Wotan himself is morally stricken and won't eat Freia's apples, which keep him perpetually young; Jokanaan in *Salome* preaches unavailingly of Christ's miracles at Galilee. The dethronement of Virtù makes possible the coronation of Poppea. Amore, the heroine's protector, is the busybody omnipresent in opera, an impulse rather than an angel. His pardoning of Poppea makes way for the apologies of Norma, or Violetta in *La Traviata*, or Manon Lescaut, who all expect to be forgiven—even canonized—because they have loved. The gods of Monteverdi's last opera are the magnificent embodiments of human lusts.

The gravitational tug which is the morality of music in *Ulisse*, rooting all things in the ground bass of their home, no longer works in *Poppea*. As the opera begins, Ottone is singing of a return like that of the line to the center, the fire to the sun, the stream to the sea—or that of Ulisse to Penelope. But his trust in physics is mistaken. What brings him back to complain outside Poppea's house is obsession, not a homing inevitability; and though he prides himself on his fidelity, he proves inconsistent, later transferring his affections to Drusilla.

These characters don't wait upon divine intervention. Instead of the deus ex machina of the masque, flying in to aid them, they rely on their own machinations. They elect the gods they will choose to believe in. The ambitious Poppea nominates Fortuna as her patroness. Ottavia, spurned by Nerone, harangues Giove and orders him to send down an avenging thunderbolt. If he won't make his power manifest in this way, she upbraids him for impotence. Instead of that vertical order of existence which ensures the lofty rescue of Orfeo, the only scale here is social, or vocal. The characters are climbers—not into the sky like Calisto, but onto pinnacles of earthly privilege. Poppea's scheming advance is matched by her nurse Arnalta, who looks forward to being grandly bossy; Amore saves Poppea's life and pipes that he'll make a queen of her, just for the satisfaction of winning the quarrel in heaven. The ladder of rank and esteem is a vocal hierarchy. Seneca's sententious bass voice is the basis of the action, resigned to the limits of mortal existence. Poppea's soprano is the sound of her flightiness and greedy aspiration, delighting in the rarified air further up the chain of social being. She kills the reproving Seneca by remote control when she slanders him to Nerone, because her sensual freedom and his baleful conscience are ethically, as well as vocally, incompatible. This is an opera about the triumph of vice, and it seems to foreknow the form's propensity to affluence, satiation and orgy. Ottavia's exile from Rome is followed at once by Arnalta's gloating promotion, Seneca's death by Nerone's carousing with Lucano. Opera is partial to such apotheoses: Salome kissing the severed head, Lulu copulating with Alwa on the divan where she killed his father.

Poppea sets free the shameless hedonists who populate opera from now on. At the same time it is sternly honest, admitting the futility of the dictatorial caprices which its characters indulge. It abrades and levels them by the contradictoriness of its construction. Every character systematically crosses every other. Every scene negates its predecessor, tragic grief countered by comic mischief. For some characters, love is devotion and sacrifice. Ottavia scorns to revenge herself on Nerone by committing adultery in her turn. But for others—the page skirmishing with his girl in the garden—love is just a physical itch. To the guards, it is above all a professional inconvenience, since they have to spend their nights uncomfortably on duty outside Poppea's house, while Nerone is within enjoying her. Nerone, accustomed to absolute power, is maddened by the spirit of contradiction which prevails in the work, first in his argument with Seneca, later when Ottone and Drusilla noisily disagree, vying to claim responsibility for the attack on Poppea. Seneca's disciples comically contradict his tragic resolution to die, and protest (despite their stoic principles) that life's too agreeable to be thrown away. Nowhere is there a place of safety or surety, a conclusion which can stand unchallenged. Ottavia is offered two opposite kinds of consolation, and rejects them both. Her nurse advises her to cuckold the husband who has betrayed her; Seneca advises her not to question a torment allotted to her by fate. It might seem that Seneca, philosophically armed against the miseries of the world, is the opera's wise man. Yet his voluntary end hardly qualifies as an apt or an honest response. He goes about it pedantically, welcoming death because it enables him to practice the virtue he extols. Suicide is a schoolroom demonstration for the benefit of his pupils (who, aghast as they are, will now all no doubt desert the cause). Even Arnalta at her moment of giddy success is undeceived and inconsolable. She will not be taken in by the flattery of hangers-on, for she knows herself to be as ugly as a sibyl; and next time around, if she returns to earth, she would prefer an inverse fate, to be born a lady and die a slave. Now that she is comfortably off she will be sorry to die. But a serf, she reasons, dies gladly, having nothing to live for. This sad footnote to her last aria comes immediately before the final scene, when Nerone invites Poppea to "ascend the sublime summit" with him, and it must sour the political jubilee. How long can such gratification last?

Opera seria in the eighteenth century comes to be the preserve of tyrants like Nerone. They supply Handel with his heroes—another Roman emperor, annexing new colonies and gathering up Cleopatra as sexual booty, in *Giulio Cesare in Egitto*; the Scythian warlord Tamburlaine in *Tamerlano* (first performed, like the opera about Caesar, in 1724); the Persian despot Xerxes in *Serse* (1738). An earlier work, *Rinaldo* (1711), is also about conquest. The crusader routs the infidel magicians Armida and Argante, and converts them to Christianity. In Handelian opera, the totalitarian authority is song. These are works about the politics of the voice, and they became, to Handel's dismay, occasions for the tyranny of the singer; at last the exorbitant vanity, feuding and competitiveness of their performers drove him to give up writing for the theater.

Treating the voice as an instrument, Handel's virtuosity makes it politically instrumental, defying and intimidating all opposition. Rinaldo goes into battle singing "Or la tromba," in alliance with the brazen, exulting trumpet hailed by the aria. It's the voice, in this show of force, which wins the war. When the Met staged *Rinaldo* in 1984, Marilyn Horne sang "Or la tromba" high on a military parapet. Between her verses, to demonstrate the new physical puissance of song, a team of gymnasts did somersaults and backflips in time to the trumpet's arrogant acrobatics. Handel's Cesare also sings politically. At Tolomeo's court, he is menaced by conspirators. In his aria he likens himself to a hunter, declaring that you must tread softly and keep out of sight when stalking your quarry. To begin with he is the prey, but by singing he turns himself into the predator and the hunt into a political battle of wits. At first his rhythmic pace is hesitant, his delivery unemphatic. Then as he ventures into those multiple repetitions of the three lines which constitute his text, he grows bolder. He communicates this new assurance to the battery of horns accompanying him. They had pursued him; now, rallied by him, they do his bidding. Song is his superb defensive bluff. The coloratura of Cleopatra's arias is just as tactical: a tinselly show, meant to allure. She deploys the voice as the most versatile and irresistible of her sexual charms and diplomatic wiles.

By the time of *Serse*, the sound and fury of song has become a comic matter for Handel. His Persian autocrat is titanically petulant, sentencing his own brother to death for presuming to love the girl he himself fancies. Serse rants for three acts, then finds that he has no choice but to surrender Romilda to his brother after all and marry the heiress who has dogged him throughout. Rinaldo's bellicosity is far in the past. The characters of *Serse* care more for the pursuit of pleasure than for power. The hero's conquering will is fragile, because he's so frivolous and whimsical. Serse pompously opens a bridge across the Hellespont, making way for his advance into Europe; in the next scene, it's struck by lightning, and collapses.

Despite his murderous rages, Serse is happier relaxing into lyricism and escaping into nature. The opera begins with the infatuated love song he addresses to a tree—"Ombra mai fù," known (without the voice) as Handel's largo. Monteverdi's Penelope relied on nature's moral regularity. Its music is still that of Apollo's orderly, chiming planets. Serse feels through his music a more intimate, affectionate empathy. Perhaps he likes the tree because it won't answer him back (as Romilda does), or because it is blissfully insentient, spared the vexations of human sentiment. Flowering from inside the body, the Handelian voice itself constitutes and carpets a landscape. In arias constructed around similes, his characters ally their emotions with natural impulses and processes. Bertarido in *Rodelinda* (1725) is exiled in a remote place. He sings of the disconsolate springs and streams, which weep with him; disjunct echoes are returned by the hollow caverns and unfeeling hills. The vocal decorations are pictorial—the liquidity of his phrase "ruscelli e fonti," for instance, where the rolled "r" sounds like that brook interrupted by stones, or the tremulation in "fonti" which suggests the spray of water. Bertarido also likens himself to a wild beast with its leg in a trap howling for freedom, and he wails melodically. From this dreary horizon, the voice takes flight when he is assured of Rodelinda's good faith. Rodelinda becomes the "rondinella," or swallow, of which he sings, and his voice begins to wheel and trill in imitation of the bird's elated motion. These people can't make nature obey them, as Orpheus could with his lute (or, later, Tamino with his magic flute); they can, however, train the voice to imitate that nature.

In Handel's *Alcina* (1735), the Orphic mystery returns as black magic. The witch Alcina, a colleague of Circe, has trapped her victims in a compulsory pantheism, transforming them into beasts, or into a stone or a bush. Alcina's enchantments introduce a new sense of the stage as a place of inescapable obsession. The second act ends with a ballet in which the incubi of dreams and nightmares do battle. Hence opera's interest in Alcina, or in the sorceress Armida, a character in *Rinaldo* who is treated to musical dramas of her own by Lully, Gluck, Haydn and Rossini; these women are the evil genii of opera, which is their sinister theater of fantasy.

Whether or not Handel's characters are constrained by a spell, like Oberto searching forever for the father whom Alcina has changed into a lion, song is a mental condition in which they're becalmed. From such stillness, Handel's Samson derives his moral fortitude. Nothing can happen while he sings; if he wants to topple the temple, he must leave the stage to do so. Alcina's captives are as helpless as Serse's tree, or as statues. One of opera's most terrifying traumas is this freezing of vital life, which changes a body to stone—the Commendatore on his plinth in the graveyard in *Don Giovanni*, the calcified Kaiser on his throne in *Die Frau ohne Schatten*. Are Handel's operas caught in the same paralysis?

The directors who stage them suggest as much. The characters, fixed inside their attitudes, resemble monuments. The scenic emblem of Elijah Moshinsky's *Samson* at Covent Garden in 1985 was a chipped black basalt column, standing for the eroded but upright spirit of the hero. Characters who lack dramatic volition can only be given motive and mobility if you put wheels underneath them. Joan Sutherland's Alcina, in Zeffirelli's 1960 production in Venice, was a singing armchair, mounted on a decorative float which was propelled on and off without her needing to bestir herself. The Covent Garden *Samson* chained Jon Vickers on a cart, like one of the ambling wagons on which medieval morality plays were performed. The giant Harapha was pushed on to confront him in a white pulpit, and their argument consisted of a skirmish between those dodgem chariots. Philip Prowse's *Tamerlano* for Welsh National Opera in 1982 took place in a junkyard of brick, where ephebic grandees in gilded robes flounced through the rubble. These were the ruins of the Ottoman empire, sacked by the Mongol chieftain Tamburlaine. The exhibits which defined the opera were statues: the bronze horses from the Basilica of St. Mark's in Venice, here ridden by corpses. In this setting, operatic emotion had succumbed to the rigor mortis of masonry.

The society of Monteverdi's operas maintains a tense truce between contending forces. Peter Hall's production of *Ritorno d'Ulisse* at Glyndebourne in 1972 placed the Penelope of Janet Baker on a black-and-white-tiled floor which looked like a chessboard. As in that game, her every move had to be premeditated—during long vigils of watching and waiting—because it would generate a series of consequences. The world is made from the equilibrium between warring agents: men and gods, the four elements, time and eternity. Opera, uniting the arts and making them coexist, is for Monteverdi a model of that ideal but fragile concord.

No such diplomatic balance survives in the operatic society of Handel. Absolute for whatever mood they're vociferously in, his characters resemble monoliths. Unlike Monteverdi's tacticians, they are intemperate, or even distempered; their singing is capricious, but ferociously so, like Tolomeo's in *Giulio Cesare* who in one of his most floridly angry arias warns his minions to fear him when he frowns, or Juno in *Semele*, whirling off in a fury to revenge herself on philandering Jove. The recitative to Juno's aria "Iris, hence away" dizzily scales an entire universe, in its lightning bolts and torrents of decoration. It plunges from the height of Mount Cithaeron to the flood of Acheron into which, with ever lower repetitions of the word "fall," Juno thrusts Semele. But this is not Monteverdi's ample universe. It exists only in the geographical mimicries of Juno's voice. High notes are its jagged peaks, her chest its underworld. Declaring, as she swears by hell, "Tremble, thou universe, this oath to hear," she is merely an opera singer indulging a temperamental fit and exaggerating her grievance. Handel's characters may not be gods; they are, however, sacred monsters.

The next phase of opera's evolution occurs when those arrogant, impervious classical statues acquire a vulnerable and romantic interior; when they lose their Handelian rigidity and begin to move. This happens in Gluck's *Alceste* (1776). The High Priest, entreating the oracle, actually sees the change taking place. Staring at Apollo's statue in the temple, he says, amazed, "Le marbre est animé! Le saint trépied s'agite!"—the marble stirs, the sacred tripod trembles.

Gluck reformed opera, controlling vocal excesses and introducing a solemn simplicity to the drama. But reform in his case meant a resort to origins. Monteverdi and the scholars of the Camerata saw opera as the revival of Greek drama. Gluck revives Greek tragedy a second time, and recalls through it the even more primal and primitive source of drama.

Drama originates in a ceremony of sacrifice, and Gluck's operas are preoccupied with that rite. Orfeo volunteers to die for Euridice, Alceste ventures into the underworld to exchange her life for that of her husband Admète. Gluck's two operas about Agamemnon's daughter, *Iphigénie en Aulide* (1774) and *Iphigénie en Tauride* (1779), concern such sacrifices. Agamemnon slaughtered Iphigenia to buy from the gods a wind to speed the Greek fleet on its way; it was this cruelty which his wife Clytemnestra, in the Sophoclean play adapted by Hofmannsthal for Strauss's *Elektra*, avenged by slaying him on his return to Mycenae.

The chorus of ancient tragedy convenes to protect the community by casting out a demon, or expelling the individual who pollutes it. *Alceste* is about that massed demand for a victim. The priest calls this the "mystère" over which he presides. The double choir addresses Admète and Alceste as its succoring parents, though for its own sustenance and salvation it must destroy one of them. The structure of opera, ranging a soloist against the impersonality of a crowd or an orchestra, re-creates this ritual trial. Alceste, "mourant pour vous, pour la patrie," is Aida lamenting the pain her country has cost her. In Gluck's second act, the mob heedlessly rejoices at its escape from calamity, while Alceste privately grieves. Faltering, her only moral support comes from the orchestra, as the upward figures of the strings reembolden her after her description of the infernal landscape. Transactions like Alceste's remain the concern of opera, whose characters regularly offer themselves for execution to reprieve another—Norma replacing Adalgisa on the pyre, Gilda in *Rigoletto* choosing to be murdered to spare the Duke, Maddalena in *Andrea Chénier* securing the release of Idia Legray so that she and Chénier can be guillotined together.

Though Gluck returns to this first dramatic ceremony, he refuses (or is unable) to accomplish the rite, to shed the blood opera requires. In *Orfeo*, Euridice is resurrected thanks to the interfering partiality of a cupid, and Alceste is rescued by the boisterous intervention of a giant. A moral crisis is solved by a sentimental miracle, or by force. In both of the Iphigenia operas, the goddess who demands the sacrifice relents. In Aulis, Diana takes pity on the sufferers and agrees to let the Greeks proceed without the death of Iphigenia; in Tauris, where Iphigenia is now a priestess who must sacrifice her own brother Orestes, Diana rebukes the savage Scythians, prohibits their religious carnage and frees the heroine from her vows. Nevertheless, the complaints of men aren't entirely appeased. Admète in *Alceste* accuses the gods of inhumanity. Whereas Monteverdi's Apollo divinizes Orfeo, when Apollon appears in Gluck's opera it is to commend Hercule, the son of Jupiter, for fending off the demons and saving Alceste. He assures the bullyboy's immortality, while leaving the mortal couple to their own devices and their own earthly realm. Admète comments "les Dieux sont adoucis" (the gods have grown sweet, or perhaps soft), but henceforth humans must do without divinity. There are, as Strauss's Elektra declares in her anguish, no gods in heaven.

To the nineteenth century, Gluck's resolutions seemed halfhearted. Wagner and Strauss therefore rearranged and rewrote Gluck to free the romantic spirit from his classical form. Wagner produced a version of *Iphigénie en Aulide* in 1847, Strauss revised *Iphigénie en Tauride* in 1889.

The sacrifices in Gluck enjoin a resigned calm, which is that of Iphigenia surrendering herself to Agamemnon. This is the demeanor admired by the eighteenth-century antiquarian Winckelmann in Greek statues. Wagner rids Gluck of this composure, fomenting turbulence. His Greeks positively bay for Iphigenia's blood. Rather than the servants of a social duty, his characters are mystics or magi, claiming for themselves the foresight or potency of gods. Iphigenia agrees to her own death in music as rapt and visionary as that of Elsa in *Lohengrin*; when she assures Achill that through her intercession Greece will vanquish Troy, she becomes a midwife to history, like Brünnhilde incinerating the gods or Didon in *Les Troyens* anticipating her vindication by Hannibal when he advances on Rome. Wagner's Klytämnestra summons Zeus to overwhelm the Greek fleet, and sings with the vehemence of Isolde pleading for a storm to sink Tristan's ship.

In Gluck, the deity's change of heart is meekly reported by Calchas the soothsayer. Wagner introduces the goddess to the action, and his Artemis turns out to be a romantic redeemer like Parsifal. "Nun seid ihr versöhnt" she announces: now you are purified. Not a stickler for tributary blood, she is a force of spiritual transcendence, like Wagnerian music. She prizes Iphigenia's exalted spirit (her "hoher Geist"), and personally delivers her to Tauris, where she will enroll her as a priestess. Wagner's new dispensation also allows history to unfreeze. The final cry of "Nach Troia!" as the armada sets off again suggests the pilgrims in *Tannhäuser* issuing their summons "Nach Rom!" or the iterated reminders of "Italie!" which keep Enée on course in *Les Troyens*.

The classical serenity is already disturbed in *Idomeneo* (1781) when

Elettra, raving of Oreste, delivers herself to the torment of psychological furies. She is preparing for her metamorphosis into the maniacal Elektra of Strauss; and Strauss made his own performing edition of *Idomeneo* in 1930. The oddity of Strauss's version of *Iphigénie en Tauride* is its anachronism. Gluck's opera is an epilogue to the events dramatized by Sophocles and Hofmannsthal in *Elektra*. Orest arrives in Tauride after killing Klytämnestra, and is now himself pursued by the Furies. But for Strauss in 1889, it's an unwitting prologue to his *Elektra*, first performed twenty years later.

Strauss acclimatized Gluck's work to the neurotic romanticism which follows Wagner. The opera begins with a storm, a psychic "Schrekensnacht" (night of horror) as Thoas says. Mozartean music calms storms, during the embarkation in *Idomeneo* or in the trio from *Così Fan Tutte* praying for the safety of voyagers; romantic music incites them, as do Wagner's Klytämnestra, Isolde and Donner pounding the rock with his hammer in *Das Rheingold* to strike sparks of electricity. As in *Elektra*, the characters of Strauss's version are afflicted by mental agonies, persecuted by ingrown furies. The priest Thoas has imagined his own death at the hands of Orest's companion Pylades, Iphigenia dreams of her father's murder, Orest continues traumatically to reenact his slaying of his mother. The recognition—Iphigenia's of Orest, anticipating Elektra's of Orest in the later opera—is a shock of guilty psychic kinship: Iphigenia sees Klytämnestra in her ravaged fantasy as "diese Furie!" and she enters the cell immediately after Orest cries out "der Mutter!" as if she were her mother's emissary, a fury willed by her to punish him. Strauss retains the clement Diana who ensures salvation for all; he had to wait for *Elektra* to restore Gluck's characters to the primitive truth of the tragedy. Elektra has no squeamishness about completing the sacrifice, and is obscenely specific about the protocol of the bloodshed. She warns Klytämnestra that she'll raise the ax above her head but won't strike immediately, leaving her an interim of sick remorse and retrospection: "die Bräuche sind noch nicht erfüllt," she says—the rites are not yet fulfilled. As she consecrates a killing, Elektra creates opera all over again. Tragedy is reborn from the spirit of a musical madness.

TWO

Mozart

THANKS to Mozart, the jealous gods and vindictive absolutists of the first operas lay down their arms. In *Idomeneo*, Idamante slays the ravening sea-monster, while the god who sent it to do his vindictive work, Nettuno, relents and forgoes the human sacrifice he has demanded. Bassa Selim in *Die Entführung aus dem Serail* (1782) threatens torments to his captors but then decides to release them; the Roman emperor in *La Clemenza di Tito* (1791) spares the conspirators who bungle the assassination attempt on him. Sarastro in *Die Zauberflöte* (1791) is accused of being a monster and a tyrant. In fact he is a benevolent, doting parent.

Pardon is indeed the dramatic motive of Mozart's operas: it is the emollient word uttered by the Countess in *Le Nozze di Figaro* (1786), which instantly secures an end to the misunderstandings in the dark garden and the remission of all sins. This clemency is a benediction of music. It no longer, as in Monteverdi, sounds from the remote and ideal spheres on high; it listens in on the tribulations of human beings, articulates the tender desires and fears they cannot own to in speech—the plaintiveness of Barbarina in *Figaro*, whose loss of the pin is the first grief she has known, the ache of self-doubt and sadness beneath the high spirits of *Così Fan Tutte* (1790)—and therefore extends understanding and forgiveness to them. Music is a mollifying, tempering force. The anguished characters of *Idomeneo* invoke it as a soothing breeze: it is Elettra's "soave zeffiri" and Ilia's "zeffiretti lusinghieri."

Yet this humane mercy visits a world in disruption; and the music which brings with it concord and harmonic peace is also capable of dissonant uproar and obsessive fury—the storm in *Idomeneo* or the hoarse growling described by the chorus when the ogre surfaces, the thudding apocalypse of the first chords in *Don Giovanni* (1787) and the terrified velocity of the overture which follows, describing man's effort to outrace death.

Mozart's operas exist precariously at a moment of transition, between old and new regimes in society and in music. They begin from classical formality, but they are agitated by a romantic impetuosity of emotion. The Crete of *Idomeneo* is a wasted land, its streets coursing with blood, its citizens exhaling poison; the Rome of *La Clemenza di Tito*, despite the marmoreal fixity of the emperor's gestures, is mined by treason, hysteria and arson. Mozart's two great characters are revolutionaries. Figaro wants to change society and abolish feudal prerogatives like that which gives the Count a prior claim to his bride. Don Giovanni, more radically, threatens to destroy society altogether by exciting in it a desperate instinctive greed which topples hierarchies and confounds identity.

Idomeneo is about the paralysis of the classical world. It begins with the demand for an offering of flesh—a holocaust as Idomeneo himself calls it, when he explains his bargain with the god. He will save his own life by taking that of a stranger (who turns out to be his son). At such ceremonies, classical tragedy was inaugurated. For the precocious Mozart, the ancient rite of slaughter had an up-to-date psychological significance. In secret, *Idomeneo* is about the composer's relation with the adoring, domineering father who invented him, promoted him and had—if the boy were ever to be himself—to be rejected. Idomeneo's vow to kill Idamante stands for the classical world's ambition to control the future, perpetuating itself by prohibiting the existence of a hereafter. Patricide is the emotional necessity of the young in every generation. The romantics in particular were imitators of Oedipus, destroying a past which they considered oppressive because patriarchal. Fathers and sons are locked forever in this primal battle. The sweet reasonableness of music extricates them in *Idomeneo*. The oracle at last prompts Idomeneo to abdicate power in favor of Idamante. He accepts his own natural fate of supersession, and permits the life of the young to continue in his absence. This is not the embarrassed afterthought of the gods which excuses Gluck's heroines from their sacrifices; it is a biological inevitability, accepted thanks to the healing, tranquilizing intercession which throughout *Idomeneo* is an effect of the weather (the "dolce calma"

of the sea after the shipwreck), of emotion ("serena il ciglio irato"—
smooth that angry brow—say Ilia and Idamante to Idomeneo in the quartet, as if addressing a clouded, turbulent sky), and of music.

In a later romantic study of the classical downfall, Berlioz's *La Prise
de Troie*, change can only happen after conquest and carnage. The founding of Rome requires the incineration of Troy; the mission of Enée requires the abandonment of the Carthaginian queen Didon. Sacrifices like
hers, when she kills herself after his departure, are now made not to jealous
gods but to the will of history. *Idomeneo*, an epilogue to the fall of Troy,
has a humane compromise in view—voluntary renunciation, and an appeal to the pacifying agency of nature. Hence the pantheism of Ilia in the
garden, confiding her troubles to the trees and flowers, hearing the landscape as a rustling Aeolian harp. Idomeneo is prepared to slay Idamante in
order to appease the elements, and he begs the winds to return to their
caves. As in Beethoven's pastoral symphony, music rehearses a new meteo-
rological power, stirring up storms—the shrill winds, rumbling drums and
harried strings which urge on the chorus when it flees from the monster—
in order to allay their discord and restore the Orphic serenity of music.
Where the classical demons live on, it is as mental distempers. The hellish
furies Elettra sings of in her first aria, its coloratura turning vocal decoration into shrieking derangement, still plague a modern girl like Dorabella
in *Così Fan Tutte*: her scooping, wailing fits in "Smanie implacabili"
make her, she says, a candidate for persecution by the Eumenides, just as
Elettra in her last spasms sees the torch of the fury Aletto scorching her.

In *Idomeneo*, a god is disestablished, vanquished (as Nettuno himself
admits) by love. In *La Clemenza di Tito*, there's a belated attempt to construct a god by deifying a man. The Romans have built a temple where
they intend to worship Tito as their divinity, but he shrugs off their homage and redeploys the treasures he is offered to help the victims of erupting
Vesuvius. He prefers fraternal humanity to autocratic godliness. A god can
happily exist in detached self-sufficiency. Tito, however, must practice
painful self-denials, giving up first Berenice and then Servilia, restraining
his initial impulse to punish Sesto. The monarchs of classical opera, like
Handel's Serse or his Cesare, achieve such self-mastery easily, and broadcast it in grandiose flourishes. Monteverdi's Nerone pardons Drusilla, who
has encouraged Ottone to assassinate Poppea, but he does so to make
propaganda for himself. Live on, he tells her, in order to make my mercy
famous. A good deed is only worthwhile if it carries a political benefit.
Tito's moral victories are harder won, and their cost is counted by the

music. His arias are reflective, and the effortfulness of their delivery transcribes his difficulty in convincing himself.

Gluck makes the classical statue move. In Mozart's last opera, the
classical statue crumbles. Sesto, sent off to kill the emperor, falters in irresolution. Prowling the inflamed Capitol, he describes the weakness which
makes him so sympathetic—he trembles, he shivers, advances, draws back,
and the orchestra punctuates each of those false starts. Incapable of action,
he's preoccupied with the study of his own symptoms. In his most elaborate aria, "Parto," he ventures to leave, but is immobilized in anxious pensiveness. The imperturbable classical faces have grown lines of worry and
acquired a romantic introspectiveness. Self-examination, pitilessly putting
the mind on trial, is the rule of these people. Vitellia announces that she
must examine her own constancy, and she does so in a rondo, "Non più di
fiori," because she must go on repeating the scenario of her shame until it
becomes real to her and breaks her. Metastasio's text was already more
than fifty years old when Mozart set it. Revising it for him, Caterino Mazzolà interpolated ensembles which don't so much advance the plot—like
the successive revelations in the second-act finale of *Figaro*—as organize
an overlapping of consciousnesses. When Vitellia is summoned to wed
Tito moments after dispatching Sesto to murder him, she sings of her
frustration and anger in scales of savage angularity; Publio and Annio,
joining her in the trio, can't hear what she's saying and interpret her panic
as glee. What's tragic to one person looks harmlessly comic to the others.
They sing together, but can't understand or assist each other. Invaded by
ambiguity, the characters lack that willfulness which made their classical
predecessors invulnerable. In the first duet, Sesto and Vitellia sing of the
thousand conflicting emotions which quarrel within them; when Tito confronts the guilty Sesto, Publio notes that the same thousand inconsistent
feelings are in dispute, tugging Tito between rage and love. Mozart's
music makes the libretto's cliché true, with Sesto's stumbling rhythms,
Tito's alternations between remorseful asides and barked commands, and
Publio's muttered promptings. Sesto's comment that he's bathed in sweat
is set to a falling cadence on the strings which is, briefly, beatific, and illustrates the musical working of Mozart's compassion.

Like a confessor, music overhears the dismay, bafflement and misery
of men. This tactful eavesdropping perhaps explains why the chorus of rejoicing for Tito's safety in the second act is so devoutly hushed. It offers up
thanks to the creator, but does so almost under its breath, as if afraid of
voicing its relief and recuperation aloud. It also accounts for the intro-

verted muting of the first finale. The Capitol is aflame, the emperor has been struck down, yet Mozart confines the scene to dampened choral exclamations from afar and absorbs the five protagonists in a collective soliloquy which dies away into lamenting silence. The catastrophe they describe is romantically interior; the classical world ends here in a whisper.

From it emerges the romantic society of unfettered desire, powered by a libido to which Mozart's music is attuned. The overtures to his Italian operas dramatize that heady propulsion—eager for intrigue and escapades in the busy introduction to *Figaro*, rampant and sinister in *Don Giovanni*, deceptively frivolous and fickle in *Così Fan Tutte*. All three are about sex and its various freedoms. An erotic mischief unsettles social rank in *Figaro*. An anarchic license riots through the world in *Don Giovanni*. Love is a plaything in *Così Fan Tutte*: a game for the women, a controlled scientific experiment for the men. Modern man's avocation is the pursuit of happiness, and music is synonymous with that quest. Mozart's subject is pleasure, Beethoven's is joy (the "Freude" celebrated in the choral symphony), Wagner's is an insatiable yearning, dissatisfied with all consummation (the "höchste Lust" of the dying Isolde).

Mozartean pleasure is also acquainted with pain, deliciously invited by Zerlina when she asks Masetto to beat her, relished by Figaro when Susanna slaps him. *Die Entführung*, set in a Turkish harem, explores this perversity. It is about the despotism of appetite; the seraglio is a romantic haven of sensual enslavement and luxurious sloth, far removed from the family loyalties and civic responsibilities of classical society in *Idomeneo* or *Tito*. Its mood is that of a dreamy enervation, enjoyed by those who suffer it.

Belmonte's opening aria is a prayer to love, which he addresses as his god. But his "Liebe" is almost interchangeable with "Leiden," the agonies he endures for its sake. The steady pace and rhythmic deliberation of his delivery suggest his expenditure of will and effort. Love here is arduous, not the natural fermentation of Don Giovanni or the wayward impulsiveness of Dorabella. Konstanze's first aria "Ach, ich liebte" is about the transmuting of pleasure into pain in a wilting, fatigued minor key. The Bassa tries rationally to argue her out of her martyrdom, finding such an elegiac eternity insane. When the Countess in *Figaro* calls love to her aid, she at least longs for restoration to life; but Konstanze's proud refusal to forget or adapt is a contradiction of life, and it isolates her inside a psychological prison as hermetic as the harem. Susanna or Ilia in their gardens derive their emotions from nature, and they return them there. Konstanze's "Traurigkeit" aria sentences nature to expire with her: she is a rose killed by a canker, grass choked by winter moss, and the breezes when she speaks respire her woes and make her inhale them all over again. The deathliness of her negative desire seems the more extreme because of its opposition to the jaunty eagerness and optimism of Blonde, her maid. Susanna and the Countess can change places and identities, Despina can catechize and outargue her employers in *Così Fan Tutte*, but between Konstanze and Blonde there is an absolute opposition of philosophical temper, and they don't even try to remonstrate with each other.

The arias in *Die Entführung* are longer and more fanatically repetitive than elsewhere in Mozart, suiting the private fixations of the characters. Konstanze has three solos in the second act. The third, the notorious trial of "Marten aller Arten," is her laughing embrace of the tortures threatened by the Bassa. Its extended instrumental prologue hints at Konstanze's solitary self-absorption, an inverse exhibitionism which jealously clings to her feelings and resents having to express them in song. In the third act, she is overjoyed at her chance to die with Belmonte. Is she slightly disappointed when the Bassa reprieves them?

If Konstanze—in this opera about the perversity of pleasure—is a grateful masochist, then Osmin the harem guard is a gloating sadist. His bass rumblingly enumerates the kinds of pain he's expert at inflicting: the bastinado, impaling, hanging, burning, decapitation, and so on indefinitely. He's vital only when planning these deaths. The more gruesome the prescription, the more sprightly is his singing. The unwieldy bottomless voice positively capers on its way to executions. Osmin's patter is as grotesque as Konstanze's overwrought, exhausting scales. Both are excited by death. In its absence, she is languorous, while Osmin is lazy, stupidly burbling as he picks figs or carousing in stupefaction with Pedrillo.

Turkey means more here than a clash of cymbals in the overture. It is a kingdom of romantic surfeit, a headquarters of opera's alternative religion, like the sun-worshiping Egypt of *Die Zauberflöte*. Pedrillo considers slavery to be a sweet enough lot if irrigated by wine, and amends the ideology of Mahomet by introducing alcohol. The old prophet, he tells Osmin, made a mistake when he imposed prohibition. He corrupts Osmin—or converts him to opera's own gospel—when he gets him drunk on the Cypriot wine, and lures him into a hymn of praise to Bacchus. Osmin trembles, wondering if Allah might be watching. Opera is at home in the seraglio, and would just as soon not be rescued.

When Osmin treats Blonde as his slave, she reminds him that she's English, and born to freedom. Her political protest doesn't impress him, and in any case it's only a pretext for instituting her own small, shrill dictatorship: she goes on to crow that even if she loses her freedom, she's still queen of the world. The same protest, less arrogantly put, is the motive force of *Le Nozze di Figaro*. Politically, it's about the deft outwitting of the Count's domestic tyranny. Dramatically, it's about the contest to partition or share the community of the congested stage, where too many people overlap. Susanna complains of a dangerous proximity or "vicinanza," which places her bedroom within reach of the Count's. The comedy of the work derives from the doubling-up and cramming-in of people, packed in rooms which can't accommodate them all: the chair which hides Cherubino, the closet with its multiple occupants, the arbors where so many are secreted. They all have their own claims to the freedom of self-possession and social right. The closing flourish of Bartolo's aria establishes his prerogative. He's known, he declares, by everyone in Seville. Whereas he has an acknowledged power in the city, the freedom craved by Cherubino is exploratory and unconditional. He wants the run of the palace, and access to every woman in it. Even Antonio the drunken gardener is proprietorial about the patch which is his sovereign terrain, complaining that rubbish is always being hurled into it, and brandishing his injured carnations.

If the work's dramatic concern is living space, the musical counterpart to that is breathing space. *Don Giovanni* is driven; *Figaro* is breathlessly overworked. Its music isn't in desperate flight like that of *Don Giovanni*, but scrambles to keep up with the restless rearrangements of society and human relationships. The excitement of *Figaro* is the uniquely theatrical one of watching people think on their feet—Susanna's spontaneous inspiration of fainting, and her instantaneous recovery when she's led toward the chair concealing Cherubino; Figaro's quick-witted invention of excuses in the second act, and the perilous risks he takes in the third act as the Count begins to see through those lies. The excitement is compounded because they must act in time to the never-pausing music. It sets an itinerary for them, and they must dance to its tune. Figaro makes the point twice in the first act, in each of his arias: he will play the "chitarrino" while the Count trips in time to it; and Cherubino must march at the tempo ordered by trombones and cannonades. When his plot gets under way, Figaro mutters to Susanna, "Eccoci in danza"—the dance has begun. The rhythm is that of a perpetual motion, and he's saved by it at a moment of crisis. In the third act he can no longer be bothered to lie, and arrives at a showdown with the Count. The outbreak of hostilities is avoided only because a march starts up, summoning them to take their places and go through its measured temporizing motions. A musical armistice is declared. Music in *Figaro* must industriously accompany work. Figaro vocalizes "La lala la" as he goes about his chores, Susanna serenades Cherubino to keep his attention while she's dressing him up, and if she has a duet with the Countess it must be because she's writing a letter at her employer's dictation.

Every key change in the astonishing finale to the second act signals a reshuffling of the pack and introduces a new dramatic challenge or obstruction. Characters enter an ensemble—like that in which Figaro learns who his parents are, and is discovered in a compromising position by Susanna—to emerge from it, after a few minutes, with their lives transformed and their allegiances transferred. Beaumarchais subtitled the play which da Ponte adapted for Mozart "la folle journée." The events of the mad bridal day may look like farce, but Figaro, speaking of the Count's tricks, calls them "la moderna festa," and the modern version of a festive comedy is revolution. This revved-up agenda, forever in frantic action, gives a special, almost sainted peace to musical pauses when the jostling and jockeying briefly let up, and the voices can breathe: the short-lived truce in the trio after Susanna steps out of the closet, and the Count is pardoned; the time-stopping happiness which concludes the reunion between Figaro and his family; the duet about the rendezvous by the pines, and Susanna's relaxedly idyllic aria in the garden. But all such remissions are temporary, and illusory as well. Susanna in "Deh vieni, non tardar" is expressing impatience for her lover's arrival, to enrage the listening Figaro.

The society of *Figaro* is as solidly specific as that of a novel. It begins with an act of enumeration, as Figaro measures the allotment of space for his bed. Times of day matter in it, and habitual domestic routines. The Countess, her husband notes, doesn't usually lock her door. Character is defined by a minute exactitude in physical markings—the spatula on Figaro's right arm. Outside the castle are ranged the inflexible apparatuses of law and social usage, the codex and index scrutinized by Bartolo in prosecution of his grudge. But despite the substantiality of appearances, these people inhabit a house of cards. Novels happen in a founded, anchored world; in drama, everything is precarious and collapsible, because it's ruled by chance and play. The world of *Figaro* is held together by flimsy ribbons and bandages, like the one with which the Countess binds Cherubino's arm, or by pins, like those the women—as the Count comments—are always sticking into things, and always mislaying. Its promissory notes and contracts have no power because they're paper obligations, and can instantly be canceled, as they are in the third act when Marcellina drops her suit. The action's symbol is an invalid document: the patent commissioning Cherubino, which lacks its seal.

Nevertheless, the characters battle against such slippery contingency, and seek some safe basis for their lives. For the Countess, it lies irreclaimably in the past. She is no longer Rosina, she tells her husband. Since she has no emotional support, she must derive her self-esteem from her social position, and she feels herself shamed—in the climactic cadence of recitative before "Dove sono"—by having to rely on help from her serving maid. The swollen pomp and brassy swagger of the orchestra during the Count's aria denotes his confidence in his own lordly authority. He can't tolerate the happiness of a menial while he himself is denied what he wants.

This is the source of disparity between *Figaro* and *Don Giovanni*. The Seville near the castle of Aguasfrescas has law officers and a garrison; the Seville nocturnally prowled by Giovanni can rely on no such force, because its social pretenses and formulae have been jokingly demolished by Giovanni himself. Ottavio in the second act leaves Anna in the care of the others, and goes off—he says—to advise the authorities of Giovanni's crime. But *which* authorities? They have all succumbed to Giovanni's nihilistic jests. Nor does Giovanni ever make the mistake of deceiving himself. The Count means it when he sneers at the lowly Figaro as a vile object, just as Susanna does when she sees that trivial people like her don't have the leisure to suffer from the vapors. Rank has no value for Giovanni. He's scurrilously teasing when he defends his class against the slanders of the plebeians.

Susanna's exchange of clothes and roles with the Countess is an uncomfortable imposture for both of them, and they have to alter their voices to match the lyrical elocution of the class each is imitating. The Countess must try to sound as peppy as Susanna, Susanna as elegantly gracious as the Countess. The life swap of Giovanni and Leporello in the second act, however, is more than a charade designed to embarrass. It is one of those existential hazards by which the theater is so tempted and so troubled. Acting, you can become someone else. Since Giovanni is an Everyman, a universal characteristic, Leporello in performing that role is augmenting his own personality; Giovanni's impersonation of Leporello is also a strange enlargement of identity, enabling him to indulge a self-hatred and a desire for castigation he nowhere else exhibits, when he tells Masetto in meticulous detail how to arraign Giovanni and beat him up. Leporello unselfconsciously calls Giovanni "l'amico," a word Figaro could never use of the Count. They are colleagues, and alter egos.

This capacity to sidle in and out of each other's existence is the psychological affliction of the women in the opera. Once aroused by Giovanni, they can never again know for certain who they are. Elvira is betrayed by her own helpless susceptibility, rather than by Giovanni's mistreatment. Everything about Anna is invaded by ambiguity. Is she chasing Giovanni from the house at the beginning, or pursuing him because he won't stay? Does her self-dramatizing account of the incident in the recitative before "Or sai chi l'onore" match the facts? Why, in "Non mi dir," does she distract Ottavio with her ornamental flummery, and defer her promise to him? Why does she insist in the epilogue on a year's grace?—is she mourning her father or Giovanni? E. T. A. Hoffmann was so suspicious of her that he wrote a story intimating her true motives. A soprano singing the role in the German provinces exorcistically takes on the distress of Anna, and dies for her sake. Her confession to Hoffmann in a darkened box at the theater admits her infatuation with Giovanni; expiring in the night with a starry cry quoting from Anna's second aria, she consummates their union.

Set at night in alleys, empty streets and graveyards, happening in a tenebrous nowhere which is its hero's hunting-ground, *Don Giovanni* certainly lacks the social breadth and fullness of *Figaro*. But while it can't be wide, it does go deeper. Giovanni's seductions are a penetrating inquisition of character and society. He defrauds people of their cherished selves by making them want him, exciting a lust which he won't stop to satisfy. He is infallibly fatal: the exuberant life-instinct—which, to Kierkegaard, he personified—creates in those he stimulates the consciousness of their own deaths. This makes him at once comic and tragic, and though da Ponte's words may narrate a snatch-and-grab career of sordid intrigue, Mozart's music hears beneath them a drama of spiritual perdition.

The elderly, celibate cynic Alfonso in *Così Fan Tutte* is a Don Giovanni who avoids the sexual fray and the libertine's exhaustion, contenting himself with a cruel, supercilious knowledge. He constructs the opera's action as a logical demonstration of female perfidy. Again the theater is a place for psychological experimentation: a laboratory where people are analytically taken to pieces. The mood is colder than in *Don Giovanni*, and even more disquieting because of its pitiless rationality. The orchestra spells out Alfonso's formulation and its own title at the very beginning, after some bars of languishing regret. Alfonso's power is verbal; against him, the only recourse of the persecuted women is Mozart's music, which vouches throughout for feelings the drama won't accredit.

The new opera's title crops up casually in *Figaro*, when Basilio is defaming Susanna. "Così fan tutte le belle," he says, "non c'è alcuna novità": all the beauties are like that, there's nothing new in it. But each Mozart opera constitutes its own world, and has its own laws; *Figaro* has no difficulty in disproving Basilio's slur. Its first rebuttal points to differences of class. Susanna and the Countess are seen as members of two dissimilar social groups, rather than companions in the same gender. And if they pretend to infidelity, it's only to remind men of their abiding good faith. Alfonso's version of the slander is more dangerous because it's proposed as a scientific theorem, and put to the test on live, squirming human creatures. The more flippant *Così Fan Tutte* pretends to be, the more hurtful and distressing it actually is. Ferrando and Guglielmo first reply to Alfonso's insinuations by reaching for their swords; Fiordiligi and Dorabella, shamed at the end, beg to be impaled on those same weapons.

This is not fatuous overreaction. Comedy may be satisfied with easy generalities, like Alfonso's about women or Despina's about men, but tragedy knows each case is different because each being is an individual, sure that his or her own joy or pain is singular and unique. Hence Ferrando's enraptured "Un'aura amorosa," or the despair of the betrayed Guglielmo. Whereas the truth about characters in *Don Giovanni* may best be approached by mistrusting what they say—which is Hoffmann's recommendation with Anna—in *Così Fan Tutte* music beseeches us to believe them. At first, the men simulate lovelorn misery and the women stoic constancy, but the emotions acquire reality as the action proceeds. Perhaps Fiordiligi is exaggerating in "Come scoglio," though why should she wrack her voice with those punishing intervals? By her second aria, "Per pietà," there's no doubting her. She is performing to no one here, and her chesty vowels are avowals of an unassuageable sorrow. The parody is on the surface only, and so is the finely tuned comic teamwork. *Così Fan Tutte* is known as an ensemble opera, with individuals housed in chattering collectives like those in Rossinian finales or in *Falstaff*. But the concerted singing is mostly the conduct of war by other means. The men skirmish in their initial trio, and in their first duet Fiordiligi and Dorabella defy each other to the death with their sustained high notes. The ensembles couple by force (and by Mozart's ingenious modulations) utterances which are woundingly incompatible: when the Albanians stage their suicide, the guilt and grief of the sisters contrasts with the chuckling asides of the victims. Some ensembles recruit the singers against their will and better judgment. During the nuptial toast—a devout wish, again validated by Mozart's score, for revocation of the past—Guglielmo mutters a disenchanted curse. He has a good vocal reason for his exclusion, since their register isn't convenient for his baritone; however, the musical necessity enables Mozart to make an abrasive dramatic point, as the character poisons his own happiness.

Nor does the flouncing comedy of manners and mannerisms for which *Così Fan Tutte* often passes take account of the work's chilly intellectuality. Alfonso is a philosopher, sterilized by his mental rigor. The meddling Despina is an expert technician, and touts her skills as a doctor and a notary. Despite their presumption, they operate in the muddled superstitious realm of pseudoscience. Despina gives a lesson in mesmerism just as Fiordiligi deciphers Dorabella's horoscope by reading her palm. Anatomizing human frailty, Alfonso reduces love to an effect of physiology, and Guglielmo recommends himself by cataloging his bodily assets— good feet, eyes and nose, a superb mustache. But love is the junction of body and soul. Drama may understand its carnality; only music can do justice to its other half. Despina's knowingness also reaches its limits when, as the learned doctor, she gabbles in garbled Latin. She brags that she also knows the Greek, Arabic, Turkish, Vandal, Tartar and Swabian tongues. Still, this polyglot pedantry is as nothing to the orchestra, whose music is the Esperanto of emotion, comprehensible everywhere and at once.

Despina has the eighteenth century's rational view of the theater, shared by Diderot and Rousseau, as a place devoted to physiognomic lying. She is schooled in its insincerities and can counterfeit fears or laughter on request. It is all a game, kept going by bribes, its playfulness a gambling delight in chance. The affair begins as a wager between the men. When Fiordiligi and Dorabella have to choose between the Albanians, they place their bets at random. Again, music knows better than this. What begins as a masquerade ends—when Fiordiligi dresses in Ferrando's uniform and Dorabella, accepting Guglielmo's gift, changes hearts and identities—as a rite of passage, deranging and transforming. The theater is closer after all to magic than to science.

It is also close to the taboos and transgressions of myth, and in particular to a myth which warns against the demystifying knowledge of Alfonso and the encyclopedists. *Così Fan Tutte* replays events in Eden. The sisters innocently enjoy a garden menaced first by pain (when the officers quit them), then marred by death (when the Albanians mime their poisoning).

A devil lurks in the shrubbery. Dorabella calls love a serpent, and Despina (its agent) a little demon. Despina herself, case-hardened, regrets only the temptations she doesn't succumb to: her first act in the opera, since there's no apple to hand, is to taste the prohibited chocolate. She instructs her employers in a knowledge which is both of the devil and about him. At fifteen, she says with a smirk, a woman ought to know where the devil hides his tail.

These memories of a lost paradisial innocence darken the comedy; so do other ancient mythic recollections, dating back—in this consciously contemporary work, which drops the name of Mesmer whom Mozart had known in Vienna in the 1770s—to opera's beginnings. The characters are always accusing each other of being archetypes. Figaro, closing in on Susanna in the garden, modernizes the adulterous Olympians by calling himself the "nuovo Vulcano del secolo," who will trap Venus philandering with Mars. Such comparisons are endemic in *Così Fan Tutte*. Dorabella offers her agitation to the Eumenides. Awakening in the garden, the men address the sisters as Pallas and Venus; later Guglielmo snarls that Fiordiligi is his chaste Artemisia, and when Alfonso advises him to marry her all the same he says—revising the myth of connubial and musical fidelity which is Monteverdi's *Orfeo*—that he'd sooner wed Charon's boat, or the gates of hell. He is not being hyperbolic. The pagan myths stay with opera throughout its history because they are the undying, perpetually reborn fires of the flesh, recurrent like the eruptions of a volcano. Vesuvius is one of the Neapolitan tourist spots no doubt frequented by the girls from Ferrara, and Dorabella understands its meaning so well that she appropriates it, remarking that she has a Vesuvius in her breast. Apparently flippant in its adherence to the surface of things, *Così Fan Tutte* is in fact Mozart's most atavistic work, where classical gods have their second coming as romantic manias.

Its ending is a hasty, shifty compromise, intended to be unsatisfactory. After such knowledge, what forgiveness can there be? *Die Zauberflöte* tries to advance beyond these quarrelsome divisions, and to rationalize the musical pangs which torment Dorabella. Alfonso's practical joke becomes, as Sarastro puts Tamino and Pamina to the test, a purgative trial. The paradise lost when the serpent wriggles into that Neapolitan garden is here restored. The chorus of priests looks forward to a day when earth will be inseparable from heaven, and mortal men ("Sterbliche," or the dying) will be like gods. The formula which unlocks that perfection is musical: Orfeo's lute changes to Tamino's flute. Behind *Die Zauberflöte* lie the fables of Monteverdi and Gluck; after it comes Beethoven's progress from myth to history in *Fidelio*, where the earthly paradise envisaged by Sarastro's acolytes, still rallied by music, is a new political regime.

The benignity of *Die Zauberflöte* isn't within the emotional range of the operas preceding it. They have a violent intensity, which is the impetus of desire. Their characters experience that desire as madness—Cherubino in a perpetual whirl of infatuation, Elvira excoriating herself, Dorabella rushing through the house in a fit. But the motive of *Die Zauberflöte* is a gentler and more moral feeling: love, not sensual abandon. Though the magic talisman of the flute recalls Orfeo, the sun venerated by Sarastro's men is not the cold brilliance of Monteverdi's Apollo. It emanates instead a human warmth, the blessings of care and companionship. Love in *Die Zauberflöte* means kindness and kinship. It is indeed the benefaction of that deity in nature whom medieval theologians knew as Dame Kind. Earlier Mozart operas may touch on marriage—a social alliance in *Figaro*, a flimsy cover for the infidel libido in *Don Giovanni*—but none of them is concerned with propagation or with the constitution of the human family. Such matters are, however, crucial in *Die Zauberflöte*, where the most reverent praise of conjugal love—the duet about "Mann and Weib," who united will attain divinity—is sung by two characters, Pamina and Papageno, without the slightest erotic interest in each other. Love in this opera is generously parental, donating life to others. Papageno yearns for offspring; Pamina hesitates between the opposed claims of her parents, each of whom wants total possession of her. The instinct is a law of nature, synonymous with humanity. Thus Papageno can define himself as natural man, a "Naturmensch," and the Queen's most insidious threat to Pamina is the vow in her second aria to cancel those bonds of nature which hold them together. The fate worse than death here is exile from the family of human sympathy, suffered by Tamino when the serpent pursues him through a wilderness, by Pamina when he doesn't answer her pleas, by Papageno when, dispirited, he believes he has lost his biological partner.

The opera's magic totems are musical instruments: the golden flute, the silver bells, the wooden panpipes which make Papageno a feathered satyr. Music erects that dizzy vertical chain of being which joins earth to heaven. On the heights are the Queen's galactic high notes, in the depths Sarastro's bassoons and the cavernous low notes he emits on the word "Mensch" at the end of his aria, supplying the opera with its humane bedrock. Between these extremes commute the voices of the three boys—unbroken and sexually indefinite, still poised between soprano and bass.

The three ladies, handing over the flute, extol the humane ministry of music. It has the Orphic power to revive the dead, though it exercises its gift in the realm of comedy. It banishes sorrow, they say, cheers up the mourner and encourages the old celibate to take a wife. Yet if music is to be an aid to human happiness ("Menschenglück"), it must be democratized. The potion can't exclusively belong to virtuosi like Monteverdi's Orfeo. *Die Zauberflöte* attunes and harmonizes all of nature. Any sound made by man or beast may qualify as music: the yelps of Monostatos, Papageno's humming or his stuttering "Pa-pa-pa," the inane and innocent "La-ra-la!" of the slaves dancing to the bells. Silence, imposed on the men as one of their trials, is also brought within the work's sonic domain. A peace which passes understanding may be inaudible to the human ear. As a singspiel, the work dodges between song and chattering, gossiping speech, and this alternation is one of its subjects. Music and dialogue have their places on that great scale between the sky and the catacombs on which the Queen and Sarastro are ranged. Some of the opera's business is too serious to be conducted in anything but earnest speech. Tamino's mentor is entitled the Speaker because he propounds truths, and in the finale Tamino asks the armored men if he may be permitted to speak to Pamina. When speech warms into song, a moral victory or an emotional transcendence has occurred. The Speaker's stiff declamation relaxes into a comforting lyricism as he assures Tamino of friendship and protection; Papageno gabblingly demands what he and Pamina should say to explain themselves to Sarastro, and she sings a reply which is selflessly poised above his earthly calculations—"Die Wahrheit! Wär sie auch Vebrechen!": the truth, even if it's a crime. The Speaker's lapse into song and Pamina's soaring takeoff into it measure the gradations on this universal scale. *Die Zauberflöte* would make no moral sense if it were through-composed.

Theatrically, *Die Zauberflöte* has always been something of an embarrassment. How could Mozart have permitted his valediction to take the infantile form of a pantomime? Within a few years of its first performance, admirers of the opera's music were rewriting its drama into respectability. Goethe prepared a sequel in 1795, restraining the random marvels and reformulating the opera as an allegory of regeneration. Sarastro quits his holy office, and the Queen of the Night returns to kidnap the child of Tamino and Pamina. The parents can rescue the baby only by suffering new trials underground, more psychologically arduous than their fluting initiation in Mozart. Shaw in 1890 converted the opera from the mumbo jumbo of

Freemasonry to his own evolutionary rationalism. Sarastro now stands for the modern ethic of secular humanitarianism. G. Lowes Dickinson's fantasia in 1920 adjusted *Die Zauberflöte* to current spiritual disasters. The trial by fire is the trauma of war, the trial by water the welter of atheistic doubt. W. H. Auden, translating the opera for an NBC television production in 1956, rewrote the dialogue to discipline the unruly Papageno and added extra poems for Sarastro and the Queen of the Night, European deities who have taken refuge in American academe. Sarastro, a pedant and a bore, teaches ancient myth, Auden says, at a New England college; the Queen is its bossy Dean, keeping secret her recent reappearance as Wagner's prophetess Erda in the *Ring*.

Does the work need to be saved from itself by such ingenuities as these? Not at all, because it is Mozart's fullest exposition of what music and drama mean, and of what they achieve in conjunction as opera. Music is predestined, drama improvised. The moral surety of music is repetition: hence that Lutheran chorale intoned by the armed men who entreat Tamino. Against this solemn determinism, drama is more skittish and variable, tolerating the interpreter's liberty. The warriors have a duty to tread along with the measure, and their words describe just such a plodding steadfastness. But Papageno knows no such limitation. He is free to make up his dialogue as he goes, and potentially free to multiply his exclamations of "Hu!" or "Ei!" or "Pa-pa" along with his prodigious self-reproducing after marriage. His enumeration—"Eins! . . . Zwei! . . . Drei!"—could go on forever.

The same coexistence of discipline and freedom gives *Die Zauberflöte* a double life in the theater. It enacts a rite, and its trials are preordained as all ceremony must be. Though this irreversibility allies it with tragedy, it remains resiliently comic, thanks to its faith in improvisation. The rite stages death and transfiguration, as Tamino and Pamina are laved by water and purified by fire; but the pantomime treasures another, easier kind of theatrical immortality. Papageno can try as often as he likes to hang himself, Pamina can point the dagger at her breast, but they possess the charmed life of theatrical beings, extemporized and safe from time's depredations. They may seem to die, but they're always resurrected for the curtain call, ready to live and temporarily to die once more at the next performance. *Die Zauberflöte* is a Mass, celebrating human communion. It is also a game, magically artificial, a farrago of stunts and deceptive tricks. In its childishness lies its wisdom. Opera's special, reconciling task is to unify such opposites.

THREE

Romantic Opera

AFTER Mozart, opera's history goes hedonistically into reverse. The social tensions, mental anxieties and spiritual yearnings attended to by Mozartean music disappear. The new operas are incentives to a carefree indulgence of the greedy body and the wayward mind. Rossini's heroes are gluttons, the heroines of Bellini and Donizetti—following from the moonstruck priestess Norma—are mellifluous lunatics. Enjoyment in Rossini and a dreamy derangement in Bellini and Donizetti are the imperatives of romanticism, which relishes both physical vivacity and a whirligig mental agility. Mozart's dissolute Giovanni has turned into a harmless epicurean. The English critic Hazlitt, reviewing *Don Giovanni* in 1817, ignored the dark forebodings in it and heard only "a light, airy, voluptuous spirit," which he identified as "the personal character of the composer's mind."

The same genial misinterpretation of Mozart extradites him from gloomy, soulful Germany, and makes him an honorary Italian. Leigh Hunt, Keats's friend, believed Mozart was saved by being taken to Italy in infancy. There, Hunt surmised in 1817, using the Bacchic imagery which is an ideology for opera, "he drank at the winy fountain, and seems to have been intoxicated ever after with love and delight."

In the bel canto operas, music is the voice of what Leigh Hunt called the impassioned "animal ardour" of romantic Italy. In Rossini it works like sal volatile, fizzily invigorating. In Bellini it drifts off into reverie, carried away by his endless, enraptured melodic lines. In Donizetti it is more agitated and crazy: the harangues of Anna Bolena, the deadly rages of Lucre-zia Borgia, or the untuned squawkings of the hoarse singer in his 1836 comedy *Il Campanello.*

Because history has run backward, in quest of eternal youth and the "sprightly turns or lapping pleasures" Hunt heard in *Le Nozze di Figaro,* it's fitting that at the center of this new group in the repertory there should stand an opera which is a belated prologue to Mozart—Rossini's *Il Bar-biere di Siviglia* (1816). The Beaumarchais play Rossini set is about the early days of characters who have grown sadder and more worried in Mo-zart's opera. Rossini's Figaro is a nimble procurer; Mozart's has the more onerous responsibility of holding society together—or choosing to let its makeshift order break down. When Mozart's Count calls his wife Rosina, she says she's no longer that person. The rebellious verve, transcribed in Rossini's "Una voce poco fa," has died in her. The farce of the earlier play still rankles with the losers in Mozart's opera. Bartolo wants revenge on Figaro, whom he won't forgive for having prised Rosina away from him for the Count. Though written a generation after *Figaro, Il Barbiere* is an in-nocent unselfconscious prelude to it, ignoring the perplexities which lie ahead of its characters in Mozart.

It derives its confidence from Rossini's romantic interpretation of *Don Giovanni.* The subject of *Il Barbiere* is that vital ardor which throbs through Giovanni, and which powers the imprisoned Rosina's lust for freedom. Rossini's comedy, in the phrase Hunt wrongly used of *Don Gio-vanni,* asserts the "fair play of nature." The moral world has narrowed. The sexual compulsion of Mozart's hero changes to sensuous delecta-tion—the fashionable vanities pandered to by Figaro's shop, or else more edible, potable pleasures: the snuff to which Berta is addicted, the sweets Rosina pretends to send to Marcellina, the wine which is Almaviva's rowdy camouflage when he reels in pretending to be drunk. Whereas Gio-vanni suffered spiritual damnation, in Rossini's Seville the fate worse than death is social ostracism, rehearsed by Basilio in the scandalmongering crescendo of "La calunnia." The rap on the door which terrifies Bartolo isn't a divine summons, like the knocking of the Commendatore; it an-nounces the arrival of the police to put down a domestic fracas. And when they attempt to arrest Almaviva, like the ineffectual maskers at Giovanni's party, he disarms them by flourishing a piece of paper. No one in Rossini remains accountable for long.

The animal spirits which rage in *Il Barbiere* and demand their free-dom are stimulated by the singing voice. As Rosina explains in her aria, it's a voice—Almaviva's, serenading her—which has awakened her, and she uses her own voice as a means of teasing bodily exploration. Her excursions into a husky lower register warn of the fury beneath her polite docility (hence that ominous drop on the word "ma" in "Una voce poco fa," and the viperish flickerings of her next lines); top notes are her gestures toward a flighty escape from restriction. Singing Rossini is the tongue-twisting articulation of more or less nonsensical synonyms for joy: Figaro's exultant "lalalalalalalalalala," the gurgles and bleats of erotic anticipation in Almaviva's aubade under the window. Or it is the production of uninhibited, cacophonous noise, like the fusillade of concerted whispers in Basilio's aria. No wonder that a crucial scene is Rosina's singing lesson, where what she learns is how to cancel words and make them semaphore the body's longings. She sings one aria, stiffly formal, to Bartolo, another seditiously between its lines to Almaviva.

Music, rid of that fatal urgency it possessed in the overture to *Don Giovanni*, has settled into a physical pleasure. Figaro insists like Giovanni on music's brisk present tense, chiding Rosina and Almaviva when they lag behind for some private spooning and won't keep to the faster tempo he sets for their escape. He is essential to Seville, as he boasts in "Largo al factotum," because like music itself he's a supplier of instant gratifications.

Rossini has his comic deaths, when the scurrying pulse is jarred from characters and they're momentarily stalled and metaphorically killed. One such moment comes when Bartolo is petrified by consternation, another in the diagnosis of Basilio's scarlet fever. In both cases, musical life resiliently starts up again. Pleasure is inexhaustible, so long as there's money to pay for it. *Il Barbiere* notices how expensive this emotional affluence can be: Almaviva has to tip the street musicians and bribe Basilio; Figaro's bounteous creative imagination works best, he explains, if charged by the idea of gold. Yet sooner or later the glutted body will wear itself out. Berta's wonderful lament, an afterword to romanticism, admits the inevitable sagging of this musical liveliness into halting debility. She, an old maid, will die in desperation. Don Giovanni burns in hell, but Rossini's comedians have their equivalent to his plight—the libertine's misery of jaded exhaustion, the sated expiry of the capacity to feel.

The comic operas of the romantic period recommend music as a universal panacea. Though the potion sold by Dulcamara in Donizetti's *L'Elisir d'Amore* (1832) may be a fraud, the music he sings does possess the magic properties he claims for his brew: it startles paralytics into life again, as he says; it is, in another of his slogans, a benefactor of mankind. One of the apothecary's clients in *Il Campanello* demands a similar remedy, mixing all the ingredients known to pharmacology together with an essence called Dulcamara (the name means bittersweet) and, for good measure, the navel of Venus. Again the prescription is rattled off in a patter song which is itself the cure. This elixir welling from Leigh Hunt's "winy fountain" is the musical motive of Donizetti's *Don Pasquale* (1843). The hero, an elderly celibate, is rejuvenated and made fertile by music. As he sings of the "foco insolito" or sensual fire which has blazed up inside him and numbers the half-dozen "bamboli" he expects to sire, his chortling patter is his means of reproducing himself, gabbling in his effort to outrun time. *Don Pasquale* contains its own Dulcamara, the quack doctor Malatesta who supplies Pasquale's bride. Malatesta does music's medicinal work, and reprieves characters from death by organizing sensual fulfillment for them. Pasquale, assured of a spouse, declares "Son rinato," I am reborn; when Ernesto writes to Norina saying he's near death, Malatesta briskly promises "Lo farem vivo," we'll revive him. The excitability of the music—pantingly urgent in Pasquale's "Per carita, dottore," brilliantly showy in Norina's tantrum—is the rejoicing of romantic energy, which William Blake called eternal delight.

Adina in *L'Elisir* reads and laughingly amends the romance of Tristan. Norina too is first discovered with a book, a chivalric love story. She laughs at the posturings of the cavalier Riccardo, yet she knows how to translate the courtly manners of romance into her own slier romantic allurements: she understands the secret of that "virtù magica," which is in her case a teasing vocal artfulness. Lucy in Walter Scott's novel *The Bride of Lammermoor*, who was to become Donizetti's Lucia, goes mad because the romances she reads unsettle her sense of reality. Adina and Norina, her more comically temperate sisters, adjust those antique fables to the promptings of the body. Lucia takes refuge in a deadly fantasy, killing an unwanted husband in order to imagine marrying her lover; Adina and Norina bully and connive so that reality makes their dreams come true. For Norina, whose animal spirits have been suppressed by her impersonation of the simpering convent-bred Sofronia, to liberate the senses and the imagination means to go on a spending spree. Her first action after her wedding is to double the servants' wages, then she sets about using up Pasquale's fortune on a new wardrobe for herself.

Romantic music serves her, like all Donizetti's heroines, as a wish fulfillment. The madness of Scott's Lucy is ugly and disgusting. She dab-

bles "her bloody fingers, with the frantic gestures of an exulting demo-
niac"; Delacroix painted her as a satiated killer, a lioness at feeding time.
In Donizetti, though, her insanity is angelically serene, calm in its gratification. *Lucia di Lammermoor* was the right opera for Flaubert's Madame
Bovary, herself an overeager fantasist, to attend.

Tragedy is overruled by the comic buoyancy of this music, which
charms reality into submission. When Rossini sets a Shakespearean tragedy in his *Otello* (1816, seventy-one years before Verdi's version), it
emerges as a comedy of musical sentiment and sympathy, incongruously
ending in deaths. Rossini's Otello is a juvenile version of the Shakespearean and Verdian hero: a sprightly wooer who wants his naval victories
crowned with the reward of Desdemona. He's indistinguishable from Almaviva, since both are examples of that Rossinian Everyman, "l'homme
moyen sensuel"; he's indistinguishable too from the other male characters
in the work—the duped Rodrigo, and Iago, a spurned suitor of Desdemona's. Otello, Iago and Cassio are hedonists squabbling over the same
female symbol of happiness, so it's psychologically apt that all three should
be tenors, more suited to the graceful, tremulous confession of their erotic
symptoms than to the rending outbursts of Verdi's characters. Verdi's
Iago blasphemes, his Otello despairingly prays. Rossini's men are world-
lings, intent on earthly satisfaction. There's a similar unison, at once emotional and vocal, between his women. Desdemona and Emilia don't
belong to different spiritual realms, the saintly and the humdrum. Both
quiver and shudder with the pangs of love, and sing of their common predicament in a duet.

Tragedy is about isolation and singleness; Rossini's music is comic
because it's about what everyone can and does feel. Whereas Verdian ensembles measure the incompatibility of characters—the quartet in the second act of *Otello* twines together the hero's inconsolable introspection and
Desdemona's lyrical generosity, Iago's muttering trickery and Emilia's
helpless resistance—Rossini's ensembles equate them. The same words do
for all his people in the first finale, because they're all brothers and sisters
under the skin. The tragedy in Verdi is a metaphysical warfare, between
the interceding Madonna to whom Desdemona addresses her "Ave
Maria" and the uncreating demon who is Iago's sponsor. Rossini operates
at the cheerfully busy level of farce. Like Rosina in *Il Barbiere*, Desdemona is a domestic intriguer, whose father intercepts a letter she is smuggling to Otello with a lock of her hair enclosed; and Iago, because the
characters are interchangeable, can use a letter written to him to trap

Otello simply by claiming it was addressed to Rodrigo. Otello kills Desdemona in a temper tantrum, accompanied by one of those orchestral thunderstorms which in Rossini's comedies describe an imbroglio in nature.

Talking to Wagner in 1860, Rossini called Mozart "l'angelo della musica." In sanctifying Mozart, Rossini had sanitized him. His Figaro lacks revolutionary rage, his Don Giovannis are smug gluttons not the enemies of prohibitive heaven. Rossini's version of Cinderella, *La Cenerentola* (1817), uses the fairy tale as a symptom of that wishful thinking which motivates all his plots, and which bids even Otello announce as he returns from battle that he wishes only to be a citizen of Adria and to fall in love. The libertine's worst crime is a greedy avaricious self-indulgence. Dandini in *La Cenerentola*, the servant disguised as his master, is a collector of tidbits, a connoisseur of savory sensual morsels like Mustafà relishing his harem in *L'Italiana in Algeri* (1813). His promiscuity is innocent, like that of a bee in April, as he sings when sniffing out the attractions of the ugly sisters. His lazy, lolloping vocal line pauses to ingurgitate every word as he drinks the contents of Don Magnifico's cellar, belchily regurgitating when he protests that he can't marry both the girls. The charade appeals to Dandini because power means the privilege of filling your belly: now he's a prince, he announces, he will eat enough for four. He is content as well to allow others to feast on him. As the sisters buzz round him, he mutters that he must be made of sugar.

After imbibing thirty barrels, Dandini appoints Magnifico president of the grape harvest and director of Bacchic vows. It is an operatic office, woozily saluting Dionysus, and Magnifico is the ripest and most swellingly benign of Rossini's musical monsters—a Don Giovanni who, overweight and dotingly pleased with himself, is near to that smiling toper, Verdi's Falstaff. Magnifico's arias are multiplication tables, as prolific as Don Giovanni's catalog of conquests or Falstaff's bill at the tavern in their plurality of pleasures. The first, "Miei rampoli femminini," extrapolates the number of grandchildren he expects, and in its burbling approximates to baby talk; the next, celebrating his appointment as overseer of Dandini's winery, publishes his titles, offprints six thousand copies of the patent, and loses itself in an endless future of bureaucratic repetitions, "et cetera, . . . et cetera, . . . et cetera" and so on indefinitely; another, fantasizing about the powers of patronage he'll enjoy after Clorinda or Tisbe marries the prince, both gabbles and gobbles, masticating words as he describes the sweets he'll be stuffed with and singing as fast as he can eat; in the duet with

Dandini, he reels off the infinitudes of attendants who comprise his court—thirty servants, a hundred and sixteen horses, dozens of guests, and suppers with ice cream upon request. This is the carnival of romantic imagination: the "poetical appetite," in Keats's phrase, gains its food simply by dreaming of it.

Cenerentola's triumph is equally automatic. The musical scale is the ladder up which she does her social climbing, negotiating ascents of more than two octaves in the quintet. She shakes the words "Fortuna capricciosa" with her own arrogant, capricious confidence, and in her final rondo dispenses vocal decorations like favors or badges of merit. This is a very different character from the same fairy-tale heroine in Massenet's *Cendrillon* (1899). Cendrillon has none of Cenerentola's swagger; for her, Massenet writes music of a sweetness which, like her moody erotic dreams, is about to turn rancid. She suffers from the Wagnerian sickness, and her fairy godmother is an expert at distilling love-drafts. Cendrillon's love for the prince seeks expiation and consummation in death. At the fairy's oak she begs to take his agony on herself, and in sacrificing herself she wins him. By contrast with this hypochondriac soulfulness, Rossini's characters help themselves to their physical deserts, and the music they make while doing so is the reflex action of their bodies. Rossini rhythmically mimes a heartbeat in Ramiro's aria and the liquidity of laughter in his chuckling asides, or sets all the characters tiptoeing through the stealthy deliberation of "Questo è un nodo" in the sextet; he remembers always, in Magnifico's lip-licking "son tutte papa" (I am all father) or Mustafà's litany of "Pappataci," that language and song are both oral products, salivary joys.

Rossini's most contagiously hedonistic comic society—where all that matters is food, drink, time-passing dalliance and song—is that of *Il Viaggio a Reims*, composed for the coronation of Charles X of France in 1825, performed a few times and then withdrawn, only to have its musical contents mashed, remolded and served up again in 1828 as *Le Comte Ory*. The characters are on their way to the ceremony at Rheims, but are let down by their horses; stalled in their spa hotel, they occupy themselves in maniacally doing nothing and getting nowhere—flirting, quarreling, taking inventory of their possessions, and (since they are a European flotsam, comprising among others a Russian general, a Polish widow, an English milord, a German musical enthusiast and a Spanish admiral) in singing their various national anthems. The piece is a gratuitous riot: musically delicious, dramatically vacuous.

The travelers are at the spa to pamper and purge the organisms they treasure. A doctor prescribes their regime of bathing and supervises their meals, since they are picky eaters. Their hostess Madama Cortese knows their ailments are mostly voluntary mental addictions, and instructs her staff to humor them by talking about their obsessions—fashion with the Contessa di Folleville, antiquarianism with Don Profondo, contrapuntal techniques with Trombonok. Their romantic pursuits are subsidized by their affluence. The Contessa delivers herself of a heroically fatuous mad scene when her modish new bonnet suffers an accident. Their journey is a tribute to the digressive, adventurous, expensive pleasure principle. Unable to get to Rheims, they settle for a party in Paris, which Belfiore describes as "d'ogni piacer l'asil il più giocondo": the asylum of all delights. Appetite is here a rampant possessiveness, engorging an entire world. Don Profondo, listing the armada of their baggage, trots through everyone's trophies in an epic of patter, naming and numbering the Frenchwoman's jewels, the Englishman's teas and parliamentary bills, the Spaniard's heraldic emblems, his own classical curios. His aria is a speeded-up encyclopedia, but for all its exuberance it is a tally of dead things, relics and fetishes, as abundantly unnecessary as everything else in this amazing work.

The music of *Il Viaggio* is static in its very dynamism, indolent despite its bustling energy. A grand sextet introduces the characters, who are all chafing to depart; still they get nowhere, and run impatiently on the spot. Music's service, in the medical routine of the spa, is as a condiment or a restorative for their jaded minds and bodies. When the Contessa faints, the doctor diagnoses a syncope; Trombonok assumes her illness is syncopation. The inspired singer Corinna calms the discord with an Orphic improvisation on her harp. Yet is this benediction, or only a random twittering? When she gives Belfiore a lesson in lyricism, it's the trickery of rhyming—music's preference for the sound of words over their sense— which she chooses to show off. Her muse accepts the whimsy of Rossinian play, and for her last aria she performs on a subject chosen from among the hobbyhorses of her companions by lottery. Their very politics are musical: the anthems they render are to them simply tunes.

This life of sensations and self-soliciting excitements exhausts them. They are a neurasthenic company, and music registers their febrility. Rossini's fretting of the vocal line with shakes and flurries is a nervous graph, its pulsation often near to hysteria. His characters constantly sing of their symptoms. Their cue is the racing palpitation of the body: the "tanti palpiti" of the crusader's final aria in *Tancredi* (1813), the same tattoo of the nerves described by Arsace in the aria "Si, vendicato" from *Semiramide*

(1823). Over plucked strings, Nemorino in *L'Elisir d'Amore* sings of the "palpiti di core amante," and the ensemble he starts up develops into a collective cardiograph. Amina in Bellini's *La Sonnambula* (1831), quaking with anticipation of Elvino's arrival, asks a friend to place a hand on her breast and feel its throbbing: "palpitar, balzar lo senti." The radiant hops, skips and jumps of her coloratura transcribe this physical impetus.

Romantic opera is a symphony of sensibility, and in the second duet of Semiramide and Arsace the most tremulous and overstimulated vocal runs come on the words standing for that condition, "in cor sensibile." Donizetti's characters live by unsettled fits and starts, in rhythmic spasms. Nemorino moons inertly in "Quanto è bella," frantically races in the duet with Dulcamara, droopily decelerates again in "Una furtiva lagrima"; the giddy rapidity of Lucia's madness contrasts with the lachrymose faltering of Edgardo among the tombs. Music might almost be called their metabolism.

For Bellini's Romeo and Giulietta, in *I Capuleti e I Montecchi* (1830), song is a vital sign, a matter of life and death. Bel canto is their fluttery respiration, and its interruption gives warning of their expiry. Bellini's Giulietta is a victim of romantic sensibility, worn out by the strain her feelings exact. Already at the beginning of the opera she seems moribund, pining and fearful that the excitement of seeing Romeo will kill her. Her singing is the expenditure of life itself. "Respiro," she says when she knows Romeo is safe; she can breathe again.

She lacks the reckless flair of Gounod's heroine in *Roméo et Juliette* (1867), who defines her character in a whirling waltz which speaks of intoxication. Gounod's lovers are elated by a musical life-spirit: theirs is the springtime of the body. Juliette says "laisse mon âme à son printemps," and the score is a lyrical aviary, resounding with nature's mating calls. The duet at dawn concerns their dispute about the nightingale and the lark; Stephano sings of a white turtledove. The music glows with what Roméo and Juliette, at the time of consummation, call their "volupté de vivre." Stephano declares the same when he shrills "J'aime la musique!" to taunt the censorious Capulets. But Gounod belongs to a later, bolder phase of romanticism, and understands Shakespeare's Romeo and Juliet by way of Wagner's Tristan and Isolde. Bellini's pair are not voluptuaries, but colleagues in emotional fragility. For this reason, they're both played by women: Bellini's Romeo is a mezzo-soprano, and the role's early interpreters included Grisi and Malibran. The contrivance joins them in a sorority of weakness and shared confidences like that of Norma and Adalgisa, who see into one another's hearts, echo each other's words and breathe in unison as they sing the same line an octave apart. In the melodic fragments of the tomb scene, Romeo and Giulietta achieve a tenuous last understanding as each completes the other's gasped and enervated phrases.

Gounod's Frère Laurent stages the sham death of Juliette as a recoverable liebestod. After all, in the oblivion of sex, lovers die and rise again every night. Bellini's librettist Romani avoids this coital fulfillment, and when the time comes for Giulietta to die in earnest, he fails to supply her with a means of doing so. Romeo refuses her his dagger, and has drunk all the poison himself; she has no recourse but to collapse on him, inexplicably lifeless. She hasn't died from pleasure, like Juliette, but from the depressive pain of her own sensitivity. Hinting as much, Romani alters the profession of her adviser, Shakespeare's Friar Laurence. For Gounod, as for Berlioz (in whose *Roméo et Juliette* he sings a requiem over the two corpses), he remains a friar. Bellini's Lorenzo, however, is a doctor (who in *West Side Story*, demoted, becomes the proprietor of a New York pharmacy): less a spiritual than a medical counselor, intent on calming the overwrought Giulietta, his specialty the treatment of those psychic maladies which are the debility of romanticism.

Learning of Giulietta's feigned death, Bellini's Romeo raves suicidally in a harmonic labyrinth of major and minor variations, begging his rival Tebaldo to kill him. Madness is a natural state for these bel canto characters, because theirs is a music of distraction and mental vagrancy. Insanity is the virtuosity of consciousness, freed by music from the drab rigor of logic. Hence the tyrannical tantrums of Donizetti's Tudor heroines, female versions of earlier operatic despots like Monteverdi's Nerone or Handel's Serse—the slanging matches between Henry VIII's wife and his mistress in *Anna Bolena* (1830) or between English and Scottish queens in *Maria Stuarda* (1835), Elizabeth I's fits of murderous pettishness in *Roberto Devereux* (1837). To sing means, for Donizetti, to behave captiously, unreasonably. When, in his comic opera *La Fille du Régiment* (1840), the tomboyish Marie is given a singing lesson, lyricism is her excuse for a domestic tempest: a motiveless mad scene, concluding in a folly of doodling vocal twiddles. Joan Sutherland always accompanied this ornamental exhibition with an attack on her sheet music, sending an avalanche of paper into the orchestra pit.

In Mozart's *Figaro*, the bells at night made ominously symbolic sounds: "din-din" from the Countess, chirpily feminine; "don-don" from the Count, threateningly masculine. For bel canto comedy, these are noises with no ulterior meaning, contributions to the orchestral uproar of the world. Don Pasquale's servants rush back and forth between contrary commands, "tin tin" and "ton ton," as they complain in their chorus. The same comic delirium overtakes Rossini's characters, turning song into a drilled, senseless din. *Cenerentola* makes its best musical jokes out of interminable, consonant-ridden jargon words like "conciossiacosacché" (meaning inasmuch as) or from the infantile alphabet soup of Magnifico, babbling "che . . . co . . . chi . . . si, che bestia!"—what . . . how . . . who . . . well, damn! The maddest and most mechanized explosion of pure noise occurs in the first-act finale of *L'Italiana in Algeri.* Stupefied, the characters chant variants of "din din," "cra cra," "bum bum" and "tac tac," imitating the jingling of bells, the hoarse cawing of a rook, the thudding of a hammer and the boom of a cannonade. The orchestra becomes a factory of confused and intolerable sound: during the first-act finale in *Il Barbiere di Siviglia,* the characters call it a smithy, where the anvils keep up a barbarous harmony. A musical instrument can torture its hearer. Magnifico hears a double bass sawing away in his head. The industrial imagery of *Il Barbiere* returns in the first finale of *Cenerentola,* where the characters first whisperingly describe a sylvan idyll, then erupt in astonishment at the earthquake which destroys it. To begin with, they imitate the music of nature—chirruping birds, murmuring streams. But the fire below the ground forces itself out, and the ensemble concludes in a spouting maelstrom of smashing, crashing noise. The Rossinian orchestra is a comic dynamo, untiringly energetic and unstoppable, indifferent to human reason.

Elsewhere, the serene Orphic spell, calming discords, still prevails. Bel canto can treat the voice as an effusion of nature. Elena in Rossini's *La Donna del Lago* (1819), boating on her Scottish lake, showers it with vocal cascades. In *L'Elisir d'Amore,* when Adina compares herself with the fickle breeze, her voice has the mazy straying indirection of the wind she describes; Nemorino's voice, in reply, curls and curves like the rivulet he speaks of, seeking out the sea. Maria Stuarda addresses her first aria to a cloud which she tracks across the sky over Fotheringay, and the sound she emits etherealizes and evaporates in homage to the specter above her. Anna Bolena in her last scene yearns for a lost innocence, and retrieves it by singing a plaintive reprise of the ballad "Home, sweet home"; Donizetti thereafter allows her to die of homesickness, not by the executioner's ax.

The greatest bel canto aria—the priestess's invocation of the moon,

"Casta diva," in *Norma* (1831)—is also the one most dreamily inseparable from the landscape it inhabits. It is a nocturne; the romantic poet Théophile Gautier, translating its sounds into colors and sights, didn't so much hear it as see it, and described Norma's voice as a wind rustling dewy leaves, stirring shades which are alternately silver and blue, cool yet velvety. Norma is a Druid, and her religion suits romantic opera because it worships nature: the moon, an oak, the bough of mistletoe she scythes during "Casta diva." The Scottish bards, hailed as "sacri cantori" or holy singers in *La Donna del Lago*, are prophets of the same cult, thundering encouragement to the military clans and eliciting support from heaven in the form of a meteor.

Romantic imagination in Rossini ravenously eats up reality. In Donizetti, it zanily cancels that reality, like the mad Lucia. In Bellini, it sings reality to sleep. His opera about the sleepwalking Swiss peasant girl, *La Sonnambula*, so often dismissed as silly, is his defense of that imagination's visionary faith, and of its capacity to make dreams come true by the intercession of bel canto. It is Bellini's transalpine answer to *Der Freischütz*, first performed ten years earlier, in 1821.

Weber had found the romantic mind to be a grotto of guilty fears and superstitious credulity. Bellini, less aghast at the romantic traffic with demons, has his own view of this irrationality, in the fables of the villagers about their local phantom. The urbane Count derides their folklore but capitulates to it when he mistakes the sleepwalking Amina for the legendary ghost. In Weber's German forests, imagination conjures up devils; Bellini's spirits are benign. The Count romantically suspends disbelief for a while, but analytically demolishes the illusion when he explains to her neighbors that Amina is a "sonnambula": they don't understand the term, and are told that it is compounded from the words "andare" and "dormir." All charms fly at this touch of cold philology. Yet Amina's experience remains a magical initiation. She envisions something and—like Adam craving and thus inventing Eve, in the biblical dream which Keats called an allegory of imagination—awakes to find it granted to her. Having lost Elvino, in her second sleepwalking scene she fancies they are reunited, and when roused finds him waiting to reclaim her. *Der Freischütz* ends with the hermit's pious exorcism of the fiends which lurk in the romantic subconsciousness; *La Sonnambula* ends by placating those bogeys and investing them in the surrounding landscape as familiar gods. There they will, as Amina sings, make the earth on which we live a paradise of love.

In *I Puritani* (1835), Bellini confronts the enemy of this blissful imaginative hope: a censorious, puritanical reality. The opera is set during the English civil war, and concerns the love of Elvira, who lives in a Cromwellian garrison, for the cavalier Arturo. He temporarily jilts her to rescue the widow of Charles I, beheaded by the Puritans. Deserted, she seeks comfort until he returns in a melodious madness. The implacable reality in *I Puritani* is politics. Elvira's respite from it is song. Exempted from the drama, alone in her private musical domain, she almost ceases to be a character. She is a spirit or, simply, a voice. Often indeed she is a voice off, heard not seen—inside the castle at her morning prayers; wandering the halls intoning her lament before she arrives for the mad scene; later, errant and invisible in the woods. Disembodiment makes a ghost of her, a lunar revenant who is the mere shadow of an earthly being. Giorgio and Riccardo, Elvira's uncle and her Puritan suitor, have a duet in which they describe her and Arturo as sad, wandering, moaning phantoms.

Song gives voice to what can't normally be heard: the language of the soul, or of the unconscious mind. The lyricism of Bellini, placid and unimpeded, is the self-immersion of his characters. His bel canto has its own time-span, since it exists in an immobilized, suspended eternity, like Amina teetering on the plank above the millstream in *La Sonnambula* and literally walking on air as she sings, or like Norma spinning out forever the floating cadence of "son io" as she accuses herself and volunteers to die. Absorbed by music, Elvira falls behind the urgent tempo and onward momentum of drama. She asks Arturo near the end how long they have been separated. Three months, he says. No, she replies, in a beautiful and heartfelt phrase, it was three centuries, an aeon of pain. This is more than operatic overstatement; it's a fact of bel canto life. To sing is a way of preventing things from happening. Elvira stops the clock at the instant of Arturo's betrayal, and retires inside herself to sing about the wedding the plot has denied her. Deliriously repetitious, she does elongate Bellini's cantilena until it could occupy three hundred years.

She is restored to Arturo in and by a song—the troubadour's ballad, which he used to sing to her, and which she encores when she hears him in the forest. The troubadour uses music to complain about vexatious reality. When it's evening, he longs for sunlight, and vice versa; spring to him is winter, and pleasure is pain. This helpless contradictoriness, though it suits the emotions of Elvira and Arturo at this point in the opera, is inefficient bel canto. It self-pityingly rails against the way things are, yet can't alter them. Bellini can achieve those reversals for which the troubadour pines. When Arturo resumes the song he converts its woe into joy, and magically changes what Elvira calls her memories and futile dreams into truths. He sings her out of her depression.

Doing so, he revives the past. This is one of the heartening bounties of Bellinian song. The meandering fluency of his melodies carries his people back into themselves, as on that double stream of reverie in the duet between Norma and Adalgisa which sings the praise of memory: "Oh! rimembranza." The romantics defined genius as childhood recovered at will. Bellini's characters exercise that nostalgic genius when they sing. Recognizing the landscape of his birthplace, the Count in *La Sonnambula* as he begins "Vi ravviso" travels an unruffled, unending avenue of sound toward a destination inside himself; the refrain of Elvira's madness, "Oh! rendetemi la speme," is a prayer for the restoration of a vanished time.

In *Norma* the singers, intent on this open-eyed retrospective dreaming, seem to be mystically entranced, mesmerized by their own voices. The mnemonic spell of "Oh! rimembranza" works on the warrior Pollione as well, when he describes his dream to Flavio, and Norma's prayer is for the return of a lost, paradisial joy in "Ah! bello a me ritorno." Despite the shock of dramatic events, she remains fixed on the ritual of disconsolate remembering, sustained by her long breath or by the unbroken arcs of the cello before her soliloquy in the third act. The worst crime Norma can accuse herself or others of committing is to forget. In the trio she defies Pollione to forget his children, his promises and his honor; indicting herself, she says that for a moment—when she considers killing the children—she could forget to be a mother. Drama is suspended by the different summons of music, internal and reflective. Norma's dagger is poised to strike Pollione, but she can't go on; she must clear the stage for another meditative review of their complicity. Having sentenced herself to die she drifts abstractedly back down two further streams of consciousness: another remembered summary of Pollione's betrayal in "Qual cor tradisti," an appeal to Oroveso's memory and his paternal responsibility in "Deh! non volerli vittime." Before she can mount the pyre, she has retreated forever into the remoteness and immunity of the past.

Song for her is both psychological defense and spiritual sublimation. Venerating the moon as her "casta diva," a chaste goddess, the singer is herself an operatic diva; she and the moon are colleagues in divinity, for while Norma is a priestess, the soprano who performs the role must be just as ascetic and devout about her own vocation, dedicated to the production of superhumanly perfect tone. Bel canto, so boisterously carnal in Rossini, has in Bellini become a religion.

FOUR

Beethoven and Political Opera

REVOLUTION is near in *Le Nozze di Figaro*, though it is staved off by the Countess's clemency and by Mozart's peacemaking music. In 1789 it broke out, abruptly accelerating the tempo of history. Opera assumes a new mission—to embody that urgent time-spirit, which throughout the nineteenth century demands change and evolution. Music, operating as it does in time, has a unique ability to dramatize this idea, and it does so in Beethoven's only opera, *Fidelio* (1814).

From the timid, almost stealthy beginning of its overture to its hectically joyful, unbraked conclusion, *Fidelio*'s orchestral rhythms are the powers impending over the destinies of men—repressive and obstructive at first, wildly freed at last. Its musical drama describes the toil and travail of human striving: advance countered by conservative reaction, or postponed by mere exhaustion; the allegro of progress—for allegro means both speed and happiness—relapsing into the safe andante of cowardice or self-satisfaction.

The overture states the terms of this historical struggle. The opening thumps are a peremptory command to hurry up. The horns appease this fretfulness and appeal to a bucolic peace; the strings are pensive. Gradually the initial momentum returns, irrepressible as the human demand for freedom, and the overture ends in a rush, almost a stampede. Alone with their domestic chores, Jaquino and Marzelline in the first scene debate this musical and political agenda. Jaquino, importuning her, is moving too fast;

she holds him off by time-killing repetitions. Though always busy—he's ordered about by the knocking at the door; she keeps to the measure and dares not interrupt her work—they achieve nothing. After each of their numbers, music sighingly gives up hope.

Like Sisyphus, the opera rolls a boulder uphill only to watch it roll down again, frustrating all effort. The quartet after Leonore's arrival is about fixed positions, a situation which is oppressive because static; when the voices cease, the orchestra dies again into silence and impotence. Each of *Fidelio*'s separate numbers starts out boldly, only to find it can't continue. Music must surrender to hesitant, stumbling speech. Rocco rouses the others from the ruminative immobility of the quartet in his aria about riches, but the throbbing, excited future his crescendo foresees is a false start, stopped short when Leonore challenges him. A dialectic is established which controls the rest of the work: music instigates a motion, speech checks it; a voice ventures forth, only to be reined in. Leonore lunges into the trio with elation, and her vocal line strains both ahead and upward; Marzelline with her practical fears lowers the vocal altitude and restrains the rhythmic pace. Between their different proposals, Rocco can only contrive a spurious synthesis, good for the time being, when he changes gear in "Nur auf der Hut, dan geh es gut" (Be on your guard, all will be well). Every number defers a conclusion until the next, which is likewise unable to reach a decision. The singspiel follows the jerky stop-and-go motion of history.

A march is a byword for historical propulsion, brassily keeping Enée on course toward Italy in *Les Troyens*. But the march announcing Pizarro in *Fidelio*, snaky and covert with its furtive drumbeats, isn't the will of history; it's creepy and defensive, just as the vocal prowess of Pizarro's aria is a falsely confident bluff. His voice races ahead, panting in anticipation of Florestan's last moments. But this is not a revolutionary encouragement of time. Pizarro, as he admits, will be safe only when time has a stop, with Florestan's death. His climactic triumph is hushed at once by the guards, who hurry up only to get away from him, and in the subsequent duet the more furiously he gestures Rocco ahead, the more skeptically Rocco hangs back. Again the musical drama is made from a failed momentum. Describing Florestan, Pizarro cannily throttles the speed of his utterance, enticing Rocco to complete his thought when asking if this is the man who has wasted to a shadow. Rocco's interjection is rhythmically moribund, a premature funeral march. Once he has concurred, Pizarro pounces onto his next note—"Zu dem . . . !" To him!—and presses the issue to a pat and breathless conclusion. A little later he teasingly delays the word "schlei-chen," which describes his slithering entry into the cell, only to speed it up unexpectedly as he leaps on its last syllable. Character in action (the ancient definition of drama) here finds its musical correlative: voices in motion.

Leonore's aria "Abscheulicher!" (Monster!) is plotted on the same self-contradictory principle. It's swaggeringly angry at first, then stayed by detachment and moral forethought. Her appeal to hope is her attempt to calm herself. She is thrust out of this repose by the admonition of the horns. Onward, as always in Beethoven, means upward, and the testing scales on the word "Gattenliebe" (married love) are vocal exercises for a female Sisyphus. Emotionally, politically and therefore musically, the aria ends by soaring over hurdles or scrambling up ladders.

Yet there is, all the same, no advance. When the prisoners are re-leased, their reawakening to life enjoins a gradual increase in musical vol-ume. Both processes automatically turn tail: the two prisoners who have sung out from within the crowd vanish into its anonymity again; the brave forte is dampened as they huddle, whispering, and are shooed back to the dungeon. Nor can the finale of the first act permit a musical outburst. It's another catacomb of separate, soliloquizing privacies. Leonore is reduced to muttering asides while the ensemble's top line is claimed by the brightly superficial Marzelline, who sets about embroidering it. In the orchestra, when the voices give up, there's a brief epilogue—a fading, dispirited fall. The act is a treadmill; it ends with a merely circular progress made.

Florestan is a victim of this musical and dramatic law. In his aria a rebellious protest starts up, then falters. The vehemence of his appeal to "Gott!" lapses into a small pastoral symphony of resignation—like Leo-nore's landscape with the rainbow in "Abscheulicher!"—as he remembers his springtime days. A vision rejuvenates him and agitates his voice, then leaves him bereft and prostrate. The last instrumental bars of his aria taper out like the cardiogram of a dying patient.

The next number in the score, as Leonore and Rocco arrive to dig his grave, is a melodrama—dialogue with orchestral punctuation. It brings into confrontation the two constituents of *Fidelio*: song and speech, the headlong drive of music against the laggard, quibbling resistance of human language. The orchestra prompts Leonore and Rocco, but they're too dis-mayed or too cold to accept its challenge. In their duet, Rocco sets an in-dustrious gait to match their digging. Music is movement and thus a disbursement of energy; it's synonymous with work, as for Figaro measuring the room, for the gypsies in *Il Trovatore* pounding their anvils, or for Hans Sachs hammering the shoes in *Die Meistersinger*. Rocco stammers and stutters in rhythmic trepidation. Leonore, meanwhile, grows vocally ambitious, and executes a set of grandiose flourishes above and around the word "befrei'n." That word means freedom, and by ornamenting it she is exhibiting the quality she extols. Virtuosity serves her political dedication, as the voice rhetorically cheers itself up.

Her first contact with Florestan restates the opposition between airborne song and earthbound speech which is so central to *Fidelio*. Rocco is disarmed by Florestan's voice ("seine Stimme")—but by the voice in speech, not song. Hitherto, dialogue had been timidly murmured, with music as the prerogative of those bold enough to raise their voices in accusation. Florestan's few sentences question that judgment. Lyricism is after all a gift unequally bestowed; the language we speak and teach to each other, on the contrary, is the ground of our human equality and community. Once this democratic shared medium is established, the trio which follows can justify music all over again, for its ingredients—breath, air, motion—are those of life itself. Leonore's "Wie heftig pochet dieses Herz!" (how fiercely my heart beats) takes its shape from the most primary of the body's rhythms, and Florestan's "O Dank!" demonstrates how the voice should be used: in prayerful gratitude, respiring in thanks to the agency which first inspired it. Here that animating force is no god, like Monteverdi's La Musica, but another, fraternal human being. The signal to Pizarro, however, obliterates uplifting music and substitutes shrill noise. The two most troubling sounds in *Fidelio*—the initial raps which startle Jaquino, and the whistle here—lie outside the conciliatory domain of music, and are also inexplicable by speech.

The sudden alarms and defeated reversions of this musical pulse persist through the drama's conclusion. The ensemble in which Leonore challenges Pizarro charges at high speed until the trumpet stops it short, then the voices retract into pensiveness and song relapses again into dialogue as Jaquino and Rocco arrange the denouement. Leonore falters when Florestan asks what she has suffered for his sake: "Nichts, mein Florestan!" is all she can say. But the voice modestly lowered in dialogue at once unabashedly peals out in song as their duet begins. Between its choruses of galloping jubilation, the last scene also interpolates a passage of slower introspective summary, "O Gott! O welch ein Augenblick!" (O God, what a moment). This, however, is no sagging fatigue. The rhythmic backsliding has been overcome. Though the characters pause here in thoughtful reverence, they proceed when Leonore prompts them, directing the chorus to sing loudly and lovingly: "Liebend sei es hoch besungen." The multiple repetitions of the finale proclaim that revolution has achieved its messianic aim, advancing from history with its disappointments and retrenchments into an enduring eternity.

Fidelio not only transcribes the career of political history, moving through time to engineer change; it is also an opera about opera's evolutionary destiny, and it both summarizes and surpasses the history of its own form. Beginning as a chatty singspiel, it grows into music drama yet ends—beyond drama and its merely personal fates—as oratorio or choral symphony, when the whole unchained world rejoices in song.

Beethoven adjusts the mythology of neoclassical opera to a world of intractable human realities. Instead of Alceste following Admète to the underworld, Beethoven has Leonore follow Florestan to the actual and modern hell of a political prison; whereas *Alceste* ends unconvincingly in comedy, with Hercule boisterously vanquishing death, *Fidelio* begins in comedy—with the bickering of the menials—in order to outgrow it. Gluck's Orfeo returns to a dreamed-of pastoral Elysium; Beethoven demonstrates how men might construct their own paradise here and now.

Fidelio also moves on from the caprices of bel canto opera. Just before Beethoven, Ferdinando Paër set an Italian translation of the same libretto. Paër's *Leonora* is a comedy about sexual appetite. The first act ends with a jealous erotic debacle, not Beethoven's edgy political standoff, and after the rescue in the dungeon the soubrette Marcellina flounces on and bargains for a kiss before she'll consent to help Florestano. Instead of Beethoven's idealist, Paër's Leonora is a rampaging coloratura, stamping her foot in virtuoso tantrums.

Nor does the process end with *Fidelio*. The revolution must be renewed in every generation, and in 1952 Rolf Liebermann's *Leonore 40/50* relocated Beethoven's characters in the Europe of the second world war, where the German Alfred and the French Yvette fall in love across a disputed border. At the beginning of Liebermann's opera, Alfred is listening to *Fidelio* on his wireless; the broadcast is interrupted to announce the outbreak of fighting. He and Yvette are finally united by a guardian angel, whose forgiving verdict is a quotation from *Fidelio*. Don Fernando's role of deliverer has been assumed, for Liebermann, by Beethoven himself.

Because the work is always on the verge of becoming something else, Beethoven was reluctant to stop writing it. *Fidelio* exists in two different versions, and has four separate overtures. Since Mahler's production in

Vienna in 1904, it has been the practice to insert the most elaborate of these symphonic essays, the *Leonore* no. 3, between the scene in the dungeon and the finale. Played at this point, the overture narrates the metamorphosis of opera into something like oratorio. *Leonore* no. 3 recapitulates the action. It trudges back to the depressed beginning, languishes in a cavernous misery as it recalls Florestan's long-lost spring, then by a series of strenuous exertions finds the strength to resume the struggle. But it abstracts the story in retelling it. It takes the world for its theater, not a prison outside Seville. When the trumpet sounds here, it's as an apocalyptic call to judgment, not to announce a visitor's arrival. It generalizes the drama—which is what the characters throughout have been striving to do. Fidelio is Leonore's nickname but also her allegorical title, and her most generous moral resolve generalizes her personal case: she will save the prisoner, she swears, whether he is Florestan or not. He matters to her as a specimen of wronged humankind, not as a loved one. Likewise, when Pizarro insists on identifying himself to his victim, Florestan brands him with a generality. He is "ein Mörder," a murderer, just as to Leonore he is "den Frevler," a wrongdoer—significant as a principle, not a personal enemy. By the final scene, the Leonore who renamed herself Fidelio has undergone a further mutation. No longer a person, she's a moral emblem. In her duet with Florestan, she was "mein Weib"; now she is "ein holdes Weib" or "ein solches Weib," a noble wife or such a wife. And though she is praised as a spirit of eternal womanhood, even her sex and its singularity have been overcome by her disguise as a boy. More than either male or female, the character who temporizes between the two kinds as Fidelio incarnates humanity.

Leonore no. 3 declares the drama to be redundant, and what remains of the plot is perfunctorily dealt with. Gabbling to get the explaining over, the witnesses deliver a precis of events to Fernando; Marzelline's disconcertment when Fidelio is revealed to be a woman deliberately approaches farce; Pizarro no longer matters, and is waved away. And who is Fernando? He's attached to the action by being described as Florestan's friend, but that is an allegorical bond: he's the undiscriminating friend of all men. Fernando is also, now the work has ceased to be opera, the chorus master who conducts the oratorio, and treats the assembled community as his congregation.

Fidelio retraces the history of its form to end where opera began, in oratorio. But since gods can no longer be relied on to help men, oratorio seeks a substitute for religion in the homemade creed of humanism and in the shared consolation of music. Mahler wrote a song of the earth; Beethoven wrote the song of humanity, and Fernando here patiently teaches it to the creatures whose gospel it should be. Leonore and Florestan have receded into membership of this familial crowd, and the crowd itself is but a sample of those thronging millions addressed by the chorus at the end of Beethoven's ninth symphony.

The freedom to which Beethoven pledges his music meant for Rossini only a vivacious irresponsibility. His opera about a thieving magpie, *La Gazza Ladra* (1817), flaunts this careless hedonism. A servant girl is condemned to death for a trifling theft of silver, committed in fact by the disrespectful bird. The drama solicits sympathy for poor Ninetta, but the music favors the magpie, whose instincts Rossini the self-plagiarist shared. The freedom the opera celebrates comprises insubordination (Fernando the soldier has been sentenced for striking a superior officer, but gets a royal pardon) and the slippery adjustment of truth (Ninetta quick-wittedly misreads the warrant for his arrest to befuddle the Mayor).

Rossini puts an end to revolutionary aspiration. Stendhal in 1824, noting that Napoleon was dead, announced that a new European conqueror had replaced him: this was Rossini, who sang the praises of a full belly and a quiet life. The following year, *Il Viaggio a Reims* allied itself with the restoration of the French monarchy. Its voyagers are on their way to the coronation of Charles X, who had personally approved Rossini's appointment as director of the Théâtre Italien in Paris. Of course they don't arrive, but they cheer themselves up by rejoicing in the suppression of revolutions elsewhere. The improvising singer Corinna derives from a novel by the royalist Madame de Staël, and the Spaniard Don Alvaro in his contribution to the festivities chooses to salute one of Charles X's sons, who had quashed a revolution in Spain in 1820.

The idyll of peace and surfeit didn't last long. In 1830 revolution broke out in Paris, Charles X fled, and the monarchy of Louis Philippe began. The poet Heinrich Heine, writing in 1837, patronized Rossini as a relic of the old order, a composer of table music who "would never have attained his great popularity during the revolution or in the days of the empire." His music, Heine argues, is melodiously lazy, relaxing into the mood of dolce far niente, bored by the strife of political engagement. The claim fits Rossini's comedies, but not his last opera, the work whose portrayal of Swiss patriotism defying Austrian rule started opera's alliance with national campaigns for liberty, and prompted Verdi to dramatize Italy's cause against Austria—*Guillaume Tell*, performed in Paris in 1829.

The overture to *Tell* summarizes the historical predicament of *Fidelio*. It begins as a pastoral symphony of repose, convulsed by a storm; the horns are an epic summons to combat. By the end, as the sun transfigures a Switzerland freed by Tell, the orchestra pit has lifted into that radiant sky. Tell begins a choral prayer which begs liberty to redescend from heaven, and it does so as an inundation of music.

The wavering Arnold, harried by Tell, comments "Quel sévère langage!" Rossini's language is indeed unwontedly severe. Music has assumed a responsibility for political organization. The first chorus sings serenely of "nos concerts," but it means a concerted social effort as much as a blithe occasion for song. In *Guillaume Tell,* song is likely to be an accompaniment to work, as it is for the fisherman on the lake or the villagers in the mountains hearkening to the bell which ends their day of labor. Tell interprets all emotions politically, and when Arnold blushes because he loves the Hapsburg princess Mathilde, Tell reads this as remorse for a treacherous division of loyalties. Personal emotions and possessions must be offered up to the cause. Mathilde, rather than singing love duets with Arnold, lectures him on the need to enlist, and promises to visit him in his tent on the battlefield; Jemmy, Tell's son, sets fire to the family home when there's no other way of signaling for the uprising to begin, and consoles his father by saying that he has at least salvaged their weapons.

The formulae of opera undergo a similar conscription. Processions, like that of the hunters across the peak of Rütli, are a show of power, meant to intimidate. Tell plans the merriment of the wedding games as a screen for his conspiracies. In the archery competition at Bürglen, ballet is target practice, a training for combat; at Altdorf, when Gessler's soldiers stamp out opposition, dance is again militarized. The Rossinian crescendo, once a collective dementia, here amasses forces and winds them up for a clash, as at the end of the first act. Ensembles are musical parliaments: the second act arrives at a battle plan after a coordination of representative voices. In the dark forest, Tell chairs the assembly of three choral deputations. The men of Unterwalden trudge through the woods, those of Schwitz arrive from the mountains, and those of Uri sail across the lake singing of parliamentary speech: "Parle! parle!" Once all three cantons have convened, Tell prompts them to a unanimous vote: "Aux armes, aux armes, aux armes!" This is a long way from the babel of nonsensical idioms in *L'Italiana in Algeri*; it claims for opera a new power to mobilize society, as when the united Catholic vigilantes consecrate their swords on the eve of the massacre in Meyerbeer's *Les Huguenots* (1836).

The example of Meyerbeer is used by Heine to reproach Rossini. Gormandizing has been replaced by a more high-minded, abstemious diet. For Heine, one of Meyerbeer's moral credentials was a liking for dried cod. Rossini's fondness for private sentiments gives way to Meyerbeer's concern with partisanship and social cohesion. Heine detests Bertram in *Robert le Diable* (1831) because he remains undecided, like Arnold in *Guillaume Tell* with his contradictory loyalties. Such irresolution is the mood of romanticism—of moral weaklings like Pollione in *Norma* or Arturo in *I Puritani*. Hamlet is the patron saint of their uncertainty. Meyerbeer, the man of imperial confidence and conviction, must advance beyond introversion. His later protagonists are therefore bureaucrats, experts at organization: Marguerite de Valois arbitrating between the religious factions in *Les Huguenots*, Jean de Leyde institutionalizing a bogus religious faith in *Le Prophète* (1849), Vasco da Gama in *L'Africaine* (1865) planning argosies for the enrichment of Portugal. The great scenic stunt of *L'Africaine* is its cross-sectioning of Pédro's ship, revealing its tiered arrangement of decks and cabins. The sailors sleep above; below there are separate areas for Inès and her attendants, and an office for Pédro, who leads the colonial expedition. Meyerbeer exhibits society as a systematic filing cabinet.

Heine elects Meyerbeer as the musician of the Napoleonic empire, and *L'Africaine* is his attempt at an imperial opera. Its subject is the imperialism of Portuguese navigation in the fifteenth century, pressing round the Cape of Good Hope toward treasure in the east; its own techniques are imperious—batteries of effects, an abundance of expensive exoticism, a stage aswarm with battles at sea or heavy with Hindustani monuments. The people are as grandiosely impersonal as the sets. Indeed they're piqued by the imputation of personal motives. When the captive chieftain Nélusko tries to kill Vasco, he declares, with the ideological zealotry of a true Meyerbeer character (shared by the Carlists in *Les Huguenots* and the Anabaptists in *Le Prophète*), that the man's a Christian, and he hates them all. Sélika the African queen, who knows he dotes on her and is jealous of Vasco, taunts him by asking whether he has no other motives. Vasco overtakes Pédro's ship to warn him of danger ahead, but Pédro discredits his zeal by suggesting that he cares only for saving Inès.

Mendelssohn said that the music of *Robert le Diable* had everything but a heart. Vasco shares that heartlessness. He is both an imperial profiteer and a self-obsessed operatic tenor: he reserves his highest notes for the praise of prosperity (when he hectors the council in Lisbon, demanding support for his voyage) and for his claims to immortality. In prison he keeps a map by his bed, and dreams exclusively of glory; he promises himself to Sélika if she will help him with his cartography, and trudges off with Inès when that is the only way to stay alive. His lyrical meditation "O paradis" is a survey of colonial real estate. This new continent belongs to him, and his voice reaches its peak at the moment of appropriation: "Sois donc à moi!" Murmuring of his country, "ma patrie," he has no sense of it as an extended family, like Verdi's characters with their filial tenderness toward the fatherland. His country is his employer, certifying his worth and augmented by the booty he brings it. As an organization man, he can't exist without it. Sentenced to death by the Indians, he sobs in annoyance because his career will be halted, and bargains for a chance to report his discoveries before they sacrifice him. He can't die, he protests, until he has secured his immortality.

Politically, grand opera means noisy grandiloquence, backed by a policy of greedy aggrandizement. Beethoven heard in revolution a song of humanity. Leonore's yearning for freedom is an impulse of love. But the epic mission of empire demands a rigorous inhumanity, and opera acquires a new breed of ruthless politicians to replace its earlier cast of vindictive gods and autocrats—Vasco sailing back to Lisbon as Sélika, shamed by the use he has made of her, dies; Siegfried in *Götterdämmerung* deserting Brünnhilde after a single night to embark on the Rhine; Enée in *Les Troyens*, urged on to Rome despite the grieving Didon.

FIVE

Berlioz and Historical Opera

MEYERBEER made opera massive, able to contain entire societies. After his inflated grandeur, opera attempts an epic dramatization of history. In the two parts of *Les Troyens*, Berlioz narrates the fall of Troy and the exploratory journey of Virgil's hero Aeneas toward his Carthaginian idyll with Dido, and on to found a new civilization in Italy. From the collapse of a classical order the modern world is saved. Russian opera extends across the long struggle to define and defend nationhood. Borodin's *Prince Igor* deals with the campaign against the Tartars in 1185, Mussorgsky's *Boris Godunov* with the regicides and uprisings of the years from 1598 to 1605, his *Khovanshchina* with the dispute between the mystic Asiatic Russia of an old belief and a newly European dispensation after 1682; Prokofiev in *War and Peace* recalls the war against Napoleon in 1812 and connects it with the effort to withstand another invader, Hitler, who threatened Russia as he was composing the work. Opera, established as a rite, can now celebrate a communal identity and make musically manifest the destiny of a people.

Before Berlioz, the Virgilian characters had made an operatic appearance in Purcell's *Dido and Aeneas* (1689). They are as yet innocent of the historical fate Berlioz devised for them. Indeed Purcell's Dido, deserted by the conquering hero, melodically entreats her confidante to "remember me! but ah! forget my fate," whereas the Didon of Berlioz goes to oblivion hoping that she will be forgotten but her fate—as one of history's casualties—remembered, and avenged when Hannibal in the future travels from

Carthage to menace Enée's new citadel, Rome. Even an incriminating historical fate can be amended in Purcell's opera, made to comply with the erotic desires of the characters. "Fate your wishes does allow," Belinda chirpily assures Dido, and Aeneas vows he has "no fate but you!" For him, her refusal of his advances would be itself a historical calamity, making "a hero fall, and Troy once more expire." The Enée of Berlioz is pursued by ghostly historical mentors, who urge him to be true to his mission and press toward Italy. The opera is his tragedy, because he must sacrifice emotional trust to a political glory. In Purcell, the intervening gods are not moral tutors but mere pranksters—mischievous witches who play tricks on Dido and Aeneas to procure their consummation, an elf disguised as Mercury who fraudulently reports that Jove commands him to set sail. The epic, miniaturized, begets a comedy of foolish misunderstanding and easy infidelity. Dido's only solace is self-indulgence: when Aeneas offers to stay with her after all, she sends him packing and offers herself to another ravisher—"Death invades me."

The people of *Les Troyens* (composed 1858–60) are not permitted to take refuge in sentiment. They are the creations of their society, which they must resign themselves to serving. The prophetess Cassandre forgoes happiness with Chorèbe. Enée tells his son Ascagne that he must learn from others the art of being happy: his warrior parent can teach him only valor and the piety of ancestor worship. Enée is a father to the refugee Trojan clan, Didon a succoring mother to Ascagne (when Enée places him in her care) and to her grateful Carthaginian subjects. These individuals emerge from and are absorbed by the crowd. Cassandre materializes among the heedlessly happy Trojans on the plain outside the walls, and is the voice of historical conscience, which they can't hear; she dies into that indiscriminate mass, rallying the women of the city to suicide. Enée bounds on to announce the slaughter of Laocoön by the sea beasts, in advance of a panicking throng and charged with the responsibility of uttering an epidemic terror. In Carthage, he holds himself in reserve, pretending to anonymity among the ranks of his own men, stepping forward and unveiling the armor beneath his sailor's rags only when history—in the attack on Carthage by the Numidians—has need of him. Didon's entrance is preceded by a chorus declaring her to be queen because legitimized by the love of her people; death is her transit to a visionary future where she foresees the recuperation of Carthage, and her own vindication by Hannibal.

They are deputies of the people, whose hopes and miseries are the immemorial substance of history. The hydra-headed protagonist of *Les*

Troyens is the chorus, and beneath it the orchestra, brazen in tone and exultantly energetic despite its unwieldy size. *Les Troyens* begins with the explosion of a pent-up population, racing into the fields as the siege is lifted. It ends with retreat and consolidation, as the Carthaginians close ranks to curse the Trojan horde. Its first sound is a contagious laughter, its last a howled imprecation. In between, the chorus is our induction into the collective life of family, society and race: our means of experiencing an oceanic immersion both in music and in history, carried along by a torrential energy which exhilarates but also exterminates the individual. This is the case with the antique, off-key sonorities and thumping rhythms of the Trojan hymn to the city's gods, as a society exerts all its rough efforts to make music, or the stark cries and guttural undertones of the priests of Pluto before Didon's death, addressing the spirit of Chaos in morbid dissonances. Enée proves his leadership by drilling the mass to make music, calling for the trumpet and lyre to accompany the wooden horse through the gates, or cementing a new alliance of Trojans and Tyrians by setting a march tempo in which all are compelled to join.

Verdi's ensembles are enlivened by individual dissension. While the chorus of *Aida* unfeelingly rejoices in an Egyptian victory, or that of *Don Carlos* in a bigoted sacrificial justice, solitary voices protest on behalf of an injured personal feeling. The ensembles of *Les Troyens* do without this argumentation; individuals are unified by the fear or the desire they share. Once Enée tells of Laocoön's death, the augury is ingurgitated by everyone present. Eight voices ponder it in a communal monologue, repeating it over and over to consume it as the serpents have done to Laocoön, then transmitting it to a double chorus which goes on devouring and recycling the same words. Berlioz has made audible the dread and disturbance of a society's unconscious mind, babbling as if in its haunted sleep. In the moonlit gardens of Carthage, another society—in the murmuring soporific septet, joined by a chorus which pulses as gently as a becalmed sea—relaxes into a delicious stupor. Spellbound by music as the waves dreamily harmonize, the characters float out of themselves, lulled and at peace. The night of which Didon and Enée sing, their "nuit d'ivresse et d'extase infinie!", is not the instinctual darkness of Tristan and Isolde. It's a benign state of rest, safe from the conflicts and agitations of daily living. Troy's dreams are tormented, and as Enée writhes on his bed the orchestra rumbles and crashes, its stabbing chords and jagged flares describing the destruction of the city; the soothing sleep of Carthage is a respite—momentary only, yet prolonged by a timeless repetitiousness—from history. Sleep teases us with the remembrance of a period before history began, when we were paradisially happy: hence the song of the sailor Hylas in his cradle high in the riggings, dreamily crooning of his mother, of the homeland he'll never see again, and of the eternal, rocking, amniotic sea.

Nietzsche supposed that opera began in the frenzy of a mob, deranged when the god possesses it. The rollicking haste of the crowd is judged in the same way by Cassandre: its riot, she says, is a drunken madness. She is in turn seen as a Dionysian, one of opera's own hysterical muses, during her suicide at the altar of Vesta. A Greek soldier admires her fervor as she sings of death with a lyre in her hand, and calls her a Bacchante inebriated by her own music. This political orgy, goading Trojan society to self-destruction, recurs in Carthage as a saturnalia. Didon and Enée go hunting in the forest and, trapped in a cave by a sudden storm, make love. The episode is an orchestral ballet: Didon and Enée don't sing because they are now purely physical beings, driven by erotic compulsion; and this carnality has made Olympian gods of them, omnipresent in the turbulent landscape. He, the son of Venus, rides in the guise of Mars, wearing his warrior's costume; she is dressed as Diana, the patroness of the chase. Their orchestral coition is feted by a gang of Dionysian creatures in the undergrowth. After they retreat into their grotto, satyrs and fauns caper grotesquely in the murk, and when lightning ignites a tree they gambol about with the flaming branches.

The jubilation of the chorus has its equivalent in the orchestra. Wagner laughed at Meyerbeer for having put onstage a scenic counterpart to the noisy, congested, gimmicky big band of Berlioz. His jibe contains some truth, for the score of Les Troyens is a sonic replica of the society Berlioz represents. It gets its sheen and its harsh brilliance, like the glare of the cloudless sky over Troy as described by Chorèbe, from the brass; it resounds with the clatter of weaponry, as when the clank of armor is heard from inside the wooden horse. In Carthage, Panthée tells the chieftains that invisible blows make their disused arms ring, and Mercury uses the shield of the laggard Enée as a gong, smiting it with his herald's wand and, as it reverberates, repeating the summons to Italy. A debris of metal, giving off the clangor of the Berlioz orchestra, is the first and last exhibit in Les Troyens: at the beginning, the crowd plays games with the leftover helmets, spears and javelins of the Greeks; at the end, Didon sentences the rejected armor of Enée to incineration on the funeral pyre, then unsheathes his sword to stab herself. Virgil began his Aeneid by declaring that of arms and the man he sang; Berlioz, setting the epic to music, makes the arms themselves sing.

Voices are forged into the semblance of steel: how else can the tenor who sings Enée reach those gleaming, lacerating high notes? Though pastoral Carthage has refashioned its swords as plowshares, replacing the arsenal with agricultural and architectural tools—Didon distributes sickles, set squares, rudders and oars to her subjects—the orchestra remains a factory of muniments, turning out instruments for the conduct of war. The phrase Cassandre uses of the horse as it rolls through the gates, "l'énorme machine roulante," could serve for *Les Troyens* itself, that outsize musical and dramatic mechanism which Berlioz keeps perpetually and tirelessly on the move.

It isn't, however, an imperial contraption like Vasco's ship in *L'Africaine*. The shade of Hector sends Enée from Troy to found an empire which will in future dominate the world, and Anna salutes Didon as the queen of a fledgling empire which each day grows richer, but the characters of Berlioz are not Meyerbeer's profiteers. Enée berates himself for making use of Didon, and her eventual realm is underground: she explains her death as a sacrifice to the somber deities who preside in the empire of the dead. History is less the annals of adventure and conquest, progressive because greedy, than the record of the earth's survival and its yearly replenishment. Hence the small pastoral symphonies which question the strife of the epic—Chorèbe's appeal to Cassandre to forget the war, watching the flocks and listening to the birds proclaim a hymn of peace; Didon's gratitude to the fertile goddess Cérès, and Iopas's song which reckons her blessings in the fields. While men exert themselves to rule the world, women are content to be guardians of the earth. Didon's is a maternal monarchy, nurturing her people, and in promising to care for Ascagne she tells Enée he should not doubt her motherly love. Her most wounding insult when he quits Carthage is to call him unworthy of his own mythological mother: he is not the son of Venus, she cries, but of some wolf in the forest.

Virgil's subject was the heroic prowess of the male. To this, Berlioz added an image of female tenderness and solicitude borrowed from his other literary idol, Shakespeare, in whose plays women are the agents of healing and of nature's redemption. The rural festival in Carthage suggests the sheepshearing in *The Winter's Tale*; for their love duet, Enée and Didon paraphrase the mythological fables traded by Lorenzo and Jessica in *The Merchant of Venice*. The Virgilian epic worries about bolstering up a power which will never be stable or permanent. Shakespearean comedy has no faith in political arrangements, and proposes surrender to nature's reconciling power over us. Throughout *Les Troyens*, the moral is recovery and continuation, the need to resume the simple business of living despite the terminal pessimism of epic with its sacked cities and toppling masonry. Troy, as Hector predicts, will have its renaissance in Rome; the classical world is born again in the romanticism of Berlioz, who lovingly revives the defunct antique characters of Virgil. As history continues, tragedy settles down naturally into comedy. This is the experience of Hector's widow, Andromaque. In Troy, she leads her son to the altar while the chorus comments on her mute grief. Since she doesn't sing, she seems a classical statue, mournfully self-contained. As she lays down her wreath, a clarinet is liltingly happy for a moment, recalling past joys—or anticipating those in the future? For although Andromaque doesn't reappear, she is mentioned in Carthage, as one whose tragedy has been mitigated by the glad optimistic comedy of nature. Enée tells Didon the epilogue to her story: she has at last succumbed to Pyrrhus, and agreed to marry her father's assassin. Didon is shocked by such inconstancy, but it's an augury of her own, and a tribute to the biological prompting which is the veritable will of history. Classicism is saved from its marble rigor by the new life of romanticism.

The deaths of Cassandre and Didon are not an annihilation, like those of Wagner's heroines who delightedly cast off their existence—Senta leaping into the sea, Brünnhilde riding into the fire. Death is their admission to an extended family, the tribe of their ancestors and of their progeny. Thus Cassandre dies in company, comforted by the sorority around her and confident that Enée will save the sons of Troy; Didon gains solace from a future which will vindicate her. Wagner's epic about the machinations of history, the *Ring*, reaches a different conclusion. Here the family is a device for the perpetuation of power, a jealous dynastic immortality: Wotan breeds the Wälsungs, Alberich begets Hagen as his avenger, and the upwardly mobile Gibichung clan in *Götterdämmerung* schemes to co-opt Siegfried. The future is mortgaged to our possessiveness. In Wagner there is no fructifying goddess of the fields like Cérès in *Les Troyens*. Freia's apples, which in *Das Rheingold* ensure the eternal youth of the gods, are the diet of those afraid to relinquish power. Human society doesn't tend nature, like Didon's husbandmen with their scythes, but ravishes and exploits it. Alberich tears mineral wealth from the innards of the earth. There can be no pastoral compromise between men and that abused earth, such as Berlioz expounds in the song of Iopas; nature instead, when Walhall burns and the Rhine floods its banks, must scorch and submerge a parasitic human life. The Trojan march in Berlioz—though it's heard in an eerie, elegiac minor key in Carthage, as if ashamed of the damage it will do there—urges society ahead. The corresponding march in Wagner, accompanying the funeral of Siegfried in *Götterdämmerung*, is a threnody which treads backward into the past. Its procession of motifs is a review of time irretrievably lost, and hopes betrayed.

Verdi too makes an epic summary of history, which he sees as a cycle of mischance and malicious coincidence: the force of destiny. Writing an opera for St. Petersburg in 1862, he fixed on the subtitle of the play he adapted—the Duke of Rivas's *Don Alvaro o La Fuerza del Sino*—and called his opera *La Forza del Destino*. That force is unintelligible and accidental, ruining the lives of the three protagonists because a pistol goes off when Alvaro throws it down, killing Leonora's father and rousing her brother Carlo to a pitiless vendetta. The history which persecutes individuals also hounds the mass of men. The same mob of pilgrims, carpetbaggers, muleteers and gypsies which quarrels and carouses in the Spanish inn at Hornachuelos turns up on the Italian battlefield of Velletri. The warmongering Preziosilla cheers on the recruits with promises of military honor; she leaves behind an abattoir of wounded men in Italy, and a jostling, squawling congregation of beggars outside the monastery in Spain. The busy panorama makes no sense at all, and in Verdi's original ending Alvaro, spurning the religious resignation of the Padre Guardiano, hurled himself over a cliff to an absurdist death. Because Didon has herself been a refugee adrift on the sea, she resolves to help Enée. But everyone in Verdi's opera is homeless, friendless—Alvaro is an exiled Indian prince, Leonora even before her father dies calls herself an orphan—and instead of sympathy and fellow feeling they must rely on the grudging charity of the church and its regime of penance. Melitone ladles out soup and sermons, the Padre Guardiano forces the dying to their knees in unavailing prayer. Nor can Verdi believe in Wagner's ecstatic obliterations. Here there are only the cries of human misery, like the wail of Leonora when her brother, whom she has rushed to care for, seizes the final opportunity to stab her.

In both Berlioz and Wagner, history has its own good reasons, obliging Enée (as he tells Didon) to obey a divine command and inciting Siegfried (when he shatters Wotan's spear) to disobey one. Verdi can discern no such logic. History for him is noises off, an irrelevant victory parade like that overheard acclaiming Otello, who lies prone on the floor, unable to hear it; the private affections and anguish of his characters are impervious to political successes or defeats. The monastery in *La Forza del Destino*, where Leonora and Alvaro seek refuge, is less a religious establishment than a place of disenchanted seclusion, exempting them from the violent muddle of history outside.

Like Berlioz, Verdi models his history on Shakespeare's chronicle plays. The grumbling sentries in *Les Troyens*, who don't want to resume the quest and prefer to stay in Carthage teaching Phoenician to their new girlfriends while eating venison with the local vintage, are insubordinate underlings from Shakespeare, as skeptical about the purposes of war and empire as the cowardly Falstaff in *Henry IV*. The military episodes in *La Forza del Destino* are indirectly Shakespearean, deriving from Friedrich Schiller's play *Wallenstein's Camp*. But Melitone is no Falstaff: he condemns the vicious world, rather than seeking a compromise with it; and in his own opera about Falstaff, Verdi ignores the political and military intrigues of *Henry IV* and puts the fat knight out to pasture in the forest. The goodness and comic wisdom of Verdi's Falstaff demand his withdrawal from history.

The Shakespearean chronicles are a prototype for Russian opera. Borodin's *Prince Igor* has a pair of inglorious Falstaffs, the deserters Skula and Eroshka. Igor's brother-in-law Galitzky takes greater pleasure in roistering than in ruling, and the opera stays at home with him and his revelers rather than going to war with Igor against the Polovtsians. Mussorgsky based *Boris Godunov* (1868–72) on a play by Pushkin which imitated Shakespeare's histories, and selected as the chronicler of Russia's futile ups and downs a Shakespearean fool—the simpleton whose lament for the weeping people ends the work. Tchaikovsky's *Mazeppa* (1884), dramatizing a Ukrainian rebellion in the eighteenth century, has a similar ending, as Maria, deliriously indifferent to the carnage around her, sings a lullaby to the dead Andrei. Russia has its own gloomy interpretation of Shakespeare's protracted civil wars: history is a tale told by an idiot.

It therefore must be unconsecutive, episodic, apparently without purpose. These operas make a virtue of their own incompleteness. *Prince Igor*, its scenes alternating between the sturdy Russian folk and the wild Polovtsians with their tribal dances, remains inconclusive. This, Borodin thought, was its truth to history—"there was no final victory over the Polovtsian Tartars," he noted. He hadn't finished the work when he died in 1887. Mussorgsky left *Khovanshchina* unfinished at his death in 1881, a loose conglomeration of anecdotes. It teems with musketeers and mystagogues, a sorceress and a sect of Lutherans, aristocratic conservatives and Westernizing reformers; no single character or group occupies the center. The opera's title is appropriately vague and improvised: the word is a neologism of the Tsar's, who when informed of a conspiracy against him labeled it "Khovanshchina," which meant "the goings-on of the Khovanskys." History is all plotting and no plot, a mess of snarled, simultaneous actions. To follow one line of cause and effect, as drama conventionally demands, would be a lie.

The same is true of *Boris Godunov*. It is not exclusively about the Tsar; he appears in only three of its scenes, with a walk-on in a fourth outside the cathedral, and he is disengaged from the opera's thronging forum, singing mostly in soliloquy. Even in his isolation, he is less a person than a personification. The people invent him, electing him their father as they cry at his coronation. But the beloved patriarch must then be rejected: Boris is invested with power by popular love, and destroyed when that worshipful affection turns to resentment and hatred. Like the shaman, he is created to bear and expiate the community's woes. When he sings of Russia groaning ("stonet Rus!") he voices the agony of the country. He has a tragic contract with the land, unlike Didon's motherly care for Carthage. The god must be slain so that his country can survive. Mussorgsky's score, adapted to the long travail of Russian history—in the trudging, exhausted rhythms of the prologue or the sawing string figure which introduces Pimen's interminable writing; in the bells of the coronation scene, the pendulum beat of Boris's delirium and the tolling as he dies, all dolefully marking a time which goes on forever—treats the career of Boris as a ritual sacrifice, repeated over and over through the centuries.

"Man is a social being," said Mussorgsky. Though Boris can have no relationship with other individuals, he contains them all. He is the mass, and its inconstancy is matched within him as he lurches unstably from glowering despot to craven weakling; he is every other character in embryo. He has a memory of suffering as long as Pimen's, and a guilty sense of his own illegitimacy which makes him a pretender like Dimitri. Varlaam is a Boris whose autocracy has been reduced to bragging, and whose conscience can be quelled by drink. The simpleton is the frightened, helpless child Boris conceals inside his omnipotence. Marina too, coveting his throne, is his female counterpart, and stages her own coronation at her dressing table when she calls for her diamonds. He's a composite in himself, an anthology of Shakespeare's tortured monarchs. Like Richard III he's a child-killer, and Mussorgsky's prologue, when Tchelkalov and the police tease and bully the crowd into acclaiming Boris, recalls Buckingham's manipulation of the citizens by pretending that Richard shuns the crown. Aghast at the thought of the dead rising from their graves to accuse him, Boris is the haunted Macbeth; tolerating the fool's insults and protecting him from arrest, Boris is the penitent Lear. It is as if he undergoes serial reincarnations in the work, like Russia itself.

Mussorgsky was a student of Darwin's theories, and his score registers the strain and weariness of a personal and national evolution. Its tempo is characteristically worn-down, flagging, in need of threatening stimulation from the drum when the officer outside the monastery shows the crowd his truncheon, or from the bells and glaring horns which impel Boris's ovation; the opera seems to comprise not seven years but the seven ages of a man's life and of a country's. The history of Berlioz and Virgil has a messianic end in view. Enée can look forward to his promised death on the Ausonian fields, and hasten toward it. Russian history is experienced by Boris as a purgatory: an eternity of pain, where time will never have a stop because there will always be another existence for him to toil through. It's the sight of a clock's unstoppable workings which provokes his collapse. Didon's confident foresight is Boris's despair. For him as for Macbeth, the succession of tomorrows can only prolong his life sentence.

In the second act of *Boris Godunov*, the Tsarevich studies a map of his Muscovite domain, pointing out its choicest spots. Boris admires it too, and says you can look down from the clouds and see the entire kingdom at a glance. But though geography can cope so easily with space, history is an enduring apprenticeship to time. Geography sees the world from the air; history must slouch along the ground. On the map, everything comes together at once. In history, events don't occur once only but are reviewed, remembered and repeated without end, and this is the nightmare which music, based on inescapable recurrence, terrifyingly acts out.

History can't only happen. As a story, it must be written. This penitential business of chronicling, which corresponds to his own labor of musical composition, is one of Mussorgsky's subjects. The writing of history is Pimen's soul-saving chore, bequeathed to him (he says) as punishment for his sins. He has had two lives: one of savage, sportive action in his youth, another of lamplit literary reflection in old age. As the orchestra mimics ebbing water, he describes the power of history and of music to recycle in the mind a time which is running out. Writing is his insomniac discipline. He has spent the long-ago days unconsciously living; the nights are sacred to remorseful memory. While he writes, Grigori sleeps, and dreams of power. Pimen wants to hand on to him the task of completing the chronicle, but Grigori would rather perform in history than write about it. Impersonating the murdered Dimitri, he treats history as theater not narrative. Already in the frontier inn, he has begun the business of falsifying himself which will transform events into play. As he reads out the description of himself on the warden's warrant, he changes each of the itemized features to end with a verbal picture of Varlaam. The Polish scenes see history as the sum of such fantasies: Dimitri's dreams of military success, Marina's of brocaded robes and coronets, Rangoni's of a religious crusade.

When the Tsarevich relates the tale of the parrot pecking the nannies, Boris praises the narrative art which organizes his story, accredits its truth and compliments the boy's education. His faith is misplaced: the anecdote is endless and pointless, like the sequence of non sequiturs in the nurse's songs about the gnat or the hen which bore a bullock and the pig which ate an egg. Boris needs to believe that history has a beginning, a middle and an end, that it can be written into coherence after the event, but these nursery rhymes or the simpleton's refrain know better: it's a chaos of happenings which signifies nothing. Though the boyars order Tchelkalov their clerk to write down their anathema against Dimitri, it's a self-deception to imagine that they can stop him by promulgating or publishing words. After Pimen resigns his pen, the narrators in *Boris Godunov* are hearsay, gossip and many-tongued, unreliable rumor—Varlaam's tall story about Tsar Ivan at Kazan, the boyar's scurrilities about Shuisky, Rangoni's whispered propaganda, the babble of the peasants outside the cathedral. Boris walks into Shuisky's performance of his superstitious torment: Shuisky imitates Boris shooing away the dead child as Boris enters, still shooing the specter. History is not drama but a specious charade. When Pimen reappears in this scene, he has adjusted his tactics accordingly. Earlier he told Grigori to set down the truth without art; now that he no longer writes, he can be theatrically artful, terrorizing Boris with the tall story of a miracle wrought by the dead Tsarevich, which he takes on trust from a shepherd.

In the first patriotic Russian opera, Glinka's *A Life for the Tsar* (1836), the peasant Ivan Susanin dies to save his monarch from the Polish invaders. After the 1917 revolution, a new libretto was fitted to the work, proposing that Susanin sacrificed himself for the preservation of the fatherland. The new proof of heroism is service to society. Already in *Khovanshchina*, the characters belong to social categories. The librettist Stassov intended a contrast between opposed encampments—the prim German pastors of Emma's clan against the ribald squalor of the barracks. The princes are contradictory social forces—Khovansky the inflexible Muscovite with his feudal costumes and his retinue of Persian dancing girls, against Galitsin's foreign schooling and inclination toward Teutonism. The fundamentalist Dositheus, who chooses the funeral pyre rather than recognizing the anti-Christ, exemplifies another type: he was compared by Stassov with Mohammed, John the Baptist and Savonarola.

War and Peace, on which Prokofiev began work in 1941, retains the episodic shape of Mussorgsky's epics, making a more or less random choice of thirteen scenes from Tolstoy's novel. Yet its society, unified by the twin emergencies of 1812 and 1941, regains that faith in history which Mussorgsky questions. Mussorgsky's operas are about people making up history—Shaklovity in *Khovanshchina* dictating his libels to a mercenary scribe, or Kouzka narrating the career of the vicious hag he calls Gossip. For Prokofiev, the Tolstoyan history is as unchallengeable as holy writ. The Russian people in *Boris Godunov* are indifferent to politics but opportunistically eager to survive, so that the Falstaffian Varlaam ends as one of Dimitri's cheerleaders; "our great people" in *War and Peace*, as Kutuzov calls them, attain an anonymous, democratic heroism.

The crowd is concerted and regimented by music. Prokofiev's scenes of peace are about dances, those of war about marches. Russia at peace resembles an opera, absorbed by flirtation and social frippery. At war, it has closed its ranks and re-formed itself as a choral oratorio. The music of courtly Russia is a social amenity. The host at a ball commands the choir to sing as his guests troop down the receiving line, and orders Lomonosov's ode when the Tsar appears; Dolokhov rounds up the partygoers for waltzes or a mazurka. All is elegance and superficiality. This first section is Prokofiev's criticism of Tchaikovsky's operas, already reviled by Mussorgsky and his colleagues for their un-Russian cosmopolitanism. The naive, deluded Natasha is Tatyana from *Eugene Onegin*, wasting herself on the wrong man; the ball attended by the Tsar recalls Catherine the Great's arrival at the party in Tchaikovsky's *Queen of Spades*, and the fondness of the characters in that opera for the French rococo is denounced by Prokofiev's patriots, who despise French emotions and fashions. In *Onegin* the dancing master M. Triquet sings some fatuously stylish French couplets, and in *The Queen of Spades* the grandees entertain themselves by staging a pastorale with the earnest affectation of Marie Antoinette pretending to be a dairymaid. Prokofiev ends that game by setting fire to the French theater in Moscow as Kutuzov orders the city's evacuation. The imported actresses rush squealing into the streets, still made up and in costume: operatic artifice is shamed by historical reality.

Once war is declared, the dance, futilely rotating, gives way to the purposeful, straight-ahead march—parades of grenadiers and chasseurs, a jaunty quickstep of hurrahing foot soldiers. Individuals retire into the mass, which can be indefinitely multiplied. When Denisov says he needs five hundred men to break through the French lines, the peasant Tikhon says he can have thousands and thousands. Prokofiev's choir is his militia. In the epigraph to *Peace* it sings of the club raised by the Russians to bludgeon the enemy. That weapon is the percussive force of those outraged, upraised voices. *War* begins with an episode of choral training which is also an exercise in sweated military labor. Digging a bastion and carting off barrows of earth, the men are instructed to heave like bargemen, "all together, as hard as you can." A people's war must be won by the chorus.

Mussorgsky called *Khovanshchina* a "folk drama." The same description suits Prokofiev's *War*, so much so that he allowed the folk to compose a good deal of it, supplementing Tolstoy with the journal of a guerrilla poet and the songs created to boost morale during the 1812 campaign. In less belligerent mood, the people are the subject of Janáček's *From the House of the Dead* (1930), based on the Siberian prison diary of Dostoevsky. Janáček's communal hero is not Prokofiev's proletariat, mobilized and like-minded, declaiming its talismanic slogans: his music treats mankind rather than a mass; it generalizes without collectivizing.

The family of man remains quarrelsome, eternally at odds with itself. Janáček's text for the opera allotted each of the prisoners his own language. Some sang in Russian, others in Czech, with a babel of extra Slavic dialects; only after Janáček's death did the work's first stage director translate it uniformly into Czech, thus blunting its meaning. For in this opera, music alone can manage an impartial sympathy and comprehension which is denied to words. *From the House of the Dead* is Janáček's lament for argumentative, inarticulate humanity, as *The Cunning Little Vixen* is his anthem to speechless nature.

The internees of *From the House of the Dead* still have a touching confidence in language. Jenůfa in an earlier Janáček opera teaches the herdboy Jano to read by drawing the letters for him; here the political prisoner Goryanshikov educates a young Tartar. Alyeya, having learned to read and write, quotes the prophet Isaiah, through whom God utters the command to forgive and to love. But writing can equally be an instrument of torture, a forced labor: immediately after Alyeya's delighted showing off of paper, pen and ink, another prisoner recalls being arraigned before a district commissioner who made him write and write without reason as he was whipped. Though the characters pass the time telling stories, their narratives are as inconsequential as those in *Boris Godunov*, and are recited at cross purposes. Shishkov reviews his own record of homicidal jealousy without recognizing that his rival Filka, another prisoner, is among the listeners. No communication or forgiveness is possible: Filka dies, and Shishkov curses his body.

What words cannot say, Janáček's music finds sounds for—Alyeya's yelps of anguish during Shishkov's narrative, and the last spitting gasps of Filka; the vocalized moaning of the prisoners, like the sighing of the Volga in *Kátya Kabanová*; the strings taut with grief at the beginning of the opera, vibrating above a clank of chains, painfully high-pitched when Goryanshikov is dragged on. Those with nothing else to hope for derive courage from music. On their holiday, the prisoners perform a play about Don Juan, who braves the lecherous devils and calls for his Elvira. The whistles, leaden drums and fraught strings could not be further from Mozart, but this Juan like Don Giovanni stands for resistance, ebullience, the erotic and musical irrepressibility of life. This crude little opera is followed by a pantomime about a miller's lustful wife, who secretes her lovers around the house. Juan returns from hell to add her to his list, and they dance until they die of exhaustion, along with the devils. Janáček sets the episode as a scurrying orchestral farce. It is his admonition to the prisoners, who survive their tragedy by vowing to see it as a comedy. Music's special ministry here is to those without a political voice, and without a history.

SIX

Verdi

VERDI set the entire world to music. His operas encompass the theocratic ancient Egypt of *Aida* and the bigoted Babylon of *Nabucco*, the imperial Spain of *Don Carlos* and the licentious Italian Renaissance of *Rigoletto*, the provincial German courts of *Luisa Miller* and the contemporary Parisian demimonde of *La Traviata*. In him the operatic world theater, universal in Monteverdi, becomes truly global. The composer of *Macbeth*, *Otello* and *Falstaff* is opera's Shakespeare: Verdi the populist is an expert on the human heart, who commiserates with the slave Aida, the courtesan Violetta and the cheerily dishonorable Falstaff, with the wandering mendicants of *La Forza del Destino* or the universal chorus whispering its prayer for peace in the *Requiem*. Like the chameleon Shakespeare, Verdi hears everyone at once and distributes music impartially to all men alike. His ensembles compound opposite emotions, as if a god were listening to the polyphonic hubbub of the human race. In the quartet from *Rigoletto*, Gilda's lament and her father's curses, the Duke's philandering refrain and Maddalena's chuckling patter entwine and overlap; musically they are equivalent, and while they are singing, Verdi withholds judgment.

Music is the gift he lavishes on these people, and it is their only means of salvation. Dumas, in the novel which was Verdi's source for *Traviata*, says that the lady with the camellias will be pardoned because she has loved; Violetta earns pardon with her singing, which is changed by her sacrifice from the glassy brilliance of her first aria to an angelic plea for

147

mercy. The only heaven Verdi could believe in was one constructed by music, and his operas lead inevitably to the secular Mass which is his *Requiem*. From it emerge his two summings-up—the infernal, ironic creed of Iago in *Otello* and the comic forgiveness of *Falstaff;* first an opera in which the antagonistic spirit of drama derides the balm of lyricism, then one in which all dramatic misunderstandings are resolved by the lyrical coordination of a fugue.

Music is the motor of Verdi's dramas because it is the life-force of his people, cascading through Violetta's praise of pleasure or starting up in the trill which revives the dunked, dispirited Falstaff, gurgling in the laughter of Riccardo in *Un Ballo in Maschera* as he scoffs at a prophecy of death, boldly sounding in defiance when Posa challenges tyranny in *Don Carlos*. To sing is a symptom of vital courage, when Aida taunts Amneris by declaring herself an equal in rank or when Amelia resolutely arrives beneath the gibbet in *Ballo*. The voice which is the body's proud possession also serves as a conduit for the spirit. Elvira in *Ernani*, pleading for her lover's life, says heaven utters through her. As well as blessing—which it does in Desdemona's entreaties, or Nanetta's serenade to the fairies in *Falstaff*— the voice can assert its power by imposing an anathema. Rigoletto is haunted by the fatal word of malediction, while the monks in *Forza* protect the hermit Leonora behind a barricade of impenetrable noise when they sing their curse on intruders. Like all operas, Verdi's are mystery plays, and the mystery is vocal. The characters of *Don Carlos* are admonished by a bass who echoes invisibly from the cloistered tombs and a soprano, also miraculously unseen, who pronounces comfort from the sky.

At first, Verdian opera is a clamorous free-for-all. The plot of *Ernani* (1844), notoriously clotted, exists only to provoke vocal confrontations. The singing is the drama, because it's the arousing of rebellious instinct, the jealous insistence of desire. The characters in *Ernani* are emotional states, absolute yet unstable, altering at a moment's notice if their musical biorhythm demands it. Ernani's moroseness in his lair changes to rollicking optimism once he decides to abduct Elvira. In Silva's house he appears as a humble pilgrim, only to reassume the role and the vocal swagger of the bandit. Elvira lunges from anger to penitent expiation when she produces the dagger. Carlo, as soon as he's crowned, exchanges vendetta for compassionate amnesty. The characters reel from one crisis to the next—Elvira's room is invaded by three rival wooers—but always have an energetic musical response to the dramatic emergency. Elvira fights off Carlo by outsinging him, capping his every phrase in their duet; when he turns

148

plaintive, she replies with a set of frisky vocal leaps reminding him of her hot Aragonian blood. Political alliances are made and unmade according to the same impulsive whim. Ernani and Silva, mortal enemies, fraternally team up against Carlo, then revert to their ancient feud. The logic is that of the passions.

Music foments this sexual competition. A Verdian opera, as Shaw said, is a dispute between the tenor, who wants to make love to the soprano, and the baritone, who objects; and here the bass also swears to prevent consummation. Music delights in the political affray, with its tumult of raised voices. Ernani is a song of vigor and anarchic liveliness. The only tragedy it acknowledges is that of growing old, the subject of Silva's misery in the second act and of Carlo's resignation when he looks back on what he calls his green years.

The voices in Ernani belong to healthy young animals, wild enough to love noise for its own sake. The jollity of the outlaws, gambling and carousing in their den, sets its tone. Macbeth (1847) has already been overtaken by vocal superstition. Some Verdian singers console from on high, like the intercessor in Desdemona's "Ave Maria," while others occupy the lower depths, that primal mud which is Iago's element; in Macbeth too, song is supernatural. Its motto might be the phrase Macbeth and Banquo use to describe the predictions of the witches—"Accenti arcani!" It is a work of arcane accents, of shrill, harsh sounds like the owlet's cry heard by Lady Macbeth, like the ravaged, shrieking voice Verdi wanted for Lady Macbeth herself, or like the pinched, piping utterance of the phantom child with his "occulte parole." Its most disturbing note is heard not seen, left behind by the sleepwalking Lady Macbeth as she glides offstage: the dwindling D-flat which is her elegy. Stridently colored or malevolently overcast, the voice in Macbeth is a landscape. Banquo sings in reverberant gloom as the assassins gather round him. Lady Macbeth must sound metallically bright, to slice or jab through the orchestra like the knife she wields, yet is hoarse and ravenlike too. When he revised the opera in 1865, Verdi appropriated Macbeth's speech about dusk in the play and gave it to her as the text for a new aria, "La luce langue." In it, she makes audible the darkness he looks at.

Because Verdi finds in Macbeth a wolf's glen of spooky untamed sounds, the scene central to his opera is one which in Shakespeare scarcely matters: Macbeth's second encounter with the witches, when they cavort with Hecate and concoct visions from their caldron. In Verdi the episode is a show of vocal conjuration, making voices materialize from the air.

Thus the first exhibit is a severed, helmeted head. The witches summon up these freaks to illustrate the "incognite Posse" or unknown powers they serve, dramatizing the nether world in a pantomime. Referring to "il nostro oracolo," they mock the pompous oracles of classical opera. The speculative metaphysics of Shakespeare's play, investigating problems of free will and predestination, have been forgotten. Instead Verdi composed an infernal prelude to that *Requiem* which was to follow twenty-seven years later. Lady Macbeth almost enviously intones for her victims "un requiem, l'eternità," revering the dead because their sleep is untroubled; after Duncan's murder, she, her attendant, her husband and Macduff form a pious quartet and mutter "Gran Dio!" among an earthquake of choral and orchestral crashes. Opera ventures a black parody of the Mass.

The theater began as a place of contagious insanity, and music can still press dramatic characters to acts of reckless extremism. This inspired rampancy is Verdi's subject in *Il Trovatore* (1853): the self-forgetfulness of Azucena hurling her baby into the fire, of Leonora swallowing poison and rejoicing in a decorative cadenza, of Manrico bravely leaping toward the unauthorized and probably deadly high C at the end of "Di quella pira." These are people driven by music. They obey the bell which startles Ferrando's troop, the anvils which order the gypsies to work, or the trumpets which marshal the soldiers. They have no dramatic reality beyond their obsessive, competitive activity of singing.

Trovatore is a war between vocal archetypes. Manrico is mettlesome, because that's the heady imperative of his tenor range. Luna broods as baritones must, skulking further down the scale; Ferrando derives his personality from his cavernous bass, which fits him for the mournful recitation in the first scene. Leonora the soprano specializes in ecstatic flights, Azucena the mezzo-soprano in an angrier and chestier passion. Leonora's mood is still that of a bel canto heroine, mellifluously drowsy; Azucena the howling animal looks forward to the physical violence of verismo. Since song is the subject of *Trovatore*, it turns sound into spectacle. Its great moments are occasions of vocal disembodiment—the unseen Manrico's first ballad or his appeal from the tower, the choir of nuns, the slaughtered gypsy's command of vengeance or the quavering voice from heaven which tells Manrico to spare his brother.

Action is banished; the crises happen either long before the opera begins or between its acts, and are recounted in scenes of musical reverie—Ferrando's ghost story, Leonora's swooning erotic vision, Azucena's reliving of her trauma. Manrico isn't seen rescuing his mother: he sings of his resolve to do so, and proves vocally equal to the adventure, in "Di quella pira." At its most imperative, music is its own justification. *Trovatore* deprives the characters of motives for the fanatical missions which engage them. The libretto is a tangle of genealogical mix-ups, its most dramatically pertinent questions left open. Ferrando can't satisfactorily cope with the queries of his retainers. Azucena answers Manrico with contradictions. Is he her son? First she denies it, then reassures him that she was raving when she said so. Luna demands where she's going when she strays into his camp; she shrugs that she doesn't know.

The individual purposes of drama are of no account in this opera, where everyone is causelessly agitated by music. The orchestra sets them on fire. Azucena's crackling narrative "Stride la vampa," describing her mother's funeral pyre in a voice which spits and lashes like tongues of flame, could represent the psychological condition of every character in the work. They are on heat, inflamed and at last incinerated by the score. The libretto's images flare into life when this incendiarism burns through them. Luna calls his love a fire, and Ines says Leonora is feeding a dangerous flame and asks how the first spark ignited her. These elemental beings are planetary sources of warmth, sometimes of light but more often of combustible fury. Luna rhapsodizes about Leonora's smile as starlight, and calls her glance a sunbeam. If she is the solar center of the work, he is the moon after which he is named, coveting a heat he cannot share. "Di quella pira" measures the enfevered temperature of *Trovatore*: it's a work of musical pyromania.

Here opera is the outcry of a frantic irrationality. Azucena's "urlo feral"—the bestial screech remembered by Ferrando—is a primal scream. The mother who destroys her son is a fiend from the Dionysian rites. There are other, Orphic occasions in Verdi when music tempers and harmonizes human distress. His *Luisa Miller* (1849) is based on a play by Schiller, *Kabale und Liebe*, in which music has an enlightened embassy to men. Schiller contrasts the artificial divisions of class with the natural affectionate equality between people, and in a spoken drama invokes music as a symbol of this accord. Miller (in Verdi's opera a retired soldier) is in Schiller a fiddler in the municipal orchestra; Ferdinand (Verdi's Rodolfo) ingratiates with Luise by signing on for flute lessons, and she entertains him by playing the piano. In the play, music regulates insurgent passions. Ferdinand, enraged when Luise apparently betrays him, seizes a violin and tries to play it, then punishes it when it cannot soothe him, ripping the strings and smashing it on the floor.

In the opera, music is more than a metaphor. Verdi bestows it on his victimized characters as their means of spiritual redress. Schiller's Luise looks forward to a judgment day when hierarchy will be confounded: the opera is that second coming. In singing Verdi's generous melodies—Luisa's prayers, Miller's swelling praise of paternal love—Schiller's characters become uprisen souls, glorified by lyricism. Against the restrictions of social caste, Schiller proposes an aristocracy of mind. On that judgment day, Luise says she will be accounted rich, for tears will be treasures and fine thoughts noble ancestors. Verdi creates instead a democracy of song, rewarding characters for a simplicity and sincerity proclaimed by their music. The opera's ensembles have their own version of Schiller's political reckoning. In one of these, Luisa's lone voice begs God to shield her from her accusers, while her father appeals to divine retribution; in another, when Luisa is made to perjure herself before the Duchess, Verdi leaves the voices to overheard reflection on their shame or gloating relief. Unobscured by the orchestra (which returns only to place a full stop after their a cappella meditation), they are souls bared for judgment. On the final day, Ferdinand promises in the play, the varnish will be stripped from every lie. The opera doesn't need to wait so long: music is truth, for no one can tell a lie while singing. Verdi sanctifies Schiller's grotesques. In the play Miller is selfishly grumpy, and when Luise threatens suicide he asks who will look after him in his old age; Verdi's character is a selfless patriarch, God's deputy on earth (as he says). In the play Ferdinand poisons Luise so they can share a mutual damnation. The opera musically amends their fate. The poison releases Luisa from the need to pretend that she is unfaithful to Rodolfo, and they swoon in a delirious love-death.

Luisa Miller craves the consolations of religion, but alters them to suit its own musical theology. Luisa defies criticism by saying that her soul and Rodolfo's recognized each other: God created them to fall in love, and after death they'll resume their affair in heaven. The god to whom her pleas are addressed doesn't come when called, like the mechanical helping hands of classical opera—Hercule in *Alceste*, Nettuno in *Idomeneo*. The blessing sought by Luisa and Rodolfo derives not from the church into which they troop but from the score's inexhaustible sympathy for them. *Luisa Miller* proposes opera as a New Testament. In Miller's duet with Luisa about a life of happy beggary, or Luisa's melting forgiveness of her persecutors, it pours forth music as the medium of its love.

In *Simon Boccanegra* (1857), music descends like a messiah to make peace between warring men. The opera is about the reunion of families.

Boccanegra regains the daughter lost to him when her mother died twenty-five years before; his adored Maria is reborn in the next generation as Amelia, and her lover Gabriele, named Boccanegra's successor as Doge, is himself a young Simon; Fiesco, Maria's father, grows through time from Boccanegra's enemy to his adoptive parent. The same loving communion must extend to embrace all of society. Verdi achieved this by adding to the opera in 1881 a scene in Boccanegra's council, for which Boito wrote the text.

The plebeians and patricians are at odds, and disrupt the council with their exchange of insults. Boccanegra, quoting Petrarch, implores an end to external hostilities, since Genoa is at war with Venice. The two cities, he argues, are brothers with a common Italian paternity. Their conflict is fratricide. He calls for peace and for love, and his appeal is effective because of its musicality, not its statesmanlike rhetoric. In the opera's prologue, Boccanegra's election is rigged by a coerced and conducted vocal demonstration. His manager Paolo bribes and manipulates the chorus, telling them to cry "Simone ad una voce." Boccanegra delights in this bombastic publicity. "Suona ogni labbro il mio nome," he says—his name sounds from every tongue. The unanimity in the council is no such facile singalong, and though it is propounded by Boccanegra, the character who gently enforces it is Amelia, singing "Pace" above the ensemble. She has promised to be a dove in Boccanegra's palace; she makes good her vow in a beatific trill, hovering between two notes as she is pacifying two factions.

Political dispute is here resolved by ritual—first Amelia's appeasing trill, which turns the mob into a communing mass; then the curse of exclusion from this commune, which Paolo is made to pronounce against himself. Verdi's operas return to the form's origins in rite, though their ceremonies are darkened by mixed motives—the orgiastic capers of the Duke in *Rigoletto* (1851), Flora's gambling party in *La Traviata* (1853), the conspiratorial masquerade in *Un Ballo in Maschera* (1859), the solemn benediction of a military campaign by a retinue of temple ballerinas in *Aida* (1871).

The festivity is at its most troubling in *Rigoletto*, alternately morbid and jocular. The prelude begins with baleful prognostications, then turns frivolous. The work has the eerie gaiety of a scherzo, and Rigoletto wants to believe that the kidnapping and rape of Gilda was a practical joke—"fu scherzo, non è vero?" Blindfolded by the plotters or served up the wrong body in the sack, he is the victim of a murderous farce. *Rigoletto* dares to be a comic opera gone wrong. Though the hero's profession is jesting, he lives in horror of defamatory laughter, afraid that the courtiers will mock his deformity. His own foolery is potentially deadly, when he jeers that the Duke should slice off Ceprano's head. The comic spirit here has no Falstaffian mellowness: Rigoletto's clowning is as rabid as the erotic fires of *Il Trovatore*.

At first he veers between gloom and exhilaration; later he comes to unite tragedy and comedy inside himself, singing of revenge with what Gilda calls a fierce joy. If Rigoletto is a comedian raised to tragic authority when he condemns the courtiers, the Duke is a villain of irresistible comic grace and glee—one of Verdi's most disturbing characters, because his effervescent music seems to excuse his callousness, and far from being arraigned for his crimes he is allowed a lyrical apotheosis: a last reprise of "La donna è mobile." He conceals his name from Gilda, then palms her off with the alias of Gualtier Maldè; his real identity might be Don Giovanni, with Rigoletto as his unwitting Leporello. Certainly the blend of cruelty and gallantry recalls Mozart's opera. The Shakespearean wisdom of *Rigoletto* perceives likenesses between such contrary moods, and between inimical people. "Pari siamo" says Rigoletto of Sparafucile: we are alike; the one kills with words, the other with a blade. Monterone sees the same parity between Rigoletto and the Duke, colleagues in infamy. The comparison eventually links Rigoletto and his accuser, for the Duke has debauched Monterone's daughter too. Gilda altruistically recognizes that her own case isn't singular. Overhearing Maddalena weep for the Duke, she is touched by the plight of one who suffers as she has done, and resolves to save the lover they share by taking his place. Human fates are interchangeable. In *Rigoletto*, all are equal in the sight of music.

Traviata brings the operatic rites up to date, restaging them in the society of Verdi's own time. The dances given by Violetta and Flora are raffish Bacchanals. Violetta's party throbs with a delight which is, as Alfredo says, the palpitation of the entire world. The modern courtesan doubles as an ancient priestess: pouring wine for Alfredo, Violetta calls herself Hebe the libation bearer. Flora's gathering, with its games of chance and its chitchat about infidelities, exchanges Violetta's life of enjoyment for a ruthless, mercenary pleasure-seeking. Here the rite is performed in fancy dress by the ballet of matadors. Flippant as they are, their work of slaughter does recall the sacrifice underlying *Traviata*: society's demand for a victim, in whose agony everyone else can exult. Violetta expires during the Parisian carnival, and the song of the crowds outside takes up the matadorial idea in a heedless triumph. They sing of killing the fatted ox, his head crowned with Dionysian vines; Violetta, the true candidate for the sacrificial altar, wastes away with none of this gross and overfed enthusiasm.

Like Rigoletto, Violetta grows from comedy into tragedy. He advances beyond scurrility to become the conscience of his society; she renounces hedonism and martyrs herself to the happiness of others. Music converts the carnal woman to spiritual charity. She imbibes life from Alfredo when he serenades her, and breathes that glad vibrancy back into him. Against a racing accompaniment of strings, he sings in the second act that she has tempered and soothed him, and she softens Germont too, commenting that his voice—startled into sensitivity by her insistence that she loves Alfredo—now sounds sweeter to her. In the last scene, trying to revive her, Alfredo claims to derive his life from her. She is "sospiro e luce" to him, air and light, or "mio sospiro e palpito." Singing, she transfuses herself into those around her. This life-giving force is derided by her brief resurrection before the final collapse ("rinasce," she cries). The Duke in *Rigoletto* rises from the dead for an encore of his immortal tune, but in Violetta's case the reinvigoration is a clinical symptom only, and a misleading one.

D'Annunzio called *Un Ballo in Maschera* the supreme opera. It is so because of its musical hilarity. The festive mood infects it with playfulness, but its games are dangerous because lives are placed at risk by them. Riccardo leaves his court to visit the witch's den for a lark, Amelia keeps a midnight rendezvous at the gallows when dared to do so; even the choice of an assassin is gamblingly made by lot. Tragedy and comedy fugally intertwine. In the first scene, Riccardo's supporters calmly greet the day while his enemies mutter their plots. The ensembles collate the most diverse reactions—the ebullient page Oscar sings along with the prophetic Ulrica, the one treating the action as comic prank, the other as tragic fate; on the heath, when the unveiling of Amelia changes an erotic tryst to a domestic mishap, the conspirators marvel that tragedy has lurched into comedy and chuckle in sarcasm while Amelia moans in fear. The dancing giddily continues even after Riccardo has been attacked, and the band onstage tapers off in embarrassed reluctance: music's instinct is to ignore a solitary death, since its own liveliness is so indiscriminate and unstoppable.

Riccardo personifies this ribald delight. He is a Dionysian joker, telling his friends to abandon themselves to folly when they visit Ulrica. His emotions are as mutable as music. He feels faint when Amelia's name is first mentioned, and in their duet he is by turns worshipful, distraught and riotously happy; then, having worked through all these emotions, he vanishes, consigning her to the care of her husband. The barcarole he sings to Ulrica's customers when pretending to be a sailor states his comic creed: he believes in buoyancy, in his capacity to stay afloat and to negotiate the scurrying wavelets of crescendi which assail him. He is a harmless Don Giovanni, whose only qualm is an intermittent spasm of playboy's guilt. In his busy punctuality he also anticipates Falstaff. He reaches Ulrica's hideout promptly at three, and is at the gibbet at midnight as arranged. Like Falstaff with his reiterated date at Alice's house between two and three when her husband is absent, the comic hero with a lot of escapades programmed relies on keeping to his schedule.

Rigoletto, Traviata and *Ballo* are Verdi's social operas, aware of opera's equivocal function as an amusement. Society enjoys Rigoletto but doesn't care about him; it trifles with Violetta and hypocritically discards her. Riccardo treats social duty and political office as pastimes; the reality he flouts strikes him down. The characters of these works don't belong in tragedy: Violetta protests against having to die so young. Their successors in Verdi's political operas—*La Forza del Destino* (1862), *Don Carlos* (1867), *Aida* (1871)—lack this resilience; their societies defeat them in advance. The world in *Forza* is given over to war, extolled by Preziosilla as a convenient mass suicide. Through it an ambulant population of penitents and mercenaries trudges without a destination. Exiled from happiness, Leonora and Alvaro imprison themselves in hermetic solitude, like Charles V in *Don Carlos* celebrating his own funeral and retiring to the monastery. Orfeo overcame death. These Verdian characters prematurely surrender to it, and choose residence in the tomb, where Aida returns to join Radamès. Their existence is a long expiation—Leonora's increasingly wretched prayers; the farewells of Elisabeth in *Don Carlos* to Fontainebleau, the banishéd Countess, Carlos, and to life itself; Aida's appeals to divine pity.

In the early Verdi, song was a bodily power, the instrument of Ernani's insolent challenge. The people of the later operas have lost that lyrical vigor. Alvaro must refuse Carlo's challenge to a duel, and ignore the offered weapons; Don Carlos is neurotically ineffective, passing out at Elisabeth's feet. The power denied to individuals is monopolized by the state. Preziosilla recruits a rabble for the army. The Inquisitor in *Don Carlos* counsels repression. The triumphal scene in *Aida* is a totalitarian rally, all trumpeting pomp and strutting circumstance.

These political dramas demolish the panoply of grand opera because they deplore the spectacle of amassed, arrogant power. Consecutive scenes of *Don Carlos* reveal the gap between institutional might and the haunted, impotent reality. The coronation happens in a blaze of sun, brass and punitive fire, with Philippe II disclosed within the cathedral as an icon of holy terror; in the next scene, guttering candles show the unhappy private man in his study before dawn, awaiting death and rebuked meanwhile by the Inquisitor. There is a section of martial confidence in the final duet between Carlos and Elisabeth, as she hails his foray to Flanders. But it soon loses heart and turns weepy: they are singing of an implausible glory to cheer themselves up. In this mournful opera, the two most incongruous characters are those who trust in the rewards of this world, or believe that it might be changed—Eboli with her erotic schemes and her gossip about the latest silken French fashions, Posa with his political ideals.

In *Aida* the grandiose operatic society has suffered a sclerosis. Inflexible, rigorously hieratic, it takes everyone captive. Radamès is enslaved by his ambitious dream, defined by the fanfares he imagines before "Celeste Aida." The code of classical heroism is brutalized: military honor overrides personal loyalty. Aida's crisis comes when, bullied by Amonasro, she is made to betray her lover rather than her country. Emotions are politically controlled. Amneris tests Aida by pretending Radamès is dead, and Amonasro blackmails her with a gruesome reminder of her dead mother; Aida convinces Radamès to flee by blaming him in advance for destroying her if he doesn't. Orchestral battalions and rowdy choral throngs encroach on the quartet of soloists, instantly materializing to announce the Ethiopian sortie and disappearing just as rapidly. A weight impends above everyone, finally made visible when the stone is lowered to seal Radamès in his tomb. The collective power bludgeons individuals into obedience. Aida joins in the cry of "Ritorna vincitor," even though she is supporting a crusade against her own people.

There are no monasteries here to retire to; truth must take refuge in fugitive vocal asides. Aida's is the still small voice of personal affection, trying to make itself heard through cohorts of opposition—reduced to ineffectual pleading when she realizes that she can't claim equal rank with Amneris, briefly jubilant when she recognizes Amonasro, only to be at once hushed by him. During the triumph she finds a few bars of empty space where her voice can hang in the air imploring mercy, but her wordless cadence of pity is pushed to the margin when the choral troops take up their repetitions of "Ma tu, Re." In her aria beside the Nile she creeps stealthily up to her high C, and having got there sings it with cautious softness: this is an emotion afraid to speak out. Ultimately, in this world of sound and fury, the only vocal integrity lies in silence. Aida is self-protectively mute, prevented from owning to her identity; Radamès joins her in that condition when he won't reply to the accusations of the priests. His silences during the offstage trial mark another of Aida's oases of sound, intervals of a peace now known to reside only in the grave. This grandest of operas ends almost in a whimper, with the last suffocated duet and the muffled interjections of Amneris.

The Requiem in 1874 is an epilogue to Aida, and to all Verdi's operas. From the first he was concerned with religion, and with transferring to music its work of human ministration. Nabucco in 1842, about the impious coup of Nebuchadnezzar in Babylon, criticizes dogma and idolatry. Its religious characters are megaphonic impostors. The demagogue Zaccaria indoctrinates the Hebrews and rouses them—with the aid of clashing cymbals—to support his visions of extermination. He seizes Nabucco's daughter Fenena as a political hostage, swearing to kill her if her father profanes the shrine. The opera's first action is the invasion of Solomon's temple. Abigaille charges in to announce the victory—but is she serving a religious cause, a political career, or her own sexual jealousy? In the trio which follows, Fenena calls on the god of Israel while Abigaille keeningly unleashes an operatic god: the "furia" of her despised love. The religious war is an excuse for vaunting self-promotions. Abigaille the slave bustles onto the throne, while Nabucco, not content to be king, proclaims himself god on a perilous escalator of semitones, striding up to vocal extremity and mental breakdown.

Authority in Nabucco is imposed by decibels. The Hebrews, commenting on Nabucco's megalomania, say that he fulminates: the voice thunders or detonates from him. Abigaille too, slashing across two octaves or ripping the parchment and canceling her own birth in those razor-edged roulades, emits lightning flashes. Deity is made manifest by noise. Carrying the Mosaic tablets, Zaccaria announces that god has fulminated in the mouths of the prophets; and when he foretells Babylon's devastation, he commandeers the loud-hailer to insist that the Lord is dictating his aria to him. These singers imagine themselves to be omnipotent divinities.

Later operas still use the rhetoric of religion, but adapt it to a human and earthly love. Probably there is no one to hear the prayers of men, so the music to which they are sung must itself be the remedy. We elect our own angels: in Boccanegra, Gabriele calls Amelia angelically pure, and she adds that his image is lodged within her as God is in the temple. The heart constitutes the only inviolable sanctuary. Opera began with Orfeo's research in the underworld; *Boccanegra* anticipates the day when all graves will open to disgorge those we have lost. Amelia is restored to Boccanegra as from the dead, and Fiesco stages his own resurrection: the dead salute you, he tells Simon. The purpose isn't wrathful judgment, as on the "Dies Irae" of the *Requiem*, but reconciliation. In *Forza*, the exhumations are grimmer. The time lapse here doesn't allow for healing, as does the gap of a generation within *Boccanegra*; it's a purgatorial vigil, kept by the ghosts of defunct and despairing selves. The Padre Guardiano warns Leonora that she will henceforth see no living being, and should ring her bell only to receive the sacraments. When she reappears, it is as a gaunt revenant. "Uno spettro," says Alvaro, and he's equally aghast at Carlo's return to life—"voi vivente!" Both are reborn, however, only to be killed.

Don Carlos and *Aida* separate the sanctimonious preachings of established religion from the more forgiving alternative faith of opera. For Philippe II and his Inquisitor, the Church cements a political system; but the monk, a disinterred Charles V, exists outside the world and broods knowingly over it, commiserating with men and intervening to rescue Carlos from his persecutors. Amneris denounces the priests, begging a heaven which houses a god other than theirs to take vengeance on them. The *Requiem* follows logically. Indeed the music of its most plaintive section, the "Lacrymosa," was cut from the original Paris version of *Don Carlos*, where the sobbing melody is introduced by Philippe as a requiem for Posa, executed by the Inquisition to punish his anticlerical zeal.

The *Requiem* is an anthological opera, with limbo as its setting. Its soloists compound all Verdi's dramatic protagonists. The soprano contains recollections of characters as different as Gilda (who assures Rigoletto that she'll await him in paradise beside her mother) and Elisabeth (who more dolefully forswears earthly vanities). She is Leonora from *Trovatore* stirred by the monkish "Miserere," Leonora from *Forza* amending the prayer of the pilgrims at the inn to fit her personal case, or Amelia from *Ballo* pleading as she confronts death for a glimpse of her son, remembered in a wistful postscript to her aria by cello, oboe and clarinet. She is the unseen priestess from *Aida* who names Fthà in the temple, gliding above the foundation of the basses like a bright, germinating light, and who is heard again in the Nile scene, softly describing the incestuous union of Isis with her brother and lover Osiris.

In the *Requiem* the soprano melts hard hearts, seraphically floating above the tumult in "Quid sum miser," soaring in "Salva me," introducing her archangelic colleague Michael in the "Offertorio." The final section, "Libera me," belongs to her. Left behind on earth, she must overcome her fears on behalf of us all. She does so by singing an aria. Her agitated prayer is the recitative, her tremulous account of her dread is the cavatina, but she emerges from these shadows to a glowing cabaletta, where a new confidence enables her to reach the radiant pinnacle of a B-flat. Cabalettas usually race toward consummation; here the chorus sets a breathless pace, only to be checked by the soprano who calmingly sings the fugue at half speed. Yet is the music which emboldens her a permanent help? In the last bars she is grounded in speech once more, still asking to be freed from her mortal alarm.

Verdi's operatic tenors are willful and impetuous, from Ernani to Radamès. Their successor in the *Requiem* has been purged of such egotism; his forebears, when he humbly petitions for assistance in "Quid sum miser," are Macduff mourning his slaughtered children in *Macbeth* and Riccardo magnanimously absolving the conspirators as his truant sons ("miei figli") in *Ballo*. Yet Verdi finds a self-reliant value in the tenor's swaggering. While the soprano timorously wrings her hands, the tenor demands salvation. "Ingemisco" is his aria, and when he asks to be placed among the sheep not the goats and to be honored on his maker's right hand, he assumes that his serenade will earn him priority on high. The tenor teaches a legitimate human pride, unbowed by death.

Verdi instructed his librettist that Amneris should sing a requiem during the tomb scene, and in 1875 he added a solo to the *Requiem* for Maria Waldmann, who had sung Amneris in 1872 at La Scala. The new section, "Liber scriptus proferetur," belongs to an enthroned and stentorian Amneris, declaiming from the book of laws in a voice which peals across infinite space. The mezzo-soprano here is Verdi's only trustworthy oracle, ending a line of occult frauds. Verdian mezzos, because of their baleful voices, are often touted as soothsayers: Azucena sees visions in the fire, Ulrica bays for Satan, Preziosilla is supposed to tell fortunes. The singer in the *Requiem* calls their bluffs, reading from the book in which all deeds are recorded. She takes no angry pleasure in the distresses of others, like Azucena crowing when Luna beheads his brother; she is a reformed character, penitent in "Quid sum miser." This is one of two sections in which she is paired with the soprano, in opera always the mezzo's rival, enemy or antithesis. They are still competitive, vying for the last word in their repetitions of "ante diem," and in the "Agnus Dei" they keep the diplomatic distance of an octave apart, but they have made their peace.

The Verdian bass always had a religious conscience—Zaccaria with his smug imprecations, the Padre Guardiano with his platitudes. The rumbling voices of Ramfis or the Inquisitor entitle them to lecture an Egyptian or a Spanish monarch. An expert on eschatology, the bass is given the quaking account of the "Dies Irae" and the cataclysmic "Confutatis maledictis." But he lacks the self-righteousness of Ramfis decrying treason or the Inquisitor routing heresy. He includes himself among the sinners, and kneels to plead in "Ora supplex et acclinis." Like Silva begging for Elvira to gladden his declining years in *Ernani* or Philippe II contemplating his gray hairs, he is an old man, sorrowfully readying himself for his end and hoping that he need not die alone: this is his request in "gere curam mei finis."

The *Requiem* is an opera because it is so emotionally plangent. Its dramatic urgency contrasts with the *Requiem* of Berlioz, first performed in 1837 at Les Invalides in Paris. Berlioz called this an architectural work, because of the echoing antres its sonorities require; those spaces are its windy universe where—in protracted pauses, swallowing and dampening all sound—music hopelessly dies away, like the hero plunging into the crater at the end of *La Damnation de Faust*. Berlioz omits the "Libera me," which is Verdi's most touching revelation of character. When his tenor soloist does appear, in the "Sanctus," it is as an anonymous worshiper, one among an innumerable many. As in *Les Troyens*, Berlioz deals with the fate of mankind, not Verdi's effusive individuals pressing their personal cases. Verdi's soloists get their way by lyrical insinuation. In the "Offertorio" they eagerly cite God's promise to Abraham because it is evidence that their wish has been granted, and they repeat it as a reminder to an unreliable deity; at "fac eas, Domine," asking for the passage of souls from death to life, they plan a concerted campaign—the soprano and tenor wheedle irresistibly, while the mezzo and bass more sternly point to an obligation.

Yet this is a requiem for opera as much as for the novelist Manzoni (whose death it commemorated). The accord between the two women, or the cooperation of all the soloists in the "Offertorio," suggests why Verdi, in the sixteen years between *Aida* and *Otello*, was so reluctant to go back to the composition of opera. The form meant contestation, the violent clash of opposed wills and voices. Having achieved the *Requiem*'s armistice between the four participants—the integration at last of his vocal family—how could he once more disrupt it?

He was persuaded to do so by Boito's libretti for *Otello* in 1887 and

Falstaff in 1893. *Otello* sums up all the previous tragic operas, and from the traditional vocal typology makes a map of the moral universe. Desdemona the soprano is an angel, Iago the baritone is a devil. Between them the tenor Otello constitutes the turbulent nature in which they do battle, rent not by the epileptic fits of the Shakespearean hero but by cosmic convulsions. *Falstaff* brings this metaphysical strife to an end with comic grace and musical discipline. It rewrites the *Requiem* as a divine comedy. All will be pardoned, because we are clowns not sinners. When the merry wives set upon Falstaff in the forest, with the imps pricking and pinching him into repentance, they sing a mock-liturgical requiem and pray that the Lord may make him impotent, or else chaste. Falstaff amends their judgment in an aside, asking for his belly to be spared. The mood of *Falstaff* is that of the "Sanctus" in the *Requiem*. Like that light-footed galloping choral fugue, *Falstaff* sees life contrapuntally, as the overlapping of all existences, good and bad. The opera's fugal conclusion adheres to the strict musical form because it could otherwise scarcely contain its joy.

Before the collaboration with Verdi, Boito had written a libretto for Ponchielli's *La Gioconda*, in which this last reunion of Shakespearean tragedy and comedy is anticipated. *Gioconda* is set in Venice, where *Othello* begins. Verdi and Boito eliminated Shakespeare's first act, to begin with Otello's arrival at Cyprus; *Gioconda* therefore functions as a prelude to the later opera. Its Venice is a city of beauty and squalor, of circuses and political despotism. After the gondola races, the mob sings and dances with careless glee, but as the minstrel Barnaba points out they are dancing on their tombs. Alvise's party is halted by the tolling of a death knell, and the courtly reception turns into a wake for Laura. This self-divided tragicomedy is exemplified in the title. The heroine is nicknamed "the Merry One," but she is never jocund, except just before her suicide. Hers is also a down-at-heel lyricism, no longer able to manage the saving flights of the Verdian soprano: Gioconda is a street singer who sells her vocal wares throughout the city. Operatic sublimation—Amelia's trill during Boccanegra's council—has been tethered in a real and mercenary world.

Boito was a nihilist. The devilish negations of his Mefistofele or Iago are echoed by Falstaff, in the derisive "No" which runs through his monologue disparaging honor. In opera, Boito pits words against music, and verbally teases or torments the simpleminded optimism of song. Hence the quizzical jeering of Mefistofele, or Barnaba's mockery of his nautical tune. Thus *Otello* became a quarrel between drama and music—the witty speech of Iago (who at first was to have the title role) against the lyrical rhapsodies of Desdemona; Boito against Verdi.

The struggle in *Otello* is less for the hero's soul than for the possession and definition of opera. Boito saw the work in a characteristically schizoid way. He called the finale to the third act—with Desdemona humbled before Lodovico, pouring out her grief while Otello rants and Iago continues plotting—"a lyrical melodic piece beneath which runs a dramatic dialogue. The principal figure on the lyrical side is Desdemona, on the dramatic side Iago." These spiritual foes are the twin constituents of opera.

Instead of Boito's dualism, Verdi saw the work hierarchically. He knew it had disassembled the old operatic form, but he intended it to be a justification of music against the assault of drama. He ranges the characters on a vertical scale from speech to song. Iago, as he said in a letter to Boito, "should only *declaim and sneer.*" Otello "must sing, must *shout*"—or rather he should alternate between song and shouting to express his degeneration. He begins as a one-man orchestra, with the trumpet tones of "Esultate!" or the heady astral harmonies of the duet with Desdemona. In the middle acts he is rabid, out of control vocally and psychologically. His jealousy, like the delirium of Tristan, is a melodic breakdown. By the end he has worn out his voice along with his life. When he learns the truth about Desdemona, Verdi said, "Otello has no breath left in him; . . . he cannot and should not sing with more than a veiled, half-dead voice." Verdi set his expiring moans with sounds which, in his own view, "have *almost no musical value.*"

At the pinnacle of this melismatic ladder is Desdemona. She has been lifted above the drama which destroys her. In contrast with Shakespeare's rebellious daughter and obstinate wife, Verdi wanted his heroine to have as little specific character as her predecessor in the *Requiem:* he called her a symbol "of goodness, of resignation, of sacrifice," endowed with what he saw as all the soprano virtues. Her transcendence of drama frees her for a pure lyricism. She alone "must always sing, *sing.*" That singing resounds from heaven, for the voice was the only article of religious faith Verdi could accredit. Just as Monteverdi made the sun sing through Apollo, Verdi hears Desdemona supernaturally. For her willow song, he instructed, she "must have a Holy Trinity of three voices: one for Desdemona herself, one for Barbara the maid, and a third for *Salce, salce.*"

Othello is a domestic drama, fussing over handkerchiefs and bed sheets. The music of *Otello* makes it elemental. Otello is the storm out of which he hurtles like a cloud-borne god, Iago is the sparking fire beside which he sings his praise of drink, and with Desdemona at the end of the first act Otello listens to a shining music of the spheres: describing the galaxies, they are showered by the stardust of a harp. In the play, Othello lopes on, casual and relaxed. In the opera, he arrives as a portentous savior, whose appearance turns agony to ecstasy and causes massed humanity to exult. The hurricane is as grandiose as judgment day in the *Requiem*, overwhelming the earth; Boito's Cypriots sneer that the Muslim fleet will find its requiem at the bottom of the sea. Otello triumphs over this tumult as an agnostic messiah, yet also as a latter-day Orpheus. He creates the world anew out of the tempest of matter; from the undifferentiation of terrified noise he rescues music in "Esultate!" His creation is parodied and undone by Iago—the fire scene shows the world to be combustible and unstable—only to be lyrically soothed once more by what Desdemona calls her sweet murmurings. The first act concludes with a prayer and an "Amen." The blessing sought and gratefully acknowledged is that of music.

All this Iago nullifies, because his techniques are verbal. He is the evil genius of spoken drama—a witty mimic in the second act, echoing Otello's words, or a scurrilous gossip in his later scene with Cassio. Words, which are Iago's medium, terrorize Desdemona because they are so brutally explicit. When Otello calls her a courtesan, her defense is to cry that she doesn't know what the horrible word means. Iago's triumph is to reduce Otello from heroic song to sputtering, half-articulate speech: he collapses while gabbling about the handkerchief. Listening to Desdemona's hymn of praise as the Cypriots present her with flowers and play their mandolins and harps, Iago explains his campaign against music. Beauty and love have joined in harmony, he says; he will disrupt their sweet accord. Otello meanwhile, also listening, has forgiven Desdemona because of her singing. "Quel canto mi conquide," he admits—the song has won him over, as it should.

Despite Iago, *Otello* is the apotheosis of opera. Desdemona's "Ave Maria" contains a moment of vocal annunciation which hints at the birth of opera as it describes the conception of Christ. She begins by uttering the words in nervous, reticent speech; then, just as she names the fruit of Mary's womb, her voice blossoms into song, as if spiritually ascending. The angel who announces the Virgin's pregnancy has been replaced by music, fertilizing the word. Otello's last hope comes from that same source. Music, organized by repetition, can recall the happiness we have lost, and he dies in a brief, gasped reprise of the love duet.

Falstaff has left behind the old Verdian opera of belligerent will. Only Ford in his jealous tantrums still behaves and sings in the conventional way, and his rages are factitious. Outside the inn, Alice takes up Mistress Quickly's narrative of the night-prowling huntsman and finishes it as a fairy tale, giggling at its absurdity. Quickly sounded as spooky as Azucena; Alice might be reinterpreting *Trovatore* as a comedy.

Boito perhaps saw Falstaff as another spirit of negation—Quickly calls him by the devil's pseudonym, "l'Avversiero" or the adversary—but Verdi endows him with such rhythmic verve and vocal energy that he becomes a god, one of those pagans who have been opera's sponsors throughout its history. Antlered in the forest, he compares himself with Jove bullishly pursuing Europa; Meg says she is Juno, crushed by his bulk. Alice suggests they should roast him in the fire—is he the fatted ox carried through the streets at carnival in *Traviata*? When he swills down the wine or rejoices in the liquor streaming from Mastro Fontana (Mr. Brook), he is a paunchy Dionysus, and like the dying and reborn god he can rejuvenate himself at will. He survives his drowning; describing to Alice the springtime of his life, he slims and refines his voice until it is that of a youth once more, preserved inside this mound of sagging flesh. His signature is the indefatigable upbeat which starts the score into life. He transmits this zest to all the other characters, even when they are plotting against him. It wells up in the concerted laughter of the wives, and it makes the sextuple "No" with which Alice and Nanetta dispute Ford's plan to marry the girl to Dr. Caius resemble a lively affirmation. Like the exultant Otello, Falstaff is a profane savior. He has wisely revised the edicts of the *Requiem*. When his cronies sing their sarcastic "Amen" at the inn after Caius swears off alcohol, Falstaff corrects their tempo, and when they return professing penitence he knows better than to believe them: they are simply resuming their lives of petty, jocular crime.

Verdi's final opera is a drama in praise of music. In the bulbous crescendo which concludes the first scene or the revivifying trill when Falstaff doses himself with wine, the orchestra's biological vigor raucously outsings death. The shabby schemer of Shakespeare's *Merry Wives of Windsor* is transformed by music into that force the nineteenth century called "the comic spirit." This gives Verdi's Falstaff an impersonality which corresponds to but restrains the driving frenzies of *Otello*—the billowing sea, the fire and lightning. The Victorian novelist George Meredith saluted the comic spirit as a humane agent of good sense, softening the "big round satyr's laugh" to a "slim feasting smile." Falstaff has the satyr's randy, capering elation, and he communicates to the orchestra those "volleys of silver laughter" which to Meredith were the noise of comedy doing its good works in the world. When Ford offers Falstaff the Cypriot wine, the strings burble liquidly; when he disburses money, a spangly tinkling suggests Jove's golden shower over Danaë. The score has the elusiveness of love as described by Falstaff in his madrigal, assuring us of nature's rebirth and of a freshness which will never stale. *Falstaff* proposes a comic alternative to the musical philosophy of *Tristan und Isolde*. Verdi's orchestra keeps up with the flux of sensation, rather than lapsing into a trough of apathy where pleasure sickens to pain.

Falstaff has a moment of reflection on speech and song like Desdemona's account of the time when the word became flesh as Christ, and when the letter was changed to spirit by music. It comes in his monologue about honor. He asks what substance that word contains, and says that it is made of air—"c'è dell'aria che vola." An etherealizing twiddle in the orchestra illustrates this aeration, which is the bequest of opera: song gives wings to words. Nanetta promises that she will sing "parole armonïose," harmonious words. Like her mother she is a siren, dispensing musical enchantment. Alice prepares for her tryst with Falstaff by getting out her lute and strumming it. Fenton's aria in the forest is another ecstatic apology for music. He describes his song taking to the air to find a partner who'll join in it; when it does so, the very air is enamored, and vibrates with happiness. Voices unite as in a kiss, and the most musical noise in *Falstaff* is one to which both voices and orchestra, silent for an instant, defer: the puckering smack as the lips of Fenton and Nanetta meet behind the screen. After Fenton has made nature sing, Nanetta in her aria as the queen of the fairies urges it to dance, telling her attendants to move in time with their tune.

It is Verdi's last wish, as affectionate a musical hope for humanity as the gospels of *Orfeo*, *Die Zauberflöte* or *Fidelio*. The ambition of opera is nothing less than the reconstitution of paradise.

SEVEN

Wagner

AFTER *Orfeo*, opera chose to be discreet about the mystery which lies behind it. Wagner changes that, and brings about another rebirth for the form. He is opera's most daring and compulsive mythmaker. The myths he makes, in succession to that of Orpheus, are celebrations of opera and of his own heroism as a composer.

The Camerata had attempted to revive the union of the arts achieved by Greek tragedy. Wagner managed this union in himself. He wrote the poetic dramas he set to music, oversaw their staging, and constructed at Bayreuth an ideal theater for them. *Tristan und Isolde* derives its myth from the merging of drama and music which is opera: the rationality of drama, concerned with action and social identity, subsides into the instinctive underworld of music. Drama drowns in music, as in the watery consummations of *Der Fliegende Holländer* (when the ship sinks) or *Götterdämmerung* (when the Rhine overflows). The dramatic hero in *Siegfried* kisses the musical heroine awake, and learns from her a fearful sense of the limits to his own active power; their love is drama's copulation with music.

Wagner is all his own heroes, from the heaven-descended deliverer of *Lohengrin* to the magus Klingsor in *Parsifal*. Identifying himself with them, he amends the character of Orpheus. Monteverdi's Orfeo earned immortality from Apollo. Wagner's Orphic vocalists follow the different worship of Dionysus—the bard in *Tannhäuser* is aroused to song by the erotic witchery of the Venusberg, the minstrel in *Die Meistersinger von Nürnberg* scandalizes the guilds with his metrical and melodic innovations. Song in Wagner is a spell. Elsa summons Lohengrin by her infatuated musical dream of him. Senta's ballad about the Dutchman, with its weird hummings and hallooings, its windy howls and shrieks, is an exercise in vocal sorcery. When Erik worries over her obsession, she asks whether he is afraid of a song, but his holy dread is justified. The Wagnerian singer raves: Ortrud's appeal to defiled gods in *Lohengrin,* her voice shrilling malevolently through the night; Kundry's screams of rage and groans of anguish in *Parsifal.*

Opera was to Wagner a political creed and a spiritual gospel; its aims were revolution and/or salvation. His music, as he said while composing *Tristan,* would transfigure the lives of those who heard it—or else make them mad. His epic *Der Ring des Nibelungen* adapts the Teutonic myth to dramatize this convulsion in society. The *Ring* has been called a history of the modern world: Alberich, stealing the gold from the Rhinemaidens, industrially ravages nature to establish an economic reign of terror. But the ring he fashions from his booty is also an emblem of art, and Wagner here investigates the collusion between art and power. Wotan's citadel of Walhall is Wagner's own aesthetic shrine at Bayreuth. *Das Rheingold* proudly builds the castle; *Götterdämmerung* burns it down in expiation.

As if with the aid of the Tarnhelm—Alberich's magic helmet which can transform him into any other creature—Wagner distributes himself through the entire cast of the *Ring,* and in different characters unleashes his own mixed creative motives. He is Wotan the god, Alberich the ogre, and also Siegfried the political agitator who ends their old order. Of all the arts, opera is the most materially lavish, the most dependent on the wealth seized by Alberich and fortified by Wotan. *Götterdämmerung* concludes the cycle by showing how Siegfried and Brünnhilde have been trapped by the false values of opera itself. The hero who shatters privilege and precedent in *Siegfried* is here a vain operatic tenor, in love with his reputation as the greatest hero in the world (and, according to Gutrune, the most handsome); the heroine who is Wotan's accusing conscience in *Die Walküre* is now a jealous and vindictive lover. Both die for the sake of a grand gesture.

Parsifal is intended as opera's redemption. Wagner called it a festival play to consecrate a stage ("Bühnenweihfestspiel"); as well as blessing the new theater at Bayreuth, it consecrates opera. It's Wagner's equivalent to Verdi's *Requiem*—but whereas Verdi adjusts Christianity to a tearful human world, and offers his art as an emotional solace, Wagner reinterprets Christianity as autobiography, and makes it the messianic glorification of that art. For Verdi there is no god, so music must fill up the absence; for Wagner there is no god, so he must personally assume the role.

Wagner begins to dissolve the operatic form he inherits in *Der Fliegende Holländer* (1843). It is literally a dissolution—drama's submergence in music. Wagner directs that, in the first scene, the sea should occupy most of the stage. The action is set afloat because opera has inundated drama, opened a channel in it for the tidal, musical flux of passion: the Steersman's song of the winds and waves, Senta's ballad with its gales and storms. Drama wants to be landed, anchored in reality. Hence the Steersman's announcement that they're on a firm bottom, the crash of the Dutchman's anchor, and Daland's confident identification of the harbor as Sandwike. This grounding in a world he believes to be solid is enforced by Daland's materialism when he ogles the Dutchman's jewels. Senta's friends busily spin, cocooning themselves inside a domestic fortress. Erik the hunter prowls the borders of this little precinct to ward off predators; the Steersman too keeps watch, maintaining the vigil of reason.

But these dramatic groundlings are uprooted by music. The Dutchman can set foot on earth only once every seven years, and at last rejects the terrain of the real forever when he is drowned in the sea and then lifted into the air with Senta. Though drama counsels them to watch and ward, they're liable to nod off into a musical somnolence—the Steersman's catnaps, Erik's prophetic dream, Senta's delirious absentmindedness when she should be spinning. When the Dutchman appears to her, it's not the portrait which has stepped down from the wall into reality but she who has gone to join him in his entranced unreality, adrift in space and impervious to time. During their duet she wonders whether she has sunk into a dream, where she sees an illusion.

The stage, deluged at the beginning and end of the opera, has here dimmed into an arena for ghosts: a phantasmagoria. So it is always in Wagner, with Loge's barricade of fire, Venus in her rosy mists, or Klingsor's garden planted with nubile girls. In *Tristan* the illusion is acknowledged to be insane, when the world is refracted and distorted by the hero's dementia; in *Parsifal* the illusion is a divine gift of grace, when the dove hovers above the hero's head. Erik's distraught questions "Ist's Täuschung? Warheit? Ist es Tat?" (is this fantasy? truth? is it a fact?) are the litany of the rational man, dismayed by Wagner's theater of trauma; and after *Der Fliegende Holländer* no such mundane objection is ever permitted.

Wagner's music drives drama toward extinction. The Dutchman's voice is annihilated in the orchestra at the end of his aria, his prayer for nothingness hollowly echoed by his unseen shipmates. When, as he says, the world cracks asunder on that last day, it voids its contents in the seething inchoate Wagnerian orchestra. The hurtling conclusion of Senta's ballad crashes there too: words precipitate themselves into the watery grave of music.

In *Lohengrin* (1850), the musical mystery has become forbiddingly silent. The swan-knight cannot say who he is, or why he has come; Elsa must not ask. The king casually remarks that it appears he has been sent by God. Lohengrin doesn't demur, and demands the prerogatives of a god for himself—to be the unknowable one, the inscrutable first cause, and to command unquestioning devotion.

The legend, like that of the Dutchman, has been adapted into a myth for opera. The Dutchman's curse is that of dramatic performance. He is bound on the wheel, made to perform his life over and over until reprieved by and obliterated in Senta's song about him. In *Lohengrin* the first creation, personified by the hero, is musical: the advent of a sound, not a word—the quivering, shimmering strings voicelessly confide the knight's origins in the prelude, and are reduced to words and robbed of their mystery only at the end in his narration. Elsa too, as a visionary, reverently guards her silence. Her processional entry is mute, and the wind instruments answer the king's queries on her behalf while she bows, nods and gestures that she has nothing to say. Urged into song, she presents her dream as the sight of a sound: she prayed for aid, heard the cry echoing away, then fell asleep and before her closed eyes the cry took on a body as the enigmatic knight.

Music arrives in the world as an arcane and absolute power. Wagner, like Lohengrin, concealed his source, sinking his orchestra in the roofed Bayreuth pit, so the music stole into audibility—a spring from beneath the earth in *Rheingold*, a shower from above it in *Parsifal*. Words in *Lohengrin* are the atheistic enemies, analyzing and thus destroying the lyrical missives of spirit. Ortrud's is the satanism of faithless intellect. She derides taboos and laughs at divine prohibitions; her magic is a matter of technical skill, as she boasts when sarcastically complimenting Telramund on his understanding. Her blasphemy is verbal utterance—her curdled exclamation "Gott!" which as Telramund says sounds terrible when intoned by her; her wailing "Elsa!" which startles the girl because the word is so painfully distended. Outside the minster, her harangue abruptly stops the music, halting the endless melody of Elsa's advance. While she rages about the unknown name, the chorus, aghast, tries to prevent her speech: "Was sagt sie? . . . Sie lästert! Wehrt ihrem Mund!"—what's she saying? she's blaspheming! stop her mouth! The false cadence which wrenchingly concludes the second act, as Elsa hesitates again, reveals how far the peace of music has been perturbed.

The wedding march and the well-wishing choruses in the third act hope to reestablish that effusive certainty. But opera is made from drama's interrogation of music. The Orfeos of Monteverdi and Gluck are most affecting when their mellifluousness deserts them; Wagner too must destroy his own lyrical creation. Lohengrin begins the duet by saying that the sweet song has faded, leaving them alone. Now dialogue starts, and with it disagreement. The concord of music yields to drama, which takes its energy from conflict. Though Lohengrin sings Elsa into compliance, she demands to know his identity and his purpose; a duet founders into an argument. Her craving is for words, to impose names on music's states of feeling. Is this love? she asks, wanting to know what she should call it, "dies Wort, so unaussprechlich wonnevoll"—this word so unspeakably wonderful. Lohengrin ruefully satisfies her, and paraphrases the sonic mirage of the first shiningly hazy prelude; then he withdraws his music from a world too dramatically querulous for it.

His secret is that of opera. He comes, he tells her, from light and joy; he might be Monteverdi's Apollo. The heaven which sends him, however, is of Wagner's own construction. His home is Montsalvat, the Grail castle of his father Parsifal. If Montsalvat is the artist's ivory tower, a pinnacle of lofty self-sufficiency, then the Venusberg is his bordello, where he distills a decadent inspiration from the senses. Lohengrin's music offers salvation, Tannhäuser's a salutary damnation. *Tannhäuser*, first performed at Dresden in 1845 and revised for Paris in 1861, is about the apostasy of opera: the abdication of God, and his replacement by the artist.

After the promiscuity of Don Giovanni, the romantic hero embarks on a career of sensual derangement, committing himself to a Venusberg which—for poets like Baudelaire, Rimbaud or Verlaine—is a brothel of recondite specialties or an opium den, but which could equally well be the performance of a Wagner opera. The Wagnerites pictured by Aubrey Beardsley at Covent Garden in the 1890s gorge on the music as a forbidden fruit. Baudelaire, writing about the Paris *Tannhäuser*, applauds its assault on a hypocritically decorous society; Dorian Gray, attending a performance at Covent Garden in Oscar Wilde's novel, sees Tannhäuser's perversity and his moral backslidings as a biography of his own lost soul.

Tannhäuser is the romantic artist, vowed to self-exploitation and self-destruction. More specifically, because he is a singer with a talent for profanity, he symbolizes the unholy art of opera. Disrupting the sedate ceremonial at the Wartburg, he recollects opera's development out of sacred music and thrusts it toward a parody of that sacredness. He has his own religion, selecting Elisabeth as its divinity and asking her to pray for him. Instead of piously venerating a god outside him, like the orthodox Wolfram, Tannhäuser experiences that god's invasion of him when Venus commands him to sing. Inside her realm he too is a god, as she tells him: one for whom wishing suffices to make things so. The legend condemns Tannhäuser; Wagner, as his artistic colleague, exonerates him. Amplifying the Dresden overture for Paris, he changed the Venusberg into an ecstatic hell, as chromatically feverish as the rhapsodies of Tristan and Isolde. In 1845, the plodding tread of the pilgrims returns to trample the voluptuous music underground. In 1861, the revels continue unchastened. The Venusberg is the cleft in earth where the Wagnerian orchestra is housed. The title of Beardsley's novelette about Tannhäuser, *Under the Hill*, anatomically identified the place: that jungly grove is the mons veneris. Venus is also a theatrical impresario. Her grotto—with its pink twilight and its fuzzy dioramas representing the rape of Europa or Leda's insemination by the swan—is a lair of playacting fantasy.

Venus describes the human world with revulsion, calling it the place from which the goddess has fled. But the reality which to her is so chill and dreary can be redeemed by imagination, infused with vitality by song. Elisabeth's entrance aria, addressed to the auditorium in the Wartburg, is about this gift of life. The hall seemed paltry to her in Tannhäuser's absence; now that he has returned, her singing breathes life into it again. Her resuscitation of the bare room is repeated every year when human beings, by their wishfulness, resurrect a dying earth. The shepherd in the valley dreams of spring and causes it to happen: at once, on cue, the pilgrims sing their chorus, for that time of year makes hope spring eternal in men and sends them on pilgrimages. By the third act it is elegiac autumn, but Wolfram keeps the cycle going when he says that, since the leaves have fallen, the pilgrims will soon be home. If winter comes, can spring be far behind?

Christian morality is bent into agreement with pagan myth, and with the theater's inexhaustible rebirths. The token of this operatic cult is the blossoming staff. The Pope tells Tannhäuser that he won't be absolved until his rod of office sprouts into leaf. Such a feat is problematic in nature;

for the Wagnerian theater it's easy. In any case, the unforgiving Pope has been replaced on the seat of judgment by Elisabeth. In the third act she prays at the wayside cross to the Virgin, "Allmächt'ge Jungfrau," but already in the second act she takes over from that interceding maiden when, calling herself a "Jungfrau," she withstands Tannhäuser's assailants. Her prayer lacks the plaintiveness of Desdemona's "Ave Maria" or Leonora's appeal to the Virgin and angels in *La Forza del Destino*. Verdi's heroines implore a power somewhere above them; Wagner's absorbs that power into herself. The dying Tannhäuser prays to Elisabeth, and she sponsors the theatrical miracle which the Pope had declared impossible. The pilgrims report that the barren, reproving stick gripped by the priest has bloomed.

Wagner planned *Die Meistersinger von Nürnberg* (1868) as a comic epilogue to *Tannhäuser*, like the satyr plays performed after Greek tragedies. When he confronts the mastersingers, Walther von Stolzing announces that his model has been Vogelweide, one of the contestants at the Wartburg who is denounced by Tannhäuser for his timid piety. But Walther's artistic vocation involves no education in vice. Tannhäuser the renegade is punished with ostracism; Walther is rewarded with membership of the guild. Tannhäuser sings ranting irreligious hymns, Walther a prize song whose dream of Eden is gratified at once when he finds his Eva before him. The savior hailed by the pilgrims at the end of *Tannhäuser* and in the chorale which opens *Meistersinger* is a musical poet: Walther or Wagner, not Christ. The spiritual warfare between papacy and paganism changes to a dispute over aesthetic methods between masterly precedent and creative subordination, but the two are reconciled by the diplomacy of counterpoint in the overture or in the polyphonic brawl of the second act. In the crowded, bustling urban orchestra, there is room for both.

Meistersinger takes place in Nuremberg near the time, at the beginning of the seventeenth century, when opera was being invented in Florence or Mantua; it elaborates a German myth about the form's origins which can be set against the Italian fable of Orfeo. The singer here is more aggressive, compared (when Eva mentions Walther's resemblance to the painting) with Dürer's David who slays an institutional Goliath. With the same zest for combat, Wagner justifies opera by once more reviving the pagan mysteries and altering Christian theology to suit himself. Walther's first song is of spring. Like the shepherd in *Tannhäuser* or Siegmund in *Walküre*, he associates opera with Renaissance in history and rebirth in nature. "An stillen herd" is winter's dream of spring, allying song with the sappy upsurgence of our emotion and desire. Like Siegfried tuning his pipe, Walther learns to sing in the forest, and the orchestra intimates that the birds were his tutors. In "Fanget an!" he is himself the voice of spring, rousing jubilee in the landscape just as he later incites a festive fracas in the city. The Pope's stave now has a musical meaning. Song grows out of speech like a flower, twisting its harmonic tendrils with the curly organicism of the treble clef. Most of *Meistersinger* is chatter, disputation, pedantic lecture, or mere noise like the scratching of chalk on the slate or the banging of the hammer. Walther's music calms this babel, and shows language how it might lyrically flourish.

He still has the rebellious instincts of Tannhäuser, flaunting an illicit poetic faith. When asked to choose a sacred theme for the contest, he selects love: sacred to him, but profane to the masters. Yet there is no moral showdown, because Christian theology has been revised to accommodate him. The prize song describes Adam's vision of Eve. No god intervenes to fashion the beloved object from a rib; Walther wins Eva by the persuasiveness of his art, and their union, like all sexual matches in Wagner, is that of words and music. When Sachs says more work is needed on the song, Walther impatiently exclaims "Wo fand'ich die? Genug der Wort'!"—where can I find her? enough of words! The musical poetry of opera is once more our recoverable paradise. Sachs says that in verse many find again what they have lost. His cobbling song interprets biblical events from a shoemaker's point of view, arguing that shoes were a divine consolation to soften our eviction from the happy garden; Walther replants Eden, expunging all guilt from the myth when he sets in that garden a tree not of poisonous knowledge but of fruitful, inviting life. The rite of Christian baptism, hailed by the congregation at the beginning of the opera, has by the end been commandeered for the greater glory of opera, when Sachs solemnly bestows a name on Walther's song. He calls it "Die selige Morgentraum-Deutweise," the blessed-morning-dream-interpretation-melody. Walther and Eva are its father and mother, David and Lena its godparents, Sachs the officiating priest. Like the consecration of a stage in *Parsifal*, this christening of song is Wagner's ordination of his art, and it prompts a devout anthem in praise of music—the quintet.

Equating classical and Christian, paradise and Parnassus, *Meistersinger* discovers a key to all mythologies by making them aspects of Wagner's own myth. It revises *Tannhäuser*, and revokes the hero's damnation; it also revises the other operas which precede it. All poetry, says

Sachs, is the interpreting of dreams. Thus he explains and apologizes for the crazed fantasies which generate the Wagnerian theater. Senta dreaming of the Dutchman and Elsa of Lohengrin are both artists. Though beginning from *Tannhäuser*, this revision of tragedy as a wish-fulfilling comedy includes *Tristan und Isolde*, first performed in 1865. *Meistersinger* quotes *Tristan* when Sachs gently refuses Eva's offer of love. He is, he tells her, a Marke without remorse or anger. The "Wahnsinn" he diagnoses in the third act is the erotic mania which impels Wagner's other characters toward oblivion; Sachs regulates and harmonizes the madness. The second act, overseen by him, is an affectionate parody of the corresponding act in *Tristan*. The passionate tryst in the darkness is here a farcical imbroglio, set in a congested alley not a garden. Isolde is inflamed by the night, sensually stirred by nature; Sachs however is soothed by the elder tree under which he sits. Walther begs Eva to elope with him to freedom, but doesn't, like Tristan, propose the easeful remedy of death. Sachs keeps a lookout more efficiently than Brangäne, and the Watchman's booming cowhorn orders the nocturnal rioters indoors. Was not the fatal outcome in *Tristan* due merely to carelessness? Like Verdi in *Falstaff*, Wagner in his single comedy calls operatic tragedy's bluff.

Monteverdi's Orfeo was an aristocrat who vanquished by sheer panache. Wagner's defense of opera relies on the industriousness of bourgeois man, saluted in Pogner's propaganda for the burghers and their guilds. The artists here are craftsmen, worried about the technical manufacture of songs. David the apprentice busies himself with the scenic labor required by the theater, rearranging the furniture for Walther's audition and choosing the correct chairs and boxes. This operatic festival is no hermetic otherworldly affair, like Parsifal's Mass at Montsalvat. It is a boisterous public holiday at midsummer, Johannistag. Far from sanctifying the drama by confining it to the elect, Sachs insists that the public should vote for the winning song. This is the plebiscite Heine applauded in Meyerbeer, who made sure that his operas contained something for everyone. *Meistersinger* develops its myth from the technology of Wagner's own century, and treats opera's unification of all the arts as a one-man factory. David explains that the junction of singer and poet produces the master. Opera too depends on a division and cooperation of labor, like the industrial production line. Sachs's metrical cobbling is close to the mass-produced creativity of the *Ring*—the mine in *Rheingold*, the domestic forge in *Siegfried*.

The *Ring* (1876) is currently taken for a political allegory, an autopsy on the fatal greed of capitalism whose settings are the citadels of modern economy. Wieland Wagner said that Walhall should be understood as Wall Street; Patrice Chéreau made the Rhinemaidens guard a hydroelectric dam. But there is another possibility. The myth Wagner works out here concerns his own art. The tetralogy is a history of opera, and of Wagner's effort to use it as a revolutionary criticism of society. It admits the failure of that revolution. In *Rheingold* music teases the drama, exposing the fatuity of characters who think they have purchased immortality: Loge laughs at the gods as they strut across the diaphanous bridge to Walhall. Yet this irony doesn't persist through the cycle. The *Ring* outgrows its political program; music increasingly overwhelms the diagrammatic drama.

Rheingold is no tract about heavenly tycoons, gigantic trade unionists and dwarfish proletarians. It is a return to the operatic world-theater of the baroque, extending vertically from the thundery sky to the riverbed or the catacomb of the mine, with music traveling between these distant regions. The orchestra forms chimerical landscapes, wavering and surging beneath the Rhine, thickening in a panoply of brass as the gods appear, igniting for Loge, sparking for Donner. It constructs castles in the air or images in sound, and this artistic idolatry is the subject of *Rheingold*.

The cycle begins with the taboo-infringing acts which create art: Alberich's theft from nature when he pillages the gold, Wotan's attempt to cheat nature by making himself eternal and secure from life's distresses in his aerial villa. Fasolt envies Wotan because he rules by beauty. Freia's apples, which keep the gods young, make the ruling class itself a work of art, as if fitted with monkey glands or cosmetically nipped and tucked. *Rheingold* scrutinizes Wagner's own motives by acknowledging that art is in league with the quest for power. He who forswears love can use the ring to be lord of the world: art effects the triumph of a deathly will. Mime says that he and the Nibelung hordes at first were innocent smiths, shaping ornaments for their women and other pretty trifles, delighting in their craft; Alberich, armed with the ring, turned their toil into slavery. Art, like Tannhäuser's blasphemies, is a means of revenge on the world. Freud might have been describing the accursed ring when he analyzed the artist as one who denies himself satisfactions in actuality so he can enjoy them in fantasy. Because Fasolt doesn't want to give up Freia, he stipulates that the pile of gold for which she is exchanged must obscure her from sight. Her form is to be the measure of his compensation ("Freias Gestalt" as Wotan puts it), a substitute, as art always is, for something lost or unattainable. The Tarnhelm is another of the artist's tools. Allowing the wearer to stand invisibly outside life or to enter another body, it instigates the dangerous masquerade of Wagner's theater and the shape-changing insinuations of his music, which can depict a slithering snake, a fugitive toad, a bird or a dragon in the forest, or Brünnhilde's frisky horse. *Rheingold* is about Wagner's own devious, compulsive magic.

Walküre deals with another aspect of his art: music's explosion of boxed-in, domesticated drama. It begins with the outlaw Siegmund's invasion of Hunding's household; its moral crux is Fricka's righteous defense of marital property. The door which suddenly admits the spring, and with it Siegmund's erotic impetus, is forced open by music. Characters in drama employ the stage as their shelter. They want upholstered lives, excluding uncertainty. Mozart's Figaro measures the room, Rossini's Figaro celebrates the fittings of his shop. The untamable energy of Wagnerian music incinerates such flimsy cubicles. Siegmund's narration describes the burning of his family's home by the Neidings, Sieglinde raves of a house on fire. Society cannot withstand the insurgency of nature. Wotan admits the futility of the fortress he designed in *Rheingold*, envisaging an end and the collapse of all he has built. Siegmund rejects Brünnhilde's invitation to refuge in the cenotaph of Walhall, and Sieglinde flees into the wildest part of the forest to bear her child. Wotan, no longer trusting in architecture, can protect the sleeping Brünnhilde only within a perishable fence of flame.

Drama in *Walküre* has narrowed to the study of a compulsory social existence. Sieglinde is bullied by Hunding, ordered to prepare the food then wait for him in bed; Wotan escapes to the mountains to be rid of Fricka's nagging. Opera gets close to the insidiousness and obliquity of actual talk—the circuitous politeness of Wotan's first replies to Fricka, archly concealing his contempt; Brünnhilde's wheedling and bargaining during her last duet with him. Social propriety is outraged by the free spirit of the incestuous Wälsung twins, and drama in the same way resists the elemental life of music, which rises like sap in Siegmund's song of spring, rampages through the cyclonic weather of the riding Valkyries and overflows (in a melody used again for the flooding Rhine in *Götterdämmerung*) in Sieglinde's cries of maternal gratitude. "Hojotoho," Brünnhilde's rallying call, is music's most exhilarated expression of this Dionysian delight in combat, danger, stormy weather. Having delivered it, she swoops off on the winds because she doesn't want to be entangled in one of the drama's domestic arguments. In the third act her vocal recklessness infects the other Valkyries, their screeches and giggles encouraged by thundering drums and the brash clamor of the brass. No wonder Fricka disapproves of these uncouth warrior girls. Their musical uproar flouts the bourgeois demeanor she imposes on the drama.

Hunding's authority is supported by social customs and sexual bans. Fricka gives these habits divine sanction, and even Brünnhilde is shocked by Siegmund's undutiful rejection of service in Walhall. The characters are straitjacketed by the conventional postures morality requires of them. Music is their means of liberation, because it attends to the cravings they dare not enunciate. It becomes, in *Walküre*, a streamy commentary on their subconscious motives and misgivings, an underground river. When Brünnhilde begs to know the cause of Wotan's dismay, he wonders whether he should voice it aloud. Would it not slacken his will? Brünnhilde declares that she is his will, invented to act on his impulses: in confessing to her he will be talking to himself. Speech and silence are the same. The orchestra therapeutically prompts the characters when they are reticent or afraid, so that violins anticipate Sieglinde's serenade when she first gives Siegmund the water; it intimates truths they can't know or don't wish to acknowledge, as when the whispered Walhall motif reveals the secret of Siegmund's paternity or when the name of Siegfried wordlessly quenches the fire as Wotan leaves. Brünnhilde's dispute with Siegmund when she announces his death is a psychological encounter, and the message she relays matters less than the transformation in her from militaristic goddess to commiserating woman. Music topples the indoor enclave of drama, as the door opens to let in nature; at the same time, it enables drama, which in the past could only observe actions, to enter the mind and trace the processes of thought.

Siegfried advances a stage further. It is about the social production of music, and its conquistadorial powers. The sword-forging, dragon-slaying apprenticeship of Siegfried is Wagner's account of the artist as a young man, and it leads to Strauss's dramatization of his own battling career in the symphonic poem *Ein Heldenleben*.

Wagner likened Meyerbeer's parade of sound effects to a battalion of Prussian guards, and *Les Troyens* with its gongs clattering on shields makes music from the clash of arms. *Siegfried* is Wagner's experiment in this epic orchestration. It may be a pastoral, but it begins in a factory. The first act develops from Mime's tinny, irritable hammering to Siegfried's industrial dynamism at the foundry as he pounds his father's shattered blade into shape.

This steely weapon is Wagner's image of his orchestra, beaten and honed into an indissoluble amalgam. Siegfried smashes the remnants of Nothung, then in the crucible solders it again, withdraws the molten mess and—as Mime gasps at his violence—percussively batters the hissing metal into submission. This drama of manufacture exactly corresponds to Wagner's musical technique. He smelts instruments into a whole which absorbs their individualities. Though he was acutely sensitive to single tones or textures—Cosima's diaries pick out the harp in *Rheingold* which sprinkles incense, or the glockenspiel in *Götterdämmerung* which catches the flickering glee of the funeral pyre—these solitary sounds are allowed no life of their own, like that possessed by the horns challenging Mozart's Fiordiligi or Beethoven's Leonore during their arias. They must be melted down into the collective like the fragments in Siegfried's forge, so the Wagnerian orchestra can be as inscrutable and irresistible as a force of nature, imitating maelstroms or conflagrations. The music wants to sound as if it comes from nowhere and is made by no one, like the liquid chords at the beginning of *Rheingold* or the imprecise, impressionistic glare of throbbing heat at the end of *Walküre*; all the while, however, it is being synthesized and molded by Siegfried.

His musical education continues in the forest, as he whittles a pipe to echo the bird's song. The dragon's blood enables him to understand the speech of birds, and this too commemorates an operatic achievement: in Papageno's twittering, in the discussion of larks and nightingales by Gounod's Roméo and Juliette, in the feathered congregation tended by Messiaen's Saint François d'Assise, opera envies birds their unverbal eloquence. Music longs to speak their universal language; Siegfried learns how.

Still it remains a simpleminded chirruping, akin to the yelping hilarity of his own "Hoiho!" or "Heiaho!" When he awakens Brünnhilde and for the first time experiences fear, he is exposed to a more difficult idiom—the language of complicated human emotion, as she vacillates between joy and outrage, the pride of the warrior-maiden and the sensuality of the woman. Siegfried is charmed but confounded. He tells her that he hears her sweet singing, but can't understand what she says to him. Their duet arrives at an accord between his riotous instinctive music and her reflective words, just as that of Tristan and Isolde brings about the consumption of words by music. The final scene of the opera suggests the cosmology Cosima derived from operatic history. Mozart, she said, was the naive perfection of paradise; with Beethoven human beings intruded into music; Wagner follows as the advent of religious revelation. Siegfried progresses from the primitive, unkempt garden through the problematic human world, vanquishing Wotan and arousing Brünnhilde. As he acquires muscular power over nature, then fearful comprehension of it, he becomes Wagner: Orpheus with a horn and sword instead of a lute.

What follows is apocalypse: *Götterdämmerung*, the decadence of the gods. From *Orfeo* to *Die Zauberflöte*, opera's ambition was to make men like gods. Wagner, however, reduces gods to parity with men. In *Rheingold* they sicken and age without their diet of apples, in *Walküre* Brünnhilde is expelled from their company and left to a pitiful human fate. Wotan declines from a man of power in the first opera to a henpecked husband and bossy father in the second; by *Siegfried* he is a dispirited magician whose spells no longer work, in *Götterdämmerung* the absent observer described by Waltraute and sentenced to death by Brünnhilde.

Musically the greatest of the cycle, *Götterdämmerung* is dramatically the meanest, attributing the end of the world to a squabble over a connubial trinket. Bernard Shaw thought that Wagner had reverted to the old operatic conventions he began by despising. Certainly this is opera at its grandest, full of rowdily Italianate situations. The blood-brotherhood duet could be from *Don Carlos*, the rollicking Gibichungs from *Ernani*, the conspiratorial trio from *Un Ballo in Maschera*, the purgative pyre from *Norma*. There are rapes, oaths, drinking songs, weddings and funeral marches; it all ends with the collapse of the theater—and this is the point of it. Shaw mistook Wagner's intention. He was not relapsing into opera but showing how the world had lapsed into it. *Rheingold* is about the economy which will eventually produce opera, as its chosen means of exhibiting and expanding wealth. *Götterdämmerung*, with its venal and ambitious Gibichung siblings, reaches this society of ostentation and passionate extravagance. It is about the material splendor of opera, as *Parsifal* is about the spiritual refinement of the form.

The characters are corrupted. The twilit gods are Siegfried the divo, conscious of having to live up to his reputation for derring-do, and Brünnhilde the murderously temperamental diva. Siegfried is smugly prepared to entertain all comers with the narrative of his exploits; being a celebrity, he expects sexual favors, as his banter with the Rhinemaidens discloses. Brünnhilde sends him off, after an exchange of trophies, to perform new astounding deeds. His career, she knows, must overrule their love. She too has changed. In *Walküre* she spent most of her time listening and watching; in *Siegfried* too she was detached and pensive, holding off the hero's assault; in *Götterdämmerung* she is a rampant fury, abusing all who have offended her. Siegfried laughs off her tantrums as the behavior of a girl down from the mountains, whom Gunther must set about civilizing. Moments before the immolation she is still berating Gutrune for having stolen her man. Her extroversion suits the mood of the work. Music here is no mental inquest, as in *Walküre*; it advertises events, as in the noisy scandals aired before the vassals. Isolde's death is a soliloquy, Brünnhilde's an oration.

The gods fall when, to these operatic monsters, the ego becomes a god. Brünnhilde scorns the entreaties of Waltraute and destroys the world in tribute to her infatuation. Siegfried, ignoring the Rhinemaidens and discarding his life like the clod tossed over his shoulder, destroys the world for an adventure. Nothing could be further from the lassitude and renunciation of Tristan and Isolde. *Götterdämmerung* is Wagner's testament to the profane values of opera, as entrancing as ever the Venusberg was—its joy in excess, its emotional surfeit, its taste for cosmic hyperbole.

Tristan und Isolde (1865) and *Parsifal* (1882) both restore sacredness to opera. Each adheres, in its different sphere, to the religious transactions which inaugurated the form. In *Tristan* the mystery is erotic, in *Parsifal* spiritual; but as always, opera doubts that the two can be separated.

In *Tristan*, Wagner extends that journey through the underworld taken by Orpheus. His music—at once frantic and listless, compounding desire and desolation—investigates the secrets of orgasm, that explosion of life which results in a small and temporary death. Strauss, imitating Wagner, describes only the business of intercourse: the blustering prelude which accompanies Matteo's deflowering of Zdenka in *Arabella*. This physical satiation is not Wagner's concern. Love and death are here engaged in a metaphysical strife, resolved only when they perceive that their motives are the same. Tristan tearing off his bandages and Isolde causelessly expiring answer at last the demand of Plato for an Orpheus who would remain among the dead, rather than briskly proceeding upstairs to a connubial happy ending.

Since Wagner's music is itself transitional, forever recombining its elements to weave or wind them into something else, it is the logical medium in which a rite of passage can occur. The drama of *Tristan* is made from such transitoriness: the death of one state of mind or phase of existence, the growth of another life from it. Each act conducts a psychological adventure or initiation. The first takes Isolde from hatred to adoration, the third takes Tristan from misery to a fatal joy and then (after his death) leads Isolde from bereft solitude to submergence in him. The second act begins and ends with sundered selves, but in between contrives a union so intimate that the lovers can't tell where one existence ends and the other begins. These almost chemical processes of modulation could be narrated only by music—because of its mutability, because it happens darkly and invisibly, because it need never be confined to single meanings. The score is at once serene and achingly tense, ecstatic and agonized; all emotions are suspended in it. It resembles a fluent consciousness, or an organism of throbbing, thronging sensations: the mind as represented by the novels of James Joyce or the body in those of D. H. Lawrence, both of whom wrote under Wagner's influence.

The music of *Tristan* dissolves dramatic identity. The lovers exchange names, and every dialogue is a colloquy within a single, manifold person. Brangäne and Kurwenal are the cautionary moral watchdogs within Isolde and Tristan. Like the interchangeable potions, the orchestra mixes disparate ingredients and opposite instincts. Strauss pointed out that while traditional counterpoint engineers agreement between warring themes, in Wagner the entangled melodies remain "intractably opposed." Tristan's delirium consists of four incompatible musical ideas, and their polyphonic discord transcribes the clash in him between love and loathing, the deceptive will to live and an eagerness for oblivion. Any note or chord or melody is striving to flex into something different; the text of *Tristan* has the same musical ease at metamorphosis, using words as if they were mutant genes. When Tristan reverses his name and persona to call himself Tantris, his thematic signature is also switched back to front. The language thrives on a punning ambiguity. Marke calls Tristan his "treulos treuester Freund" (his most truly truthless or unfaithfully faithful friend), twining together superlative and negative like major and minor keys to suggest the snarled combination of injured sexual pride, fraternal rivalry and paternal forgiveness in his attitude toward the betrayal. Music destroys the verbal clarity of drama. All the words in the first act, before the drugged lovers rapturously utter each other's names, are untrue—relayed messages, shifty excuses, oblique hints; all those in the third act are approximate and inadequate. The duet nags at syntactic and semantic impediments, like the baffling "und" which comes between them. Tristan, dying, can only explain his experience to Kurwenal in metaphors, which he knows will not be understood.

To accommodate this musical introversion, the drama must be nullified. The meaning of *Tristan und Isolde* lies in the things its characters don't do and don't say. Drama aspires to the condition of music, which in turn aspires to the perfect ambiguity of silence.

The stage vibrates with the stillness of the characters, poised for actions whose performance they postpone indefinitely. On the ship Tristan won't come to Isolde when summoned, and she won't kill him when she has the chance. Nor will he defend himself against Marke's accusations or Melot's assault. The interruption of the rendezvous in the garden happens in a scrambling moment; there follows, during Marke's long monologue, a paralyzed pause, as each character retreats to ponder the internal changes provoked by the event. These people think themselves out of the drama, whose crises are to them irrelevant. Isolde doesn't know where they have arrived when the ship docks, or which king greets them. Kurwenal cheeringly recollects place and possession for Tristan, telling him he is on his estates, among his flocks, with his ancestors. Tristan dimly demands where all this is, and Kurwenal replies "in echten Land"—in reality. Tristan recognizes no such location. Denying the solidity of drama, *Tristan* also derives its music from silence. Isolde says she has learned how to sing in silence. The first bars of the opera sound almost surreptitiously out of that unechoing void, the last bars at length find their way back there. Drama and music have together, like Tristan and Isolde, passed through a rite of death and rebirth.

The outcome is *Parsifal*: opera midway between Mass and orgy, asking again the question which has perplexed the form since its beginnings—is this the consecration of a theater, or the desecration of a church? Music here is both salvation and venereal perdition. *Parsifal* is set in a temple, and also in a magician's den; hortatory voices sound in the heights, but in the depths there are howling miseries and feral laughter. Titurel calls down grace from above, Klingsor hauls up fiends from below. The realms intersect in Amfortas, the sinner who must, despite his self-scourging, perform the priestly office. This is Wagner himself, whose operas redeem by corrupting.

After his tormented night, Amfortas seeks relief by bathing in what he calls the sacred lake. The score of *Parsifal* is itself immersive. But this is not the sensual ocean of *Tristan*. The textures are thinner, matching the imagery of streaming blood or suppurating wounds, Kundry's balsam or the dewy repentant tears of the Easter meadows; the fluidity is that of life running out.

The contours of individual existence are washed away in this liquid element. Working on the opera, Wagner was surprised when two different characters—the Grail-messenger and the erotic temptress—coalesced in Kundry. These separate identities remain distinct, so that as Klingsor's agent she craves Parsifal's destruction while as the servant of the Grail she seeks through him her own absolution. Still, the dramatic incoherence makes musical sense. Kundry's oscillation between irreconcilable sources demonstrates the interdependence of good and evil: lashing her in contrary directions, the score exposes in her a schizophrenia which is the state of the entire opera. Because she is an eternal woman, whose reappearances through the ages Klingsor lists, she can change from one female persona to another within a few bars. Thus she is both sacred mother and profane whore. She announces the death of Parsifal's mother, and shocks him into moral adulthood; then, when she kisses him, she teaches him the difference between a maternal embrace and a sexual seduction. Bathing his feet and humbly drying them with her hair, she is Christ's mother, preparing her son for his personal calvary. All the characters secretly share in one another's lives, thanks to the psychological insinuations of music. Kundry's kiss causes Parsifal to become Amfortas, whose name he cries and whose sins he assumes. In this continuum, moral opposites come treacherously close together. Klingsor designing the pleasure garden is the other side of Titurel building the sanctuary; both are aspects of Wagner's own creativity.

Immobilized in space on Wagner's stage, these people seem to travel through time, making *Parsifal* the history of an eternally frustrated, protracted human quest. Kundry was Herodias once, and will be again when Strauss composes *Salome*. When Gurnemanz asks Parsifal's name, he replies that he has had many, though he has forgotten them all. Kundry christens him Parsifal, but like Tristan's name it is a reversible caption: she coins it from "fal parsi," which she says means pure fool. He has a series of existences—oafish innocent, chivalric adventurer, martyr to the world's woes—which seem to extend through centuries, like those journeys which take Kundry to Arabia and back. She has, she declares, been waiting an eternity for the moment when he appears at last in the garden. Their careers are those of the dying and reborn god: the seasonally slaughtered Dionysus, killed so the earth can thrive anew; Christ expiring on Friday to rise again on Sunday. During the Mass, the young knights sing that Christ's body lives on in them. He died so that they might consume him each day, and sustain themselves.

This is a religious mystery, but it is also—as Wagner uses it—a specifically theatrical mystery, and it claims immortality for his own art. *Parsifal* attempts a solemn contemplative stasis. Arthur Symons at Bayreuth in

1897 marveled to see "for the first time, people really motionless on the stage." Time too has been stopped, by those reflective pauses in the first prelude. After Gurnemanz's initial narration, the same story is recited over and over. Wagner is imitating and equaling the incarnation: the moment when eternity descended into time and, with the advent of Christ, history at once ended and began again. Drama occupies space, music happens in time. Rituals, like those staged in *Parsifal* and like *Parsifal* itself, arrest time by spatializing it. Repetition ensures that an instant lasts forever, and that we can travel round the world without needing to stir from home. This mystery, in the transformations from the forest to the temple in the first and third acts, is devoutly rehearsed by Wagner's scenery, and choreographed by his music. The set moves, while Parsifal and Gurnemanz walk on the spot. Parsifal asks what is happening; Gurnemanz explains that space is becoming time. If they wait, the temple will come to them. The theater has miracles of its own.

The Easter of *Parsifal* belongs in all mythologies at once. It is a pagan rite of spring and a Christian promise of resurrection; it also hints at the almost supernatural power of the theater, where every performance is a reenactment, restoring life to the dead letter of the score and the text. The holy day, as Gurnemanz calls it, is a theatrical holiday. It marks the festival decreed by Wagner on the stage which *Parsifal* consecrated, and it seeks to ensure that the feast is immovable: Wagner ordered that this opera should never be given outside Bayreuth. Art has not succumbed to religion, as Nietzsche claimed when expressing his dismay about *Parsifal*; the art of opera has itself been established as a religion.

EIGHT

Realism and Puccini

REALISM does not come naturally to opera, whose dimensions have from the first been those of myth or religious mystery. Bringing opera up to date and down to earth—as the verismo composers at the end of the nineteenth century wished to do—meant that it must be demythologized, by force if necessary. The gods were to be grounded, the rite defiled.

This happens when the operatic realists adapt the myths of Wagner. Realism can't help but be a travesty of heroism. Puccini's *La Fanciulla del West* (1910) is wild West Wagner, with Minnie the saloonkeeper a gun-toting rather than spear-wielding Brünnhilde, her home a cabin in the mountains. Puccini quotes *Die Walküre* when the door bangs open in the blizzard during Minnie's rendezvous with the bandit Johnson, and the Californian redwoods, as the prelude to the third act suggests, grow in Siegfried's forest. Demoralized by verismo, the characters shrink from claiming operatic grandeur. Minnie writes herself off as a nonentity, "oscura e buona e nulla," and Johnson begins anonymously, dismissed as the "signor di Sacramento." Yet they dream of regaining the Wagnerian exaltation the drama has denied them. Minnie reads books, conducts Bible classes, and turns Johnson from an outlaw into a damned soul redeemed by her love. The sudden, stunning high notes of her part leap like Brünnhilde toward a heroic musical altitude from which the drama, anchoring her in a world of squabbling miners, venal sheriffs and promiscuous redskins, tugs her down: one of these desperate vertical climaxes—in the aria "Oh, se sapeste"—actually attempts the levitation she longs for, reaching into the sky from the Sierras.

Brünnhilde, who dreads the shame of being cast out into the human world, finds herself exiled in the reality of pioneering America. Tristan and Isolde, in Charpentier's *Louise* (1900), recur in contemporary Paris. Charpentier wanted what he called his "musical novel" to combine the squalidly realistic drama of Zola with the sublimity of Wagnerian music. Louise is a humble seamstress, Julien the poet who lures her away from the factory to free love in Montmartre. His aubade in the first scene is as grandiose as the dawn in *Götterdämmerung*, and Louise's repetitions of "Paris! Paris!" at the end, as she flees the parental home, have the urgency of the dying Isolde. The enshrouding metaphysical night of *Tristan* is here an urban reality. A seducer nicknamed Le Noctambule prowls Montmartre, and he symbolizes the erotic enticement of the dark: "Je suis le Plaisir de Paris!" Julien and Louise sing a duet as rapturous as that of Tristan and Isolde, but its uproar is powered by the city—"la chère musique de la grande ville!"—and they conclude with a hymn to that industrialized dynamism: "Paris! Cité de force et de lumière!"

At every point the myth is adjusted to an earthier truth. Louise like Elsa awaits a chivalrous rescuer, as promised in the books she reads; she takes Julien for her Lohengrin, but when she says it's like a fairy story he corrects her: "Non, c'est la vie! l'éternelle, la toute-puissante vie!" Her parents are derelict gods. Julien brands them as leftovers from Wagnerian legend. "La mère la Routine, le père le Préjugé," he says; they are the oppression of custom and stereotype, and he is the ardent Siegfried who will overthrow them. The mother has the voice of a nagging Fricka, the father is a world-weary Wotan—except that in Wagner they wouldn't have to set the table and drink up their soup.

Although the setting of Zandonai's *Francesca da Rimini* (1914) is medieval, it too is about a Tristan and Isolde realer than their models in Wagner. In Dante, Paolo and Francesca succumbed to their adulterous passion while reading a romance about Lancelot and Guinevere. In d'Annunzio's play and the opera Zandonai based on it, the blame belongs to a different text: Wagner's infectious *Tristan*, venerated by d'Annunzio who made the hero of one of his novels murder his mistress after a performance of the work, to save her from the malady of mortal life. The room where Paolo and Francesca discard the book to make love is painted with frescoes narrating the romance of Tristan.

Nevertheless, Zandonai's lovers are a Tristan and Isolde with a difference—carnally ravenous Italians, not abstruse, intellectualizing Germans. They hunger for blood. Francesca climbs the tower during the battle, aroused by the slaughter. Isolde lets the sword drop; but when the ravings of a prisoner beneath the floor annoy Francesca, Paolo's brother Malatestino at once beheads the man on her behalf. Though she disowns the deed, he claims it was her wish, and hurls into evidence the bleeding head. Isolde's nursing of Tantris happens in recollection, not onstage; Francesca is seen tending Malatestino's wounded eye, dabbling in the gore with her fingers. Just before Paolo's arrival at Ravenna, Francesca quotes the dying Tristan who, when Isolde calls, says he hears the light. She tells Samaratana that the light is resounding like a peal of trumpets. Despite her fidelity to Tristan's words, she alters their meaning: he shuts out a bright, irrelevant reality; she welcomes it, because it brings sexual fulfillment.

The love draft in *Tristan* is a mystic opiate, a dose of the negation Wagner learned from Schopenhauer. For Paolo and Francesca, slaking their thirst with wine after the battle, it is simply an aphrodisiac. Isolde, signaling Tristan, quenches the torch. Her action announces their symbolic commitment to night and to extinction. Francesca, however, ignites a torch which signifies her physical ardor. She is fascinated by the flaring caldron, and draws a firebrand which she launches to scorch the enemy. Death comes to Tristan and Isolde when called for, because they have chosen and embraced it. Realism makes the end of Paolo and Francesca more violent and muddled. He scrambles through a trapdoor, but his fancy cloak catches on a bolt: Francesca's breast receives the thrust intended for him. The meditative self-obliteration of Wagner's lovers changes to a gory double murder.

The characters of heroic opera lived on the heights—Monteverdi's gods in their winged cars, Wagner's goddesses on their flying steeds. Realism aims to pull them down. Eugen d'Albert's *Tiefland* (1903) is about this process. The title means "lowland." Pedro the shepherd, who loves the freedom of the hills, must descend to the valleys, where he suffocates in a world of sordid deals and sexual brutality. *Tiefland* is a low-down version of opera's congenital myth, with Pedro as the Orpheus who ventures into that geographical underworld to retrieve his Eurydice, Marta, and take her to the upland. He kills the wolf who menaces his flock and the wolfish landowner Sebastiano who has enslaved Marta; escaping prosecution, he has like Orpheus vanquished death.

The motif which stands for d'Albert's lowland has a downward propulsion like an angrily banged fist, bludgeoning the airy clarinet of the mountains. Verismo also lowers the vocal center of gravity. Song becomes chestier, more guttural and expletive. The singer no longer rides the air like Verdi's sopranos; Santuzza's curse is wrenched from her in *Cavalleria Rusticana* (1890) and Tonio unlyrically snarls "la commedia è finita!" in Leoncavallo's *I Pagliacci* (1892). Music, the precious resource which once allowed operatic characters to set themselves among the gods, is cheapened in *Tiefland*. Sebastiano uses it to demean Marta. The symbol of her subjection is his guitar, which he plays when he wants her to dance for his pleasure. She sings the narrative of her mistreatment over a barrel-organ-like accompaniment: the utilitarian hurdy-gurdy matches the banality of her case.

Puccini's operas humiliate his own music. The tragedy of Mimi in *La Bohème* (1896) has been commercialized in *Il Tabarro*, one of the *Trittico* operas (1918), where a song seller churns out an extract to working girls and their boyfriends along the Paris quays. A singer performs a madrigal in Puccini's *Manon Lescaut* (1893), but Manon, bored and sexually restive, pays no attention. The same heroine in Massenet's *Manon* (1884) slights the entire institution of opera. Her doting elderly admirer hires the ballet troupe from the Paris Opéra to entertain her at the Cours-la-Reine; asked whether she enjoyed the expensive show, she yawns that she saw none of it. In its turn, Massenet's opera is realistically devalued. Murger, on whose stories of bohemia Puccini based his opera, had called the flirtatious Mimi and her wanton friend Musette "vulgar Manons"; Massenet's Manon is vulgarized all over again when the girls at the sweatshop in *Louise* gossip of having been to see Ambroise Thomas's *Mignon* along with *Manon*. Camille says she thought *Manon* was lovely, especially when the heroine dies. Opera here looks askance at its own tawdriness: it manufactures sentimental tunes for us to snivel over.

This degradation is the rule of realism. It happens to Manon between Massenet's version and Puccini's. Massenet's girl lives on the surface, dedicated to that "pursuit of happiness" which was the creed of the eighteenth century, when the Abbé Prévost wrote his novel about her. Puccini makes this frivolous hedonist real by making her a monster—vicious, grasping, yet sustained by a will to live which, when she protests against death in the desert, has an almost Darwinian force. She is a man-eating Isolde, and Puccini's score has been invaded by the languishing disease of the *Tristan* chord. The worst Massenet's Manon does to des Grieux is to entice him away from taking holy orders at St. Sulpice to play faro at the Hotel Transylvanie. Puccini's heroine destroys her des Grieux, who begins

189

as a nonchalant boy and ends a groveling wreck, begging for a menial job on the ship which takes her to imprisonment in America. *Tristan* is reinterpreted by Puccini as a study of the sex war: a merciless combat between the woman and her male prey. An Italian critic said after its first performance that *Manon Lescaut* was the "song of our paganism." That's what opera had always been, from the return of the pagan gods sponsored by the Camerata; but in Puccini, renaissance has given way to regression. His characters are pagan because they are emotional primitives, sensual savages.

Massenet's *Manon* is aware that it's the kind of opera Brecht was to label "culinary." It begins with the innkeeper's recital of his bill of fare, and when his customers scoff at the duck pâté, he assures them that it's a work of art. Manon herself is a tasty morsel, all sugar and spice. Her most heartfelt aria is her farewell to the little table she shared with des Grieux. Massenet's characters are connoisseurs. Lescaut recommends the inn with the best claret in Amiens; the female worshipers at St. Sulpice murmur their admiration for the sermon des Grieux has preached, and compliment the sweetness in his voice. Though Puccini's hero feels he has been sullied by his gambling, in Massenet it's a rational way to get rich quickly and to maximize pleasure. What good does it do to economize? asks Lescaut in one of his arias. The most dubious activities can be excused if conducted elegantly enough. The cardsharps at the Hotel Transylvanie have a chorus praising their own nimble art.

Puccini presses the issue infinitely further. Whereas Massenet's Manon wiltingly expires at Le Havre before she can be shipped across the ocean, Puccini's ends in a parching American desert. The hiccups in the libretto of *Manon Lescaut* serve the remorseless logic of this downfall. To avoid charges of plagiarism from Massenet, Puccini cut the intermediary episodes, like Manon's impoverished sojourn in Paris with des Grieux or the quarrels in the Louisiana prison colony which explain their presence in the arid wilderness. The elopement from Amiens is a youthful prank; already in the next scene Manon has aged into a case-hardened courtesan. The embarkation at Le Havre is an outburst of joy; the next scene strands them in a scorched waste, dying in the dry heat of their own compulsion.

Realist opera is almost sadistic in its defiling of people. The Japanese heroine of Mascagni's *Iris* (1898), abducted for sexual abuse by Osaka, is smeared with mud for her harlotry. She hurls herself from the window of the brothel and lands in an open drain, to be fished out by scavengers beneath Fujiyama. Even in comedy, there must be a dirty secret: for instance that after which Wolf-Ferrari names *Il Segreto di Susanna* (1909). Susanna's vice—perhaps remembering the cigarette factory in *Carmen*, often considered the origin of verismo—is an addiction to nicotine. Dionysus no longer recruits operatic followers with alcohol; he now employs the weed. Susanna's husband, however, makes the connection with the Nietzschean god: "odor, per Bacco," he sniffs, "ch'è di tabacco!"

The subject of realist opera is a pathological desire. For José it is the disgrace of loving Carmen, for Santuzza the excommunication which punishes her love for Turiddu, for Puccini's Manon the stigma of the roll call when she is rounded up with a motley pack of prostitutes. These abnormal passions demand medical diagnosis: Mimi's breathy ecstasy is a symptom of tuberculosis.

Romantic emotion has itself become a sickness. This is the judgment of Tchaikovsky in his two operas based on Pushkin, *Eugene Onegin* (1879) and *The Queen of Spades* (1890), or of Massenet in his study of Goethe's romantic poet *Werther* (1892). Goethe's Werther and Pushkin's Onegin are figures from the first age of romanticism. Werther kills himself to be rid of an individuality which keeps him apart and alone. Onegin is too worldly to do any such thing, and proudly, miserably guards his loneliness in the middle of an incessant social whirl. Now, at the end of the nineteenth century, these poetic solitaries are redefined by opera as neurotics.

Tchaikovsky's operas are terrified of a dangerous desire which in the composer's case (and in that of his brother Modest, the librettist for *The Queen of Spades*) was homosexual. The more violently the musical emotion pours out—in Tatyana's impulsive love letter to Onegin, or the obsessive vows of Herman in the later work—the more prudently or vindictively society in the drama represses it. Herman interprets the world as a conspiracy to deny him the love of Lisa and the knowlege of the occult card trick with which he hopes to buy it. An obstinate reality at last drives him mad. Tatyana is aloofly spurned by Onegin, and in turn regretfully spurns him; they must both learn to live without desire. It is as if Tristan and Isolde had agreed not to love each other in deference to Marke. The unoperatic conclusion is dictated by Tchaikovsky's dread of feelings which can be expressed in music but not in action.

At first Onegin is frigidly proof against emotion. He mocks the susceptibility of his friend Lensky, and Olga teases her sister Tatyana for wandering off into literary and musical fancies. A superficial life is best. The long scene in which Tatyana writes her reckless letter telescopes a whole night from bedtime to dawn, and thus listens in on her unconscious mind. She ought to be asleep and harmlessly dreaming, rather than entrusting her fantasy to print. Her aria ends in a swelling musical triumph; any other operatic heroine could look forward to having her wish come promptly true. Tatyana, instead, is cold-shouldered by Onegin. Later she is grateful: his cruelty has taught her the self-preservative virtue of the social forms. Her elderly husband Gremin extols in his aria a very unoperatic kind of love. He admires her goodness, and is cheered by her kindness; neither feels passionately about the other. Social duty is their salvation. The only outlet for musical impulse which society approves is dance, because it obeys strict rules and precludes intimacy—the rustic jigs of the peasants, the jolly waltz at Larina's party, the strutting polonaise which leads a conducted tour of the nobleman's house in St. Petersburg.

Tchaikovsky saw opera as a fatal, erotic temptation: "One must be a hero to refrain from writing operas. . . . I do not possess that heroism." Massenet had no such moral qualms about the form, but Werther interests him as a musical tempter: a character of tempestuous emotional intensity—revealed when he translates the verses of Ossian about the breath of spring—who unsettles the bourgeois society of suburban Frankfurt and excites an illicit longing in the married, maternal Charlotte; an operatic outsider in a real world whose reality excludes and eventually kills him.

Goethe's novel, published in 1774, was about Charlotte's effect on Werther, who meets her once only; Massenet's opera is about his effect on her. In the novel, he writes letters to this unattainable object of desire; in the opera, she receives and furtively rereads them. Goethe was concerned with a metaphysical puzzle. The egotistical hero envies the tranquil unselfconsciousness of Charlotte. He wants to lose himself in her, to disappear into her family. Massenet's interest in the relationship is exclusively erotic. Werther draws Charlotte away from her stolid, grumpy husband. For Goethe, the tragedy lay in the frustrating limitations of the mind. Massenet deals with the delicious weakness of the heart (and, in Charlotte's "Air des larmes," with the use of tears as a covert relief). Charlotte relies on religion to save her from herself, like the penitent Thaïs. Her strength, she says as she emerges from church, is redoubled by prayer. As soon as Werther shoots himself, she can own up to loving him, reward him with the postponed kiss, and join him in enjoying his agony. "On est si bien ici," he remarks, bleeding to death on the floor. The realism of *Werther* is in its analysis of Charlotte's tactics for punishing the pleasure she must deny herself.

Herman in *The Queen of Spades* is maddened by his quest for that prohibited pleasure. He kills the old Countess to secure her infallible formula for winning at cards. Tchaikovsky's music sympathizes with his frenzy, yet the drama counts its psychological cost. The rule is once more the unoperatic one of repression. Pauline sings a conventional melody about Arcadian love, accompanying herself on the harpsichord; her friends call for something sprightlier, and start up a rowdy folk song. The governess interrupts their frolics, and says they should be ashamed to dance in the crude Russian fashion. The Countess, who long ago lived down her scandalous past, is a symbol of locked and bolted restraint. She barks orders at Lisa to close the window (through which Herman has entered) and go quietly to bed.

The Queen of Spades pays envious homage to romantic opera, where desire encountered no impediments and suffered no insidious guilt. In particular it yearns for the liberty enjoyed by Don Giovanni and Carmen. Tchaikovsky begins with a pastiche of Bizet's opening scene, as passersby stroll in the park and a chorus of boys performs a military drill; the Countess is the figure of that fate read by Carmen when she turns over the card emblazoned with spades. Mozart is lovingly imitated in a pastoral intermezzo about Daphnis and Chloë. His music hides its own sensual secret: Tomsky reports that the Countess's lover, bargaining for sexual favors, whispered the card trick into her ear with words sweeter than the sweetest Mozart. Herman is a demented Giovanni. Mozart's hero menaces the paternal Commendatore; Tchaikovsky's outrages the matriarchal Countess (who returns to haunt him, like the Commendatore). The change fits Giovanni's psychological profile. Otto Rank, after seeing *Don Giovanni* in Vienna in 1921, wrote a study of "the Don Juan complex" suggesting that the libertine's career of seduction was a search for the one woman denied to him by taboo: he killed the father not so as to have the daughter (which is how Mozart's opera begins) but because he wanted to sleep with his own mother; he shares the ailment of Oedipus. Herman and the Countess seem to be partners in some sinful knowledge which the music hints at—in the shivering strings as he sneaks into her bedroom—though the drama will not name it. The Countess's refrain, remembered from one of the operas by Grétry heard in her courtly youth in Paris, enforces the ban. "Je crains de lui parler le nuit," she hums: I dare not speak to him at night. It could be Herman's motto too. Tchaikovsky's operas are about the silencing of a nocturnal speech like that of *Tristan*. The pleasure principle, opera's imperative, must surrender to the reality principle.

Realism puts an end to romantic opera, in which the characters sing as naturally as birds. Music is the energy of Mozart's people, or the fermenting lifeblood of Wagner's. Now such lyrical expression seems unrealistic. Opera must justify itself, and it does so by choosing artists for its protagonists, creatures who can't be expected to behave realistically and are at home in the shoddy artificiality of the theater: Puccini's opera singer Tosca, Leoncavallo's grimacing clown Canio, the Comédie Française actress who is Cilea's heroine in *Adriana Lecouvreur* (1902). Opera demystifies itself by showing the paltry feigning which goes on behind the scenes, as in Strauss's prologue to *Ariadne auf Naxos* (1916). Someone chattering backstage in *Adriana Lecouvreur* says that the actress Duclos is dressing. A colleague giggles that she is actually undressing, in order to be more celestial than ever. Deity is being denuded.

Everyone in *Tosca* (1900) employs that theatrical false front designed by Scarpia when he orders the simulated execution of Mario: "Occore simular," he says. The law and religion, like Tosca's operas, are deceptive performances, masking the cynical machinations behind the scenes. Scarpia's most nastily acute comment on Tosca is his pretense that her hysteria in the second act is painless art: she was never more tragic onstage, he sneers. He proves his suspicion correct, for he traps her by appealing to her enthusiam for playacting. She eagerly rehearses Mario for his death, and applauds the artistry of his fall. Soon after murdering Scarpia, she has rewritten the event as an aria. When it happens, she tonelessly screams at him; telling the story to Mario, she dramatizes it with sound effects from the rapping drums, suspensefully holds back the climax, then caps it with a vocal stunt. In "Io quella lama gli piantai nel cor," describing how she drove in the knife, she hurtles from the top to the bottom of her range, and almost begs for an ovation.

Canio in *Pagliacci* is less fortunate. The cuckolded clown is a low-life Otello, deprived of the authority with which Verdi's hero, farewelling glory or swearing revenge, ritualizes his predicament. Nedda sneers at Tonio's inept lovemaking as "quanta poesia!" and Canio's grief is insulted by an audience which treats it as part of the play. Opera may have been a rebirth of tragedy, but those origins are parodied by realism. Tonio in the prologue announces that the author is reviving the masks of antique drama. Whereas the classical mask made the actor's face sternly immutable, in *Pagliacci* the only mask available is the greasepaint Canio smears on during "Vesti la giubba," and it defames his face, denying the anguish beneath.

Cavalleria Rusticana, set in Sicily, is a Greek tragedy restaged by peasants. Though the anecdote about Turiddu's philandering is rude and earthy, it is treated to all the classical formalities. The unities of time and place are respected, a chorus sits in gossipy judgment on the action, the final violence happens offstage and is reported by a breathless messenger. Drama even acknowledges its source in religious rite: the opera happens at Easter, and the congregation proclaiming the resurrection of Christ and of nature also salutes the theater's power to bring the dead back to life at every performance. The mystery is that of *Parsifal*. However, Verga's story describes a rustic version of chivalry—Turiddu is about as chivalrous as a barnyard cock—and Mascagni's opera rusticates or vulgarizes tragedy. Santuzza veers between pleading and vixenish hatred; in her emotional rawness and mental muddle, she is too real to be tragic.

The refined and sophisticated Adriana Lecouvreur, though she interprets classical tragedy onstage, is somehow not real enough to deserve comparison with the heroines she plays. She knows she is their ancillary, "l'umile ancella" as she says. Canio's grief is truer than the pique of Pagliaccio, and Tosca when beset by Scarpia emotes as grandly as she does in the theater. Adriana lacks their furious conviction. Her reality is only the shadow of her performances, and these occur elsewhere. She arrives rehearsing a speech from Racine's *Bajazet*, but the operatic setting is the greenroom and to deliver the monologue she disappears from view; we are left with a commentary by Michonnet, the stage director who watches from the wings. At the Princess's reception, prodded by a sexual rival, Adriana does declaim a tragic speech—Phaedra's self-reproach when Theseus returns to discover her passion for Hippolytus—yet it's still not operatically the real thing. The scene is an essay on vocal and dramatic technique, rising from speech to song to a last shout of execration. The emotion she counterfeits is not her own. Phaedra is genuinely disgusted by her moral crime. Adriana is blameless, and in quoting the speech attributes it to the adulterous Princess. Her oration done, she receives her applause and stalks off, walking out of a tragedy which belongs to someone else. Her dying delirium is another performance. She lifts herself from her couch and announces to the bystanders, "Scostatevi, profani! Melpòmeno son io!"—Away from me, profane ones! I am the tragic muse! Allying herself with the muse and sanctifying her distress, Adriana remains an artist: a professional tragedian immune to actual tragedy.

Puccini's bohemia hints at the aesthetic bad faith of realist opera. His characters are amateurs pretending to be artists. They lack talent or persistence, and sacrifice their creations to more creaturely comforts. Rodolfo the poet burns his drama to keep the attic warm, and is diverted from his essay by Mimi's knock on the door. Marcello the painter complains that his fingers are too numbed to work, and exchanges his epic canvas of the Red Sea for the chore of daubing the inn walls. Bad workmen, they blame their tools in their duet: Rodolfo curses his pen, Marcello his brush. Schaunard the musician buys a cheap horn from a peddler, and discovers when he tries it that the D is out of tune; he earns an income giving music lessons to a parrot. The symbol of their endeavors is the false flowers Mimi embroiders: not art but a decorative fiction. The artist's existence appeals to them because it's the prolongation of childhood, delaying adult responsibility. They spend their time playing games—slap-up feasts, comic duels; their revenge on society, when they cheat the landlord or leave the café bills for the state councillor Musetta has picked up, is to ensure that someone else pays. Rodolfo explains in his aria that poetry allows him to live beyond his nonexistent means. He's poor, but he builds seignorial castles in fantasy. Poetry consoles Mimi, as she says in her reply, because it supplies an illusion to mitigate reality. In the second act, Rodolfo declares that if he is a poet, then Mimi must be poetry: a bloom as fragile and ephemeral as youth, or health.

In Charpentier's Montmartre, Julien's friends propose electing Louise the muse of their bohemia, but a philosopher objects that "Les Muses sont mortes!" and goes on to explain aestheticism as a social virus. The workers want to be bourgeois, the bourgeoisie to be aristocrats, the aristocrats to be artists and the artists to be gods. Louise's father believes that, given the choice, everyone would quit work and opt for idleness. Her mother agrees, adding that everyone would be an artist. Bohemia for her is poverty set to music. Opera is traditionally an art of affluence, of economic and emotional surplus. Rossini's Figaro covets gold, Wagner's gods build pyramids of it. La Bohème is about those who can't afford to live operatically. The arts the bohemians practice are fanciful or fraudulent; they are rich only in useless sentiments.

Realism treads down the artifice of opera. In Madama Butterfly (1904) the heroine asks Suzuki, as they do their household accounts, whether poverty is far off. Verdi's Luisa Miller and her father plan to wander the countryside as beggars, blithely singing; Violetta rewards the revelers with the last of her savings. These romantic dreamers don't understand financial stringency. Puccini's characters can never ignore niggardly facts. They must be starved into truth, as they are hurt into song.

Butterfly, like Canio or Michonnet who tells Adriana that they are poor folk and shouldn't meddle in high society, understands the humiliation of performance. She became a geisha when the family lost its fortune, but she warns Sharpless that she'd sooner die than return to that career: singing for her is the fate worse than death, because it trades in factitious emotions. Her own sacrifice to realism occurs when she throws out her pot of rouge.

Butterfly is tragic because she insists on believing the words Pinkerton so glibly sings at her. Opera has been infiltrated by people for whom song is insincere, like Carmen and the two Manons. Pinkerton's feelings are casual, as he admits in "Amore o grillo," and he finds the tackiness of the theater morally convenient. When Goro rearranges the house by maneuvering the screens like a set dresser onstage, Pinkerton notes that in Japan houses and contracts are equally elastic. For his homecoming, Butterfly and Suzuki carpet the floor with petals and blooms, but they're pathetically bedecking a place which is in truth bleak and ugly. Lyricism is no longer an excuse for misdemeanors, as it was in Verdi. Puccini added a last aria for Pinkerton, "Addio fiorito asil," but a good tune doesn't exonerate him. Song must be extorted by emotional duress, or physical agony. The butterfly impaled on a pin and fixed to a board is Puccini's image of operatic character crucified. Music has reality only if it's the sound of a body in pain. It must be justified by the display of weaponry—the sword with which Butterfly kills herself, the spiked crown which draws blood from Mario's head in Scarpia's torture chamber, the hooks and pincers applied to the squealing Liù in *Turandot* (1926).

Realism intended to bring about a revolution in opera, democratizing its gods and heroes. An opera about a revolution, Giordano's *Andrea Chénier* (1896), shows the process in action—and shows how it failed. Chénier was a poet put to death by the terrorists of the French Revolution. The opera translates his verses into arias and makes a singer of him, who treats first a party and later a courtroom to exhibitions of his golden voice. When Chénier is tried for treason, Gérard receives a letter from Robespierre remembering that Plato cast the poets out of his ideal republic. But music reverses that decree: opera casts the republicans out of its empire, and in doing so vindicates Chénier. André in Massenet's *Thérèse* (1907) belongs to the Girondist party, the moderate republican faction of 1792. When the revolutionaries turn against him, his wife Thérèse, eager to join him, flamboyantly taunts the mob with a cry of "Vive le Roi!" and marches off to the guillotine. She too, like Chénier, has exchanged political radicalism for a proud operatic intransigence.

Moving furniture before the Coigny reception, Gérard tallies the labor which sustains this "casa dorata" and its vain, powdered society. The gilded mansion might be an opera house. He declares it to be doomed, but is converted to its values before he can bring that doom to pass. He succumbs to what he calls, as he spies on Maddalena, "l'eterna canzon": the operatic cult of erotic song. He tells her later that "la poésia" in her has inflamed him and defeated his political principles; he goes on to protest against the infamy of executing poets.

The first scene of *Andrea Chénier* is a demolition of grand opera. Maddalena complains of her corseting and the tiresome pretenses of society; Chénier's improvisation accuses her genteel world of rapacity; Gérard opens the doors to the hungry and wretched, who ruin the party. The second scene moves from a palace to the streets. The Arcadian shepherds of the masquerade at the Coigny house are replaced by an unruly metropolitan mob. The fancy dress of operatic character now serves as camouflage for the dandified "incroyables" or hedonistic "merveilleuses" of the town. Bersi interprets revolution as the liberation of the instincts, and toasts the tumbrils with champagne. But her corruption, according to the spy who keeps her under observation, is unspontaneous. She has adopted a role in order to merge with the crowd. For Chénier, a romantic hope has been tainted by reality—which is what the 1890s saw as the tragedy of the nineteenth century. He no longer believes in the poetry of existence; the opera's purpose is to restore his faith. Maddalena comes to meet him at an altar erected to the new custom-made god, Marat, and the last scene is set in what she calls the degraded cloisters of the St. Lazare prison. Together they reconsecrate these demeaned places, asserting—in defiance of realism—the old operatic religion of sublimation, consummating love in death. When Maddalena quotes Chénier's question "Non conoscete amor?", that love no longer means social compassion: it is the luxurious death-wish of Tristan and Isolde.

Gérard too is reconverted from political reality to the operatic extravagance of romance. His aria "Nemico della patria" rejects institutional power and transfers allegiance to a sensual god, "il Senso!" He decides that all else is lies, "sol vero la passione!" This was the revolutionary agenda of verismo; yet when Maddalena sings "La mamma morta," Gérard forgets the satiation of the senses and vows, for no reward or reason at all, to save Chénier. However, Chénier, as indifferent as Tristan to physical fate, doesn't want to be saved. Maddalena in her aria describes love descending to transform earth into heaven. Gérard says he expected revolution to change men into gods at once, in a single embrace. As Giordano demonstrates, only opera can do that.

Puccini's last operas abandon realism. The *Trittico* rebuilds the old vertical, spiritual theater, encompassing all the gradations of nature. Puccini's original plan was to make the three panels episodes from Dante; though that didn't happen, they still constitute a divine comedy. *Il Tabarro* is set in an urban inferno, *Suor Angelica* in a convent which serves as the heroine's purgatory, *Gianni Schicchi* in a mercenary Florence which from the heights of Fiesole looks like a radiant paradise. Because Dante's was a journey through the undiscovered country, all three works map Orphic voyages into the underworld. The Seine of the bargeman Michele in *Tabarro* is both Lethe and Styx, a sluice of oblivion consuming the autumn sun at the day's end and freighting corpses like Luigi's. Angelica brews a painless poison for herself and by a scenic miracle calls back her dead child. Frugola the ragpicker in *Tabarro* longs for death as a release from work and weariness; Angelica confidently assures the other nuns that "la morte è vita bella." Gianni Schicchi learns the secret of a comically reversible and profitable death, impersonating Buoso to dictate a new will with himself as the beneficiary. "Da morto," he says, "son rinato," and the doctor credits the prodigy to Bolognese medicine. Schicchi's daughter Lauretta vows in "O mio babbino caro" to drown herself in the Arno, but she is bluffing to wheedle a favor from her father.

The hell of *Tabarro* is a proletarian prison: the stifling hold of the barge where the stevedores work. Luigi's aria "Hai ben raggione" is a song from underground, the complaint of those who toil in the earth. Music too is cranked out laboriously, churned from a street organ to accompany the leaden-footed dancing on the barge. In the city, the truest and most exiguously realistic music is noise, like the hooting, whistling sirens on the river with which *Tabarro* begins. Whereas Angelica's maternal love fulfills itself in sacrifice, here sexual love seeks its outlet in violence—Luigi's threat to carve Giorgetta's flesh with his knife, Michele's strangling embrace. Though they live in hell, these brutalized characters remember a paradise located in the suburbs. Luigi and Giorgetta sing rapturously of the sidewalks in Belleville. Pursuing that ideal place, the *Trittico* recedes in time, from contemporary Paris in *Tabarro* to the late seventeenth century in *Suor Angelica* to the year 1299 in *Gianni Schicchi*; and it retracts in space from the metropolis to a cloister to a medieval town glimpsed through an open window.

Tabarro makes do with the cheap tunes which are within the budget of its characters—the song about Mimi peddled on the riverbank, the "ron, ron, ron" of Frugola's cat. The music of *Suor Angelica* is the onomatopoeia of nature. It is a pastoral symphony, with piping birdcalls, heehawing donkeys, bleating lambs, tweaked strings to represent wasp bites, and the lilting giggles of the sisters as they gobble red currants. Angelica says that the Virgin anticipates desires and grants them before we can utter them. The theater has the same power to make dreams come true: dying, Angelica sees the figure of Christ held by the Madonna turn into her own baby. This is opera's claim to sacredness. Angelica understands that the penance forced on her by religion is mere hypocrisy, and herself appropriates the right of judgment. She damns her aunt for her callous silence; in *Gianni Schicchi* too the monks are greedy parasites from whom Buoso's property must be kept. Angelica, whose sin was love, wishes herself into paradise because her child calls her from there, and Schicchi in his spoken epilogue disputes Dante's relegation of him to hell and hands over the right of last judgment to the audience, which will pardon him with its applause.

The *Trittico* begins in reality, but it ends in the theater. *Gianni Schicchi* acknowledges that opera is a province of faked emotions. Buoso's relatives profess their sorrow to the sound of lachrymose falling seconds which soon become automatic; Zita marvels that they are able to produce real tears—but this is only after they read the will. Schicchi compliments them for acting better than strolling players. Yet beyond these pretenses lurks a magical power to transform life. The theater enables Schicchi to perform his own croaking death and ebullient resurrection. Soon his legacy will prompt a similar renaissance in Florence, for he is hailed in Rinuccio's aria as one of the new men who are changing the city; and when that cultural nativity happens, it will bring with it the rebirth of opera.

Puccini arrives at last in the realm of myth where opera belongs. In *Turandot* he sanctifies a monster—the woman who warps love into hate, attracting men because they know she will destroy them. The Chinese princess, given a music made of jagged icicles to sing, is less a character than a complex: a vagina dentata.

Turandot is a mental nocturne, a dream play of fantasy. Its atmosphere is defined by the moon, as fascinating here as it is in *Salome*. The moon negates the reasonable daylight of Apollo, that "sol" which is the classical source of music. Puccini's chorus addresses it as "testa mozza," a severed head in transit across the sky, and calls it bloodless, a pale lover of the dead, gleaming on graveyards. It is the negative of the sun, as power—

in the lunar tyranny of Turandot—is of love. Its blankness indeed suggests the illusion which is Turandot, who exists only in the haunted minds of men. Ping, Pang and Pong claim there is no such person, that she is only the void in which Calàf will be annihilated—or the vacancy in which he sexually spends himself. A patriarchal rule has failed. Timur is dethroned, the emperor Altoum is senescent. Turandot is enskied in their place as an absent, homicidal deity.

She is also the despotic artist, who creates in order to destroy: Puccini himself, who called his characters, in a letter to one of *Turandot's* librettists, "my puppet executioners." Her command of "Nessun dorma" is also his. No one must sleep in Peking because opera is about the noctambulism of desire. Liù is in haste to die before the break of day, for fantasy vampirishly flees from enlightenment; Timur tries to rouse her, saying that it's dawn and time to wake up, and then, realizing that she is dead, he decides to follow her into "la notte che non ha mattino." That dense "notte nera" is the shadow box of Puccini's cruel theater, sealed off from reality and reason. *Turandot* discloses what happens in Scarpia's invisible torture chamber, or behind the screen when Butterfly unsheathes her sword.

Calàf, who wins Turandot by solving her riddles, attempts to rationalize this psychic enigma and to overcome his terror. It is fear which makes a goddess of Turandot, and she calls his assault a sacrilege. Like Adriana ordering the profane ones away, Turandot shrills "Non profanarmi!" Puccini obeys, for he couldn't bring himself to humble his venomous goddess. He said that "these two almost supernatural beings descend through love to the level of mankind." That, certainly, is the delevitation planned by verismo. But Puccini died before he could compose the final duet in which Turandot was dragged to earth, and the opera had to be lamely completed by Alfano. The mystery remains inviolate.

NINE

Wagnerism and Strauss

WRITING what he called the music of the future, Wagner preempts that future. Everything after him risks seeming an unworthy epilogue. Like the myths they are, his operas are rewritten by his successors, who justify their own existence by extending or contradicting Wagner's meaning.

Opera first tries to recover from Wagner by composing a prologue to him, a fable whose innocence knows nothing as yet of Wagnerian lust and longing. This is Humperdinck's *Hänsel und Gretel* (1893), recognized by Wagner's son Siegfried as the most important opera since *Parsifal*. Humperdinck had actually written some of *Parsifal* himself, supplying a few extra bars (later cut) to cover one of the scene changes at Bayreuth; and he set the Grimm story to a medley of quotations from Wagner. The domestic chores of the children are introduced by the *Meistersinger* overture: Hänsel is making a broom and Gretel is knitting, both at home in Hans Sachs's world of handicrafts. The witch is an unhinged cackling Brünnhilde, riding a broomstick not a winged horse, and dawn comes to the forest with a reminiscence of the Norns from *Götterdämmerung*. In *Parsifal* a dove descends in blessing; Hänsel and Gretel are protected at night by fourteen angels in a charmed circle. Humperdinck weds the various Wagnerian mythologies—the singing artisans of *Meistersinger*, the elemental nature of the *Ring*, the religious revelations of *Parsifal*—and from them makes a fairy tale, where the gods are gruff parents and the monsters infantile bogeys. He has made Wagner fit for children, and writing about their games can pretend he exists before rather than after Wagner: the child is the father of the man.

In Debussy's *Pelléas et Mélisande* (1902), Golaud banishes the thought of sexual treachery by saying that his wife and his brother are children playing in the dark—"Quels enfants!" Again the effort is to anticipate Wagner, to prove his characters innocent of the aphrodisiac music he writes for them. Pelléas and Mélisande are Tristan and Isolde in embryo, apathetic, timorous, inarticulate. They make love in fragmentary whispers. When they embrace on their last night, the orchestra briefly foams up as it does in *Tristan*, only to be cautiously silenced; Pelléas is killed, and Mélisande flits off, gasping that she doesn't have the courage to stay. They understate their emotions and so does Debussy, mistrusting Wagnerian hyperbole. The reticence of his score, murmuring between the lines of Maeterlinck's prose, matches his tact and his compassion. He will not permit the self-dramatizing of Wagnerian tragedy: Tristan's curses, Brünnhilde's abuse of the gods. Arkel, the patriarch who corresponds to Gurnemanz in *Parsifal*, quietly sighs over the sadness one sees everywhere.

Golaud orders Yniold to speak more softly, and Arkel tells Golaud to lower his voice as Mélisande dies: the human soul is itself silent. Debussy's aim was to muffle the tumult of Wagner. When Mélisande says she loves Pelléas, he doesn't hear her and asks her to repeat it. The music is hushed so that it doesn't disturb the shy tremors of emotion or the repose of nature. At the fountain, Pelléas says the silence is so extraordinary one can almost hear the water sleeping.

Maeterlinck's play abounds in images of oppression. The characters live as if underground, and rarely see the sun or sky. When Golaud is thrown from his horse, the whole weight of the forest seems to sit on his chest. Yniold can't shift the boulder. For Debussy, that lowering, stifling obstacle is Wagner, whose orchestral textures—imitated in the interlude describing the journey of Pelléas and Golaud into the choking stagnant vaults of the castle—are so heavy, thick and leaden. "Ah! je respire enfin!" cries Pelléas when he surfaces on the terrace, climbing into the air up the brightening ladder of a musical scale. Debussy too can only breathe musically if he lightens or alleviates Wagner.

He does so by liquefying the clotted symphonic style. This suits the wateriness of Maeterlinck's images. The impressionists immersed objects to wash away their hard contours. Debussy wrote a piano prelude about a flooded cathedral, Lalo an opera (*Le Roi d'Ys*) about a drowned city. Mélisande threatens to throw herself in the water when Golaud approaches her, and later drops his ring in the pool; her love, says Pelléas, is a hot iron which breaks ice. Debussy's lyricism has the same liquidity. Wagnerian melody, confined to static formulae and motifs which worked like calling cards, could never respond to what Debussy called "the mobile quality of souls and of life." Debussy's characters rely on half-made admissions and incomplete gestures, and he writes for them a music which respects the hesitations of their prose and—in the interludes—wanders and wavers, drifting with plaintive uncertainty rather than treading solemnly toward its destination like the processional scene-changes in *Parsifal*. Inconclusiveness is Debussy's rebuke to Wagner: why should he have presumed that his own music was a terminus to the art? It is also a clue to the resigned sorrow in *Pelléas*. The opera ends with the arrival of a child, who must now follow the dead Mélisande's path through the woes of the nowhere which is Allemonde. Life continues, as it is never allowed to do by Wagner's apocalyptic climaxes.

Debussy said that his procedure in *Pelléas*, "which consists in dispensing with Wagner, owes nothing to him." But since *Pelléas* is the denial of Wagner, it owes everything to him: it couldn't exist if he hadn't been there to reject. "We must look forward from Wagner and not back to Wagner," Debussy declared. Yet the way forward is opened by a retraversal of opera's history, and Wagner seems to have written the works which precede him as well as those which come after.

This is the case with Gabriel Fauré's *Pénélope* (1913), which couples Homeric legend and Wagnerian myth. Remote from the astute worldly Penelope who in Monteverdi's *Ritorno d'Ulisse* is one of opera's first heroines, Fauré's Pénélope is a mystical Isolde, who draws Ulysse back to her by ecstatically envisioning and invoking him. She is in fact a Wagnerian musician, for the tapestry she weaves by day and unplaits by night to deceive the suitors is the orchestral fabric. She speaks of her skill in twining threads together as if it were contrapuntal: "je suis habile à joindre les fils." The shroud she embroiders is polyphonically dense, thematically knotted. When she unveils it, a mystifying chord spreads through the orchestra. Her chromatic plaiting is imitated by the stealthy metamorphoses of Fauré's score when she describes the disguises of the Uranian gods; it also supplies the opera with its obscuring atmosphere. Eumée speaks of dusk as a violet mantle draped over the mountains, and the beggar remembers the double-thick cloak of purple wool worn by Ulysse. The characters wear this musical web like a garment. It envelops them: Ulysse says he must remain within it if he is to relieve Pénélope—"que le mystère m'enveloppe"—and in her soothsaying outcry she sees the suitors "enveloppés de nuit," by which she means extinguished.

Fauré called *Pénélope* not an opera but a "poème lyrique." The heroine refuses to take part in a drama. Intent on her dream, she ignores the persuasions of Antinoüs; her thoughts are in and of the music. Wagner's successors free his characters from the petty intrigues of opera, and transfer them to the illimitable theater of symphony. Orchestral song-cycles like Mahler's *Das Lied von der Erde* (1909) and Schönberg's *Gurre-Lieder* (composed between 1900 and 1911) universalize Wagner by releasing the dramas into nature—Mahler's flowering earth, Schönberg's resurgent sunrise.

Mahler's soloists in *Das Lied von der Erde* are not the anonymous sermonizers of oratorio. The tenor might be the young Siegfried, ardent, ingenuous, drunk with joy. The mezzo-soprano could be the maternal earth itself: Wagner's Erda. The man sings of a reckless lust for life; the woman intervenes, like Brünnhilde in the immolation, to inter him and to preside over the regeneration of nature. At the end of the love duet, Isolde's climaxes break like waves on the word "ewig," as she wills this pleasure to go on forever. That word, emitted by Isolde as an almost orgasmic scream, is given by Mahler to the mezzo-soprano, who intones it softly again and again in a lower register during her fading farewell. Once more the purpose is to demonstrate that there is life after Wagner. Isolde sings of annihilation; Mahler's woman smilingly venerates the world even though she will soon no longer exist in it.

The *Gurre-Lieder*, based on poems by a Danish botanist, also converts Tristan and Isolde to a new religion of pantheism. The work begins with a duet between Waldemar and his Tove, as erotically fatal and as orchestrally flushed as that in Wagner. She sings of drinking death gladly, exterminated by a kiss; they enjoy an idyll more prolonged and sated than Wagner's characters. When Tove is killed, Waldemar curses the god who has deprived him of her. In expiation, he is made to ride at night across the sky with a ghoulish pack of vassals (more uncouthly riotous than Hagen's in *Götterdämmerung*), seeking the woman he will never find. His punishment is that of Wagner's Dutchman. But he is released from it, and not by the sacrifice of a Senta who chooses to share his damnation: he discovers Tove's visage in nature, and his tragedy is absorbed into the revelry of earth. The twilight of love and the midnight of superstitious hauntings are vanquished, in the final chorus, by dawn.

Schönberg allows the minor characters, slighted by Wagner, to pronounce a verdict on his Tristan and Isolde. The role of Brangäne passes to a wood-dove with the voice of a mezzo-soprano, who describes Tove's funeral. Brangäne is ignored by Isolde during the liebestod. Here, given wings, she observes the tragedy from on high, then flies away from it. Waldemar's grisly carousings disturb Klaus the fool, who chatters about his master's violence, and cause a peasant to recite Aves in self-defense: these commentators might be the shepherd in Wagner's Kareol, sent to keep watch for Isolde's ship but excluded from the drama because, as Kurwenal says, he could never understand it. The bird or the bucolic simpletons measure Schönberg's detachment from the Wagnerian frenzy. The last of his characters has even escaped from the compulsiveness and strain of operatic song. This is a Speaker, who recites the melodrama about the summer wind; he passes beyond Waldemar's complaint and wonders at the inexhaustible energy of nature. During the decade he spent on the Gurre-Lieder, Schönberg, like his characters, outgrew Wagner. After Tove's death, he writes a new music—skeletal for the night ride, with rattled chains and a chiming xylophone; frisky and shrill as the wind for the Speaker's monologue, with wisps of Tove's themes fluttering through it, since the woman is now an evanescent bloom on the landscape.

Tove is Schönberg's voluptuously romantic Isolde. His monodrama Erwartung (composed in 1909) diagnoses a more modern version of the character: a jealous neurotic, who has probably killed her Tristan. The title of the work means expectancy; its nameless heroine stumbles through a nocturnal thicket searching for her lover, and finds his corpse. She rages at the cadaver and—in a psychotic variation on Isolde's address to the dead Tristan—kicks it. She wants to bring the man back to life so she can punish him further for his infidelity to her. In the center of the opera, she musically quotes another Wagner heroine. Her cry for help, "Hilfe!", when she first prods the body to rouse it, copies Kundry's octave drop as she describes to Parsifal her derision of the crucified Christ. The superimposition of Isolde and Kundry suits Schönberg's analytic purpose: the lover from the first opera has sickened into the guilty witch of the second. The music of Erwartung passes beyond Wagner's lyric modulations to the clamor of expressionism, directly translating the woman's shocks and emotional schisms into sound. She can't see in the darkness; the landscape is pictured by the orchestra with its rustlings, screeches and flickerings of light. The tone painting at the same time sketches internal symptoms—the music shudders when her foot touches the body, whirs to wind up her nerves, and bangs in time with her thumping heartbeat.

Isolde here collapses into atonality and derangement. Wagner's hero suffers a similar crisis in Hans Werner Henze's *Tristan* (1974). Henze calls the work "preludes for piano, electronic sounds and orchestra," though it is also a disenchanted postlude to the opera. Isolde is present only as synthesized noise, in a computer analysis of a high note sung by a famous interpreter of the part. The orchestra lushly alludes to Wagner's harmonies, but the piano clatters in panic and the tapes blare to shout down all man-made music. Tristan's delirium is Henze's political nightmare: composition of the work coincided with the assassination of Allende and his supporters in Chile, and "the beginning of the darkest reign of terror that now exists in the world"; the electronic hubbub is the assault of a vicious reality, stamping out romantic reverie. A century after Wagner, Tristan's concern is not sexual frustration but the failure of revolution.

The young Strauss believed himself to be Wagner's heir, the legitimate Richard II. The hero of his early opera *Feuersnot* (1901) berates the citizens of Munich for their hostility to Meister Reichhardt, by whom he means Wagner. Later, Strauss had more mixed feelings. Was he merely Wagner's invention, a parasite on the past? His uneasiness is characteristic of opera as it develops through the twentieth century: the art turns retrospective, engaged in revising or parodying its own tradition.

Strauss's suspicion that he had been preempted by Wagner, reduced to a parodist, is already evident in *Salome* (1905). Once Wilde's play has been set to music, it acquires meanings the dramatist could never have foreseen; it becomes a parable about the composer's relegation to the aftermath of musical history. The decapitation of Jokanaan—John the Baptist, who announced the coming of Christ—has an unexpected relevance to Wagner. Parsifal's first action, once anointed by Gurnemanz, is to baptise Kundry with water from the spring, telling her to believe in the redeemer. He is a latter-day installment of the Christ predicted by Jokanaan. By confining the prophet to a cistern and then executing him, Strauss is destroying a Wagnerian myth, rejecting his own redeemer.

The theological disputes in Herod's court, laughable to Wilde, comment on this Straussian sacrilege. Herod believes Jokanaan has seen God; one of the Jews says no man since Elias has had that privilege, while another doubts even the claims of Elias. A Nazarene declares that the Messiah has arrived; a Jew denies it. These quarrels provoke the most technically adventurous and comically adroit sections in the score, because they disrespectfully deal with Strauss's own uncertainty: is he an artist with a divine mission like Wagner, writing music of and for the future, or only a skilled pretender? Herod is alarmed when told that Jesus raises the dead, and fatuously commands that he shouldn't do so. His absurd fear is also Strauss's—it would be terrible if the dead came back, because the past would then arraign the meager present. The return of Wagner would mean the elimination of Strauss.

The scandal of *Salome* is less its corruption of Christianity than its joky disgracing of Wagner. Salome is Strauss's perverse adolescent Isolde, the address to the severed head her pathological liebestod. Isolde's singing restores life to Tristan; Salome nastily gloats that she is still alive while he is dead, and she can throw away this portion of him—if she wishes—for the birds to peck. Isolde dies of her own accord, painlessly exceeding the limits of mortal nature; Salome has to be killed on Herod's orders, crushed beneath the shields of the soldiers in the last wrenching bars of the score.

Strauss's next opera, *Elektra* (1909), contains his abridged, distracted Brünnhilde, ferociously cavorting in three-four time. In a hundred minutes, Elektra careens through the different phases of her predecessor's life in the *Ring*. Mourning her father, whose conscience she is, she recalls the faithful filial Brünnhilde of *Die Walküre*. The war maiden recruited dead heroes for the defense of Walhall, and Elektra too scavenges among corpses. Orest's arrival, softening her, allows her to experience the relief of the awakened Brünnhilde in *Siegfried*. Her scolding and spitefulness belong to the bloodthirsty Brünnhilde of *Götterdämmerung*, though she ends in insane glee, not the all-knowing calm of the immolation.

Hofmannsthal's adaptation of Sophocles in *Elektra* confirms Nietzsche's theory. The rebirth of tragedy means the invention of opera. The Greek characters shed blood in accordance with moral law: Electra put to rights the crime against biological and social order committed by Clytemnestra when she slew Agamemnon; Clytemnestra in her turn was avenging Agamemnon's sacrifice of their daughter Iphigenia. Orestes, who killed his mother as Electra urged, was afterward harried by the Furies until—in the trilogy by Aeschylus—the blood feud yielded to the justice of the Athenian state. No such dynastic history of penalty and expiation survives in Hofmannsthal. His Elektra is a madly isolated Dionysian woman, imagining carnage. In the operas which Gluck modeled on Greek tragedy, the protagonists still served the community. Iphigénie agrees to die to purchase a wind for the fleet, Alceste will happily do likewise to save the king who is her husband. Hofmannsthal ignores these social imperatives. The Greek chorus expressed the general will and argued for a moral norm. In Hofmannsthal's *Elektra* the only chorus is the gaggle of shrewish maids, or the offstage voices which come in any case from inside Elektra.

Music completes the transformation: the score is the sound of hysteria. The shrieking Elektra, the wailing Chrysothemis and the moaning Klytämnestra are a tribe of Bacchantes. Strauss's orchestra accompanies the massacre which was the instigation of tragedy, called a goat song because goats were slain at the altar of Dionysus. Elektra's first monologue enumerates the funeral offerings to Agamemnon: she will kill his horses and hounds, she says, and Strauss makes them neigh or bark in elated agreement, like Grane riding into the fire in *Götterdämmerung*. Klytämnestra rounds up a herd of lowing beasts for the sacrifice, and they are whipped along protesting in the orchestral prelude to her appearance. From animals, Elektra advances to human victims. The violence in Greek tragedy happened elsewhere, and was reported after the event; it didn't need to be seen, because it was the impersonal administering of justice. Elektra has none of this forbearance: the violence must be anticipated in fantasy, obscenely applauded when she calls for Orest to strike again, and made vivid by the music with its gushers of blood and croaking death-rattles.

The opera is a psychiatric tragedy. The Greeks of Nietzsche have been redefined by Freud. For Nietzsche they were children of nature; Freud saw them as emotional casualties, whose myths dramatized human neurosis. The Greeks give names to the complexes which fester in the human family, and to the outlawed instincts which are the subject of opera: Medea the mother who kills her sons, Agamemnon the father who kills his daughter, Orestes the son who kills his mother, Oedipus the son who kills his father and marries his mother. The Elektra of Strauss and Hofmannsthal is a female Oedipus. An excessive love for her father drives her to wish for the death of the mother who is her rival; in addition she tries to seduce her sister, and conceals her spoiled body from her brother. She even sets herself up as a Freudian diagnostician, inviting Klytämnestra to relax while her bad dreams are analyzed and then cured with the ax.

Elektra returns to the Greek tragedy which Nietzsche believed to be Wagner's source, and composes a sequel pressing Wagner toward derangement and disintegration. After this, Strauss relied on Mozartean comedy as an antidote to Wagner. The collaboration with Hofmannsthal on *Der Rosenkavalier* (1911) was planned as their version of *Le Nozze di Figaro*. The setting is the Vienna of Maria Theresa, whose reign ended in 1780: the rococo eighteenth century, as a refuge from both the primitivism and the modernity of *Elektra*. The Marschallin is modeled on Mozart's Countess. In the third of his plays about Figaro, *La Mère Coupable*, Beaumarchais embroiled her in a love affair with the page Chérubin; this role is played in *Rosenkavalier* by Oktavian, written like Mozart's Cherubino for a mezzo-soprano in travesty.

Still Strauss cannot keep Wagner out of his gracious eighteenth century. The orchestra is that of *Tristan*, tumescently supporting Oktavian's lovemaking with its horns. Puzzling over "du und ich," the pronouns which are the captions to an indescribable love, Oktavian attempts to solve the conundrum Tristan and Isolde discuss when they question the "und" between their names. From one point of view, the erotic intrigue follows that of *Figaro*; from another, it copies *Tristan*. Oktavian comes to Sophie as a deputy for her elder suitor Ochs, as Tristan wooed Isolde for Marke. Like Tristan, he betrays his commission by claiming the bride for himself. Or perhaps the role of Isolde belongs to the Marschallin. Though she dreads decay, she doesn't have to die; she has learned the art and the guile of survival, gently surrendering Oktavian and turning her mind—no doubt—to a replacement. This is *Tristan und Isolde* with a happy ending.

Strauss experimented with the same compromise between Wagner's opposites of love and death in *Die Ägyptische Helena* (1928). Magic saves Helena from a tragic retribution. Isolde calls in vain for a storm to wreck Tristan's ship and drown them both; the enchantress Aithra actually whips up a storm to divert Menelas and prevent him from killing Helena. Then, like Brangäne mixing the potions, Aithra serves Menelas a brew of lotus juice to sedate his memory, so he forgets his wife's adultery. A servant muddles up the drinks and gives Helena another phial which reverses this amnesia. For these characters, fickly living down their sordid pasts, to remember is the fate worse than death.

The Marschallin understands the wisdom of looking neither back nor forward. She dismays Oktavian when she recalls an earlier scare caused by her husband's unexpected arrival home; she prefers not to think about the tomorrow when her lover will leave her. Her predicament is Strauss's. She feels prematurely old just as he senses that he has been made obsolete by Wagner. Though she learns a final resignation to time, exiting with a weary "Ja, ja," Strauss refuses to be so stoical about his predestined place in musical history. He seizes for himself the freedom of anachronism, inhabiting all periods of the past at once.

Thus *Rosenkavalier* overlays three different eras. First is the eighteenth century—or rather a pair of eighteenth centuries, the elegant culture of Mozart and the venal society of Hogarth's satiric etchings, which suggested to Hofmannsthal the crowd of touts at the Marschallin's levee (and later provoked Stravinsky's *Rake's Progress*).

After the ornate Vienna of Maria Theresa comes the second of the opera's strata: the bourgeois city of the nineteenth century, set to music by the waltzing Strausses. The waltz is the most impudent anachronism in *Rosenkavalier*, because it postdates by almost a hundred years the period in which the work takes place. Its swaying lilt enables the characters to glide out of their problems. Alfred introduces one of the waltzes in *Die Fledermaus* with some lines which sum up the easygoing morality of the dance: "Glücklich ist, wer vergisst, was doch nicht zu ändern ist—trink mit mir, sing mit mir"; better forget what can't be altered. The Marschallin falls into waltz time as she slithers around obstacles, for instance when she tells Oktavian to disguise himself by dressing as her maid. The waltz is an anodyne version of Wagner's musical intoxication, and it pervades the society of *Rosenkavalier* like an addictive eroticism. Wagner himself called the first Strauss waltzes he heard in Vienna in 1832 "a more powerful drug than alcohol," and described the dancers as Bacchantes: "this demon . . . shook like a Pythian priestess on the tripod, and raised veritable groans of ecstasy."

On top of the eighteenth and nineteenth centuries is the Vienna of Strauss's own time. *Rosenkavalier* lurches into modernity at moments of farcical abandon. Oktavian jaggedly fractures melody when singing Mariandel's off-key responses at the inn; the prelude to the third act, mapping the underworld of bogeys and freaks with which the room is mined, is a nocturne as gruesomely discordant as that of *Erwartung*.

Strauss tries to outwit history by being Mozart and Wagner at once. The Composer in *Ariadne auf Naxos* (1916) is as fanatical as Wagner, and has written an opera in homage to the Nietzschean begetter of opera, Dionysus; he is also another replica of Cherubino, who tries out his "canzonetta" in the second act of *Figaro*. *Die Frau ohne Schatten* (1919) began as Strauss's *Zauberflöte*, an ingenuous fairy tale, but ended as something more like his *Ring*, a top-heavy treatise on cosmic biology. This opera continues the continuation of *Zauberflöte* Goethe had written in 1795. The subject of Goethe's sequel, and that of *Die Frau*, is continuity: the extension of human life through childbearing. Goethe doesn't believe that the quest terminates where Mozart left it. Tamino and Pamina have a child, but lose it and must set out in search of it; Papageno and Papagena are denied children at first, and must prove themselves worthy of parenthood. Hofmannsthal's characters match Mozart's twin pairs: the Emperor and Empress are infertile because too loftily inhuman; the dyer Barak is denied offspring because his wife is disgusted by natural functions and the servitude of the body. But the moral extends beyond these Mozartean couples into an evolutionary fable like Wagner's. In the *Ring*, the world's salvation lay in love. In *Die Frau ohne Schatten*, it can be replenished and saved only by procreation.

Strauss originally planned the work for two separate bands. The transparent chamber ensemble of the extraterrestrial episodes was to alternate with a murkier orchestra expanded to incorporate riotous human emotions. Starry Mozartean radiance would be shouted down by the Wagnerian noise of mankind. This indeed is what happens between the first and second scenes: the Empress, who sings like a bird in remembering her prehuman incarnations, quits her aviary in the sky and alights in the din of Barak's house, where the brothers yelp and squeak. For Hofmannsthal the fable was about the development of humanity; for Strauss it recited the history of opera—Mozart falls to earth and is brutally deafened by Wagner.

That history is summarized in *Ariadne*. In his orchestral suite for Moliére's *Le Bourgeois Gentilhomme*, intended as a pendant to *Ariadne*, Strauss included a pastiche of a minuet by Lully, the first French composer of opera. Yet when Bacchus reaches Naxos, the seventeenth century hastily arrives in the nineteenth, and baroque stateliness changes to Wagnerian fervor. *Ariadne* foresees as well the future shame of opera, that "culinary" music which chokes the glutton in *Mahagonny*. Strauss's accompaniment to the Molière play included a section of "Tafelmusik" to ease the digestion of M. Jourdain's guests, and a dance for his cooks; his most famous ballet is named after Viennese whipped cream, *Schlagobers*. The Composer in *Ariadne* is furious that his opera is being used as after-dinner entertainment.

Bacchus here hardly justifies Nietzsche's nomination of him as the founder of the form: the prologue exposes him as a preening, brainless tenor. He is compromised further by the way *Ariadne* superimposes Wagnerian legend and Greek myth. Bacchus has the voice of Siegfried, but does his deliverance of Ariadne correspond to the awakening of Brünnhilde in *Siegfried*, or her ravishment by the hero in the guise of Gunther in *Götterdämmerung*? The second incident in the *Ring* parodies the first: a delighted recall to life is followed by a casual rape. Like Brünnhilde in *Götterdämmerung*, who expects Siegfried but is greeted by the stranger in the Tarnhelm, Ariadne mistakes Bacchus's identity. She expects Hermes, hails him as Theseus, and is never quite clear who he is. She imagines he will help her to die, yet he introduces her to a very different kind of dying. The Wagnerian precedent undermines Strauss's version of it: the new, young god—as Zerbinetta calls Bacchus—is an impostor. Both scenes in the *Ring* are about the forfeiting of divinity. Siegfried reduces the impregnable Valkyrie to a woman when he woos her, then insults her by treating her as sexual booty. Strauss's characters pretend to a godliness which Wagner has already revoked.

Strauss again attempts to create a god worthy to be opera's patron in a later mythological work, *Daphne* (1938), his footnote to the earliest Florentine opera, Peri's *Dafne*. Once more he combines Grecian and German mythologies: the opera's setting is the foothills of Olympus, but the heaven from which Daphne's father Peneios has descended is—to judge by his Wotanlike somberness—more likely Walhall, and her earth-mother Gaea is a booming Erda. The opera's occasion is the feast of Dionysus; the shepherds sing a drowsy glutted hymn to him and waltz in a costume of pelts, masked as rams. Though his voice wordlessly sounds in the alphorn, he never materializes. His place is usurped by his brother Apollo. The sun-god here is no Monteverdian luminary. As irrational and vindictive as Dionysus, he slays the flute-playing Leukippos who challenges his right to Daphne. The immortalizing of the musician is only a repentant afterthought: Apollo imagines he can make it up to Leukippos by sending him to Olympus to play for Zeus. Daphne, metamorphosing into the laurel tree which sings as the wind ruffles its leaves, is saved by the camouflage of nature: she has no need of the destructive god.

Hofmannsthal explained to Strauss that *Ariadne* was about the encounter of spiritual and material worlds, "brought together: in noncomprehension." Those worlds are represented by the suffering Ariadne and the coquettish Zerbinetta; their different realms might also be those of words and music, the paired constituents of opera which can no longer understand each other. The poet's words are "recht gute" as the Composer admits, but they are too rational and referential. Music elides them with its mellifluous nonsense, in the Composer's pensive "Tra la la la," the chirpy "Ai! ai!" of the comedians, Echo's birdlike mimicry of Ariadne, or the sequinned coloratura of Zerbinetta's tirade. The two theatrical camps which are ordered to perform simultaneously—the pompous opera seria troupe and the improvising vaudevillians—dramatize the tensions within the partnership of Strauss and Hofmannsthal, and within the unstable compound of music drama. Hofmannsthal admired Ariadne's fidelity and disparaged Zerbinetta as "earth-bound." Strauss, on the contrary, called Zerbinetta his favorite character: she is the genius of the theater, a libertine like Carmen and Don Giovanni who makes herself and her play up from moment to moment. Maybe the introverted Composer is Hofmannsthal the poet, while Zerbinetta is the heedless sensuality of Strauss's music; on Naxos, perhaps Hofmannsthal plays the reclusive, disdainful Ariadne, roused by the boisterous passion of Strauss's Bacchus. Either way, opera has come to seem a rebarbative coupling of opposites.

The caprice in Strauss's last opera, *Capriccio* (1942), is this problematic hybrid of opera, debated in a château near Paris soon after Gluck's reforms. The poet and the musician argue over the prior claims of their separate arts; the Countess proposes the truce of an opera, where each art will find its completion in the other. Since both men are in love with her, they concur in serving her as the muse who harmonizes their combined labor. Yet the dialectic is not so inevitable as it was when Nietzsche united Apollonian language with Dionysian melody. The Countess merely arranges a temporary peace, and herself can't decide between words and music. The stage director La Roche believes that both words and music exist to show off his spectacular productions, and the prompter, wriggling out of his burrow, declares that he is omnipotent in performance. Meanwhile the Italian singers hired for the day trill empty-headedly, gobble cake, and quarrel about their fees. Strauss's orchestra ranges versatilely through musical history, and imitates Couperin, Rameau and Gluck; it waves away his own previous operas, in brief quotations from *Ariadne* and *Daphne* when these subjects are proposed and rejected. They have been done already, says the musician. Everything has been done already. For Strauss, opera ends in a museum of tenderly affectionate, regretful parody.

TEN

Past and Present

FOR STRAUSS, opera's destination was the museum. For Bartók, it ends in a mausoleum: the black theater of fantasy where he set *Bluebeard's Castle* (1918). The castle is a sanctuary of operatic secrets. Its bolted doors, pressed by Judith's curiosity, open onto a musical imagery which discloses the guilty mysteries of opera.

The first door reveals instruments of torture, the second an armory. There is gore on everything: opera is synonymous with bloodshed and erotic violence; its arena is Scarpia's hidden back room. Behind the third door is a stockpile of gold and gems: Fafner's hoard in *Siegfried*, supplemented by the jewels which tempt Marguerite in *Faust*, Giulietta in *Les Contes d'Hoffmann*, and the Dyer's Wife in *Die Frau ohne Schatten*. The fourth door conceals a garden of trilling birdcalls, a paradise omnipresent in opera from Monteverdi's Arcadia to Walther's suburban Eden in *Die Meister-singer* or the summertime of Gershwin's Catfish Row. The fifth door opens with a triple forte blast of C major and an organ volley. Its vista is that of annexed territory, the ambit of Bluebeard's reign; opera indulges the conquistadorial man of power—Monteverdi's Nerone and Handel's Cesare, Vasco, Enée and Siegfried. The sixth door unlocks a lake of coldly rippling tears. Opera's emotional reservoir is fed by Charlotte's lachrymose aria in *Werther*, by Desdemona's first tears, wept as Otello spurns her, or by the distraught Elsa, when Lohengrin leads her to the minster to shed her tears in joy. Beyond the seventh door, which is the last, is the infirmary of opera's victims. Judith sees there the specters of Bluebeard's wives, whom she joins in the darkness. The company includes Don Giovanni's innumerable discarded women and Carmen's used-up men, Puccini's butterflies pinned to their boards and Wagner's self-sacrificing saviors. All operatic experience coexists in Bluebeard's lair.

Bartók has summed up the psychopathic fixations of the form. Throughout the twentieth century, opera adheres to a past which it rewrites but can never reject. The dramatic missions of music stay the same. In *Jenůfa* or *Wozzeck* it lends a voice to those who are without words; in *The Cunning Little Vixen* or *L'Enfant et les Sortilèges* it is nature's self-expression, feebly imitated by men. In *Dialogues des Carmélites* music is the sound of a sweet reasonableness, tempering the noise of revolution; in *Mahagonny* it is an idle distraction that revolution must silence. In *The Turn of the Screw* or *Death in Venice* it is the truant prompting of the senses, in *Lulu* an inescapable judicial fate: a trap of punishing repetition. Orpheus still presides, though under duress—confined to a madhouse by Stravinsky in *The Rake's Progress*, dismembered again by the Bacchantes in Harrison Birtwistle's *The Mask of Orpheus*.

Though opera began at court, Monteverdi's fable of Orpheus bestowed it on the shepherds. In *Jenůfa* (1904), Janáček renews the myth by treating music as the homemade consolation of the folk. The comfort is less facile than it was in the singing, dancing society of Smetana's *The Bartered Bride*. There the exuberance of music matched the reliable cycles of nature, always rebounding. In *Jenůfa* the repetitiousness is that of unremitting labor—the circles of the millwheel, which supply the opera's first motif, or Laca's whittling and Jenůfa's potato peeling; the proverbial repetitions of her grandmother, or Kostelnička's fear that history will go on helplessly repeating itself, with Jenůfa's ill-considered marriage duplicating her own mistake. The grandmother starts an ensemble with a moral tag about getting over your troubles. Everyone joins in, and the rhythm is that of the doleful churning mill: these people are themselves being ground down. The nervous chatter of the xylophone suggests the mechanical dictation to which they are subjected. Though the second act happens away from the mill, the sawing of the strings and the regular thud of the timpani turn the regime of numbing work into a mental torment: the purgatory Jenůfa and her foster mother share. The third act returns to the industrious mill, whose wheel now pedals more unevenly and dizzily in the orchestra, to hint that the jollity of the wedding is as effortful as the toil in the earlier scene.

Used without respect, music is a trivial palliative. Števa bombards the band with money and orders Jenůfa's favorite song to appease her anger. The dance is interrupted by Kostelnička, for whom music is a waste of time. Jenůfa's own strict moral economy persuades her to do without music at her wedding, to spare expense; the chirpy Karolka thinks it a very niggardly show. Jenůfa can't be content with a tuneful absentmindedness like Števa's. Her baby also keeps its emotions to itself, and hasn't cried in the eight days since its birth. This vocal frugality matches Jenůfa's reticence. Her music must be articulate, aware of and responsible to human distresses and vexations: hence her achievement in teaching the shepherd boy to read.

Song is an offering of love to soothe a fraught child, like the lullaby for Jenůfa's baby; it is the recourse of the infant in us all, wailing for help or pardon, and in the matriarchal society of the opera everyone shares this need. Jenůfa prays to the mother of God on her child's account, and is comforted by Kostelnička who killed him; later she comforts Kostelnička for having committed the crime, as she comforts Laca for having slashed her face. Every son scars his mother, and Laca is himself Jenůfa's abject, grateful son. The music we make when crying in the night provides the opera with its simplest and most morally beautiful moment: the intersection of Kostelnička's scream of distress as Števa abandons Jenůfa with Jenůfa's call as she wakes in her room and calls for her mother; the sounds, both made by lost and traumatized creatures, are two prayers which cross in transit.

By the end, the music which paced exhaustingly on the treadmill has regained its old power of emotional release and sublimation. A fount of C major is unleashed in the orchestra by Jenůfa's loving mercy; it ushers out Kostelnička and sweeps Jenůfa toward Laca. Music can once more effect absolution. That it does too, though more starkly, for the harried wretches of Berg's *Wozzeck* (1925), first in the iterated B natural which swells from a mumbled growl to an unbearably insistent shriek after Marie's murder, then in the orchestral inquest on the drowned Wozzeck with its angry pity and its harmonic mourning.

Schönberg warned Berg that Büchner's fragmentary play about the muddled soldier who kills his whorish mistress was "forbidding to music"—too terse in its language, never emotionally expansive. For Berg, however, music pervades it. Though Wozzeck stumbles over words, he hears a song of restitution in the air. One day the poor will be thunder makers, he tells the Captain, and he sees the fiery sun setting over the fields as a sound of apocalyptic trumpets. Music rumbles up from underground, from the perturbations of an untuned unconsciousness, when Berg transcribes the chorus of snorers in Wozzeck's barracks: an eructating, abysmal lyricism, like the night noises of the wood in Britten's *A Midsummer Night's Dream*. Music is also an opiate for Berg's people, socially dispensed. Marie pacifies her child with a lullaby, Andres sings hunting refrains which are cracked remnants of those in *Der Freischütz* or picks at his guitar, the customers at the tavern whirl in giddy forgetful dances.

In *Jenůfa* music measures the routine of the mill's rotation; in *Wozzeck* its social law is that of regimentation, beating out a martial discipline. Wozzeck's three tormentors are musical timekeepers. The Captain complains when Wozzeck, shaving him, doesn't keep to the agreed tempo. Speed terrifies him, because it means a premature arrival at the end of everything; as he sings, he whiningly decelerates life. The Doctor on the contrary enjoys the speed with which bodies mature to their putrefaction, and in conducting time accelerates it. He is exhilarated by the punctuality of a cancer, which will finish off his patient within four weeks of diagnosis. He monitors the internal metronome of his vital signs—his pulse, he announces, is steady at its usual sixty; Wozzeck's is arhythmic. Wozzeck's other nemesis, the Drum Major, is named after his strutting regularity. Marie, before she succumbs, demands a demonstration by getting him to march a few paces for her. Taunting Wozzeck, the Doctor hums to keep up the punitive unsparing rhythm and thwacks the air with his stick as if it were the Drum Major's staff, or a musical baton. Wozzeck is always scuttling about on his errands, and never has time for anything. He no sooner arrives at Marie's hovel than he has to leave for the barracks; he urinates in transit in the street. Yet he experiences this perpetual, mechanized motion as a limbo of inactivity. At the dance he says to Andres, "Die Zeit wird Einem lang bei der Kurzweile": these pastimes just prolong time, and lengthen his suffering.

Berg's abstract musical forms dramatize the plight of Wozzeck, who like a convict is serving time. The three chords of the second scene obsessively recur, sliding through tonal metamorphoses until they taint all Wozzeck's thoughts and engulf the world. The Doctor propounds his thesis over a passacaglia, which grinds out the fixed idea in twenty-one variations. This is rationality elaborated to the point of madness; the Doctor thinks he has proved the human animal's freedom by automating Wozzeck. The second act is a symphony in five movements: the musical plan has the remorseless predestination of tragedy. Opera always ritualizes life;

here, symphony is the dialectic of destruction. After this, in the third act, Berg accepts Schönberg's sense of limitation by almost forbidding music to himself. Each scene is an exiguous invention on a single particle—a theme, a tone, a rhythm, a chord, a quaver. From this musical meagerness, the drama of the episodes grows. The theme corresponds to Marie's meditation on the thematic biblical text, the tone to the mirage of nocturnal illusion before Wozzeck kills her, the rhythm to the manic polka he dances in his crazed, lethal gaiety, the chord to the disordered chiming inside his head, the quaver to the hopping game the child won't interrupt when told that his mother is dead. The more straitened the musical means, the greater the dramatic force.

The rigor of Berg's plan enforces the social stricture closing in on Wozzeck. At the midpoint of *Lulu* (1937), Berg ordered that a film should narrate the trial, imprisonment and rescue of the heroine: music unrolls at the fixed speed of film, permitting the individual no variable liberty. Meanwhile Shostakovitch in *Lady Macbeth of Mtsensk* (1934) uses music to confound the dictatorship of society, which eliminates Wozzeck and Lulu. His score, condemned at first as a lewd, rowdy "pornophony," is the uprising of hilarious instinct against repressive morality.

Katerina, the local Lady Macbeth who feeds her father-in-law rat poison and applauds her lover's murder of her husband, is another of opera's holy sinners, heroic in her blatancy and insolence. No social or theological law can presume to hold her down. The police are venal oafs, a retinue of Keystone Kops who howl in horror when they catch a socialist; the priest pronounces a rollicking requiem over Katerina's first victim, and is drunkenly salacious at her wedding. Her glory, in an operatic tradition which extends back to Poppea, is erotic sacrilege. She wants to couple so furiously with Sergei that the icons will jump from their shelves. When she first does so, the orchestra makes enough din to shake the house: a banging riot, concluded with some postcoital farts of deflation on the horns. A scruffy peasant, who stumbles on one of the corpses when stealing vodka, celebrates the hiccuping Dionysia of the drama in a scherzo which says that "singing is fine when there's something to drink." Shostakovitch takes ribald pleasure in extorting noise from his characters—the yelps of Aksinya tormented by the servants, the screeching of Katerina who clambers down the drainpipe to save Sergei, the roar of pretended regret required from the laborers when their master goes away. Boris won't forgive Sergei because he doesn't cry out when he's being whipped.

Shostakovitch writes a music which is literally surreal, sounding from the dank cavernous underground which society flimsily boards up. The orchestra pit is the cellar where the stinking body of Boris has been discarded. Claudel beautifully called the operatic orchestra a "floor that breathes"; but in Shostakovitch that floor shudders and cleaves in an earthquake. This is why he was interested in the Gogol story which he made the subject of his first opera, *The Nose* (1930). Gogol's fable about a civil servant who mislays his schnozzle is a diabolical jest, confessing sexual terrors and the precariousness of a personal identity which can be canceled if one organ goes missing. The percussive fury of Shostakovitch inflates Gogol's bad dream into an exhilarating delirium. The winds squeak, the brass brays or snorts in nasal derision, the singers yell high Ds and Es. The story is Shostakovitch's invitation to a zany, dissonant license: he looks forward to a future when the nose may well displace the mouth—not the only bodily orifice able to make sounds—as the source of song.

More paradisially, modern opera has questioned the human monopoly of song by returning to the happy garden where all birds and beasts could speak. Thus the operatic myth is rewritten by Ravel in *L'Enfant et les Sortilèges* (1925) and Janáček in *The Cunning Little Vixen* (1924). Orpheus grants a tongue to the inanimate objects of Ravel's schoolroom: a teapot issues feisty challenges in franglais, an overstuffed armchair heaves a sigh; a parade of shepherds and shepherdesses step down from the torn wallpaper, chanting like Monteverdi's Arcadians to an antique tune on a pipe and tabor. They lead the way back to nature, and back through the history of opera. In Ravel's humming, droning garden, a nightingale—that most intuitively brilliant of opera singers—does its bel canto exercises. Janáček's animals, unimpeded by language, are native musicians. A cricket chirps old-fashioned tunes, and the randy tethered dog spends the night declaiming sad songs of his own composition. The vixen Bystrouška moans in her sleep, and Janáček sees what that sound means: a nubile girl, her ideal notion of herself, dances in her dream.

The single human word Ravel's animals learn from the child is "Maman!" Reverently singing it together, they announce our matrilineal membership in Eden. Janáček's landscape is different—a forest rather than a backyard park; not a nursery of infantile tenderness but a place invaded by sex and therefore by death. Bystrouška massacres a flock of hens, is deflowered by a fox and has an abundance of offspring. When she's shot by a poacher, there's another version of herself ready to replace her. Janáček arrives at a new solution to that ancient operatic mystery, the proximity of love and death. For Isolde, allowing life to stream out of her in the liebes-tod, song negates our daylight existence and introduces us to a blissful nothingness. For Bystrouška, the mystery is biological not metaphysical: love overcomes death because the species continues forever. Just because she is an animal, Bystrouška is an archetypal operatic character. Her life is elemental, impersonal. The heroine of *Kátya Kabanová* (1921) dies into nature, drowned in the Volga. But there are no tragedies among the animals, and Bystrouška's death doesn't mar the revelry of earth. Like Marty in *The Makropulos Case* (1926), she can't die at all. Marty enjoys a chemical immortality, thanks to the elixir which has kept her going for 337 years; Bystrouška is immortal by proxy, living on in her cub.

Janáček and Ravel restore opera to its home in Arcady. For other composers, such lyrical peacemaking does not come easily. Strauss in *Die Schweigsame Frau* (1935)—a comedy derived from Ben Jonson's play about a silent woman—condemns music as noise pollution. The opera begins with the barber's objections to the housekeeper's twittering. The elderly celibate Morosus has organized a domestic regime based on silence, and on contempt for opera. When his nephew reveals he has married into an opera troupe, Morosus disinherits him. Having been duped by the opera company (which foists on him the shrewish silent bride), he agrees to attend one of their performances—but as a penance. Strauss's music has quit Arcady for the hubbub of the city. His score is a cannonade of drums, trumpets, bells, rattling doorknockers and banging sticks. Morosus at last declares—now that the opera is mercifully ending—that music is most beautiful when it is finished.

Schönberg also silences opera in *Moses und Aron* when the stammering prophet laments his lack of words, and grudges his brother's proficiency with musical notes; and while Janáček and Ravel recover the idyllic source of opera, the rearguard action of Pfitzner in *Palestrina* (1917) tries to prevent opera from ever happening. *Palestrina*, set in Rome in 1563, predates the Florentine invention of opera. The hero is a master of ecclesiastical polyphony, whose pupil Silla betrays him by secretly writing irreligious erotic music based on the new monodic techniques of Florence. Palestrina is commissioned to justify the ancient style of figuration by composing a great Mass, and with the aid of some ghostly predecessors and an angelic choir he manages the feat. After its performance, the Pope arrives to bless him and to appoint him director of the Sistine Chapel. Pfitzner's historical myth is oratorio's circumvention of opera, and of the Renaissance: the problem is that it comes too late.

Another of the century's religious operas, Poulenc's *Dialogues des Carmélites* (1957), seeks to justify and sanctify the secular form all over again. Here music means rational, verbal articulation, opposed to the noise of Morosus and the silence of Moses. Poulenc's dialogues return to the first principles of Monteverdian opera: "the recitative style is when one speaks while singing; the lyrical style is when one sings while speaking." This is a counterrevolutionary work, contradicting the revolutions both of 1789 (when the Jacobin terrorists ban the Carmelite order and execute the nuns) and of Schönberg. When speech is shouted down, music subsides into clamor, and that is what revolution aurally means to Poulenc—the tintinabulation and whip-cracks as the Marquis describes the riot at the Dauphin's wedding, the thunderous fanfares of the first interlude, the vocalized roar of the mob demanding that the nuns open the door, those unmetrical thudding chops which curtail song in the last scene and mark the descent of the guillotine's blade.

Song, in accord with Monteverdi's rule, is here the tempering of speech. Against it Poulenc sets a language unorganized as discourse, crudely incapable of dialogue: Blanche's offstage scream and the brief atonal outburst which characterizes her fear; the barking offstage voice of her mistress; the prelinguistic interjections of the spectators at the guillotine, who hum on vowels while the nuns serenely chant their Latin hymn. Lacking the faith of Janáček or Ravel, the commissioner who has disowned his religion calls his lapse a reversion to the speech of animals. He howls, he tells Mère Marie, with the wolves. The scandal of Madame de Croissy's terrified death is as much linguistic as spiritual: it is about the collapse of musical speech and its self-controlled order. The accompaniment to Madame de Croissy's first utterance is chromatically woozy. Regaining calm, she is able to sing; as the pain seizes her, the voice begins to shriek, falls silent, resumes as groaning. Its sounds are averse to reason and faith, and therefore to music. That, to Mère Marie, is their obscenity; she has the window shut to bottle them up, and charges that "Votre Révérence est hors d'état de retenir sa langue." Madame de Croissy replies "Qu'importe ce que je dis! Je ne commande pas plus à ma langue qu'à mon visage." The candid, unruly "langue" (tongue) has taken over, and rather than shaping the "parole" (word) it tears apart the discipline of musical language. The expressionistic agony of Madame de Croissy is where modern music begins, and where Poulenc hopes to end it. He is, in the word the jailer uses of the Carmelites, a liberticide, though the liberty he forestalls is aesthetic not political.

Blanche's nerves are frayed by music's descent into noise. She tells her father that she can no longer stand "le bruit," which is why she has taken holy orders. The opera's spiritual triumphs are moments when music tranquilizes this bruit—the prelude to the third scene, where the growling orchestra is subdued by a high-pitched bell; the a cappella "Ave Maria" after the inauguration of Madame Lidoine. Poulenc directs that the "Mater Dei" should be voiced "bouche fermée, juste une murmure": an inner music, imperturbable. The Mass disestablished by the revolutionaries is superseded by opera. "Nous allons chanter ensemble," the Chaplain says, and orchestral arpeggios swoon as he begins the "Ave verum," with the nuns deliciously abetting his tenor. The sacrament is vocal and sensuous. This is the meaning of Madame Lidoine's long address, its two sections interrupted by the announcement of the death sentence. Her sermon fortifies the nuns because it's sung as a lullaby, and ends with her maternal benediction. Carmel has been replaced by Arcady, Christ by Orpheus.

The jailer can't sing, and blurts out a list of names over an anvil-like piano. The lyric and the recitative don't after all cooperate as they did in Monteverdi. One is devout, the other atheistic and musically inept. The officer drearily harangues the defrocked nuns, and the commissioner drones through the bureaucratic decree outlawing religious houses.

This infidel recitative becomes Poulenc's subject in La Voix Humaine (1959), whose tragic heroine is the human voice. In Cocteau's monodrama, a woman remonstrates on the telephone with the lover who has jilted her. Here is opera in extremis: a duet with a silent and invisible partner, mediated by a machine and vexed by crossed lines and bad connections. Elle has been deserted by opera as well as by her man. The human voice qualifies as a tragic character because its lyricism is unrequited.

For Britten, the dramatic problem of opera was not the incursion of noise but the insinuation of music itself. The operatic mystery in Britten's case is uniquely fugitive and shamefaced. Setting out on his puerile orgy, the grocer's son in Albert Herring (1947) imitates the whistle which is Sid's call to an erotic rendezvous; it shrilly infects the orchestra, like Falstaff's trill. But so far as the plot is concerned, Albert's sensual spree consists in giving away ripe peaches from his mother's shop to the ragamuffins. In Billy Budd (1951) drama leaves to music the scene when Vere tells Billy of the death sentence: instead of dialogue, a row of orchestral chords paraphrases events behind a closed door, thus avoiding admission of the relationship between the two men. Operatic passions are also repressed by being distanced, stranded in a past which the elderly Vere remembers or which the narrator in *The Turn of the Screw* (1954) happens upon in an old book.

The Turn of the Screw is inspecific about the "horrors" linking Henry James's seductive ghosts and the defiled children. "No, don't ask me," says Mrs. Grose to the Governess after hearing Flora's nocturnal confession. But the secret obscured by the drama is divulged by music, in the theme which slithers from the rustling orchestra, coils through variations in every scene and finally reaches the malevolence of the brass in the last serpentine passacaglia. Deriving the dramatic structure from the permutations of this theme, Britten webs all the characters into complicity. When applied to language, the principle of variation twists the norm and begets a sinister or defamatory nonsense: Miles's song of Malo which can mean whatever he pleases, Flora's precociously sensuous lullaby to her doll, their scooping, jeering parody of the "Benedicite." There is an official music in *The Turn of the Screw*, soberly spelled out by the church bells, and a regimented language too, rehearsed in the Latin mnemonics of Miles's lesson. The sonorities of opera undermine this pious formality. Peter Quint appears in a twilight of piping, cawing birds, and his enchantment sounds in the rippling glare of the celesta. He yodels when he calls to Miles, and repeats the boy's name in a yearning cadenza; tempting him to take the letter, he applies a teasing, insidious rhythmic pressure to words. His evil is an affair of musical virtuosity. He communicates this corrupt technical skill to Miles, whose performance at the piano creates a diversion so Flora can run off to Miss Jessel. When his trick succeeds, Miles pounds out a triumphant scherzo of Rachmaninov-like bravura: a concerto of brazen defiance.

The Wagnerian night is for Britten a time of deviant fantasy, not mystic oblivion. Flora commands her doll to "sleep whenever I choose," and Quint calls himself "the hidden life that stirs when the candle is out." *A Midsummer Night's Dream* (1960) finds the same slumbering disquiet in Shakespeare's wood. Theseus and Hippolyta, in one of the scenes cut from the libretto, hail music as an Orphic blessing, harmonizing the world. As the horns and hounds echo in conjunction, they praise "so musical a discord, such sweet thunder." The affray of the chase has been made tunable and cheering; the confusions of the night are sorted out into what Theseus sums up as a "gentle concord." Britten's music has no such Renaissance placidity. It is the subliminal heaving of a guilty mind: the bestial grunting beneath the frolics of the rustics, the oozing orchestral malice of Oberon's spell, the hypnosis of Tytania's coloratura. When dawn comes, music emerges from this darkness. Theseus describes his conversion from conqueror to wooer as a change in tonality ("I will wed thee in another key," he tells Hippolyta), and the interlude of transformation from the bewitched wood to the palace leads music from drowsy fantasy back to courtly officiousness. Opera has been exorcised; now it can be laughed at with impunity, in the Donizettian burlesque of the play performed by the artisans.

Opera in Britten's case is a field of sensual vice, and he revives the safer alternative of oratorio in his series of church parables. For Weill and Brecht, opera is under suspicion for a different reason, as a province of social crime. Their *Dreigroschenoper* (1928) returns to the criticism of the form advanced by Gay in his *Beggar's Opera* (1728). Gay's bandit Macheath models himself on the chivalric heroes of Handel, but his sentiments are bogus and his tunes secondhand. He steals songs as impudently as he robs coaches. The characters have no music of their own, and must make do with a random flotsam of ballads. Opera is a shoddy refuge of emotional dishonesty.

Gay's satire is used by Weill and Brecht as the pretext for a theatrical revolution. Grand opera is scaled down to jazzy cabaret; the exorbitant, luxurious art now costs threepence only. *Aufsteig und Fall der Stadt Mahagonny* (1930) devalues and debauches operatic history. The illusory town of Mahagonny, called a "Goldstadt" by Fatty and founded to prey on the wealth grubbed up by a gold rush, is halfway between Walhall and Las Vegas. Wotan was after all no more than a profiteering capitalist. When a hurricane menaces Mahagonny, a male chorus sings the Lutheran chorale from *Die Zauberflöte*; but Mozart's sermon on armed resistance is mocked by Jimmy, because mankind itself is the worst of natural disasters. A shrieky orchestra likens this storm to the romantic turbulence of the Wolf's Glen in *Der Freischütz*, and again the parody diminishes opera. In Weber's forest there are diabolical energies, but also the divine providence extolled by the hermit. Weill's nature is as fickle and unjust as his people: the hurricane inexplicably spares Mahagonny. The death of the glutton, who chokes on a fatted calf, mocks Monteverdi when the men join in a lament based on that of Seneca's pupils in *Poppea*. Jimmy before his execution prays like Tristan for a night which will never end; but Tristan's motive is mystical, whereas Jimmy's concern is to escape the payment of his debts.

Mahagonny is a monument to plutocratic opera, and its occupations—eating, drinking, loving and fighting—are the deadly sins of the form. The rise and fall of the city therefore charts the degeneracy of opera. Brecht despised a "culinary" theater, and explained that the subject of *Mahagonny* is "the cooking process itself": the operatic falsification and commercialization of feeling, symbolized by Jenny's professional lovemaking; the bloated consumerism of passion. The Nietzschean musical elixir is for Brecht no more than a cut-rate narcotic. Tired of Mahagonny, Jimmy sums up opera from the viewpoint of a disenchanted bartender: the citizens have run through the "cocktail ABC," mixed every combination of drink that's possible, and are still unsatisfied. He resolves to close down the bar of Mandalay.

Opera in the twentieth century is preoccupied with its history, wondering if it's an art whose time has run out. The Marschallin stops all the clocks in the house; Nick Shadow in *The Rake's Progress* elasticizes time by turning the clock back in the brothel. One of Ravel's "sortilèges" is a grandfather clock whose pendulum the child has torn off. Unbalanced, it speeds up in a maniacally gabbled "Ding, ding, ding!", aghast at its improper haste. This is the operatic nightmare of musical time rushing to judgment, as it does for Don Giovanni or Carmen or Falstaff when the clock strikes midnight. In *L'Heure Espagnole* (1911) Ravel regulates its passage. The watchmaker Torquemada punctiliously goes off to wind the municipal clocks, commenting that official time waits for no one; the muleteer Ramiro, whose watch has stopped, is anxious to remain on schedule. But Concepción, who in her husband's absence persuades Ramiro to carry back and forth to her bedroom the clocks which hide her lovers, knows how to delay time and deliciously profit from it. Her Spanish hour isn't frantic, like the "folle journée" of *Figaro*; it can be repeated as often as Torquemada leaves the house, and Ramiro's reappearances, she hopes, will be as reliable as a chronometer.

Ravel's score is a factory of somnolent tickings and whirrings. The voices chatter together in the last ensemble like unsynchronized clocks. He has found a way of musically dramatizing time's relativity. The farce is busy but static, and Gonzalve, inside his clock, considers it a lazy garden of hours. Opera escapes from its history by slowing that history down.

Modern operatic characters—Janáček's Marty, Berg's Lulu, Stravinsky's Oedipus or Tom Rakewell—are the victims of a time measured by music. In the overture to *The Makropulos Case*, an offstage band plays distant fanfares from a dissension-ridden past, which break in on the lyrical present. Marty lives in two epochs simultaneously: the cabalistic emperor's court and the modern city. Only when she reconciles herself to dying can the orchestra settle into a slow, wheeling waltz, which follows the rotation of nature.

In *Lulu*, drama and music belong to different moral and temporal orders, brought tragically into conflict. In the drama, Lulu is adept at wriggling out of impasses, instantly recuperating from tragedy to wonder—as she says after the Painter's suicide—what's next for her. But Berg's music, inflexibly symmetrical, confines her and weighs her down. Her dramatic credo, like Carmen's "liberté," is that dazzling cry of "Freiheit" after she escapes from prison. Yet the music belies her faith, and dooms her to a career of compulsive repetition. She tells Schigolch, with a luxurious vocal distension ending in a squawk, that she likes to stretch until she cracks. That is exactly what the opera does to her. It tortures her by elongating her life until, as her past returns, she breaks apart. Alwa describes the process as atomization: under her impact, he tells Lulu, the inner self shatters to smithereens.

For Brecht, opera works by cooking, stewing its characters in their carnal juices; for Berg, it is a matter of psychological fission. Lulu is herself decomposed into facets or aspects, appraised and used differently by everyone—a subject of painting to Schwarz, of music to Alwa, of poetry to the Schoolboy with his callow ode; a snake for the Animal Tamer, then (when the Acrobat claims her) a gymnast. Like a marketable value she is traded back and forth, unreally inflated and finally deemed worthless. Schön pays the Painter half a million to wed her, and his portrait of her sells for fifty thousand marks; eventually she shares the fate of the Jungfrau shares, discarded when no one can be persuaded to believe in them anymore.

These partial, fragmentary images or atoms of personality are also the musical cells of Berg's score. Lulu leaves a trail of casual damage behind her, but her victims regroup to accuse her. The interlude narrating her imprisonment and escape is an orchestral palindrome, running forward and then—at the precise midpoint of the opera—reversing itself to go backward; Lulu's three slaughtered husbands have spectral comebacks as her clients and her killer in the London attic. The tempo of journalism, forever in quest of happenings but liable to forget them once they have happened, matches the agitation of the action. Alwa arrives to tell his father that revolution has broken out unexpectedly in Paris, and none of the reporters knows what to write in the paper. Lulu suggests an extra edition to keep up with the news of her latest husband's gruesome demise. Journalism lives

227

down the past with obscene rapidity, and that too is the rhythm of Lulu's life in the drama. Her comment on Schön's death is "Er hat es überstanden": he has got through it, put it behind him. The drama thinks only of moments. Music, however, is the medium of memory. Schön insists, during his quarrel with Lulu, on reaching a conclusion: "Kommen wir zu Ende!" Lulu's end is musically compounded from her beginnings. The scene of retribution consists entirely of recapitulated sections from previous episodes.

The musical scheme foreordains the dramatic characters, although they don't realize it. The first act is a sonata. The ground of Schön's life is Lulu, and he tries three times to rid himself of her; but just as the sonata returns from its exploration of new material to a repeat of its opening section, so Schön must finally give in and marry her. The shape of the second act is expounded by Alwa at its lyrical climax, when he composes Lulu's body—molding her ankles as a grazioso passage, the plumpness of her leg as a cantabile, her knees as a misterioso interlude, with an impulsive andante guiding lust toward its destination. He praises her anatomical roundness, and the form in which he does so is a rondo. Again the musical shape is a moral entrapment: he revolves within the charmed circle of Lulu's physical terrain. The third act is a theme with variations. The theme is dictated by the dramatist Wedekind, whose "Procurer's Song" is cranked out in the interlude; thereafter Lulu can only despairingly vary that refrain as she scavenges on the streets for one customer after another.

Alwa says he will compose a dithyramb in Lulu's honor, just as Janáček's Marty, guzzling whiskey to cheer herself up, morosely drains the fuel of Dionysus. But the god saves neither of them. Lulu's love-death, which she owes to the surgery of Jack the Ripper's razor, isn't a melodic ecstasy. It is announced by her screams of "Nein!" and leaves behind it an insanitary mess. Marty must also do without sublimatory song. She admits in her debilitation that singing is just the same as keeping silent; and her love-death, like Lulu's, is beyond the understanding of romantic opera. She doesn't vanquish death by desiring it. Like Jimmy Mahoney, executed because he couldn't pay his bills, she has merely quit her debt to nature.

Exhuming antique forms like Latinate oratorio or Mozartean opera, Stravinsky seceded from modern musical history. His heroes live out this neoclassical anachronism: *Oedipus Rex* is about the tragic reversal of time, which moves backward as implacably as Berg's palindrome to destroy the malefactor; *The Rake's Progress* is about the comic anticipation of time, which loosens the libertine from the consequences of his misdeeds.

Oracles send Oedipus back into his past, wishes project Tom Rakewell into a gratified future. Nick Shadow makes Tom a gift of time in the brothel when he winds back the cuckoo clock: time's reversal here, unlike that of *Oedipus*, erases the moral record. Cocteau, who supplied the text for the oratorio, called tragedy an infernal machine, a snare of tight logical causation. Its engineering of judgment can be heard in Stravinsky's relentless rhythms. In the opera, Tom invents an alternative to Cocteau's contraption, a celestial machine which converts stones to bread and undoes history by making earth an affluent paradise again. Tom spurns the tyranny of time which weighs on Oedipus. His first aria casts off the predestinate supervision of heaven, and chooses the variable favors of fortune. He finds the plowman's servitude to weather and the city gent's enslavement to the "clock of Fashion" equally odious. Oedipus is ruled by necessity, Tom by randomness. Nick recommends the match with the bearded Baba, because by embracing the absurd Tom will confound time's grammar, eliminating the "unpredictable Must" of appetite and the "inflexible Ought" of conscience. Madness is no punishment, because it perpetuates this idyll. In Bedlam, where Tom and Anne are reunited, "Now" lasts forever, without "a notion of Almost or Too Late."

Stravinsky like Tom playfully exempts himself from the past. Repeating it, he turns it into the present: his musical mimicries make him a contemporary of all his predecessors, from Monteverdi onward. Whereas Berg's music has an unsparing determinism, like that judicially ponderous rhythm which beats beneath Schön's destruction of the Painter and Jack's of Lulu, Stravinsky's flaunts a heady freedom. Anne's high note at the end of her aria is as recklessly joyful a gratuitous act as Tom's decision to marry Baba. Auden declared that "every high C accurately struck demolishes the theory that we are the irresponsible puppets of fate or chance." Polevaulting above the stave, the singer has performed an existential miracle.

As the rake regresses, opera progresses. Tom begins as Monteverdi's Orpheus, who leaves his English Arcady to cross the Stygian Thames. As well as revitalizing the classical myth, he combines in himself opera's twin romantic heroes. Carousing in the brothel he is Don Giovanni, endowing humanity with that bogus engine he is Faust. He lives on into the romantic decadence. The marriage to Baba, ignoring nature and instinct, resembles the perversity of the morbid Tristan; Nick paraphrases Schopenhauer, from whom Wagner derived the metaphysics of *Tristan und Isolde*, when he says that "he alone is free / Who chooses what to will." At length Tom arrives in the twentieth century. The Hogarthian rake reaches the 1950s as a dangling man, aware that what we call reality is a game of hazard. The temptation in this accidental, aleatory world is to overthrow all ordering systems, including that of tonality. The cries in the London streets have already done so, and when Tom says to the city

> Disband your notes and let them range; . . .
> Let Tone desert the flatterer.
> Let Harmony no more obey,

he might be challenging Stravinsky to tolerate the atonal liberty of Schönberg. Stravinsky, however, runs through the operatic history which lies between Monteverdi and himself in order to joke that it should never have begun; having summarily abolished the past, he can invent opera all over again.

The mad Tom therefore instructs Orpheus to take up his lyre "in a swan-like music" which will die but rise again. The same reincarnation occurs in opera, born again when it reverts to the ceremonial celebration of its founder. Apollo and Dionysus resume their ancient battle for possession of Orpheus and of opera in Henze's *Bassarids* (1966), Britten's *Death in Venice* (1973) and Birtwistle's *Mask of Orpheus* (1985).

Between their libretto for *The Rake's Progress* and that for *The Bassarids*, Auden and Kallman had translated *Die Zauberflöte*; for Henze's opera they wrote a skeptical new installment of Mozart's moral pantomime. In the rational eighteenth century, Sarastro could automatically rout the Queen of the Night. Since then, unreason has proved less easy to overcome. "Whole societies," Auden and Kallman wrote in introducing *The Bassarids*, "can be seized by demonic forces." Dionysus for them means a totalitarian madness, which Pentheus is torn asunder attempting to suppress. In the twentieth century, the wiseacre Sarastro would probably suffer the same comeuppance from the fiendish Queen. Henze's orchestra is itself seized by the demon. This is his most explosively Wagnerian score, linking the Dionysia with a modern Teutonic epidemic which took its mythology from opera. Hitler set himself to enact in a global theater the finale of *Götterdämmerung*.

Henze conceives the Dionysian cult as a political distemper; Britten treats it as a sensual plague. Nietzsche traced "the Dionysian pageant from India to Greece." That path is followed in *Death in Venice* by Asiatic cholera, which—in time with the snaking of the orchestral bass—spreads from the Ganges delta to Europe. The pestilence is erotic, killing Aschenbach by way of his love for Tadzio. He imagines the boy to be "the soul of

Greece," but that spirit is no longer a "bright perfection." Sunny Apollo, Monteverdi's deity with the sexless voice of a countertenor, graces the athletic games on the beach, and is worshiped in a Delphic hymn; Tadzio is his deputy, playing Phoebus astride a pyramidal chariot of boys. In Aschenbach's dream, this fluting luminary is drowned by Dionysus, whose mysteries and reeling dance and sacrifice are a sexual debasement, announced by the beastly lowing of the tuba. Aschenbach likens himself to Orpheus when, in his navigable coffin on the lagoon, he remarks that the unlicensed gondolier might have rowed him across the Styx; for him as for Rakewell, the underworld is a city, and he is condemned to remain there, consumed by his obsession with an Apollonian youth.

Against a complacent bluster of trumpets, Aschenbach introduces himself as a literary man, "I, Aschenbach, master-writer." He reflects on his plight in abstemious monologues with piano accompaniment, always holding a notebook as his talisman. His vocation is verbal, and he tries to apologize for Tadzio by claiming him as a muse: "Eros is in the word." But Eros, rather, is in the music—in the falsetto ditties of the fop, the hysterical laughing song of the strolling players, or the miasma of sentimental tunes through which Venice appears, its liturgical bells unheeded; above all in the vibraphone, which makes the air tingle when Tadzio arrives. The sensuous genius of the boy, as Kierkegaard would have called it, outlaws him from the world of words: he is a dancer, inarticulately responding to the orchestra. The war inside Aschenbach between reason and instinct is a formal dispute between the two arts coupled by opera.

The Mask of Orpheus, analyzing the operatic myth anthropologically, asks whether Apollo and Dionysus might not be on closer terms than Nietzsche or Henze or Britten allowed. Perhaps they are both aspects of Orpheus. Birtwistle's is a primordial opera, restaging the rite where the form began; it tries both to anticipate and terminate the form—to be the first opera and the last. Its Orpheus is a compilation of all the characters wished on the hero since classical Greece or the Italian Renaissance, and rather than selecting one version Birtwistle and his librettist Peter Zinovieff dramatize them all, watching the process of variegation as the same story is retold with embellishments or amendments. In one episode, Eurydice resists when wooed by Aristaeus, as Gluck's heroine no doubt did; in another, she readily gives in, just like Offenbach's. Orpheus himself is alternately slain by the Dionysian women (as in Haydn) and promoted to an oracle by Apollo (as in Monteverdi).

Scrutinizing all the variants, Birtwistle and Zinovieff approach the complex truth about opera's patron. Sometimes he is Apollo's son; in a lost play by Aeschylus, his worship of the sun slights Dionysus, whose followers massacre Orpheus. He is also often himself a Dionysian, an initiate of the violent underworld. There are Orphic hymns addressed both to Apollo, "tempering the poles to the Doric mode," and to Dionysus, the "loud-roaring god of the shout." Birtwistle's Apollo booms electronically, in a gruff jargon of his own; Orpheus translates those aerial rumblings into a personal language of enchanting song. His arcane art makes a god of him, and the jealous Olympians protect their monopoly of music by striking him down. In one scene, Zeus fells him with a thunderbolt, in another Apollo silences him out of envious pique.

The crime of Orpheus is to impart divine secrets. That too, throughout its history, has been the religious misdemeanor of opera, from Monteverdi's immortalized singer to Stockhausen's luminous space travelers or Philip Glass's triad of saviors—the atom-splitting physicist in *Einstein on the Beach,* the radical saint Gandhi in *Satyagraha,* and the sun-worshiping Akhnaten, whose Apollo is the radiant Aten. Birtwistle diagnoses the divided loyalties of opera's founder. Orpheus vacillates between Apollo and Dionysus, harmony and uproar. Serving both masters, he rejoices in the ambiguity which first gave birth to the spiritual and sensual, mystic and fleshly art of opera.

III

PERFORMANCE

ONE

Phantoms of the Opera

OPERA is in origin seditious—religiously in the seventeenth century, with the resurgence of pagan gods who personify human appetites, like Monteverdi's Amore or Cavalli's Giove in *La Calisto;* sensually in the eighteenth century, with Mozart's revelation of the energetic waywardness of sex; politically in the nineteenth century, when Wagner the revolutionary adopts Siegfried as his fire-breathing Bakhunin.

All these seditions continue to enliven the form in the twentieth century. Glass and Stockhausen devise new theologies. *Akhnaten* is an overdue epilogue to *Die Zauberflöte,* banning the worship of Isis and Osiris, and Michael in *Donnerstag* is an intergalactic Parsifal, the pure fool as an evangelizing astronaut. After the aerodynamic discs of light he designed for Glass's *Einstein on the Beach,* Robert Wilson planned a *Parsifal* whose miracles would suit an age of electronics and nuclear fission, "all about light," icily white. Britten's music hears the confession of sexual renegades or repressed victims, like Grimes or Albert Herring. Henze's *We Come to the River* rehearses the revolution.

But opera is famous for its unintelligibility, and throughout its history audiences, and sometimes performers, have ignored its meanings, while the institutions founded to exhibit it have for the most part been social amenities using opera as their excuse. The opera house, addicted to routine, encumbered by bureaucracy, has been annexed by a society whose chosen rite and fanciest outing it is. In every generation, opera demands interpreters to renew, with an anger which looks like irreverence, an art which society wishes to tame.

From La Scala in 1778 to the New York Metropolitan in 1883, the first act of the newly rich urban aristocracy is to open an opera house. A high society requires a high art. Opera, for an anxiously insecure elite, is a rite of self-validation. The magnates who had made fortunes too rapidly after the American Civil War needed it as a conduct manual. It could redeem the money squandered on it and confer eligibility on those who patronized it because it's an art of splendid superfluity, enslaved (as the aristocrat must be) to keeping up appearances. Operatic characters are the last recklessly lordly creatures in a democratic world. They spend fortunes or expend their lives rather than suffer any slight to honor or reputation. Violetta pawns her belongings to pay for her idyll with Alfredo. Norma proudly declares that she never lies and nominates herself for the pyre. Even the lowly Carmen is an instinctive aristocrat, neglecting her own safety and scornful of inferiors. To their customers, these extravagant beings offered a style to be imitated—a spendthrift emotionalism, the rule of conspicuous consumption applied to the passions. The robber barons of New York relied on opera to save them from their drab pecuniary efficiency. Ensconced in their boxes at the Met they would become, like the people onstage, otiose and ornamental.

The grandly lunatic entrepreneur in Werner Herzog's film *Fitzcarraldo* devotes the proceeds from his trans-Andean railway and his ice business to the construction of an opera house in Iquitos. Opera is his mystic folly. He tells the rubber millionaires that the apparent reality of their cost-effective world is but a caricature of the true reality, which is grand opera and its compulsive dreams; he quietens the war-whooping savages, invisible in the jungle, by playing a record of Caruso's voice—Orpheus not with his lute but with a Victrola. Opera also signifies the ultimate luxury, and Fitzcarraldo hires Caruso and his troupe to perform *I Puritani* on board his boat. This is the culmination of his mountain-moving project: he props a craggy alpine set on the top deck, and has the singers posture before it as he sails down the river. Having already hauled his ship up a mountain, he now reconstructs that mountain on the ship. Opera is the most grandiose technological dream money can buy.

On the rampage, Fitzcarraldo threatens to close the church until he gets his opera house. He's imprisoned for his blasphemy, but the sacrilege which is opera's initial motive—in the new paganism of Monteverdi's musical fable, or in the Masonic campaign against Catholic superstition in

Die Zauberflöte—recurs in the institutional history of the form. Kenneth Clark notes that "opera houses came in when churches went out." They were the temples of a new religion, advertising the riches of the bourgeoisie. La Scala was built on the site of the church of Santa Maria alla Scala; the São Carlos theater in Lisbon, planned in 1792, was financed by a consortium of dealers in tobacco and leather who owed their power and wealth to the anticlerical reforms of the Marquês de Pombal. Opera houses could express their profanation either by mimicking the rococo extravagance of churches, as the architect Cuvilliés did in the theater he built in the Residenz in Munich, or by soberly criticizing ecclesiastical and courtly ostentation. The São Carlos, for instance, replaced a theater built before the Lisbon earthquake after baroque plans by one of the Bibienas, and its facade prefers bourgeois punctiliousness to regal or religious pomp: above the low-browed portico, a clock is set in pride of place.

Theaters established as clubs for a newly arrived ruling class became, during the nineteenth century, contested political arenas where that class defended its privileges and conducted national warfare at second hand. The Scala was a forum for the city, and thus a place for political proclamations or demonstrations. In 1800 a French official hastened there to announce the victory of the Napoleonic army over Melas at Marengo. It's this news which so dismays the monarchist Scarpia in the Rome of *Tosca*; to the new radicalized public in Milan, it was an occasion for rejoicing. In 1859, a performance of *Norma* at La Scala incited an outcry against the occupying Austrian army. The Milanese in their boxes and the Austrian officers in the orchestra stalls came to a showdown during the scene when Norma, striking the gong, goads the Druids to revenge themselves on the imperial Roman invaders. The chorus bayed for blood, and the boxholders joined in its cries of "Guerra! Guerra!" Oroveso sings of hurling the eagle to the ground; the audience varied the words, specifying that the Austrian eagle would be knocked from the sky. Bombarded by sound, the soldiers quit the theater. Opera and the cause of Italian unification were literally synonymous: Verdi's name spelled out the illicit movement's slogan—Vittorio Emanuele, Re d'Italia.

Later, the Scala sided with a fascist nationalism, mounting works like Mascagni's *Nerone* in homage to the latter-day emperor Mussolini. Since then, the bourgeoisie has learned to apologize for itself and for opera. La Scala, as a symbolic citadel of capitalism, was besieged by demonstrators on opening night in 1968; the administration has been careful to ingratiate with the opposition by giving concerts in factories and planning special performances for industrial workers and union members. The appeasing tactics were evident in Giorgio Strehler's production of *Simon Boccanegra* in 1971. The buccaneer promoted to Doge had betrayed his class and the sea on which he foraged; only at his death did Strehler allow the sails of his fleet to fold over him in mourning cerements. La Scala's paradoxical history epitomizes that of opera. The form which in the nineteenth century rallied its patrons to insurrection had changed by 1976 into a bunker for vested interests and subsidized snobbery: Zeffirelli's *Otello* opened at La Scala inside a cordon of carabinieri, who closed off the surrounding streets and fought back brigades of urban guerrillas.

In Austria, opera remained throughout the nineteenth century an adjunct of the court, at the mercy of those potentates who had earlier maltreated Mozart. Muskets were replaced by bow and arrow when *Der Freischütz* was performed at Vienna in 1821 because the emperor, fearful of assassination attempts, had prohibited gunfire in the theater. The courtiers came to inspect each other, paying scant attention to the stage. (The subscribers at La Scala even brought their cooks, and every opera included an "aria del sorbetto," timed to coincide with the refreshment course.) Taking control in Vienna in 1897, Mahler was the first to demand respect for music by punishing latecomers with exclusion and dimming the house lights during performances; Toscanini later followed his example at La Scala. But the grandees didn't easily forgive such presumption, and while Hans Gregor was in charge at Vienna, between 1911 and 1918, an octogenarian Princess Metternich ordered that the house lights be raised once more, so she could study the dresses of the ladies in the audience. Until the monarchy resigned control of the theaters in 1918, the Viennese opera was liable to be requisitioned for festivities of state. The new house opened in 1869 with a declaimed appeal for Austro-Hungarian unity; *Jenůfa* was staged in 1918 as a belated diplomatic gesture of amity toward the Czechs.

The plans for the theater on the Ringstrasse made elaborate provision for courtly protocol. There were two separate ceremonial approaches, one reserved for the emperor on the Operngasse, the other for the archdukes, who were to dismount from the Kärntnerstrasse. The architect Garnier's design for the new Paris Opéra stipulated a more secluded and paranoid private access for the sovereign. Napoleon III had survived an assassin's attack while attending an opera performance in 1858 in the rue Le Peletier; Garnier ensured he would never again be exposed by constructing a ramp which arrived at its own vestibule in the emperor's pavilion. There the head of state could make his entrance far from the disorderly streets, and on the other side of the building from the pavilion intended for subscribers. At Covent Garden, the problem was not to shield a monarch from terrorists but to conceal his erotic comings and goings. Beneath the theater's royal box is a claustrophobic den called the King's Smoking Room. A staircase leads to the box above but, more importantly, there's a passage linking it to the stage. Its purpose was to allow the philandering Edward VII access to the ballerinas, and its maritime portholes were intended as a homey reminiscence of the royal yacht.

Opera's ancient urge to profanation brazenly declared itself in Garnier's polychrome palace. Théophile Gautier called it the worldly cathedral of civilization; Victor Hugo saw it confronting and mocking its religious counterpart, Notre Dame. Instead of the chaste angels who guarded the facade of Notre Dame, the Opéra's tutelary deities were pagan wantons—on the front steps, a sculptural group by Carpeaux representing La Danse, with a winged Terpsichore engirdled by naked, wild-eyed cocottes; inside, lurking in a grotto under the staircase, a statue of La Pythie, the oracular priestess writhing on her pedestal, her legs and bronze breasts bared, her arm fitfully extended as the visionary spasm takes her. Garnier saw the Pythian as the spirit of art, invading an agitated human body as its medium.

This conviction that opera is a preserve of sensual violence, a religion whose demons are sacred, persists in the panel Marc Chagall designed for the ceiling of the Paris auditorium in 1964, so different in its iconography from the humane allegory of music's gift to the city in his foyer murals for the Met at Lincoln Center. Chagall's tondo covered a billowing skyscape by Lenepveu, showing the hours of day and night; in his scheme, day and night are contrary forces which clash in opera—the rationality of words perhaps, and the instinctive unreason of music. The Roméo and Juliette of Berlioz, whirling into the light, balance Tristan and Isolde, whose narcotic is darkness. The yellow radiance illuminating Pelléas and Mélisande contrasts with the red furnace of Stravinsky's firebird. At the summit, *Die Zauberflöte* and *Boris Godunov* face each other, as combatants in a metaphysical war: the cherub Mozart challenges the glowering winged devil Mussorgsky.

Garnier's conception of his theater implied a theory of opera as a luxurious and hedonistic inferno like that of Offenbach's cancan girls, a habitat for Gounod's Méphistophélès and all other worshipers of the golden calf. His task was to build a palace given over to pleasure. Gautier, writing about the competition for a design in 1861, said that a coquettish architecture would best suit the ideology of opera. Garnier called his plan "the temple of an art which spoke to the eyes, the ears, the heart and the passions": a sensory haven. Garnier despised the metallic minimalism of the Eiffel Tower, which showed its skeleton on the outside. His building was to be richly caparisoned, in an affront to what he called the drab utilitarian grayness of the modern city. Again his prescription carries with it an expectation that opera will be Bacchanalian: he emphasized, he said, "warmth, passion, bad taste perhaps, but above all color." The heat he spoke of was allegorically embodied in the foyer as light, in a row of female faces deputed to represent the evolution of theatrical lighting—first the oil lamp, then a candle, afterward gas, at last electricity. This carnal light splintered into jewelry in the chandelier which hung above the auditorium. Garnier designed it himself, and imagined it in advance as a girandole of gems. The spectators were assumed to be voluptuaries, so Garnier made sure that the foyer and promenades were theaters for their self-exhibition; on the staircase he expected them to group into compositions as sumptuous as those in a mural by Veronese. He set the architecture to compete with the dresses which would display themselves before it, and spoke of his polychrome panels of marble as huge tapestries adorning a "salle à fête" and giving it an atmosphere he called "féerique"—the same word Offenbach used to classify the genre of Orphée aux Enfers: fantastical, phantasmal.

The Opéra was therefore the logical dwelling place for a phantom. Garnier's construction was imaginatively exorbitant and excessive, pretending to mythical status; Gaston Leroux fabricated a mythology for it in his 1910 novel The Phantom of the Opera. Hugo had invented a living gargoyle to haunt the cathedral in Quasimodo, his hunchback of Notre Dame. Leroux equipped the Opéra with its own resident demon, the mad Erik who terrorizes audiences from his subterranean recess. Opera's beginnings were occult, in the hermetic researches which prompt Monteverdi's Orfeo. For Leroux the art is still, in the twentieth century, an affair of black magic.

Leroux describes the Opéra as "a palace of illusion," a laboratory of mechanical wizardry. The opera which sums up the Opéra's hocus-pocus is Faust. In the early years of the old Met, Gounod's opera had a mercenary moral: the jewel box left by the devil to tempt Marguerite was the opera house in miniature. In Leroux's novel, the same work has a diabolical meaning. The phantom is infatuated with the soprano Christine Daaé; she in her turn worships an angel of music who is her private devil. Her crystalline voice is believed to be a gift from God, though perhaps it's the love offering of her demon. One of her roles is Marguerite, and the transaction to which she's a party makes of her a female Faust, trading her soul for the sake of her career. Her licentious angel visits her in secret, and ravishes her away during a performance. The opera being staged is *Faust*, and Marguerite in the prison is entreating the "anges pures, anges radieuses" to save her. Her prayer is answered, but by the devil, not by God's ineffectual emissaries.

This revision of *Faust* coincides with the ghost's infernal vindication of *Don Giovanni*. Erik is a composer, and his masterpiece is an opera in which Mozart's libertine escapes divine judgment. "My Don Giovanni burns," he boasts, "and yet he is not struck by fire from heaven." Erik generates that fire himself: it is the ardor (Garnier's calorific passion) of opera, and also a nitrous explosive. He has accumulated an arsenal of gunpowder in his lair beneath the Opéra and intends—if Christine is not delivered to him—to detonate the building. At the end of Mozart's opera, the libertine tumbles into flaming damnation; Erik concocts the fire himself, and will use it to blow up the gods. He owes his malevolent magic to science. The simulated tropical hell where he imprisons his victims in the Opéra's cellars is heated by electricity, though upstairs the theater is gaslit and—Leroux notes—hydrogen is used for moody alterations to the lighting onstage. In this, too, the phantom is the arcane genius of the form, for as the critic Hanslick commented, Wagner's scenic miracles had more to do with electricity than with art.

Leroux interprets the Opéra as a phantasmagoria, from its raven-infested battlements to its subliminal basement. On the roof, Apollo brandishes his lyre, but it can't ward off the harbingers of Dionysian dark: the instrument is used as a perch by an ill-omened night-bird. Tipped with metal, the lyre also serves as a lightning rod. Here too the life of the building and of the art it houses is dangerous and incendiary: the sun god is to suffer electrocution. Inside, the dazzling alternative sun of the chandelier is equally fatal. The ghost causes it to fall into the auditorium, and it crushes a concierge. The ceiling is a pantheon where copper nymphs—Isis, Psyche, Pandora, Daphne and so on—disport themselves. But this is an indoor sky, and it shares the altitude with an enskied sea: the grid of pulleys and windlasses for scene shifting has the look of an aerial harbor, bristling with masts and yardarms; nature has been upended, its laws suspended. The jumble of inconsistent locations in the warehouse storing the sets introverts geography, so the Opéra resembles a muddled global museum. A scene shifter is found hanged on the level of the third cellar, swinging between a rustic farmhouse and an Indian vista from Massenet's *Roi de Lahore*. Or else nature has allowed the building to consume it. The Opéra reposes, Leroux reveals, on top of a lake, so Erik's fortress of fantasy is a moated island far beneath the rue Scribe.

Legions of elderly porters are employed throughout the building to close doors and prevent drafts. Their achievement is to insulate the artifice, seal it against the reality outdoors. Within, every aperture guards its secret. Boxes, like the one reserved in perpetuity for the phantom, are cubicles of unlicensed confession. In one of them, in a provincial German theater during a performance of *Don Giovanni*, E. T. A. Hoffmann hears the guilty admissions of Donna Anna. Behind the scenes in the Opéra of Leroux, sexual favors are bought and sold: young men are taken for their initiation to the "foyer du danse," where they're gently inducted by living versions of those Carpeaux Bacchantes. Downstairs, the Opéra conceals its private hell—the skeletons of slaughtered Communards, exhumed when the foundations were being dug; a boiler room where the stokers toil with shovels and pitchforks among the flames, like Alberich's minions in Nibelheim or devils in Giovanni's inferno; Erik's world-ending armory of powder kegs. This is a theater whose scenery is the projection of neurotic dream and desire, like the artificial grotto in the bowels of the château at Linderhof where Ludwig II of Bavaria awaited the arrival of a nubile Lohengrin, gliding across the water in a coracle shaped like a swan. Imprisoned by Erik in his mirrored maze of steamy desert, the Persian and the Vicomte find that the illusion itself is their torture, because there's no way of escaping from it back to reality.

The Opéra was planned as a monument to aquiline imperial glory, but by the time it opened in 1875 the empire had collapsed. It remained as a symbol only of itself—of opera as an illusory enchantment, more a haunted house than an official tabernacle.

In America, opera's course is the same, from ceremony to fantasy. The "vessel of social salvation," as Henry James called it, changes gradually into a vessel of sexual perdition. Opera retains its European value as a credential of swank, first for the urban plutocrats of the Met, later for a suburban middle class. America appraises opera as a means of social mobility. The exemplary case is that of Mildred Pierce, the heroine of James M. Cain's 1941 novel, who ascends from hash slinging and pie baking in Glendale, California, to owning a restaurant and proudly listening to her daughter Veda's coloratura exhibitions on the Snack-O-Ham radio program. The long-suffering Mildred is prepared to allow this operatic promotion to happen in the next generation; the ambitious Joan Crawford, who played the part in the 1945 film of Cain's novel, wasn't so humble or so patient. Encouraged to train her voice by Franchot Tone, she made test pressings of arias, proprietorially posed with her new phonograph, and after giving dinner to visiting musicians like Rosa Ponselle and Tito Schipa subjected them to Wagner evenings, declaiming excerpts from the libretti between records. Opera, she thought, would give her class.

Cain too all his life adored the form, but had guilty misgivings about his weakness for it. For the European decadents, opera connoted diabolism, and they reveled in it. Hence Baudelaire's advocacy of *Tannhäuser*, whose hero spends a season in a voluptuous hell. But in America, opera connoted effeminacy, and this is the reason for the hard-boiled Cain's fear of it. If tough guys don't dance, they shouldn't sing opera either, or be so knowledgeable about the trills and shakes and portamenti of the fat ladies who do. Cain saves the situation for himself by identifying the voice with virility. The amateur baritone in his *Career in C Major* (1938) is in the Social Register, yet he scorns anything "high-toned" and talks like a roughneck. He can reconcile himself to the possession of his talent only if—like Sherrill Milnes installing a gym in his apartment, or Samuel Ramey showing off Attila's pectorals—he allies it with manlier activities. Thus he compares going for the high notes to bird shooting, says impresarios are like baseball managers, and brags of his own endurance in an analogy with Dempsey in the boxing ring. The quartet from *Rigoletto*, when he sings in it, is driven like a racing car: "we closed out the allegro with all cylinders clicking and the show doing seventy." Art's extenuation is that it resembles sport. When the baritone dries up during *Rigoletto*, his soprano mistress taunts his crestfallen masculinity and accuses him of going yellow: "you've got to go back and lick them!"

Cain's most nuttily elaborate fable about the sexual pathology of opera is *Serenade* (1937), later filmed in bowdlerized form with Mario Lanza. It is a version of *Carmen*, repatriated to Latin America. Mérimée tells the story from José's point of view, in remorseful retrospect; Bizet gives Carmen's account of events; Cain retails Escamillo's testimony. The hero once more is an operatic baritone. He first sees his Carmen, the three-peso whore Juana, closing in on a toreador in a Mexican bar. He ousts the bullfighter, and himself becomes both fighter and bull. Educating her, he plays her the prelude to the last act of *Carmen*, and explains the bassoon's snorting phrase as "the voice of the bull." She credits him with making the same sound when they copulate, and says "when you love Juana, you sing nice, much *toro.*" The dumb ox now bellows A naturals. One of his operatic weapons augments the matador's sword: he enjoys cracking "the blacksnake whip I had used when I sang Alfio." This character, Lola's husband in *Cavalleria Rusticana,* is a mule-skinner—verismo's degraded replica of the heroic bull-slayer. Cain's hero resumes his career by stepping in (or rather charging in, straight from the audience) as Escamillo in a performance of *Carmen* at the Hollywood Bowl. His name, suiting his profession, is Sharp.

However, a psychological snag remains to cripple this American Escamillo's masculinity. The bullfighter kills the animal emblem of virility; opera likewise entails a sexual shame, which is both admitted and atoned for in *Serenade.* Sharp lost his voice when seduced by another man, and recovers it only when he ravishes the panting Juana. The art threatens him with emasculation. Hawes, the homosexual dilettante who had corrupted him, lyrically recalls the supreme sacrifice made by the operatic castrati; Juana carries with her as a souvenir the slimy, bloody ear of a felled bull. As well as hinting at opera's sexual treason, Hawes is the Don José of Cain's psychic plot. He's possessive and predatory, wanting to own music and to own Sharp, whom he sentimentally enfeebles. At a party in New York he has the temerity to change roles, and impersonates a bullish maleness he doesn't deserve. When Juana explains how trainee toreadors practice with jackasses, Hawes kneels to playact the bull, with his catamites as joky picadors, anally prodding him with broomsticks and mop handles. Pudinsky, his latest kept boy, "began to rip off the bullring music from *Carmen* on the piano." Sharp is unmanned by the derisive charade, so Juana must take over from him the role of Escamillo. As a woman, she holds his manliness in trust. For their outing to the Hollywood Bowl, she wears a bullfighter's cape instead of a coat; now she saves Sharp's heterosexual identity by spearing and killing Hawes. During their game she runs him through with the espada and Sharp, like the offstage crowd in Bizet's final scene, "wanted to laugh, and cheer, and yell *Olé!* I knew I was looking at the most magnificent thing I had ever seen in my life." In this rearrangement of the triangle, Carmen kills Don José to keep him from erotically tempting Escamillo. After this expiation, Sharp and Juana escape literally "là-bas"—down to Guatemala.

Opera itself is now the corrida, challenging its interpreters to the ultimate trial of valor and virility. Sharp has an incongruously pedantic debate with an old Irish sailor about the competing virtues of opera and symphony. He claims that Rossini is a greater composer than Beethoven; the captain, shocked, says "Lad, lad, you're profaning a temple." It's the second time in *Serenade* that Sharp has done so. In the desert during a storm he breaks open the doors of a church, drives his car down the aisle, trains the headlights on the Blessed Sacrament and couples then and there with Juana, who between her groans begs forgiveness for their "sacrilegio." But what else is opera than an act of desecration? Society may attempt to institutionalize it and render it respectable, yet it will never be subdued.

TWO

The Met and the Metropolis

IN EUROPE the court eventually yields to the city as opera's patron. The new opera house opened in Vienna in 1869 was planned to ornament the Ringstrasse encircling the city; the Paris Opéra was planted at the intersection of the boulevards, with a new avenue carved out to exhibit its facade and connect it with the Louvre, residence of Napoléon III. Hofoper changes to Staatsoper, and opera confirms the new municipal patriotism: Verdi salutes Palermo in *I Vespri Siciliani* and maritime Genoa in *Simon Boccanegra*, Wagner performs the same service for Nuremberg in *Die Meistersinger*, Charpentier for Paris in *Louise* when the lovers gaze down from Montmartre at its incandescence, Strauss for Munich in the bourgeois jollity of *Feuersnot* and for Vienna in the recondite customs of *Der Rosenkavalier*.

In America, an opposite evolution occurs. The city, haplessly democratic, feels the need of a court, and relies on opera for its invention. Thus, in New York, the metropolis begets the Met. The New York of 1883 already had an opera house—the Academy of Music on Fourteenth Street. But it was the preserve of the Knickerbocker gentry, who used its shortage of boxes to keep at bay the newly arrived class of speculators and industrialists enriched by the Civil War. One of the Vanderbilt hostesses was refused a box at the Academy; the humiliated clan made common cause with the Astors, Morgans and Goulds to build an opera house of their own, where boxes would be guaranteed to stockholders.

Their pique typified this era of purgative opulence, when wealth too rapidly and grubbily amassed was disbursed in grandly profligate gestures—buying up Europe as Henry James's characters do, or smoking cigars wrapped in hundred-dollar bills like Diamond Jim Brady. The Metropolitan Opera had its origins in American capitalism's heroic effort to change lowly use into useless beauty by the intercession of art. That process continues: in 1950 Mrs. Nin Ryan, whose father Otto Kahn had financed the Met in the 1920s, sold a Rembrandt (the redemptive spoil of an earlier generation) to pay for the production of *Don Carlo* which inaugurated Rudolf Bing's regime. Colonel Mapleson, the impresario at the Academy, defined the Met as the whim of "a number of rich people who want some new way of spending money." But the whim had logic to it. Profiteering would be excused by splurging. Men toiled so that women could transmute their gains into jewels and gowns or (in the case of Lily Hamersley) an opera box wallpapered with orchids; with the profits from railways and the industries of the new century, New York was remodeled in the image of earlier European centuries. The monopolists erected Renaissance palaces on Fifth Avenue and, at Broadway and Thirty-ninth Street, an opera house which transformed the useful into the sumptuously beautiful by cladding its iron bones in red velvet and gold leaf.

Mapleson's joke against the Met was to see the factory beneath the palatial pretense. He called it "the new yellow brewery," and indeed its founders ensured that it contained enough shops and offices to return them an income from rents. Mapleson's "yellow" jeered at the building's plebeian brick. The Metropolitan Museum had cosmetically refaced itself in limestone, concealing the shame of its native brick; the Metropolitan Opera stood incriminated by its mercantile architecture.

Despite Mapleson's certainty that "the Faubourg St. Germain of the town" would remain loyal to him, the Met opened on October 22, 1883, with Gounod's *Faust*. The choice of opera was inevitable. *Faust* is a hymn to the imperial Mammondom of this age in New York's history. Christine Nilsson, the Met's first Marguerite, sings it at the Academy to begin and end a season in Edith Wharton's *The Age of Innocence*. (Since attendance is a rite, Edith Wharton's New Yorkers prefer the operas and their performers to be reassuringly invariable.) The Met opened the rebuilt house with *Faust* after the fire in 1893, and used it to inaugurate the Brooklyn Academy of Music in 1908. The work suited the plutocrats because it's about the irresistibility of economic temptation. Marguerite is seduced by an offering of jewels, over which she coos in coloratura as tinselly as the contents of the casket. The Met itself had been designed as a macrocosmic jewel box. The voices displayed there were lapidary treasures—Lauritz Melchior differentiated between two of his partners by calling Kirsten Flagstad a diamond and Helen Traubel a ruby—and the diamond horseshoe on the parterre reminded Marion Crawford, in his novel *The Prima Donna*, of "a vast coronet set with thousands of precious stones."

Crawford is seeing through the eyes of a soprano called Cordova who, onstage as Lucia, is herself an audience, dazzled by the hall's ornate expense. The auditorium was the true stage, constructed so the stockholders on its parallel prongs could scrutinize one another rather than the singers. In 1888 the *Amusement Bulletin* published a diagram of the Met at a premiere. It bothers to identify only two of the singers who, unheeded, go through the motions of performing *Lohengrin,* but it numerically tags and names the occupants of every box; the programs too printed a roll of box-holders as a supplementary cast list. The design of the auditorium contrived to snub anyone not in a box. The orchestra stalls were the low terrain of those who'd had to buy tickets, snootily overlooked by the stockholders; above the tiers of diamond and gold, the crowds in the gallery were sentenced to invisibility. One-sixth of the seats had little or no view of the stage. Within the club there were other yet more exclusive associations. In 1899 a college fraternity leased premises in a foyer and set itself up as the Metropolitan Opera Club. Its members imbibed their suppers in the house, then dozed to the sound of music on the Grand Tier. Later Mrs. August Belmont organized a sorority to complement the male clique, and under her direction the floral-hatted ladies of the Metropolitan Opera Guild bought a crystal chandelier for one of the lounges.

Gatti-Casazza, director of the Met between 1908 and 1935, lamented the hireling status of the musicians. The management could not interfere with the stockholders, whose boxes were vacant except on fashionable Mondays. Without a subsidy, the administrators "even had to pay rent for the theater itself." It wasn't until 1940 that the Metropolitan Opera Association Inc. supplanted the real-estate company which owned the title. The social history of the Met is that of its grudging democratization: its reluctant metamorphosis from private club to public amenity.

"People don't come to the opera to listen to the music," says a visitor to the Met in Upton Sinclair's novel *The Metropolis.* They came to flirt, to reconnoiter and to conduct social surveillance, and the opera house they built for these purposes made more allowance for their exhibitionism than for the convenience of the musicians they'd paid to accompany their conversation. The Met's inadequacies reminded the artists that they were dispensable. Lacking rehearsal space, the ballet had to limber up in a bar, while the chorus vocalized in the ladies' lavatory. Sets couldn't be stored, so were parked outdoors on the Seventh Avenue sidewalk. Nellie Melba, arriving in 1893, was disconcerted by the aloofness of the boxholding hostesses. In London she hobnobbed with royalty; in New York she was a singing menial. Rather than critical esteem, she interpreted social recognition as the real measure of her success at the Met. At last an invitation arrived from the Vanderbilts, and she was received in Mrs. Ogden Goelet's box at the Met. She had graduated from the ignominy of performance to the exaltation of social membership.

The heroine of Thomas R. Dixon's novel *The Root of Evil* in 1919 objects when her escort to the Met insists on "the unusual and vulgar procedure of entering the box in time to hear the opera." (The work they are gracing is, of course, *Faust*.) The grandees had superseded the show, and to maintain their supremacy they chattered conscientiously throughout the performance. Wagner's operas annoyed them because the primordial gloom onstage interfered with their scrutiny of each other. After *Siegfried* in 1887, the *Tribune* critic reported that the audience had been "compelled to sit ... in darkness so dense that neither shapely shoulders, gorgeous gowns nor dazzling diamonds could delight the eye." Louis Auchincloss's *Tales of Manhattan* includes a cautionary fable about a genteel uncle, drafted to help run the Met in the 1890s, who deserts his own social class and sides with the musical professionals. Angered by the chitchat during Marke's monologue in *Tristan*, he orders the curtain lowered and commands his relatives to keep silent. The penalty for his protest is ostracism.

The early Met modeled the decor of its productions on the Vanderbilt mansions with their malachite statuary, stained glass and baldaquin beds. Fortuny designed a bower of filigree for Tristan's ship in 1909, and Puvis de Chavannes the next year confected an Oriental pleasure-dome for Gluck's *Armide:* the stage was a sanctuary for the gilded age, with its top-heavily elaborate furnishings. Even when economic conditions outside doomed the old plutocratic regime, the Met protected that imperiled society. This was the purpose of the Metropolitan Opera Ball, first held in 1933. The costumes that year were derived from the Second Empire, the period of the Met's signature opera *Faust*. Mrs. Belmont reigned as the Empress Eugénie, and the soprano Grace Moore came as Christine Nilsson. The occasion allowed people, for one night only and with the moral support of fancy dress, to behave operatically, which means imperiously: the art served to prop up an illusion of confident aristocracy.

At first the opera was democracy's restoration of social ceremony and deference. Henry James archly called it "the only approach to the implication of the tiara known, so to speak, to American law." It existed as well to symbolize leisure, the boon bought by capitalist toil. Mrs. Beaufort in *The Age of Innocence* takes care to be seen at the opera on the night of her annual ball, just to demonstrate her indifference to domestic worries—the backstage chores which sustain the show. But the concomitants of wealth are surfeit and excess, and because opera in New York was pledged to the celebration of affluence it became necessarily grosser and gaudier. Upton Sinclair estimated that nine of the boxholders between them sported five million dollars' worth of gems. Soon the women began to resemble totem poles for their trinkets. Mrs. Frederick Vanderbilt looped her pearls round her waist in a belt. A lump of sapphire dangled from it which, with studied casualness, she kicked ahead of her as she advanced to her box. Mrs. John Drexel tried twining her pearls across her chest and leaving them to trail indefinitely down her back. Lewd ostentation had become compulsory.

Having convened society, opera's next duty in New York was to do away with the city's provincial innocence and ignorance. If it was to qualify for a renaissance, America must fall from the blandness of puritan paradise into the degeneracy of civilization. Opera's new function was to import European vice. During the Heinrich Conried regime (1903–8), the Met's most celebrated exhibits were sensual ogres: Olive Fremstad's Salome, writhing inside a truss of jewels; Emma Calvé's Carmen, one hand on a plump hip, the other tilting a cigarette, admiringly described by a reviewer as "diabolical"; Chaliapin's Mefistofele in Boito's opera, accused by another critic of being "bestiality incarnate." In 1926 Ronald Firbank in his unfinished novel *The New Rythum* describes the Met premiere of a decadent trifle called *Paphos*. Its unveiling of Venus in her lair coincides with the uncrating on the docks of another decadent fetish—"the Prax Herc, the World's Greatest Nude," revered by Firbank's New Yorkers for its prodigious penis. Like the statue, the opera is an incitement to exotic depravity, and a distraught galleryite, torn between the worship of Venus and the rival festivity for the phallic Hercules, evacuates his supper "gently into space, to the indignation of a section of the stalls." Singers were promoted to profane and uninhibited deities, symbols of instinct and appetite. Caruso was arrested in the Central Park monkey house for propositioning a woman; Grace Moore was famous at the Met for her sexual insatiability. Physiologically too, the singers embodied affluence. At a costume party to raise funds for the Met in 1953, Melchior—huge as a girdled hippo—impersonated Shirley Temple in a pinafore and curly mop, while Lily Pons, a diminutive apache, hauled him aloft in defiance of gravity (and with the aid of some steel cables in his dress).

Once a school of courtly formality for its audience, opera now sponsored revels like those of the disbarred lawyer Richard Knight, who stood upside down on his silk topper for the photographers before opening night and somersaulted through Sherry's bar during intermission. By the late 1930s, opening night was an obscenity. Cecil Beaton describes it in 1937. The lounges swarm with widows redolent of formaldehyde, exhumed (Beaton supposes) for the event and given the brief cosmetic semblance of life by their masseurs and hairdressers. Pearls choke their skinny necks; on their tonged and tightly waved heads are the same aigrettes they wore in the 1890s. The current Mrs. Vanderbilt, presiding in her box, is a sickly pinnacle of spun sugar. The occasion is ghoulish because it's the open grave of the past: the Met is a mausoleum where these crones hole up, awaiting each seasonal resurrection. Despite the odors of death, the evening gruesomely honors sex, and on stage Isolde—Flagstad presumably—bellows what Beaton calls "a primitive imitation of a cow in heat."

The photographer Weegee trained his camera on opening night during the 1940s as part of the denudation of New York he called *Naked City*, and exposed the fashionable congregation as an orgy of guzzling and swilling. The luminaries of the Social Register are just as savage as the mobsters, harlots and urchins Weegee photographed elsewhere in New York; there's no difference between a gala at the Met and a rent party in Harlem or a ribald singalong in a dive on the Bowery.

Weegee prepared himself for his assignment at the Met by assembling a parody of the social uniform. He rented his tux from the loft of a credit clothing store, where rising damp had moldered the suits to a slimy green. His first choice of accessory was a pair of brown shoes, but he was persuaded to buy a pair of black ones for $3.50 at Thom McAn's. Once at the Met, he gate-crashed Mrs. Vanderbilt's reception and photographed Sherry's as a watering hole for overdressed predators. The women suck Coke through straws, their fur coats trailing on the dusty parquet, their high heels propped on the bar rail. Their dandified escorts look like satyrs in the infrared light which the undercover Weegee uses. Every follicle of beard on their pampered jowls is anatomized, and they leer through the murk. Afterward, abandoning all pretense of decorum, they repair downtown to Sammy's nightclub on the Bowery, where Weegee photographed a bleary-eyed patriarch fondling a piglet (which he resembles). Since Weegee's mission was the excavation of a subliminal city, patrolled by the monsters released when the reason is asleep, he especially wanted to find someone dozing at the Met. Photographing a story on the dancer Markova, he prowled the boxes in quest of a snoring balletomane. In one of them Greer Garson nodded. Startled awake, she begged him to spare her, which—with a heavy heart—he did.

He had less compunction for Mrs. George Washington Kavanaugh, who in his photograph "The Critic" is seen arriving at the Met for opening night in 1942. (The opera, ironically, was *Boris Godunov*, mounted to compliment the Russians on their wartime alliance with the United States.) Of all the Met's raddled beldames, Mrs. Kavanaugh was the most grotesque. Trotting out her sparklers for the first opening night during the war, she replied, when questioned about the indelicacy of the display, "What shall we do with these things if we don't wear them?" By 1947 she had learned defensiveness. Asked the value of her jewels at that opening, she protested, "It wouldn't do—I'm a friend of the masses!" Weegee caught her on the sidewalk as, gripping her tickets, she steps from her car flanked by the horsefaced Lady Decies. Lipstick has revised her mouth in a senescent Cupid's bow. Every wrinkle on her face exerts itself to smile. Weegee's accusing flash makes more ghastly the pallor of her ermine, her diamonds and her powdered flesh. To the side stands the critic after whom Weegee named the picture—a befuddled woman groping in her bag perhaps for her ticket, perhaps for a gun with which to second Weegee's photographic assassination of Mrs. Kavanaugh.

Mrs. Kavanaugh was in every sense a relic. Three years before, high society had divorced the Met, leaving it to fend for itself as a musical concern. The withdrawal of the stockholders forced the Met to seek out a new constituency. Gatti calculated that it was kept going by a fraction of the city's population, probably no more than fifty thousand. If the magnates could no longer be relied on, the Met would have to nationalize itself. The Saturday afternoon broadcasts, which began in 1931, made the entire country its audience, and the W.P.A. guide to New York in 1939 congratulated the Met on reforming itself as an unofficial welfare agency, dedicated to "the broad dissemination of musical culture." The guide touchingly cites the gratitude of an agrarian public: "appreciative letters" about the radio relays "were received from farmers, filling-station attendants, cowpunchers."

An earnest of this changed relation to society was the plan to relocate the opera house, now stranded between the shabby retail traders of the garment district and the neon lunacy of Times Square. During the 1920s there was a proposal to establish it in Rockefeller Center, directly opposite St. Patrick's Cathedral. Pagan and Christian temples, Firbank's salacious Venusberg and the chaste altar it profaned, would face each other across Fifth Avenue. Mayor Fiorello La Guardia argued in 1935 for its inclusion in a populist art facility to be installed in Central Park. The powerful city planner Robert Moses suggested a site on Columbus Circle in 1951 and later—prosecuting his vision of New York as a corporate utopia, resplendent with expressways, toll bridges and skyscraping garages—leveled a slum at Lincoln Square to accommodate the Met. So the company slid diagonally up Broadway, colonizing the rubble of the felled tenements with a missionary fervor. Though it was his dynastic fortune which made the move possible, John D. Rockefeller III announced at the opening of Philharmonic Hall in Lincoln Center in 1962 that "the people want art," and said that the patron's responsibility had passed from the millionaire to suburbanites lolling in lawn chairs. Thorstein Veblen's leisure class, restricted at first to the Met's founding Midases, had extended to take in the middling ranks of society, and Lincoln Center was to be their aesthetic shopping mall.

From the start this altruistic notion suffered upsets. The investors who had frustrated La Guardia's schemes for the Met allied themselves uneasily with the city's medicinal assault on what William Schuman, writing in *The New York Times* about urban renewal in Lincoln Square (and still using the idiom of affluent corpulence), called "malnutrition of the spirit—neglect of the cultural diet." The Met saw itself exiled in the wilderness: as late as 1972 its programs included a map of the still semibarbarous precinct, entitled "How to Survive in the Lincoln Center Area."

Uncertainty about what the new Met meant socially was exposed in a comic mishap of the Chagall murals. Chagall's designs for the foyer awarded the Met a mystic or metaphysical covenant, wedding it to the community. In the panel called *The Sources of Music*, the yellow Hudson River spills beneath a free-floating George Washington Bridge to inundate the city and irrigate the Tree of Life: an Orphic flood of sound deluges New York with aural gold. In the red panel depicting *The Triumph of Music*, sound doesn't drench the city but spins it in giddy circles against a rejoicing sunburst. The skyline tipsily embarks on a planetary course. Chagall wanted the yellow mural at the south end of the lobby, the red one to the north. The *Sources* would gush into the theater, while the *Triumph*—

its angels aiming their trumpets beyond the building—issued a noisy summons to the city outside. But the workers installing the panels mixed them up, and placed the red one to the south. Chagall was enraged by the mistake. Now the patrons filing past the ticket tearers would receive the salute of his brassy seraphs, not the city at large. Rudolf Bing, with his talent for compromise, persuaded Chagall to accept the reversal: "Why do you want the music to go out of the theater and into the world? Perhaps . . . the heralding angels *should* play for the people who have come to the opera house, because they do love music." The institution had already dismissed Chagall's ambition to awaken the city with music—the same dream of harmonic union cherished by Whitman who, when he heard Jenny Lind singing at Castle Garden in the Battery of 1850, imagined the sound diffused on the air until all his fellow New Yorkers could share it and chorally merge in it. The Met's triumphs, Bing warned, would be strictly self-referring, insulated within the building.

That building, despite the democratic manifestos, was as conservative as the one it replaced. Each successive reform of the Met had entailed the abolition of boxes, and when the old house closed only 35 of the original 122 were left. The new Met virtually doubled that number, and even—as a result of Bing's special pleading—kept the retiring rooms behind them. The auditorium too is a galactic version of the old jewel casket. The levitation of its chandeliers, retracting their spars toward the roof as the performance begins, might symbolize Chagall's hope that the Met would musically raise men from the earth and restore them to the sky; but it's also an absurd self-embellishment, as if the hall were clipping on earrings in preparation for an evening out. Though the front of the stage extends in a crescent beyond the proscenium, wanting to encircle the audience with the impartiality of the ancient amphitheaters, this opening of its arms was exploited only after Bing's departure when in 1973 the surviving Carthaginians in *Les Troyens* filed out along those promontories to prophesy the advent of Rome. Since then, a single director has used the theater with the imaginativeness it demands. In the marching finale to *Mahagonny* in 1979, John Dexter sent his placard-bearing agitators down the aisles and simultaneously bared the backstage recesses, revealing scene shifters and electricians at work: its make-believe demolished, the Met was redefined as a factory.

Bing temporized nimbly between the Met's old and new identities. After the event, he imagined he had been an enlightened despot, scourging the grandees who engaged him. (Mrs. Belmont made a sortie to London to check on his social credentials before his appointment was agreed.) He removed opening night from the subscription list, had himself photographed traveling by subway from Essex House to the old Met, and resigned from the Century Club once the Met's chairman George Sloan was safely dead. He even braved the outrage of Zinka Milanov when he bragged to the press that the watch a mugger had snatched from him was a cheap memento of his military service. "The general manager of the Metropolitan Opera," Milanov informed him, "does not carry a watch worth only twenty-five dollars."

But Bing also liked to play the courtier, and openly scorned union negotiators, raucous standees and ungovernable singers (who owed their fame and power, he often said, to a malformation of the throat). Gatti refused to wear frock coats, or to pose against balustrades. White-tied flunkying returned with Bing, who filled his box with junketing politicians and UN diplomats. Only in James Levine did the Met acquire a figurehead whose sweaty dishevelment vouched for his fanatical seriousness: Levine's track suits and the referee's towel he slings around his neck at rehearsals are the badges of an exhausting, almost pugilistic professionalism.

Dissevered from high society, the Met in exchange identified itself with civilization. Its marketing tactics in the 1970s made subscription a civic duty, like jury service or paying your taxes. "You are cordially invited"—as you open your wallet—"to strike a blow for civilization." These ads cunningly made the best of what began as shamefaced begging. The transition from private benefaction to public appeals wasn't easy, and Gatti felt demeaned by having to request donations in 1933. The guileful copywriters enabled the Met to cry poor without disgrace, representing it as an ennobled existence which contributors should pay for the privilege of being associated with. "The way of life called The Met," as the 1976 campaign referred to it, now offered much more than the solidarity of a club. It was an outpost of Henry James's millennial Great Good Place. Signing a check inscribed your name on an honor roll, and allowed you to share the institution's immortality: "you'll experience a sense of giving that can only be called timeless." Encoded, this was the same message about salvation which James read in the Met of the Vanderbilts, except that the redemption here purveyed was spiritual as much as social, and could be extorted by moral remonstrance. "There always has been, and always will be, a place for civilization . . . The place is in your heart."

But was this civilized life merely the luxury of the robber barons by another name? Inside the citadel, you were subjected to a means test harking back to the plutocratic Met where, as the *Dramatic Mirror* sniffed in 1883, "the Goulds and Vanderbilts and people of that ilk perfumed the air with the odor of crisp greenbacks." The programs in 1972 opened on a bank's headlined interrogation: "Well, how much are you worth this morning? More than $500,000?" The audience still strives to upstage the performers. A Zeiss Optics program ad in the same season stinted the singers to reserve its applause for the fashionable gewgaws of the operagoer. In the design, a gloved hand grips a silvery pair of opera glasses against a jeweled neck. "Clearly Bravissima!" the caption pipes up—but goes on to specify that its enthusiasm refers to "the distinguished Diadem theater glass."

Vowing to civilize the slum, the Met has in fact boutiquized it. The social bequest of Lincoln Center has been the reclamation of nearby Columbus Avenue with its sushi bars, Sunday brunches and busking string quartets. Opera can't help causing gentrification. That fate is predicted in 1957 by Leonard Bernstein's *West Side Story*, which set its gang strife in the tenements cleared for the construction of Lincoln Center. *West Side Story* Americanizes opera as the Broadway musical, and democratizes ballet as acrobatics when its toughs dance in a high-school gym. Yet once the Met replaced the mean streets, so the gritty, savage realism of *West Side Story* must be upgraded to operatic respectability: when Bernstein recorded it in 1984, he treated the rowdy score with symphonic solemnity, and secured the same upward mobility for its characters by casting the work with opera stars—José Carreras turns the Anglo Tony into a moody, orotund Latin tenor, Kiri Te Kanawa's Maria is Arabella out slumming, and Marilyn Horne, as the anonymous, offstage singer of "Somewhere," plays a hushed and awesome voice from heaven. Bernstein readies his work for admission to the palace of art built on the ruins of its original setting.

Nevertheless, the Met at Lincoln Center makes room for an urban flotsam directly descended from the immigrant mobs who crammed the Family Circle of the old house in the first decade of the century; and to its rotating repertory company of standees, the Met is not a prerogative of the rich but a charitable consolation of the city's poor, lost and sometimes crazed souls. Their day begins at dawn in the queue for a standing place in the corral behind the orchestra stalls, and ends after midnight in a crush outside the stage door.

In this underclass, the habits of the potentates who founded the Met ironically live on—the jealous exclusiveness, the air of clubbable proprietorship. They are a race of mute inglorious Mrs. Vanderbilts; shuffling into line with them once, I heard one of them curse the management's plan to increase the price of standing tickets in the next season. "Hell," she shrilled, "the standees is the aristocracy of the house!" Onto them, as custodians and trustees of the house, devolves the duty of hospitality. The boxholders favored Melba with recognition, but when Joan Sutherland made an overdue return to the Met in November 1982 as Lucia, it was a standee somewhere aloft who did the honors. Exactly inserted into the pause before her first aria was applauded, a single voice yelled "Welcome back!"; the uproar which ensued sounded as if it had been cued by that greeting. The uncle in Louis Auchincloss's story suspects that fashionable Mondays at the Met in the late nineteenth century are "a lost ritual of community living," a consolidating festivity like a village fair, when the tribe rehearses its integration. The same is true, still, for the standees. They're enfranchised in and to the Met. It's the only community or family which will own them, and they go there rather than home in the evenings. Their presence attests to the metropolitanism of the Met. To fill its four thousand seats, Mrs. Astor's quorum of the socially acceptable four hundred no longer suffices. The rest must be recruited from O. Henry's four million, the indiscriminate quantity of the city's nameless and downtrodden, raised up, as Chagall trusted they would be, by music.

Still, social incongruities persist. In the democratic modern age, opera is a hideout for the grand manner and the high style, even for haute couture. At the Met's centenary concert on October 22, 1983, the singers were festooned like Christmas trees. Régine Crespin delivered Carmen's habanera in a harlequin's outfit; Marilyn Horne's Dalila exhibited the strength she stole from Samson in biceps of powder blue; between the shoulder blades of Joan Sutherland's Semiramide reposed an elephantine lime-green butterfly. Cowboy gear became on this occasion a courtly uniform: James McCracken sang an excerpt from *Otello* in a Texan string tie fastened at his throat by a brooch.

The arbitrariness of the charade was exaggerated by the settings. Into Zeffirelli's warren of cobbled Paris streets and cavelike bistros from *La Bohème* marched Montserrat Caballé and José Carreras, inappropriately got up for a raffish corner of the Quartier Latin, she in black flounces to set off the shelf of medals on her bosom, he in tails. Finding themselves in the greasy Café Momus, they deemed it to be the St. Lazare prison, and sang the salute to death with which Andrea Chénier and Maddalena go off to the guillotine.

Late in the gala, when the curtain parted on a sulfurous pagan temple where the Met ballet was to cavort in the Bacchanal from *Samson et Da-lila*, a gasp both of pleasure and recognition fluttered through the audience like the rustling of money. That brassy edifice where material values were worshiped was an archetype of the Met these people cherished. But the spendthrift emotionalism and vocal extravagance which made opera the creed of New York's would-be aristocrats is confined today to such occasions of festive folly. Behind the scenes, the millionaires bravely keep up the show by placating their employees. The gala concert began with a speech by the Met's general manager, reporting agreement with the musicians' union on a new contract, which ensured the Met's survival until 1987. He pointed out the chief negotiator who, haloed by a spotlight, graciously acknowledged applause from a box. There were still, the general manager then added, twenty-three further contracts to be settled.

The following spring, the Met staged a second gala to commemorate its presentations of dance. A feast was to follow the performance; a team of pastry chefs in Paris made an edible Met for it, three feet long and four feet tall. One of its facades represented the old brewery in midtown, the other the arches of the Lincoln Center theater. Chagall's juggled murals from the lobby recurred in miniature, on a canvas of white chocolate. The Met cake constructed an alimentary architecture: opera for an age of consumerism, like the gingerbread house in Humperdinck's *Hänsel und Gretel*. The foundation was concreted chocolate with sinews of glucose and syrup, the stiffening of its girders accomplished by a pastillage of sugar and gelatin. A window of the Paris patisserie was removed to get it out, after which it was flown across the Atlantic, lodged on the Grand Tier and garnished with jewels (not edible) on loan from Harry Winston. But the day of the gala, May 13, was hot, and in the reflected glare from the white marquee on the plaza outside, the cake began to melt. One of the opera house's candied facades crumbled in a mess of gilt marzipan, dripping like hot wax. An electric fan was trained on it to stop the rot, but the cake had already spread its odor of decomposing confectionery—the sweet stench of death—up the triumphal staircase. Here was opera at its most culinary, and its most indigestible.

THREE

Opera in a Garden

THIS century, opera has quit its position at the center of the city. Recolonizing Roman ruins at Verona and Caracalla or roofing over the desert at Santa Fe, installed in a country garden at Glyndebourne or pitching its camp in a Finnish forest at Savonlinna, it changes from a nocturnal item on a winter's social calendar to an outing for a summer day—a musical picnic.

As it returns to nature, opera runs back through its own history. The open-air Roman amphitheaters acknowledge its source in the ancient tragic festivals. In 1975 *Die Walküre* was performed in the arena at Orange, in the south of France. The honeycombed cliff rearing above the town supplied Wagner's gods—who in Patrice Chéreau's production at Bayreuth or Nikolaus Lehnhoff's at San Francisco inhabit plush and insulated bourgeois villas—with an elemental scenery of shaggy crags and rocky mounds. Mythology here rejoined geology. The Sieglinde of Leonie Rysanek wore woolly pelts; the Brünnhilde of Birgit Nilsson, aquiline on her ledge, had a witch's peaked hat and seemed about to take flight on the hot gusts of the mistral. That wind concocted an orchestral storm of its own, and obliged Rudolf Kempe to lay down his baton, use both hands to anchor his score, and conduct by bobbing his head. Despite the accidents of the night, with a gale keening through Nilsson's war cries, the opera belonged in that landscape, its characters sculpted into form by the natural forces they defied, its music the sound of an earth in upheaval.

At Glyndebourne, where on a Sussex estate an eccentric connoisseur in 1934 added a theater to his country house, opera remembers its birth in the seventeenth century as an aristocratic whim. Glyndebourne compliments itself when performing Strauss: *Ariadne auf Naxos*, set in the palace of the richest man in Vienna, and *Capriccio*, which takes place in a château outside Paris, are about operas staged in private homes.

The English have never entirely accepted the urbanity of opera. More at home in parks than plazas, they long to pastoralize everything. The Royal Opera House had as its neighbor until recently a grubby vegetable market, and its administrative offices occupy a former banana warehouse. At Glyndebourne, opera is literally put out to pasture. Mixing a night at the opera with a day in the country produces some rich absurdities: merchant bankers with raincoats over their dinner jackets and plastic carryalls instead of wicker hampers sit among the flotsam in Victoria Station at 3 P.M., waiting for the train to take them south; once at Glyndebourne, picnics must be shiveringly consumed under tepees of traveling rugs on a wet lawn. Spindly heels sink through soggy grass, and mucky evening slippers are scraped on the rustic boot cleaner outside the house. Peter Hall's 1977 *Don Giovanni* turned on the untrustworthiness of the local weather: nemesis meant—as it certainly does at Glyndebourne—a thunderstorm, and Mozart's seducer, his sensual élan doused, ran his errands under an umbrella.

Bayreuth requires its audience to be crusaders, and to suffer privations for the music's sake. Forty years after his visit to the first festival in 1876, the composer Charles Stanford could still remember the pain of those cane-bottomed seats. Though Hanslick doubted that the appreciation of Wagner was aided "by being uncomfortably housed . . . , sleeping badly, eating wretchedly, and after a strenuous five or six hours' performance of opera, being uncertain of securing a modest snack," penance is one of the acolyte's duties. Glyndebourne demands that the operagoer double as something more arduous and unlikely than a pilgrim: a nature lover. Urban operas find themselves unexpectedly countrified there. Peter Hall's production of *Fidelio* in 1979 took place in the backyard of what appeared to be a prison farm. Rocco cultivated his vegetable patch, and Marzelline hung out her washing in a yard where chickens pecked.

The spirit of place dictates the decor. Opera in the country must be idyllic, and Glyndebourne's productions look to the memory like a series of paradises lost. Glyndebourne has twice reconstructed the pleasure garden of Mozart's *Die Entführung aus dem Serail.* During the 1950s, Oliver

Messel placed it in a rococo grove and two decades later, when Peter Wood directed the opera, William Dudley's designs shifted it to a sensual Orient of caged birds, filigree bowers and latticed peepholes, as humid as a steambath, modeled on the fantasies of a Victorian painter, J. F. Lewis. The season which began with chickens scavenging outside the kitchen in *Fidelio* ended with stuffed sheep petted by mock rustics in Haydn's *La Fedeltà Premiata*. John Cox's production evoked an artificial Eden, perhaps a prototype of Glyndebourne: Esterháza, where the opera was first performed in 1781, built by Haydn's patron in the malarial Hungarian marshes. His gardens there were a wilderness subdued to art and protected by defunct deities: statues of Diana, Fortune and Love acted as terminal gods of the walks. Wild boar prowled the denser reaches of the forest but, as a traveler reported in 1784, were "quite tame and come and nudge the walkers all the time": converted by opera's personal patron, Orpheus? The Cumae of *La Fedeltà Premiata* is haunted, like Esterháza, by a monster which at last admits to being benign. Lovers who remain faithful risk being sacrificed to an ogre; but the venomous sea-beast is a disguise for Diana, who has merely been overseeing sexual conduct. Like Watteau's island of Cytherea, spoiled by the disease of satiety, Esterháza is one of the eighteenth century's engineered and unsatisfactory pleasances, and Haydn's opera actually records that idyll's failure, because it was composed to inaugurate a new opera house built by the prince after fire had gutted his phantasmal palace. Cox's production acknowledged that we can only playact at being in paradise. The shepherds were bored courtiers, lolling on a nylon carpentry of lawn, who participate in Haydn's charade to pass the time. But the designs by Hugh Casson—serene, dreamily washed-out watercolors—suggested that the ornamental horticulture of Esterháza could be exchanged for the placid Sussex downs: the flanks of hill in Casson's distances were the landscape surrounding Glyndebourne itself, as if the back wall of the theater had become transparent.

Maurice Sendak designed a decadent late eighteenth-century arbor for Glyndebourne in the 1982 production of Prokofiev's *L'Amour des Trois Oranges*. The witchy Clarice surveyed her seedy garden from a swing, like a demonized heroine in a painting by Fragonard. Truffaldino's festival of laughter was a pornographic fête champêtre, strewn with picnic baskets like the Glyndebourne lawn. Satyrs boarded nymphs of stone, and a leering statue urinated into a pool, to the amazement of a flotilla of ducks. For an *Idomeneo* in 1974, John Cox and the designer Roger Butlin used Turner's paintings of the aristocratic house and park at Petworth, inundated by light. The Turners, seen in tunnel vision as if through the wrong end of a telescope, betokened a classical calm which Mozart's characters, agitated by romantic emotion, had already left behind them.

Whatever your image of the forfeited, longed-for good place, Glyndebourne can summon it up. When David Hockney designed *Die Zauberflöte* in 1978, he moved it from arid, Masonic Egypt to his own fabled realm of America. The first scene conflated his two favored American landscapes: stunted Los Angeles palm trees ringed one of those granitic boulders which thrust through the greenery of Central Park. Hockney worked on the designs in New York, and they referred constantly to that city. The columned staircase in Sarastro's palace copied that in the Metropolitan Museum; one of the sculptural heads lolling outside the redbrick pyramid had the stonily bland stare of the Statue of Liberty; the dragon, capsizing, puffed out a last gasp of smoke like the man on the old Times Square cigarette billboard. When, at the end of the opera, the stage opened into a solar emblem, Hockney's radial Art Deco sunburst exactly duplicated the interior of Radio City Music Hall (which someone said was the kind of place God might have built if he'd had the money). The aerial perspective of Sarastro's estate with its grid of neatly planted blocks was the view of Manhattan from the Empire State Building, and the same scene allowed Hockney to connect his cheerily depraved American hell, New York, with his bronzed and hedonistic American heaven, California. Sarastro's Manhattan tapered toward Los Angeles: near the vanishing point of the perspective, an angular swimming pool glittered in a sandy waste. But this fabled America of affluence and bodily delectation, so remote from the sparse, ordeal-ridden landscape where Mozart actually set the work, was likely to dwindle into staid, stuffy England. At the foot of the Metropolitan Museum staircase, Papageno gobbled the contents of a Glyndebourne picnic basket, and Sarastro's chariot was drawn by toy lions with rotating heads like those sold as souvenirs at Longleat. Hockney had turned Mozart's allegorical terrain and Glyndebourne itself into that indigenous American paradise, the theme park.

Opera at Glyndebourne no longer concerns the aggression and uproar of the solitary human will. Its subject is our membership in nature. The operas which have been most at home there are pastoral fables, restoring their characters to an Arcady of infancy—Jean-Pierre Ponnelle's *Falstaff*, whose hero learns about the folly of the human animal in a forest dominated by a papery cutout of Windsor Castle; in 1985, Peter Hall's *Albert Herring*, where the glowering moods of Lady Billows were registered meteorologically as a cloud blotted the sky above John Gunther's Suffolk village, dulled the spring sun and shed an ill-tempered April shower. W. H. Auden sniffed at Britten's setting of A *Midsummer Night's Dream* as "pure Kensington." Its erotic boscage can resemble a trimmed municipal garden, grazed by elves and pixies as winsome as those of Arthur Rackham. But Hall, directing it at Glyndebourne in 1981, gave it a real and sinister enchantment: this Athenian wood in gray and silver was the nocturnal negative of Glyndebourne's happy garden. John Bury's design animated the landscape. The trees were anthropomorphs, played by limber, writhing actors who flexed and twined their limbs and entangled the struggling humans in their arms.

Hall even had the courage, the next year, to direct an opera which is in origin a courtly pageant as a romp devised by the peasantry. The work was Gluck's *Orfeo ed Euridice*, chosen by Janet Baker for her retirement from the stage. Hall didn't treat *Orfeo* as a tragic monodrama; he presented it as a pastoral—and therefore a communal and comic idyll. Like all pastorals, it's about ejection from an ideal garden: the loss and reclamation (thanks to music) of paradise. Euridice drifts away from the loved and familiar countryside into a fog of nonbeing. Her revival promises the earth's annual resurrection: most opera seasons begin with the year's death, in autumn; Glyndebourne is a rite of spring. After the trio of thanksgiving, the opera extended into a bucolic epilogue, where song gave way to dance and the quickened body's enjoyment of its own suppleness and energy: a long countrified sequence of jigs around a phallic maypole. A ruddy harvest moon blessed the celebration, and children—some of them fitted out with homemade wings of straw, in humble tribute to the cherubic Amore—brought offerings of sheaves and baskets of fruit. Gluck's classicism was overtaken by an agricultural festival from Shakespearean comedy.

Hall's *Orfeo* was held together by the holding of hands; thus it performed the ancient dramatic rite of convening and sustaining a community. The production insisted on tactile values. When Amore swung down from that trapeze where the baroque gods disport, Janet Baker's Orfeo reached out to touch his chubby legs, desperate to prove his solidity and thus his trustworthiness. At the gate of hell, after Orfeo had placated the furry Furies, they repaid him with some rounds of calisthenics and then, in earnest of their conversion, shook him solemnly by the hand. Euridice's arrival in heaven was celebrated by a manual greeting. The immortals pressed their palms against hers and locked her into a frieze. Heaven is a society where, no longer needing to rely on the tenuous human accord of a handshake, we are literally members of one another. On their troubled return to earth, the touch of a hand was the only juncture between Orfeo and Euridice, since he must not look at her. But during the rejoicing which followed her rebirth, the messianic gladhanding of heaven generalized itself. A pediment of enskied gods was flown in, and they passed to the mortals a rope of silk with which they looped and bound one another. Knitted inside it, they umbilically reconstituted what they call the empire of love. Hall sent the chorus to file through the auditorium, garlanding its walls with this connective fabric and gathering the audience into its benediction.

When the gods were hauled back up to the heights, they left behind them on the empty ramp a beautifully simple scenic image. Crisscrossed on the stage was that deflated skein which had girdled and yoked all the characters together. Like myth, the silken cord is the token and the memory of a time when gods walked with men and when men could attain (as Orfeo does) godlike powers; like music, it is the fragile, fluttery bridge between heaven and earth.

FOUR

New Theaters

DURING his incendiary youth, Pierre Boulez proposed tearing down the opera houses of Europe. In the event, there was no need: opera hasn't remained cramped within them.

Migration from the cumbersome, conventional theater began when technology invented new arenas for opera. The recordings John Culshaw produced with Georg Solti during the 1960s abolished scenery and transferred opera to an invisible theater—an engineered stereophonic space behind the eyes and between the ears which Culshaw called his Sonicstage. He drew a map of it to accompany his recording of *Tristan und Isolde*, solemnly explaining that the ship should be imagined at an angle of forty-five degrees. The living room, he maintained, was the ideal location for *Tristan*, for which Ernest Newman had wanted "dimly visible actors" or "impersonal voices floating through a darkened auditorium." Culshaw's aural arena was peopled by sound effects. Hoping to "establish stereo as a legitimate operatic medium," Culshaw showed off its wizardry with feats of acoustic distortion. The trick of which he was proudest was self-consciously magical. For the Tarnhelm scene in *Götterdämmerung*, when Siegfried takes on the guise and voice of Gunther, Culshaw managed to fuse the sounds of Wolfgang Windgassen and Dietrich Fischer-Dieskau, and swore never to divulge the knob-twiddling means by which he had done so.

But this gimmickry didn't so much renew opera as bolster up old habits. Culshaw took his imaginary theater too literally: how apt that, as Nilsson finished recording Brünnhilde's immolation in their *Götterdämmerung*, he should have ushered a real horse onto the platform for her to ride into the nonexistent flames. Stereophony was just the conventional opera house with the lights turned off.

Film is able to quit the opera house altogether, and to open up new meaning within works which are limited by the stage. This, exhilaratingly, is the case with one of the earliest cinematic attempts at opera: Smetana's *The Bartered Bride*, directed by Max Ophuls in 1932. Smetana's pastoral is a celebration of the land, and Ophuls—building a Czech village in the Bavarian countryside—let the opera out into nature. Marie and Hans sing their duet drifting downstream in a flower-bedecked boat, and the news of his betrayal is relayed from house to house and on into the fields; Wenzel, silly with joy, trips through a meadow of daisies.

Ophuls used only smatterings of the operatic score, but through visual montage re-creates the music in a dance of images. The camera is his orchestra. He sends it wheeling in circles, to choreograph the perpetual motion of the circus band or of the rustic jigs. Comedy is about the reassuring cycle of nature, and Ophuls illustrates this truth with a series of circular images. His plot begins when Wenzel's carriage loses a wheel; this begets a series of visual puns, connecting the wheel of fortune on which Marie wins a prize pig, the Ferris wheel, the floral circlet on the pole decorating the arena, and the wedding ring Hans presents to Marie. The visiting circus names its entertainment after the magic circle in which it's played out. The characters themselves rotate. The marriage broker speeds round the inn table in excited arcs as he distributes documents during his aria, and Marie in despair whirls and spins inside the house, dashing against the walls like a trapped bird. The camera tracks them in 360-degree loops, swinging from Hans in his cart to the broker on his galloping horse and back, or perambulating round the circus ring as the crowd stares at Esmerelda with her head in the bear's mouth and Marie makes her getaway; in the final dance, the girls giddily revolve, their flaring skirts—up which the camera peeps—like hoops. This, like the carousel in Ophuls's later film *La Ronde*, is the circulation of desire: the force which makes the world go round.

Mobile, the movie camera can express a vital joy. Ophuls therefore interpolates into the film a defense of the new medium. Marie and Hans, evading their pursuers, go into a photographer's tent at the fair and are posed like dummies, fixed into position and forced to grin. During the half-minute of the exposure, the posse invades the tent and they have to flee, leaving Hans's parents arrested in the frame, detained by the photographer's order "Halt!" The still camera freezes people; movies, like music, thrive on kinesis. At the end of the film, the broker lines up all the parties for a wedding portrait. The photographer tells them to hold it and to laugh, and as they grin the motion picture slows down to a still, which fades and retreats into a frame. The characters vanish into an ideal, irretrievable past, preserved forever in a family album: the shot is captioned "a memory of the year 1859."

The mobility of the movies is a personal compulsion for the black heroine of *Carmen Jones*, Otto Preminger's 1954 film of the opera with a jazzy new text by Oscar Hammerstein II. Carmen here hates being cooped up; travel and transport are motifs in the action. Cindy Lou (Hammerstein's Micaëla) arrives by bus at the army camp to farewell Joe (José), who is off to flying school. Carmen works in a factory making parachutes not cigarettes, to assist the Korean war effort. This new volatility suits cinematic characters, always on the move. Carmen Jones sings the habanera while shimmying up and down the lunch queue in the factory canteen, and the seguidilla while slithering between the front and back seats of the jeep in which Joe is taking her to prison. They drive along in competition with a freight train; when they're stopped by it at a level crossing, Carmen jumps aboard and is chased by Joe, leaping between carriages. Another train waits at the station near Billy Pastor's (a transliterated Lillas Pastia's) to take Husky Miller (the boxer who is the Escamillo of the musical) from the Louisiana bayous to Chicago. Carmen is tempted by its streamlined speed in the quintet: traveling as quickly as a Kansas hurricane, it can take her a thousand miles in half a day. In Chicago, Joe hides in a ghetto room while Carmen prowls the streets, visiting Husky at the gym or in his hotel; he's tormented by the clatter of the elevated trains outside the window, mocking him with a freedom of maneuver he no longer possesses.

Bizet's music has also been made to travel. Carmen's gypsy song is given to Frankie (the character corresponding to Frasquita, played in the film by Pearl Bailey). In the swampy Louisiana backwoods, the number has gone native. Frankie tells the drummer to beat out that rhythm, replacing the operatic orchestra with millions of tom-toms. The American South reverts here to jungly superstitious Africa, and Carmen's grandmother is a soothsayer, aghast (like the citizens of Catfish Row in *Porgy and Bess*) at the sighting of a buzzard.

Joseph Losey's film of *Don Giovanni* in 1979 began with the Palais

Garnier on fire: the film is the opera house's combustion, because the music—as irrepressible as Giovanni himself—can't be sequestered inside the theater. Only traveling shots can tell the truth about the voyaging, rapacious Giovanni. During the prelude, the characters prowl through the catacomb-like corridors of Palladio's Teatro Olimpico in Vicenza, while Giovanni rides across the water toward the glassworks at Murano. Elvira sings her opening lament wandering through misty woods, circumnavigating the Villa Rotonda (where Losey lodges Giovanni). Ottavio, needing to clear his head after Anna's revelations, boats through the marshy lagoon and sings "Dalla sua pace" standing upright in his gondola; he delivers "Il mio tesoro" to the villa, stamping through the grounds and shaking his fist at it. Seduction is a journey. Giovanni beguiles Zerlina by taking her on a tour of the villa, sings his angrily effervescent aria before the party stalking through the park, and Zerlina in her turn wheedlingly pursues Masetto through the basement kitchens among carcasses of beef, airing cheeses, ropes of garlic, drying corn and racks of autumn fruit. The camera's itinerary is vertical too, plumbing the social cellarage or the molten pit—Giovanni's industrial hell—of the furnace at Murano. Only once do the urgent stalking and fleeing which are the libertine's motives and the camera's relent. In the second act, the characters return to the arcaded Teatro Olimpico for the imbroglio of their sextet, lining up to perform it before a seated theater audience. That episode of stasis and concerted judgment is essential to Losey's formal theorem: the sensual energy which expends itself in motion will eventually run out, cool off as Giovanni's hand does when the petrified god grips it; and when that happens these gladly lively beings will all congeal into funerary emblems, or Palladian statuary.

Though the liberty of film is its capacity to follow action out of the theater, Losey's decision to set *Don Giovanni* in and around Vicenza—where the Commendatore dies in the Piazza dei Signori, and Giovanni's women are distributed among the rural mansions Palladio built for the gentry—has a more than touristic justification. This external reality coincides with the inner significance, as he sees it, of the opera. Palladio's buildings are modeled on classicism, but exist to evoke romantic sentiment. In the room where the Commendatore lies in state, the veiled statues have gone into mourning; in the flare of vindictive lightning, the Rotonda is a frail, white, empty shell, no fortress for the besieged Giovanni. Leporello juggles to balance the equations of a rational classicism, and fails. "Il quadro non è tondo" he tells Elvira when explaining Giovanni's waywardness—the square isn't a circle. *Don Giovanni* is a classical cage for a romantic demon. Hence the aptness of the architecture.

Losey was fascinated by the regularity of buildings. He said of the scene which opens and closes *Accident*, showing a square brick house outside Oxford, "I wanted a completely symmetrical house, a completely symmetrical frame, because I wanted a completely symmetrical and classical film." The symmetry, however, is fearful—not the classical equilibration of an object but its romantic multiplication, tending to infinity and terminating in nightmare. Thus, exhibiting the list of Giovanni's conquests, Leporello opens a folding catalog down the villa's steps into the grounds, and could go on unfurling those regular squares of paper until they circumnavigated the world; the same perverse reproductiveness symmetrically aligns the three male predators. The Giovanni of Ruggero Raimondi and the Leporello of José van Dam look alike, and as a miniature replica of themselves they're trailed by an adolescent valet in black, a satanic Cherubino. Losey, discussing his film *Eve*, called Venice "a city of masks, a city of facades." This sense of the deceptiveness of the calm classical visage recurs in his Vicenza. Raimondi's plastery, bloodless makeup is an architectural facade not a face. Leporello wears a life mask of Giovanni while pretending to serenade Elvira, and Giovanni uses a false face of Leporello to woo her servant. The spectral glaze hints at the same romantic spirit within the classical form: the Venetian carnival has become a dance of death, with lecherous ghosts fornicating among the tombs. The landscape in which Losey cinematically plants *Don Giovanni* is at once a real place and a symbol.

This is truer still of Francesco Rosi's *Carmen* in 1984. Rosi's preceding film, *Christ Stopped at Eboli*, is about the salving encounter with the reality of a landscape: the doctor of Carlo Levi's novel, exiled from Rome by the fascists, is banished to an agrarian wilderness which even Christ stopped short of visiting; initially haughty and despairing, he learns to love these bereft and indigent people, and to be consoled by the placid, unprotesting routine of their lives. It is exactly such a reconciliation and redemption to which Rosi treats *Carmen*.

In the theater, the opera's Spanishness is falsely picturesque. Bizet after all never saw the country whose folk music he wrote so proficiently. Mérimée's characters, uprooted by music, can Americanize themselves in *Carmen Jones*, where Joe loves Cindy Lou because she's just like his ma, and wants to have lots of kids with her—when he has earned enough to take good care of them all, which is why he's so eager to train as a pilot. Carmen Jones makes herself at home in American suburbia: she shops for Joe's supper on the night she seduces him, and prides herself on cooking for her man, cleaning his boots and straightening his twisted belt. Rosi puts a stop to this migratory universality. By going onto location he can test a French opera against the truth of an actual Spain.

Rosi sees Carmen as the elusive, enchanting spirit of that country, and he sets her free to roam down its dusty streets, across its plains and through its mountains. She is as cinematically mobile as Don Giovanni, though for different reasons: he's a hunter, she's a nomad. The camera can follow her to hideouts which are off-limits to the theater because they're offstage—into the cigarette factory, where she rolls the leaves of tobacco against her inside thigh and rubs the tubes to savor their thickness; upstairs to the bedroom in the inn where she squirms on a grimy mattress to taunt José. Since she is ubiquitous, so is the cinematic eye. Rosi's first act travels along and above the walls of a drowsy hill-town, watching Carmen materialize from the mob of her colleagues and disappear again—when she escapes arrest—into that companionable throng. The second act alternates between the low tavern where she cavorts and the Moorish luxury of the Alhambra, where Escamillo is being grandly entertained. They meet in transit, on a road outside the city walls. Escamillo's wanderings are also explained by the vagrant camera. How does he come to be in the Ronda mountains, near the camp of the smugglers? Rosi supplies him with a motive by showing him as a cowboy rounding up bulls on his remote estate during the prelude to the third act.

Molded from the land, the freckled, carnal Carmen of Julia Migenes-Johnson has a genius for gregariousness, and dances to celebrate the community's adhesion. One of Rosi's interpolated scenes joins her with a tubby but terpsichorean old man, still swayed by the rhythm—agitated but elegant—which pulses through her. The character's indiscriminate-ness advertises her generosity. Ruggero Raimondi's Escamillo is her alter ego. Praying before the corrida, Escamillo suggests, as she does, the paradox of Spain—lethally suave yet superstitiously pious, gracefully affronting doom, whether that fate is Carmen's cards or Escamillo's horned quarry. Though Escamillo entrusts himself to a Christian god, he and Carmen have subjected that religion to an exotic Spanish metamorphosis: the icon of their faith is the Madonna carried through the streets of Seville at Easter early in the film, her breast punctured by swords. This injured fetish is a totem of the rite acted out again in Rosi's film, presaging the end of Escamillo's bulls and of Carmen herself.

Between the elemental energies of these twin tormentors, the José of Plácido Domingo is reduced to a blundering gawk, violent because confused. When Piero Faggioni directed *Carmen* at the Edinburgh Festival in

1977, he set the work in José's condemned cell, where Mérimée's novel of grieving retrospection also takes place. Installed there, Domingo could be a tragic hero. The prison was the huis clos of the theater: the cramped space of tragedy, from which there's no exit. But as Rosi opens up the work, José loses this centrality. He is instead a dumb ox, first grazing then rampaging through the harsh, fecund landscape of Spain embodied by Carmen. Before the music of the first prelude begins with its arrogant brilliance, Escamillo kills a bull which thrashes in slow motion, then crumples at his feet. Everything thereafter in the opera, once the music with its own fatal inevitability starts up, is an epilogue to and a repetition of that. Is the bullfight Spain's local surviving version of those ceremonies of sacrifice where drama—opera included—began?

Ingmar Bergman's film of *Die Zauberflöte* in 1974 restored the opera to a theater, on the antiquated courtly stage at the palace of Drottningholm. But film discloses a reality outside, around and behind the makeshift theatrical performance. Bergman had included Tamino's encounter with the Speaker in an earlier film, *Hour of the Wolf*, setting it in a marionette theater. Drottningholm to is a place of gimcrack illusion and crude puppeteering. The ancient scenery squeaks and rumbles as it parts to introduce the Queen of the Night; characters hold up placards with trite moral lessons inscribed on them. The camera sees through the pretense, looking back into the wings at pulleys, ropes and quivering flats, following the performers on- and offstage. Papageno, hearing his cue, jumps up from a nap, musses his hair, bounds downstairs and onto the stage; Sarastro passes the time between his entrances studying the score of *Parsifal*, while one of Monostatos's youthful henchmen reads a Donald Duck comic. Yet inside the theatrical mock-up, cinematographic miracles occur. The portrait of Pamina to which Tamino sings his aria is no cameo enamel but a moving picture, and in the magic lantern he sees her with Monostatos during the Queen's tirade.

Nor does the camera's disbelief in the theater matter, for Bergman's concern is the way Mozart's opera expands beyond the stage to encompass—and to be reenacted by—us all. One of the young Moors peers through a hole in a painted flat at the public assembled out front. The camera follows his gaze; it's always doing exactly the thing which the theater forbids—paying more attention to the audience than to the actors onstage. Thus, during the overture, Bergman studies the faces of the audience, which are excerpted from the global family of man: Swedish, Latin, African, Chinese, Indian, young and old, all of them innocently bright with hope. This conclave has been assembled by music, whose harmony (as Pamina and Pagageno say when they play the bells) should prompt men everywhere to throw away their swords. The human race's delegates are in turn surveyed by the cherubic face of Mozart. Thanks to the camera, his music pervades the park outside the theater, where the sun is setting as the overture begins, and echoes as far as the homelands of those pilgrims who have convened to hear it.

Bergman took *Die Zauberflöte* out into the world, like Chagall propounding its mission to the city in those murals for the Met lobby; music makes common cause with the internationalism of film. For Hans Jürgen Syberberg the cinematic medium points opera in the opposite direction: his *Parsifal* (1982) happens inside the head.

The head in question is Wagner's, as traced by his death mask. That blanched, rigid face supplied Syberberg with his set, and he distributed the action of the opera around its sensory zones and orifices. Kundry curls up to sleep in her creator's eye-sockets, Gurnemanz orates out of Wagner's mouth; the temple of the Grail is the master's brain, and as well the architectural child of that cranium, the festival theater at Bayreuth. The flower maidens ticklingly play around Wagner's nose, catering to his neurotic sensitivity. Thus the work becomes the autobiography of its self-pitying, self-canonizing composer, shown by Syberberg stretched on a crucifix of his own devising. As well as narrating what Thomas Mann called the sorrows and grandeur of Wagner, it sketches a psychological history of Germany, whose travails and catastrophes are foreordained by its music. On the way to the temple, Parsifal moves down an endless corridor of Prussian and Nazi banners, traveling in time through a German past which for Wagner is the future.

Syberberg chooses the head of Wagner after death because the camera, conserving moments and assembling souvenirs, compiles a dying vision of the world. The light of life seeps into a shuttered interior where there is only memory. The lake in the center of the mask, used for anointment and baptism, is a well of tears but also Wagner's last sight on earth, the final frame of his personal film: Syberberg intends it as reference to the window, looking out on watery Venice, of the room in the Palazzo Vedramin where Wagner died. Within the camera obscura, the patient has, for a while, total recall of his own life and the world's. Syberberg treats the head as a screen for phantasmal projections. Film is fantasia, he believes, so his *Parsifal* isn't a performance of the opera but a montage of images about it. Ghostly transparencies come and go throughout. When Amfortas grieves over the wounds of the world, Syberberg shows bombed Dresden. The same variable shadows play across the faces of the characters. Kundry is sometimes a Victorian Ophelia floating on the stream of tears, sometimes a Van Eyck Madonna, sometimes Christ on the Turin shroud. The base of Klingsor's throne is inlaid with the skulls of Germany's other mad magicians—along with Wagner, there are Nietzsche, Karl Marx and Ludwig II. *Parsifal* is their collective trauma.

Contemporary directors have queried the union of music and drama on which opera is based, suspecting that the two have irreconcilable aims. For Syberberg, film offers the chance to formalize that split. He has, in effect, two casts: singers to prerecord the score, actors to mime it for the camera. There are only two overlaps. Robert Lloyd both sings and acts Gurnemanz, and Auge Haugland does likewise with Klingsor. While Parsifal's voice belongs to a middle-aged East German tenor, in person he's divided between a pair of nubile adolescents—a boy for the hunter of the first half, a girl for the feminized savior of the second half. The conductor of the score, Armin Jordan, acts the role of Amfortas, because this is the character closest (in Syberberg's view) to Wagner, from whose lesions the musical blood and suffering pour. The opera's prelude is performed by marionettes, twitching on strings. Music and drama fall apart to demonstrate the separability of soul and body, which is one of the opera's pathological subjects. A puppet is a body, lent its vocal soul by someone else; body expresses soul, but is freest to do so if the musical spirit belongs to another. Edith Clever can abandon herself to Kundry—shuddering and heaving, her hands raking the air like the tentacles of a demented insect as she curses Parsifal—because the singing has already been done for her by Yvonne Minton. Film has enabled Syberberg to alienate opera from itself.

Syberberg is as right to take action within the mind as Losey or Rosi are to release it into a landscape. One of the bequests of film to opera is its demonstration that song is soliloquy, not overt statement: that the voice is consciousness—or the yearning subconscious—overheard. Thus in Ponnelle's film of *Madama Butterfly*, the love duet is shown to be a nervous double soliloquy. Neither Butterfly nor Pinkerton is seen to be singing, and they're separated from each other. She's inside undressing, while he waits outdoors, smoking a cigarette. The soundtrack is the subliminal sounding of desire. In Zeffirelli's film of *La Traviata*, the cinematic device of flashback defines the entire action as a morose review of her life by the bedridden, expiring Violetta. Zeffirelli also personifies the prying photographic eye by introducing the character of a young porter, who opens the door and peers into Violetta's weightily grandiose apartment, which he has been sent to disassemble. He is the voyeur in all of us, as Zeffirelli says—our curiosity and our amazement as we first gape at the myth of this moribund heroine. The reticent intruder, initially shamefaced and at last worshipful, is anonymous because he is the medium's deputy. I am the camera, he might be saying.

The cinema's spatial freedom has been brought back into the theater. The Russian film director Andrei Tarkovsky, staging *Boris Godunov* at Covent Garden in 1983, devised a montage of forms corresponding to the evolution of Mussorgsky's chronicle. The life of history is in process, unending and exhausting. During Pimen's narrative, sung as he pauses from his written record, a procession of history's unremembered victims crawled across the floor. The helpless peasants outside the monastery in Novodevichy remained in silhouette at the end of the first scene: the freeze-frame stood for the inertia of their predicament, from which they roused themselves as the next scene began—or rather from which they in their passivity were aroused by Boris's consenting to rule them. At first they unwound in slow motion, then as the music accelerated Tarkovsky goaded them gradually to mayhem, with banners agitated from the Kremlin walls. Life and history congealed again at the end of the opera. The stage was covered with the prostrate acolytes of Dimitri in the Kromy forest. In their dread deference, they made corpses of themselves, trampled by political events; the fool mourned over them as the snow fell. Wagner called music an art of transition. Tarkovsky edited and superimposed movement to create the same perpetual transitoriness in the dramatic action. Another cinematic imagination elasticized the stage in John Schlesinger's 1984 production of *Der Rosenkavalier* at Covent Garden. Traditionally, the third act happens in a cramped alcove of the inn where Ochs has his rendezvous with Mariandel. Schlesinger elided the walls of that chamber, distributing the intrigue around adjacent rooms and into connecting corridors, building a warren for the comings and goings of the conspirators. Though the stage may be a dead end, film can take over the whole world as its theater.

Within the theater, there have been other prescriptions for the reform of opera. If opera is a byword for luxury, it must be impoverished. Brecht stipulates an opera for mendicants, costing only threepence. If opera is synonymous with overdressed plushness, it must be brought up to date by being demeaned and dirtied. Peter Brook reveres music as a constituent of what he calls a "holy theater," because it's the sound of the invisible. However, to save opera from a phony, pompous holiness, the sacrament must be embedded in what Brook describes as "rough theater." The communion happens not in a cathedral of gilt and velvet, but in a grimy sandpit, like that on the floor of the Bouffes du Nord in Paris—a tatty, seedy old music hall in an industrial suburb—where Brook staged his *Tragédie de Carmen*. A grubby roughness always qualifies the magic in Brook's theater: the brutish fairies in his *Midsummer Night's Dream*, the food fights in his *Ubu Roi*. The gypsy in his *Carmen* scratches on the litter-strewn floor to kindle the fire which guards her domain, and Escamillo slashes open an orange to squeeze its juice over Carmen's dusty face and down her greedy throat. Carmen digs up fistfuls of dirt as she sings the habanera, and rolls in the filth as she grapples with Micaëla; Escamillo's pink cape is muddied and spattered with blood during the bullfight.

Soiling opera is a way of attesting to its reality. It assaults—and in the process wrests dramatic truth from—a work synonymous with decorative fiction in Graham Vick's 1984 production of *Madama Butterfly* for English National Opera. Butterfly calls for cosmetics when Pinkerton's ship returns, and begs Suzuki to make her pretty. Vick's production boldly intends the reverse: to make the work's society tarnished and ugly. The hillside above Nagasaki in the first act is a scorched earth, its trampled red wildflowers like bloodstains; indoors, a mess of petals covers the floor. During Pinkerton's absence, the house decays. The planks of its deck wetly rot, the floor mats look ratty, the child's toys are broken. When Sharpless comes to call, the teapot has to be unwrapped from its shroud of brown paper, and the dust brushed off it. The garden is now a field of mud, into which Yamadori throws his rejected bouquet. Butterfly's child collects the discarded blooms and recycles them to festoon the house for Pinkerton's homecoming. Suzuki pushes the tattling Goro over, and he slithers in the mud; Kate's dress trails a hem through it. The characters are literally spotted—begrimed—with commonness, and thus with reality. After Butterfly's vigil, dawn is a pitiless white light, exposing the shabbiness beneath her desperate pretense and hurting the eyes with its honesty.

Messiness is a credential of veracity in David Freeman's productions too—the making of mud pies and sand castles, dabbling in water and sculpting bricks, which occupied his ancient Egyptians in *Akhnaten;* the desecration of opera in his Paris staging of Peter Maxwell Davies's *Eight Songs for a Mad King*, which required the mad George III to sign the walls of his cell with excrement. In Freeman's staging of Tippett's *The Knot Garden*, the characters muckily delved in flower beds or scooped up sand in beach buckets. Cavalli's *La Calisto*, when Freeman directed it in London in 1984, was systematically soiled. Pan's cohorts were a grubby team of soccer-playing oafs, the Furies scandalmongering mudslingers who hauled fistfuls of filth from their handbags to smear the face, breasts and groin of the disgraced nymph Calisto; the slippery diplomat Mercury, who had abetted Jove's seduction of her, swept the remaining dust under a grassy rug. Freeman says that Cavalli's subject—the loves of the Ovidian gods—is already a "demythologized myth." He degrades it all over again by dirtying it.

If opera is to be democratized, the process must begin with the character who symbolizes the form, Orpheus. Peter Hall's rustic *Orfeo ed Euridice* made it clear that the hempen mortals were ruled by a glittery jet set of gods, who descended on skyhooks from the theater's flies at the finale. The sybaritic Olympian ladies waved and beamed like celebrities at some gala affair; an Apollo slick inside a new skin of gold paint saluted Orfeo. The aristocracy literally oversaw the peasants. Monteverdi's Orfeo even more directly owed his creation to aristocratic decree: the Duke of Mantua, after hearing Peri's *Euridice* in Florence, assigned the subject to the composer and had the work performed in his own palace. This *Orfeo* is opera's initial manifesto about itself, and to renovate the form, David Freeman—in a production seen at the English National Opera in 1983— demoted the character from a courtier to an artisan. Instead of Mantua's elegant amateurs, the work was performed by laborers in cloth caps and tatterdemalion kilts. Pluto wore blue denim; as the artificer of illusion, an electrician perhaps, he observed the action from a gantry above the shop floor. The underworld was a bare stage randomly cluttered with disused props or scaffolding, and a skyline of sets for other operas. The condemned souls were actors doing warm-up exercises. The only decor consisted of an orange sun-cloth for Apollo, or some flown-in Oriental rugs: music is a carpet of sound; aural furniture. Freeman's program note added populism to this political conscription, describing Orfeo as a pop singer. He compared the hero, as a charismatic vocalist, to Mick Jagger. Could Altamont, not opera, be the true revival of the Greek tragic festivals—a concert with deaths?

Despite Freeman's effort to rob the first opera of its pomp, the art inevitably became an overpriced trophy of the bourgeoisie. He corrected the form's shame in his *Calisto*. This had been one of Peter Hall's earliest successes at Glyndebourne, in 1970. There of course it was staged as a magical masque, with forests and fountains conjured out of nowhere in obedience to the commands of Jove. The opera is about gods who, to advance their careers of sexual conquest, commute between heaven and earth; as always at Glyndebourne, the deities alight in a garden, and compliment the place by choosing to reside there. Raymond Leppard, who conducted, imagined the action confined to the noble family: he fancied that John Christie, Glyndebourne's founder, "might have wanted to play Sylvano, the earthy woodland creature; after all his grand-daughter played the bear"—Ursa Minor, into whom Juno transmogrifies Calisto to keep her from Jove. No such country-house charade was permitted by Freeman. Rather than this astral pageant, he set the work in a television studio, where industrialism diverts its slaves by manufacturing galaxies of cheap, disposable stars. Mythology, like opera, serves the purposes of a greedy consumerism, and Cavalli's squabbling goddesses became entrants in a beauty competition. Jove is an oily entrepreneur, Calisto his latest "product," divinized only temporarily; his magic fountain was frothed from a Coke bottle. Freeman's Arcadia, its only vegetation a cluster of green balloons, was an urban pastoral whose shepherds were the down and out. Endymion wore the costume of contemporary impoverishment—jeans and a torn sweater.

For the nineteenth century, opera meant merchandise. The Palais Garnier, that emporium of scenic novelties, was nicknamed "la grande boutique." Freeman has redefined opera as collaborative, unionized labor: he calls his company the Opera Factory. The form's salvation, for him, is a salutary cheapening.

FIVE

Drama Against Music

THESE efforts to save opera by minimalizing, pauperizing or sullying it—
by a variety of desecrations—indicate what is perhaps its greatest contemporary problem: the split between musical tradition and dramatic innovation. The alliance of arts which makes up the form is in danger of collapse.
The stage director in opera was once content to assign moves; now he
worries about motives. Thanks to a new army of avant-gardists, opera has
never been theatrically livelier; nor has it ever been so disputatious and so
gratuitously bizarre. Productions achieve dramatic notoriety by their infidelity to the music: Peter Sellars has set Handel's *Orlando* at Cape Canav-
eral and his oratorio *Saul* during the Watergate investigations, and
distributed the characters of *Cosi Fan Tutte* around the vinyl booths of a
roadside diner, where their music is supplied by jukeboxes.

The director's mission is apparently to outrage. Preparing his Vienna
Faust, where Méphistophélès was to use the font as a pissoir, Ken Russell
promised the Staatsoper "the most glorious scandal in its history." The
motive is the libertine's tactic of provocation, defaming the god or insult-
ing the classic. For his Florence production of *The Rake's Progress* in
1982, Russell was the impenitent rake, deriding whatever seemed institu-
tionally smug. The brothel keeper Mother Goose was dressed as the
Queen Mother, and among the loot at Baba's auction there appeared an
inflatable sex doll with the starchy face of Margaret Thatcher. Does the
director need to shock opera into life like this?

Opera used to be the preserve of the musicians, exhibiting their art in defiance of dramatic truth. Its corseted sopranos and ponderous tenors disdained to act; the form was notorious for its theatrical nonsensicality. Peter Brook has called opera, with the inert machinery of a cultural establishment which protects it, a "monument to human stupidity," and describes its practitioners as obsolete primitives—lumbering overweight dinosaurs, due for extinction. Brook's career began in the early 1950s with a series of attempts to rejuvenate the musty classics of the repertory: a *Salome* at Covent Garden set by Salvador Dali in a web of erotic tendrils, a *Faust* at the Met located in the mercenary bourgeois nineteenth century. These productions were cried down by the critics, or simply vetoed by the singers, and since then Brook believes that little has changed. In 1983 he had to lend one of the Escamillos from his troupe at the Bouffes du Nord to the Opéra Comique, because the singer engaged for the role there had arrived wearing a beard, wouldn't shave it off, and was therefore rejected by Teresa Berganza, who on an obscure point of principle refused to sing *Carmen* with a bearded toreador.

The directors who work in opera regard it with suspicion. Brook calls it a deadly, Sellars a lobotomized, theater. They tend to experience belated, reluctant conversions. Michael Hampe, director of productions at the Cologne Opera, began his career as a musician and remembers believing that "opera was dreadful—I despised it and I didn't even look at it," until the work of Felsenstein at the Komische Oper in East Berlin convinced him that it could perhaps be saved from itself. Even so, Hampe's sympathy remains guarded and limited. "I have difficulties," he says, "with stupid operas," by which he means those whose music bombastically exceeds dramatic necessity. He cites as an example *Andrea Chénier*, which he directed in 1984 at Covent Garden. Its characters die in a fusillade of ecstatic high notes, sublimely and absurdly fearless; Hampe contrasts with this the reticence of Verdi, treating a similar extinction at the end of *Aida* and doing so, in his view, more honestly. There's even a physiological truth in Verdi's writing: instead of the bombastic noise of Chénier and Maddalena, he transcribes the exhaustion of Aida and Radamès in their tomb, as their lyricism airlessly expires.

Hampe prefers operas where the music understates, retreating almost into a subtext of implication—the Rossini comedies, or Cimarosa's *Matrimonio Segreto*; above all, Mozart. To Hampe's mistrust of stupid opera, John Schlesinger adds that he loathes what he calls "silly operas," specifying a particular dislike for Rossini, Bellini and women in helmets.

Yet all of these doubts prove worth overcoming. Schlesinger is attracted to opera as "the most liberated form of theatricality," the home of excess and bravado, while Peter Hall concurs that "the most imaginative and free form of all is opera." When it works, he says—when the dramatic performance matches the musical execution—"opera at its best is the best." Even Peter Brook, who after those early disillusionments returned to the form with *La Tragédie de Carmen* in 1981, is convinced that it repays the trouble it takes, because opera is a theater of exaltation, almost a sacrament. His reconciliation with opera occurred midway through a series of experiments with drama's origins in rite, which began with *Orghast* at Persepolis and has for the time being concluded with his staging of the Indian scriptural epic *The Mahabharata*. Brook promotes opera to membership in this sacrosanct company because its music articulates "the hidden aspects of life" or "the invisible part." Music is the stuff of mystery or miracle, and the determinant of ritual. But the heaven of the music must be grounded, for Brook, in the terrain of common sense. Opera is a Mass, but a mucky one. "The holy theater . . . is only really meaningful when it's linked with the rough side of the theater," as it is, for Brook, by Bergman's *Zauberflöte:* the spiritual parable is also a children's pantomime.

Brook venerates the immaterial idea of the music. He is less happy with the received operatic text. His own *Carmen* made a digest of Bizet, reorchestrated the score for a small band, and banished the musicians to the back of the arena around which the audience huddled, so that dramatic action wasn't mediated by the music. This is an inevitable scruple, because Brook sees the music, however potent its effect might be, as an enemy of drama; and his admission is a clue to the antagonism emerging within the notion of opera as music drama. He objects to the score's fixity. The energy of drama derives from improvisation, the taking of risks. This instinctive, vital existence is incompatible with the tyranny of the musical script, schooled, premeditated and always the same. Peter Hall defines this as the difference between directing a play and directing an opera. The spoken text is free to be manipulated, speeded up or slowed down, whereas the sung text is given and unalterable. The director is "absolutely trammeled—and should be—by the music."

A director like Jean-Pierre Ponnelle rejoices in his preemption by the score, and treats its dictation as a challenge to inventive ingenuity. He likens this to the formal regulations which govern classical prosody, with its hexameters or alexandrines, and points out that within these limits the classical line is infinitely variable: once you accept containment by the corset, "you are completely free." The clockwork precision of Ponnelle's stagings is a reaction to this constraint, fitting the characters of Rossini or Mozart into the music's schematic design. It often looks as if he is choreographing the score.

In his *Rigoletto* film, Ponnelle derives the jester's hobbling gait from the musical execution which accompanies it. As the Rigoletto of Ingvar Wixell follows Sparafucile along the bank of the steaming canal in the second scene, his hunched, loping, twistedly dancing walk is a physical equivalent to the bowing of the double bass under the duet: Rigoletto is scraping a macabre and venomous music from the instrument of his own body. Actions must be orchestrally motivated. Ponnelle's *Nozze di Figaro* film stages the overture and orchestrates relationships as if the characters (present as symbols or icons only—the Countess's white wig, Figaro's barbering tools, Antonio's pitcher of wine, the Count's ceremonial portrait) were coordinated musicians in the pit. Conducting them is Figaro, who stands guard over the opera's text. The connective motif in the overture is a paper chase of such texts, whose words or notes can't be changed though they can—as they are throughout *Figaro*—be reinterpreted. Figaro rips the title page from Mozart's score to wrap up his shaving gear and then piles on top of that musical book other texts which gloss it, and propound his own interpretation: Montesquieu's legal theory, the complete works of Voltaire. Visually, the overture is a montage of such writings, which deputize for the authoritative notes and words the performers must memorize. The Count's portrait has been fulsomely signed on the reverse and dedicated to Figaro by Lindoro, in appreciation for services to be rendered in *Il Barbiere di Siviglia*; his magisterial power is attested by dusty piles of a government gazette published in Madrid; and when Figaro pulls open a drawer he happens upon the collection of song sheets used by Don Basilio—whose name at that point appears in the cast list—during the lessons he administered to the Countess.

Ponnelle the director envisages himself as a conductor, and invents a self-image in his *Cenerentola* film: the disguised philosopher Alidoro, Cinderella's colleague in indigence and her moral tutor, metamorphoses during his aria into Rossini, and sends his protégée off to the ball. Ponnelle has the same nimble prescriptiveness which he here attributes to the composer. Regimentation is his delight, which is why he so strictly respects the orders of the score. Disciplining drama in subjection to the music, he rules with a rod of iron, and the emblems of his approach in the Met's *L'Italiana in Algeri* in 1973 and Covent Garden's *Aida* in 1984 were punitive whips. In *L'Italiana*, the eunuchs and harem girls prostrate themselves at Mustafà's entrance. Every forte note he produces causes the eunuchs to shudder, and the girls to twitch their upended bottoms. The musical measure is policed by a metronomic flagellation: as they sing their master's praises, the eunuchs graze the rumps of the captive girls with lengths of rope. Ponnelle's Amneris also punctually whacked Aida with a leather thong at every clash of the cymbals in the scene before the triumph. Like galley slaves obedient to the drum, Ponnelle's actors are indentured to the music.

To Brook and to those of his opinion, this intimidation by the music kills opera as drama. Peter Stein, formerly director of the Schaubühne Theater Company in West Berlin, argues that dramatic meaning is disqualified in opera, because "the whole structure of the work is determined by the necessities of the music." Planning the Bayreuth centenary *Ring*, which was eventually directed by Chéreau, Stein flirted with a solution like Brook's to the problem of the inordinate, hyperbolic score. He hoped to find a musician who'd make "a two-and-a-half-hour version" of Wagner's four days of music; but he admitted the impossibility, and decided that he couldn't direct Wagner for the very reason that he loved the music too much. Robert Lloyd, playing Gurnemanz in Syberberg's *Parsifal*, watched the same capitulation of a director disarmed by music. The making of the film, he says, "became a sort of battle between the film-maker and the opera-writer." Syberberg attempted to co-opt Wagner by arguing that if he'd lived today, he'd have abandoned opera for film. But Lloyd thinks that Syberberg "felt that he didn't win—that Wagner won that particular battle—that the opera prevailed over the film. I think he was defeated by the strength of the music."

Nietzsche derived Greek tragedy, like opera, from the spirit of music, violently impulsive and sensual. That spirit alarms these directors; they seek a way of restraining it, of making it responsible to the drama. Peter Stein, who staged the *Oresteia* at the same time he was meditating the production of Wagner's Aeschylean *Ring*, accordingly revises Nietzsche's theory of tragedy to give the Apollonian text priority over the Dionysian music. He insists, referring to the *Oresteia*, that "the whole of opera came out of a misunderstanding of this antique tragedy." The misunderstanding was to imagine that the musical elements dominated the verbal, and to make redress Stein prepared a prose version of Aeschylus, forbidding his actors to chant: "no music at all."

It remains important for Stein to legitimize opera by anchoring it again in Greek tragedy. He did so in *Otello* for Welsh National Opera in 1986. The production overlaid three ages of theater: Verdi's nineteenth century, with Iago as a devil from melodrama jumping out from behind a scarlet curtain stitched with licking hell-flames; Shakespeare's sixteenth century, with a set modeled on the ideal town-plans of the Renaissance, its walls battered by the elemental furies outside and mined by a pit for the bonfire in its floor; and the fifth century B.C. of Aeschylus—Stein used the communal Greek chorus as the ever-present witness and judge of the action, hailing Otello after the storm, ostracizing him when he abuses Desdemona in public, called back by Iago to see him slumped unconscious on the ground. Even in the bedroom scene Stein insisted on the presence of spectators, representing society and its institutions, and had Cassio grapple with Otello to prevent him stabbing himself.

Aeschylus and Shakespeare were made to stand guard over Verdi. Stein notes that in the manual prepared before the first performance by Boito, the principals are addressed always as actors, never singers. Peter Brook makes the same criticism of Nietzsche's theory about opera's origins when explaining the layout of his *Carmen*, which placed the singing actors in front of the musicians: "the first thing that's real is seeing a human being in action . . . But what is behind that, what is the meaning of that action?" That posterior meaning is evinced by the orchestra. Music doesn't cue or provoke the action, as in a conventional opera house where the singers are intent on following the conductor's beat; it comments after the event.

Peter Hall, having also directed the *Oresteia*, applies the analogy of Greek tragedy to opera with a difference. He proposes that "all forms of theatrical activity are in some sense a mask": a literal vizor like those worn by his Aeschylean troupe; a linguistic guise in the case of Shakespearean poetry, which controls emotion by versifying it; a lyrical discipline in the case of a Mozart aria. Thus, speaking Shakespeare, the actor doesn't need to scream but can "say a line about screaming." And singing opera, he or she can express violent and animalistic passions—Elettra's hysteria in *Idomeneo*, Azucena's baying for blood, Salome's lust—without surrendering to them, because music has imposed on them a rational form. This beautifying of the primal scream is exactly what Stein finds so false in opera. He recounts stories of people collapsing or miscarrying or dying at performances of Greek tragedy, because the action had become a collective madness. To hide behind the mask is musically to palliate and prettify the "terror and surprise" which are the dynamics of drama. Prose is raised aloft by verse, and verse in turn is elevated by song. This for Hall is opera's unique benison, because the huge emotions in which it deals have an elaborate vocal technique to discipline them. Salome isn't a squalling bloodthirsty brat; she is an artist capable of singing a vertiginous row of pianissimo B-flats.

For Stein, the same musical intervention marks opera's shame and its superfluity. He notes that "music is a very severe art," technically exigent. By contrast, as if recalling Brook's emphasis on roughness and defilement, he says that "spoken theater is a dirty art," and a democratic one: anyone who can speak can feel himself to be an actor. (In conversation, Stein illustrates the point by quacking.) The vocal refinement of singers leaves them unable to express anything at all.

Stein prefers to direct Shakespeare in German because the translation prevents the actors from singing the lines as they habitually do (he says) in England. Hall, not so fearful of music, tends to blame the drama if opera is anodyne. He cites fancy rococo productions of Così Fan Tutte, which in their flouncing and posturing ignore "the pain of the heart which is in every bar of the music." In recompense, Hall made sure that the sisters in his 1978 Glyndebourne Così were tormented, not frivolous. Fiordiligi's "Come scoglio" was her anxious self-castigation, rather than a bravura rebuff to the intruders, and Dorabella delivered "Smanie implacabili" as a distraught confession, prostrate on a sofa like a neurasthenic invalid. Hall is forever testing opera for dramatic unreality. The finale of his Fidelio was no cosmic choral symphony, with the whole world bursting into jubilant song; it began humbly and ungrandiloquently, with the officials checking the firmness of the steps up to Don Fernando's hastily erected dais. John Dexter's Met productions vouch for the action's reality by making the characters work onstage, swabbing the decks of the ship in Billy Budd or hauling the carts which are platforms for ambulatory players in Le Prophète. Dexter's Carmelites in Poulenc's opera go about their diurnal routine in the convent during the orchestral interludes, and the peasants of his Bartered Bride strain at the engines whose serfs they are—Mařenka spins Vašek on the mill wheel, and he labors to rotate the carousel.

Hampe, with the same caution, speaks of having always to justify the music. He could accept the sacrificial end of Andrea Chénier only when he recalled similar incidents in life: "I grew up during the second world war in an anti-Nazi atmosphere, and I know that there were such situations and such cases, which I have seen or at least heard about myself as a child." When the music can't be justified, it must be punished. This was the unhappy case with Tchaikovsky's *Mazeppa*, directed for English National Opera by David Alden in 1984. In a program note, Alden owned up to being embarrassed by the romanticism of the score which, confronted by terrorism and political murder, is blithely unresponsive and irresponsible. The staging in consequence was brutalized, to compensate for the heedlessness of the music. Tchaikovsky's folk dance became a slobbering drunken orgy, the vengeful ensemble a bloodletting, which spattered the walls of a bleak neon-lit interrogation chamber; executions were performed with a gore-spouting chain saw.

Seldom can there have been an uglier or more excessive retaliation by drama against music. More often, it's a matter of rationalizing opera, with its gratuitous or miraculous advents. Hence Ponnelle's invention of a character for that heavenly voice which, unseen, lectures the victims burned by the Spanish Inquisition in Verdi's *Don Carlos*. Verdi feels no need to justify this celestial serenade. Why should he, since all his heroines aspire to the sky and to the Marian function of intercession extolled by Desdemona? He writes music as a believer, in the invocatory valor of song if not in any religion. But Ponnelle approached *Don Carlos* in Hamburg as a rational man and an agnostic, characterizing its society as one of grisly religious persecution. Over the stage impends an impaled and bleeding Christ. Dotard cardinals tremble on their sticks during the auto-da-fé; the Inquisitor is a senescent bogey in a wheelchair. The heavenly voice in Ponnelle's *Don Carlos* must therefore be a spurious stunt, and he shows a monk cynically stage-managing it, handing some sheet music to a crone in nun's habit and motioning her toward the bell tower from which she'll render his extraterrestrial aria. "I am sure," Ponnelle declares, "that no angel is singing at the end of this act."

When no such ingenious justification is available, the director's stratagem is to explain the unreason of opera as dream or subjective wish-fulfillment. Drama defends itself against music by self-analysis: the opera is a psychotic dream-play, the patient's rampaging fantasy.

In Ponnelle's work, there are two notorious instances of opera diagnosed as trauma. For the third act of his *Tristan* at Bayreuth in 1981, he planned to confine Isolde to the orchestra pit. The soprano overruled him and insisted on appearing to sing her liebestod, but Ponnelle is unrepentant: "I think she shouldn't come, because she died at the end of the second act . . . It's really the high fever of poor Tristan, dying alone but with the illusion of dying in her arms." A similar rational scruple governs his treatment of *Der Fliegende Holländer*, in a production from San Francisco seen at the Met in 1979. Ponnelle declines to accredit what he calls the "emphatic ending" of this work, with the sublimatory drowning of Senta: "I don't believe that a young woman is so much in love that she dies for love. That's stupid, I think." The exaggeration prompts him to relegate the action to a dream of the work's most supernumerary character, the Steersman on Daland's boat, who projects himself into his own dream as Senta's wooer, the hunter Erik. Wagner's opera is of course about the compulsive telepathic power of fantasy, but in Ponnelle's theater dreams come true with a facility which is too slick. When the Dutchman first appeals for a savior, Senta obligingly saunters on; when she sings of him in her ballad, he steps down from his picture on the wall. As he offers Daland money, a sequined blizzard assails the ship and his cloak, thrown back, is shown to be inlaid with gems: he's a Rossinian trickster, not a Wagnerian demon. Because the characters have been automated, they can be playfully multiplied. There are a pair of Steersmen, one slumped asleep, the other capering through his own reverie; half-a-dozen stovepipe-hatted Dalands; even an extra Senta, with a death's-head for a face. The Dutchman is a manikin operated by the Steersman, and Senta too is a compliant gadget, dressed in a wimpled, brocaded cocoon and cramped throughout in postures of submission. At the end, instead of hurling herself into the ocean, she curtsies decorously to the Dutchman before stepping up to join him inside a shuttered hutch, like a pair of figurines inhabiting a clock.

The effect of intricate implosion sums up Ponnelle's work: the elemental vastness of the music has to be fitted into a neat and orderly receptacle, which is the director's brain. In his Covent Garden *Aida,* all the action emerged from the sculptural torso of the Pharaoh. Aida slid forth on a platform from her sequestration inside his body, the King popped out of another closet at the top of the effigy's crown. Always there must be involution and intricacy—Radamès pulled his sword from a ram's skull in the temple—never the expansiveness of impulse demanded by the music.

Aida was for Ponnelle another psychodrama, with the heroine's fears and yearnings shadowily enacted during the prelude. Once the dreaming begins, it proves contagious. *Der Fliegende Holländer,* for instance, can be the fantasy of anyone the director chooses: in Herbert Wernicke's Munich production it derives from Senta, whose problem is a father fixation and who enlists the Dutchman as a surrogate for the prohibited object of desire, Daland; in Harry Kupfer's production at Bayreuth it is dreamed by the Dutchman himself, strung up in chains to impotently imagine a salvation he can no longer bring about.

Shackling the Dutchman like Kupfer or boxing him as a marionette like Ponnelle, the director is curtailing the character and the actor. The concept forbids theatrical liberty to its performers. If the singer is free, then the director must be in demise. Both of Schlesinger's Covent Garden productions concluded in such directorial fatalism, as Schlesinger resigned himself to permitting what he calls "big sings." The spirit of music, so troublingly irrepressible for Syberberg, returns to outwit drama. When Antonia in Schlesinger's *Les Contes d'Hoffmann* escapes into her orotund and deadly big sing, drama changes to vocal concert. Schlesinger lit up the proscenium, and had Antonia deliver her scene from the front of the stage, crossing back and forth as she gestured winningly toward the audience. Her wish had been granted: she was singing for the first and last time at Covent Garden. The same extrapolation from the drama and from its enclosure in the room which is the stage ends Schlesinger's *Rosenkavalier*. Throughout the third act, the characters have been scuttling through the passageways of their midden, prising open doors and peering through peepholes. When the chords which announce the trio sound, they simply transcend the intrigue-ridden drama and elide the architecture, advancing through the fourth wall of the room they're in and lining up out front to sing. It's the kind of vocal apotheosis Wagner complained of when he snarled at a rehearsal "Now they *sing* again!"—an outpouring of tone, purged of uncomfortable meaning.

If music's tendency is toward seraphic nonsense, a heaven of insignificance, how can it be made accountable? This is the question on the conscience of the contemporary director—of Peter Stein, for instance, as he prepared for his *Otello*. For Stein, the existential thrill of theater is its danger, "the risk of not going on anymore," the fear of self-destruction. Most singers enrage Stein because they perform capitalistically, treating the vocal cords as their income-generating asset and spending only the interest, conserving the treasure for the customers in the next city. *Otello* was for him the chance to exhibit an exception to this mercenary rule. For him, the theatrical bravery of the work is the chaos it unleashes: its central spectacle, he says, is the collapse and epileptic gibbering of a political and military leader, prone on the floor. The Shakespearean hero's calamity is yet more acute and distressing in Verdi, because Otello is a great singer—outroaring the storm, abashing the combatants—who when this happens is choked, and loses his vocal power. An interpreter, in Stein's view, should court the same disaster. He admires the risks taken by the Otello of Ramón Vinay, in whose performance of the third act "the singing stops, and the rest is not silence but sighing, or cries or lack of articulation, like an ani mal." Music must prove its dramatic integrity by an act of vocal suicide. He stopped short of demanding this last sacrifice from his singers in the Welsh *Otello*, but did make sure that they were hurt into expressiveness. Otello, trying to extort a confession from Desdemona, hurled her against the wall, twisted her arm, grabbed her hair and—as she squealed in pain and fright—forced her to the floor where she hunched like a whipped animal.

This debate about interpreting opera has centered recently on *Carmen*, and for a good reason: the work, at least before Guiraud replaced its dialogue with droopy, sugared recitatives, is a place where speech and song, the different imperatives of drama and music, meet and maybe quarrel. Peter Hall vacillates between declaring it an opera, where music dominates, and a spoken play with interpolated songs. It is, he says, "one of the five great operas, and perhaps the greatest musical ever written in dramatic terms. It has fabulous dialogue." To illustrate this versatility in the work, he mounted the same production twice, with differing emphases: conversational at Glyndebourne in 1985, where speech could graduate easily to song but could equally subside into silence, with a pause of Pinteresque duration when José erupts into Lillas Pastia's dive and is elaborately ignored by Carmen; noisier and more populous at the Met in 1986, on a stage which needs crowds and circuses. This dual identity, dissevering drama and music, is also what attracts Brook in *Carmen*. The anecdote is "rough as only a crude melodrama can be," and Brook added some crudities of his own, staging the scene at Pastia's as a coital farce, with Zuniga ripping off his clothes to grapple with Carmen. But the music allows "the invisible—and what we've here called the tragic—elements to emerge." It's the congruent case, he believes, to Mozart's use of the singspiel in *Die Zauberflöte*. There the dramatic fairy tale supports a musical allegory; here the music is a "tragic undertow" beneath the brutal, wanton story. Either way, the music has been made responsible, because, inserted between the dialogue, it's occasional, and on each occasion is able functionally to justify itself. Carmen sings to allure victims or evade captors, José when his sentiments get the better of him, Escamillo to brag and to broadcast his reputation.

Carmen is grounded—in speech, and in earth: Brook's sandpit, or the culvert where Hall imagines her, ratlike, digging her burrow and scheming to survive. At Glyndebourne, Maria Ewing did Carmen's dance in Pastia's bar lying flat on her back on the floor. The tragedy in the work, to which the title of Brook's digest directs attention, is subterranean, and has to be disinterred. Hence the squatting and groveling in Brook's production. Before she can be musically ennobled, Carmen must be dramatically abased. This means that the truth about her, obscured by the elegance of her music, should be recovered from the dramatic source: Brook's Carmen is less Bizet's than Mérimée's, a robber and a harlot, a spitfire who bombards Zuniga with flaming matchboxes and shoves a grape into José's mouth to stop him singing. José in turn is made real by being made homicidal, again in obedience to Mérimée rather than Bizet. Brook restores, without music, the episode from the story in which José challenges Garcia, Carmen's husband, and kills him.

Jean-Claude Carrière, who worked on the adaptation of the libretto for Brook, sees Carmen as a classical tragic protagonist. Like Oedipus at the crossroads, when she turns over the cards she faces consequence, destiny and death. Her creed is a fickle, forgetful liberty. Carmen, she says of herself, was born free and will die free. But this freedom merely rationalizes a necessity read in the sequence of cards. Carrière finds here a replica of that paradoxical fate which the ancient tragedies study: the initiatives of will versus an implacable predestination.

The paradox applies as well to the constitution of opera, and is the origin of the director's problem. The fatality is music, for the score is as immitigable as the ace of spades. The countervailing freedom is the drama, since though Carmen's end is foreseen, her behavior on the way to it is entirely unconditioned. The two tenses or tempi run side by side in performance. We know, having seen *Carmen* countless times, what has to happen; we feel that it could, all the same, happen differently. If the drama has the courage to challenge the music, no particular outcome is mandated. Watching Maria Ewing taunt and torment her wimp of a José at Glyndebourne, I fully expected her to kill him in the fourth act. Of course the score too can be liberated, as Marilyn Horne's Carmen rather coarsely demonstrated at the Met in 1972 on the very word "liberté!" (which Carmen promises to José if he becomes a bandit). Horne superimposed Bizet's notes and Guiraud's soprano alternative to confound the ensemble with a vocal stunt: she soared, singing "liberté!", to a beaconlike high B, then plunged an octave and a half to repeat the word on the trombone she seemed to conceal in her chest. Finding it inconvenient to sing a *t* on the note B, she even did away with the word in the first bar, and ha-ha'd her way up the steep scale. Ostentatious and vulgar or not, the interpolation certainly expressed the liberty of this Carmen's spirit. Leonard Bernstein, conducting, protested in vain.

Brook's excavation of tragedy ordains other alterations to the score.

The earth in which his Carmen delves is that of the dark continent, the scene of Brook's ethnographic extravaganzas *The Ik* and *Conference of the Birds.* Nietzsche heard an "African gaiety" in Bizet's music, which relieved him after the somber Teutonism of Wagner. Marius Constant's orchestral adaptation of *Carmen* for Brook makes that Africa audible, accompanying the habanera on kettle drums to suggest a tribal tattoo.

All the same, Peter Stein argues that Bizet won out. As in Syberberg's *Parsifal,* music overwhelms drama. Stein believes that the acting of Brook's singers was poor, just because they had to sing: "they had to follow the measure. They couldn't go on and react to the situation." The elation and terror of chance were still absent. And when the brassy prelude to the bullfight was relayed on tape over loudspeakers in its proper operatic orchestration, Stein took the blaring quotation to be an admission of defeat. The drama couldn't tolerate the music, yet proved unable to exist without it.

There is another way of liberating the theatrical playfulness in *Carmen* from the incorrigibility of the score: this is to make the freedom of the drama an unbridled permissiveness, while mocking the repetitious fatalism of the music. The Romanian director Lucian Pintilie did so in his *Carmen* for Welsh National Opera in 1983. His method of working contradicts Brook's, which at least attempted to hold the two kinds of theater in balance. Brook says, of Escamillo's pompous entrance, that the opera shouldn't be "a big show, a carnival." This is precisely what Pintilie made it: a Mardi Gras of riotous libertinism. The scenic pretext of Pintilie's production was a carnival, careening among the sandbagged barricades erected by a troupe of Latin American revolutionaries. Carnival is to Pintilie a nonsensical revolution, and thus a means of debauching and renewing a work which has become too classically monumental, too implicated in an ancien régime of opera. "*Carmen* is not an opera," he told his singers, ". . . it is a super-opera, the most popular opera in the world." That popularity has cheapened it. When the hit tunes begin, there are knowing chuckles or cheers from Pintilie's chorus of anarchists. His theory of the opera's vain and foolish celebrity is summed up in Escamillo, who pauses to sign autographs during his duet with José.

Because *Carmen* is, in Pintilie's contention, not an opera any longer but a compendium of clichés and tired routines, he disrupts the musical necessity which is responsible for its false status. In his amateur circus, the fate motif in the overture is illustrated by a tightrope walker's negotiation of a high wire. This is a symbol of that theatrical danger Peter Stein craves, courting disaster and the possibility of not being able to continue. The musical fate is again dismissed by a dramatic freedom. Will the acrobat fall? we wonder—and, of course, as we had hoped but hadn't dared to expect, he does. Pintilie, like Brook, stages a critique of Escamillo and Micaëla, the characters interpolated by the librettists to atone for and explain the obsessive relationship of Carmen and José. Brook actually kills Escamillo off, having his gored body carried abruptly across the arena during Carmen's last showdown with José. Pintilie contents himself with making the toreador fatuous. Brook toughens up the milksop Micaëla, emboldening her to kick, punch and tear Carmen's hair. Pintilie first derides her, wheeling on a kitschy miniature of José's slumbering hometown during her rhapsody about his mother, then punishes her: he makes her blind, so she gropes through an action she's unable to understand, singing her insipid assurances in a private darkness. He comes close to the assassination of Escamillo. When José fires at him in the mountains, Escamillo jeers, in a line of dialogue unauthorized by the libretto, "A fraction lower and it would have been the end of the opera." The end of the opera is what Pintilie's *Carmen* is all about. Therefore, during the card scene, a screen descends onto which is projected the story of Bizet's end: Galli-Marié cried "Bizet is dead!" at the precise moment he was suffering his cerebral hemorrhage. The anecdote is gruesomely significant for directorial opera. Galli-Marié was the first Carmen; the creator's demise is announced—in Pintilie's case gleefully—by the interpreter. The death of the composer cues the birth of the director. With no censorious author or authority in view, anything is possible. Now Bizet rather than Carmen is the victim of the prophecy deciphered in the cards.

Drama's prosecution of its grudge against music in *Carmen* continues. In 1984, Jean-Luc Godard's film *Prénom: Carmen* transferred the action to contemporary Paris, and engaged the heroine in the service of a revolution which is more than merely (as it is in Pintilie) a joke. This Carmen doesn't deal in meager contraband, and the seduction of customs officers; she robs banks, and corrupts a José who is here Joseph, a policeman. She is the violent midwife of history, procreating to bring forth the future. And she has dispensed more or less altogether with the trivialities of Bizet's music. Some of Godard's minor characters remember the tunes from the opera. Like Coppola's Mafiosi with their Italian arias in *The Godfather*, a gangster whistles a brief extract from the score, while a hospital porter hums another. Godard's soundtrack prefers sterner, more abstracted stuff: Beethoven's string quartets.

SIX

After the Revolution, and Before

FOR DIRECTORS anxious to revolutionize opera, the logical setting for the operas they stage is a revolution.

The program for Pintilie's *Carmen* contained photographs from the firing lines in Nicaragua. Frank Corsaro, for a *Carmen* at the New York City Opera in 1984, chose the Spain of the 1930s as his theater of war, with the heroine as an undercover partisan and José a trooper in the army of Franco. The same historical convulsion did service for *Il Trovatore* in Andrei Serban's production for English National Opera North. The gypsies were refugees from combat, sheltering among the boxcars in a derelict railway yard. The *Tosca* directed by Anthony Besch for Scottish Opera in 1980 changed a Rome celebrating the Bourbon dynasty and fending off Napoleonic invasion into the brownshirted, flatulently neoclassical Rome of Mussolini; Wagner's Roman tribune in *Rienzi* was advanced from the fourteenth century to that same decade in Nicholas Hytner's 1983 English National Opera production, where he prowls through a monolith of black marble and ponders models for his reconstruction of the city in the fascist style, or is entertained by gymkhanas of racially pure, politically correct schoolchildren.

Weber's *Oberon* has been catapulted from romantic medieval timelessness into the revolutionary here and now. The work disappeared from the stage because, though the music is lovely, the libretto—a farrago of fairies, Christian chevaliers and lecherous Saracens from an incoherent

Arabian Nights' tale—is silly. For its 1985 production, Scottish Opera commissioned an entirely new text from Anthony Burgess, who altered the fabled Orient of Charlemagne to the actual Middle East of the Ayatollah Khomeini. The heroines, Rezia and Fatimah (whose name Burgess changes to Selina), are now American secretaries taken hostage by a Muslim theocracy determined to repossess the assets its deposed monarch had lodged in Western banks. Weber's jangling chorus in praise of the caliph is sung to a litany of religious and economic revenge: "Islam! Islam! / Oil and Allah build an unshakable tower."

In the same year, Handel's Caesar found himself in contemporary Egypt. Peter Sellars's production of *Giulio Cesare* at Purchase, New York, placed Pompey's funeral urn among the wreckage of a bombed Cairo hotel; the Roman emperor changed into an imperial American president on a Middle Eastern peace mission. This Caesar presided over a disarmament summit during his aria "Va tacito" and juggled ballpoint pens as symbols of nuclear weaponry, finally purveying reassurance to the world with the corny folksiness of Reagan. In 1986, Rossini's prophet was sent home to the contemporary Middle East. The English National Opera's *Moses*—a version of *Moïse et Pharaon*, Rossini's revision for Paris of the Neapolitan *Mosè in Egitto*—was a duel between shaggy guerrillas and a sleek, sleazy ruling class in Lurex lounge suits. Rather than waiting on a miracle, these Israeli freedom fighters performed a massacre, slaughtering the Egyptian army and putting it about that the Red Sea was to blame.

Revolution is an abrupt, enforced change. It's thus a shorthand for the shock of modernization to which directors want to subject opera. Revolution also means the speeding-up of history. The fusty past or ignorant present arrives unexpectedly in the future. In this respect, revolution entitles a director to treat opera anachronistically: to remove it from its appointed time and force it to take notice of what happens after its own creation; to make the production a measure of, yet a bridge across, the historical gap which divides us from the work we're dealing with. Updating is a way of endowing operas with foresight. They preview the new world which will later come into being because of them. Thus Peter Hall at Glyndebourne advanced *Don Giovanni* from 1787 to the early nineteenth century: Giovanni looked like a sallow, saturnine buck from the English Regency. The announcement of death in the opening chords of Mozart's score, and the scurrying panic those chords start up, are the inauguration of the nineteenth century in music. Even Mahler, Hall believes, is heralded here. So the production's responsibility is to show what happens to the hero after Mozart, when the eighteenth century's freethinking sensualist turns sick, kept going by an incendiary romantic quarrel with God.

At Covent Garden in 1967, Luchino Visconti found the same anticipatory vision in *La Traviata*. Verdi composed it and set it in the 1850s, though to soften its controversial modernity it was soon relegated to the reign of Louis XIV; Visconti edged it into the 1890s, with designs modeled on the fetid, entangling black-and-white illustrations of Beardsley, who died, like Violetta, of consumption. *Traviata* becomes a work about the decadent end of romanticism, as Hall's *Don Giovanni* is about its defiant liberal beginning. From Violetta's disease a morbid art is made: Beardsley's black lines stain the white of the page like spots clouding the patient's lungs. No longer a social problem, as she was for Dumas and Verdi, the fallen woman with her rancid camellias is redefined as an aesthete.

A work prior to and innocent of revolution can be infested by the director with forebodings of the reckoning to come. This was the case with Corsaro's *Amour des Trois Oranges* at Glyndebourne. Gozzi wrote the comedy, to which Prokofiev added his diabolical, dissonant score, in 1761; Corsaro transposed it to 1789, during the French revolutionary reign of terror. The violence in the music—the sinisterly jaunty march, or the furious scherzo through which the orchestra is lashed while the magus Tchélio and a war-whooping Fata Morgana copulate—could then be politically institutionalized. No longer a distempered nightmare rumbling in the pit, it had uprisen to take over the city. Corsaro set the work in a Paris street theater, where the revolution playfully consumed its offspring and executed a posturing theatrical monarchy. At the end of the opera, the Prince and Princess were pelted by the onstage spectators, rather than acclaimed; Fata Morgana returned as Madame Defarge, carrying a miniature guillotine and attended by a totalitarian armed guard of bodybuilders. The Prince's hypochondriac malady, with which the opera begins, was real after all. That mocking march is played on the way to the scaffold. *L'Amour des Trois Oranges* came to seem the prophetic bad dream of an expiring class—or rather of three such classes under sentence of death: the aristocrats of 1789; those of the Russia Prokofiev left after the Bolshevik coup, since the opera was written for Chicago in 1921; and those who happily applauded the premonition of their own overthrow at Glyndebourne, and who had an orange hurled at them by Corsaro during the curtain calls on opening night.

The operatic canon is closed, our attitude to the art necessarily retrospective. This hindsight means that an opera is modified by the historical distance it has traveled between its own period and ours. Should *Madama Butterfly*, for instance, be expected to take account of changes in American imperial policy since Puccini saw Belasco's play in 1900? Directors nowadays insist that it should. Joachim Herz's production for Welsh National Opera discerned in Butterfly a victim of gunboat diplomacy. She decorates her house with an image of Theodore Roosevelt, of whose global stickshaking Pinkerton is an agent. He arrives in Nagasaki on a warship, and when he disembarks he carries with him the supplementary armament of the ugly American abroad: a camera. Like the guns on his heavy cruiser, Pinkerton's box Brownie subdues the natives by making them acquiescently static targets. The camera first colonizes, then kills. Butterfly tells Pinkerton that she has heard of butterflies impaled on pins and filed away as entomological exhibits. Her own fate is to be glued into a photograph album. But the technology by which Pinkerton casually conquers returns, in the form of documentary evidence, to arraign him. Herz writes a letter in Pinkerton's name to Sharpless, slangily discarding "the sweet little gal I sort of married," and projects a photocopy of it on a screen as ocular proof of his treachery.

Ken Russell's *Butterfly* at Spoleto shifted the blame ahead from Teddy Roosevelt to Truman, and concluded with the bomb blast which in 1945 atomized Hiroshima. Through the radioactive murk, a galaxy of neon signs advertised a resurrected Japan, refashioned in the capitalist likeness of its destroyer. Graham Vick's production moves on to the decimated terrain of Vietnam: the children employed in it were refugees, from the Save the Children Fund Vietnamese Children's Home in London. Only Ponnelle is prepared to validate and venerate Butterfly's guileless American dream. In his film, the Cio-Cio-San of Mirella Freni scandalizes the Bonze by brandishing a postcard of the Crucifixion, and during the orchestral interlude on the eve of Pinkerton's return contemplates the equally sacred icons of her imaginary America. Pinkerton's father is Uncle Sam, and he shares his mother with Whistler. Russell supplies his Cio-Cio-San with tackier fantasies, provoked by a dose of opium—a fitted kitchen stocked with crates of cornflakes and a greasy, bulbous hamburger.

Russell has made a specialty of historical superimposition. His *Rake's Progress* in Florence exchanged Hogarth's London for the city of the 1980s, where the modish rakes scarify their flesh with safety pins and sport punk hairdos. *La Bohème* at Macerata in 1984 was his most ambitious exercise in historical synopsis, narrating the degeneracy of bohemianism from romanticism to the present. Zeffirelli's *Bohème* at the Met in 1981 dreamed of a Paris before Haussmann carved out the great boulevards, when the city was still villagey. The Barrière d'Enfer in Zeffirelli's third act—a wistful snowy park—expressed the same sense of grief for lost time as Atget's photographs of a defunct Paris. By contrast with this nostalgia, in Russell's production Puccini's opera act by act progressively outgrew its time. The first scene was backdated to 1834, when romanticism is vulgarizing itself as a fad and encouraging the talentless young to confuse fantasy with creativity. Mimi, a sagacious slut, embroiders her own "brief story," and performs in playlets of her own devising. Rodolfo and Marcello strain to make art; she *is* art, at its most meretricious. The second scene has arrived in 1914. The Café Momus is an outpost of modernism, all cubes and Picassoesque Pierrots. Musetta rides a bicycle into it, like one of the mechanized dancers in Satie's ballet *Parade*. For once, the military fanfares in the street have a purpose: the soldiers are marching off to the western front, and Rodolfo, resigning art to defend civilization, abandons Mimi to join up. By the third scene it is 1944, and Paris has been occupied by the Nazis, who use the inn at the Barrière d'Enfer as their whorehouse. Political force still constrains the bohemians, and corrupts their art. Rodolfo has exchanged poetry for the dissemination of Vichy pamphlets, Marcello instead of classical nudes daubs heroic likenesses of Hitler and Eva Braun—"these warriors" as they're called in Puccini's libretto—on the walls. The fourth scene is romanticism's fag end, in a chic and druggy 1984. Rodolfo's literary disgrace has worsened, and he now scribbles captions for fashion magazines. Marcello's garret is converted to a photographer's studio, where models now preen in furs rather than posing for the painter as stately odalisques. The others have jettisoned Puccini in favor of hard rock. Schaunard intimidates the orchestra with an electric guitar. Bohemianism at its terminus is a sordid and commercial youth culture, supplying opiates to those who refuse to grow up. Mimi is snuffed out by her heroin addiction.

Russell wanted his *Bohème* to dramatize "the death of our civilization, of our art." However that may have been, it certainly presaged the death of the opera. But Russell's postmortem on Puccini is a logical scrutiny of the work's future. Murger had already done the same, in the last of the *Scènes de la vie de Bohème* which were Puccini's source. Rodolphe and Marcel meet again years after their youthful indiscretions, which they review with amused remorse. Now they like their comforts, and are only too eager to compromise with the society they once outraged. The worst fate Murger can imagine for them is membership in the bourgeoisie; Russell knows that their destination is not the suburbs but the emergency ward.

Opera's gift for prediction matters most in works which are themselves about politics. Any political scheme has designs on the future, and that's what a director must represent. The events of *Boris Godunov* happen between 1598 and 1605. Tarkovsky's production at Covent Garden, though, showed that they have been happening perpetually throughout Russian history, before and after the unseating of the tsars. He likened Boris to Stalin, and the pretender Dimitri to Walesa. To make clear this timelessness, he set the opera in no particular place. The only background was a moldered arch, glinting with candles and tenanted by phantoms. This was the country, an outer expanse and an inner condition; in front, a shaky scaffolding suggested the apparatus of state imposed upon it.

Directorial foresight is equally urgent in *Fidelio*, because the opera is about the instigation of revolution. But can Beethoven's understanding of his own opera's subject be taken as final? Herz's production for English National Opera in 1980 adjoined some provisos. After the news of Fernando's arrival, Rocco during a scene change scrambled up a ladder on the wall of the auditorium to remind the audience—the future's jury—that not *all* the prisoners will be released. A second skeptical gloss was inserted by Herz into the final chorus: a scrim on which Beethoven's signature is scrawled dropped over and blocked off the jubilant crowd, an alienatory warning that only for the composer did the struggle end there.

Later in 1980, another East German, Harry Kupfer, directed *Fidelio* in Cardiff, and expanded it into a narrative of revolution and its disillusionments since the opera's conception in 1805. The immediate reference is to the psychology of German fascism. Searchlights glaringly inspect the panopticon of a concentration camp. Jaquino is a rigid, bespectacled clerk, one of the state's innocuous desk-murderers; Rocco creeps along ashamed, head bowed, counseling the wisdom of a low profile, as much a prisoner as the wretches he locks up. His internees likewise, rather than gladly erupting into the courtyard, have lost the habit of being free, dread Leonore (who is after all a jailer), and even when permitted to roam at will prefer to patrol in supervised circles. As soon as the guards return, they congeal to a jellied mob, collectivized by terror. This colonized and whimpering lonely crowd recovers its fortitude in Kupfer's final scene and redefines itself as the Marxist mass—the eclectic aggregate of the world's victims, united in rejection of their chains. The chorus which overwhelms the private happiness of Leonore and Florestan is here the imperative voice of historical inevitability. Universalizing the action means internationalizing it, and Kupfer's chorus comprises a global congress of revolutionaries. Ranked on a tiered platform are a coalition of Iranian agitators, Sandinistas, Polisario and delegates of the PLO, with mortarboarded intellectuals and infantrymen, peons and commissars, beatniks in baggy sweaters, all of them vomited forth from the mouth of Rudé's sculptural *Marseillaise* on the Arc de Triomphe. This is the offspring of the French revolution. The platform the chorus occupies is the secular altar of a new faith, dialectical materialism. Among the insurgents stands a jaundiced angel; the altar, however, testifies to the abdication of the gods and the regeneration of humanity. During the scene change—in which Herz's Rocco editorialized—a hail of rubble, broken chains, banners and upended torches tumbles from the deconsecrated sky, like the debris of a ruined Valhalla. Mythology has been supplanted by history. The divine edicts which governed the ancient world from above cede, in the modern dispensation, to the human initiatives of politics.

It's especially crucial for the director to ensure that the *Ring* retains its actuality. If set in the mythic past, with dinosaurlike deities and shaggily primitive heroes, it's comfortably remote from reality, and its interpretation of modern history and economics is confounded. Postwar Bayreuth felt a nervous obligation to distance it. A previous generation had appropriated the *Ring* for its own politics; making a myth of it, Wieland Wagner could denazify it. His first production in 1951 therefore eschewed Teutonism for an abstract nowhere of curving earth and radiant heaven. Its successor in 1965 found in the work an anthropological fable, allowing it to take place anywhere and everywhere. Myth didn't mean, in this production, a remote prehistory; it was the deep and secret meaning which underlay all history. No longer tribally Nordic, the *Ring* could speak to all men. The Bayreuth programs glossed it by quoting Jung: "to have a soul—that is life's great adventure."

But in the theater any style is bound to provoke its own opposite, so for the next generation of directors the urgent motive was to retrieve the *Ring* from Wieland's prehistory and apply it to the present. Or to the future, which is where Götz Friedrich's *Götterdämmerung* at Covent Garden in 1976 took place. The Wälsung radicals are defeated by the leisure class of gods and the technological Gibichungs, who inhabit a consumerist Utopia. Hagen grimaces at Siegfried through a magnifying lens, like a tycoon experiencing the world through his surveillance system; the women at Gunther's court are giggling flappers in fur coats and pink cloche hats.

The responsibility of forestalling this society of inhuman engines and appliances is transferred from Siegfried to the audience. "With what remains," as Friedrich's synopsis put it, "it is for those yet unbred to begin the endeavor anew." At Bayreuth in 1976, Patrice Chéreau's *Ring* concluded with the same exhortation. The motley witnesses who have quit their tenements to watch, amazed, as Brünnhilde acts out her suttee turn in the clearing smoke to face the other audience in the theater, their sullen faces asking a question which the Bayreuth public answered with boos. By 1983, the Bayreuth *Ring* had reverted again from history to myth. Peter Hall chose to see the work as a fairy tale, innocent of political remonstrance.

This transit of the too familiar classics back and forth through time and space can seem a reflex of the director's bored caprice, desperate for a new way to dress a work. It's justified only if it surprises unsuspected meanings from the opera. A quartet of *Rigolettos* contains two transpositions which are trivial, and two more which are serious. Verdi set the work in Mantua during the Renaissance. It belongs there: the opera's source was Victor Hugo's play *Le Roi s'Amuse*, and it sums up Hugo's vision of the Renaissance as a time at once of mental quest and sensual abandon. Jean-Claude Auvray in Basel in 1981 decided, however, to uproot *Rigoletto* to New York in 1930, where the Duke is a graduate of Capone's gang and the overlord of Manhattan, while his rival Monterone is chieftain in Brooklyn. Soon after, Jonathan Miller at the English National Opera removed *Rigoletto* to the New York of the 1950s, among the bars, vacant lots and mean streets of Little Italy. The point in both cases was merely sartorial—the joky novelty of a Duke in spats, or (in the Miller version) a leather jacket and a GI's fatigues. This was decorative opera, as superficial as its clothes.

Ponnelle's film of *Rigoletto*, shown on American television in 1985, temporized between Hugo's sixteenth and Verdi's nineteenth century by wishing the opera into Mozart's eighteenth century. His version began in a Palladian theater at Parma, like Losey's for *Don Giovanni*; capitalizing on the comic grace of the libertine Duke, who maintains a Mozartean lyrical poise throughout, Ponnelle rearranged the opera as a psychological commentary on the sexual discontents suppressed in the society of *Don Giovanni*. Pavarotti plays the Duke as a rational hedonist, disporting himself like Giovanni at his last supper. He might be a chubby neoclassical Bacchus, with vine leaves wreathed in his toupee. Ingvar Wixell's Rigoletto, meanwhile, is the Commendatore. He can play Mozart's apocalyptic censor because—in one of Ponnelle's neat doublings, like the conflation of the Steersman and Erik in *Der Fliegende Holländer*—Wixell also acts and sings the role of Monterone, Rigoletto's accuser. Monterone here is a white elder, standing beneath an equestrian statue like the Commendatore's in the graveyard. Rigoletto therefore aims Monterone's curse at himself, and in the penultimate scene, answering Monterone's imprecations, offers to be his own avenger. Compounding the roles makes the opera a therapeutic dream-play: the blanched, stony Monterone is the reproving superego to Rigoletto's ribald, jesting id. Rigoletto hallucinates a fantasy which his other half, Monterone, intercedes to punish. He has helped the Duke ravish Monterone's daughter; he must therefore want, Ponnelle deduces, to ravish his own. At the beginning of the production, he comes upon the dead, discarded Gilda, and thereafter imagines the sequence of events which may have been responsible. The hypothesis is teasing. Rigoletto after all is thought to be Gilda's lover, and assists in her abduction. Ponnelle makes him cradle her in the bed where she has been defiled, and surreptitiously alters the text to allow him that liberty. This Rigoletto demands "aprite la venta" not "aprite la porta" because he's already in the chamber, facing the curtained four-poster where Gilda lies. Is it his incestuous longing which, enlisting the Duke as alibi, sullies and kills her?

Because Rigoletto is guilty, the Duke can be innocent. Pavarotti is a harmless big baby here. He puffs and rolls his eyes in boredom as Rigoletto and the Gilda of Edita Gruberová repetitiously wind down their duet in the garden; is peeved in "Ella mi fu rapita," and comfily clutches a pillow to his bosom in "Parmi veder" as a substitute for the absent girl; chortles smuttily during the chorus's recitation of the practical joke. This view of the character releases the humor in Pavarotti, and the charming impetuosity. He stays on for a cadenza with Gilda, while Giovanna collects his gloves, hands them to him, and tries to drag him off. The reminiscence of Rossini isn't fortuitous: in *Il Barbiere di Siviglia*, Figaro hustles Rosina and Almaviva, too intent on their sweet nothings to scramble down the ladder. Ponnelle takes the view of *Rigoletto* which Beaumarchais, in the plays Mozart and Rossini set, might have done. It's about a mad day of confused identities, snarled by useless precautions. The intrigue remains comic because these eighteenth-century characters are engaged in games—flirtatious in the Duke's case, perverse but still merely wishful in that of Rigoletto, since he has his own inbuilt Monterone to restrain him—not the prosecution of crimes. Don Giovanni remains a philanderer; he has not yet been redefined as a demon.

While Ponnelle fills in *Rigoletto*'s prehistory, Yuri Lyubimov's production at the Florence Maggio Musicale in 1984 attempted to dramatize its afterlife. The Russian director provoked one of the year's noisier scandals. The conductor Giuseppe Sinopoli withdrew before rehearsals began, the Rigoletto of Piero Cappuccilli walked out after a few hours, and Gruberová consented to stay on for Gilda only after being assured that she wouldn't be hauled into the flies on a swing, then stuffed into a sack for disposal in the river. Zeffirelli denounced the production in print, though he declined to see it.

Despite the fuss, Lyubimov had a point to make about the contemporaneity of the work's spirit, whereas Auvray and Miller were only putting it in modern fancy dress. Lyubimov's is a Rigoletto accused of political venality, of collusion with the rapacious state which had recently sent Lyubimov himself into exile. In Shakespeare, the fool is the critic of power, laughing at Lear; Rigoletto the jester is, however, power's accomplice. Establishing a lineage for the character before and after his apparition in Verdi, Stefanos Lazaridis designed a warehouse stocked with dummies wearing the costumes of clowns and of the tyrants who employ them. Among Rigoletto's avatars in this museum were Don Quixote and Sancho Panza, or Arlecchino from the commedia dell'arte, who turns up again in *Ariadne auf Naxos;* the Duke's collateral descendants were represented by mannequins of Hitler, Stalin and Mao. Rigoletto himself wore a compilation of these uniforms, because he superimposed the roles. As a fool and a tramp, he sported the battered bowler and shabbily elegant cane of Chaplin. But he also swaggered misshapenly inside the greatcoat of Napoleon. Lyubimov's musty depository contained some operatic models as well—Traviata, to indicate perhaps that Gilda is another victim of social misuse, and Carmen, because as Lazaridis explained "we find that Maddalena comes through Carmen." The fact that Maddalena precedes Carmen only makes the anachronism more ingenious: in the waxworks, all times are contiguous, and Maddalena makes explicit the secret shame of Carmen, singing and dancing on street corners to trap victims for a professional assassin. Lyubimov sees Gilda supernaturally, as an untainted angel. She sings "Caro nome" on her swing, suspended above the mean muddle of a world which kills her but which she blesses all the same.

Lyubimov's store of effigies might have been a metaphor for opera. Since it's a museum art—classic, terminated, with interpreters as its respectful curators—where could it more appropriately be set than in a museum? This has been the conceit of Luca Ronconi's productions of Verdi at La Scala: *Don Carlos* in 1977, *Ernani* in 1982, *Aida* in 1985, each of them immured within a festering ancien régime.

Ronconi's *Don Carlos* treated Schiller's pageant as a Brechtian epic.

It directed the traffic of history in obedience to political imperatives. Throughout the opera, in a protracted funeral march, a crowd of three hundred plodded across the stage from right to left, disappearing to reenter and begin their unprogressive toil anew. This mob of troops, monks and grandees trundled trolleys of corpses, dragged crosses or wheeled floats with statues of the Grim Reaper: life unrolled endlessly toward annihilation. History was thus dramatized as a Triumph of Death. The stage was flanked and closed off by aluminum tombs; the funeral effigy of Charles V, unveiled when the shroud of snow was peeled back from Fontainebleau, brooded over all throughout. Only once was this dolorous procession interrupted. After Posa's death, the revolutionary insurgents advanced in the opposite direction, from left to right, soon to be halted by the Inquisitor. Claudio Abbado, who conducted, remarked that "the opera takes place on two levels," human and institutional. Ronconi made those levels the dual tiers of Luciana Damiani's set. The populous march-past occupied a ramp at the back; Verdi's characters, the belittled victims of this impersonal history, were confined to a trench in the foreground. Like the Escurial, the stage was both mausoleum and museum. Damiani saw *Don Carlos* happening in a mildewed, moldering Spain, tainted the gray of corroded metal, moistened—as he said—by "a pus that should seem to have oozed from those tombs."

Ronconi's *Ernani* also happened inside a graveyard of monuments. Ezio Frigerio's sets capitalized on the fact that the characters are always retiring into and emerging from architectural hiding-places. Silva conceals Ernani in the shiny metallic base of an equestrian statue; Carlo goes to pray inside the baroque tomb of Charlemagne. Elvira, dressed up like a wedding cake for betrothal to three successive suitors, is herself a social and artistic trophy, gaudily overwrought. What Ronconi presented onstage was an opera performance at La Scala a century ago, preserved as if by taxidermy. Bored patrons sat about watching the action, brightening up only for a masked ball in the last act. The Spain of 1519 is reviewed by the Italy of 1844. Carlo wears a Renaissance ruff and an Aragonian tunic, but Silva in his black, fur-collared coat is a nineteenth-century bourgeois republican. Next to the columns of plastic marble is the shantytown of the bandit Ernani, who enters the palace unkempt and unshaven, trailing behind him a rabble of peasants from Verdi's own time. Ronconi constructs a museum so that it can be invaded by protesting contemporary history, and ravaged.

The *Aida*, designed by Mauro Pagano, investigated a society obsessed, like Philip at the Escurial, with making mausoleums for itself. Egypt here suffered from a building mania. The temple of Vulcan at Memphis, where Radamès prays for victory, had its foundation in a trough beneath the floor, and loomed vertically into view; armies of slaves—history's anonymous stagehands, as in the procession of *Don Carlos*—hauled pharaonic heads from place to place. Like grand opera, this Egypt was intent on its own mummification.

For Ronconi, the museum and the opera house are the last resorts of an obsolete old guard. There is an opposition, however, to this demand that opera adjust itself to modern times. Other directors value it precisely because of its investment in and recollection of the past. Visconti's productions were elegies for an aristocratic existence kept alive only by the opulent furnishings and otiose style of opera. Zeffirelli's operatic realm has retreated further, fleeing from the earth. Zeffirelli says that his productions hope to make their audiences "revisit a lost planet." His lost planets are one past's vision of other more distant pasts, doubly alembicated and seen through a haze of memory like that apricot afternoon light in the church in his Met *Tosca*—a sunset imperial Egypt of rosy pyramids in his Scala *Aida*; the dim Druidic forest with its charred oak stump in his Paris *Norma*; the orange twilight of the wood in his Covent Garden *Falstaff*, marking the end of a rustic, magical Middle Ages; the Watteauesque pleasure gardens and shady groves of eighteenth-century hedonism in his Covent Garden *Don Giovanni*; the sumptuous heaviness of Second Empire decor in his *Traviata* film, revisited in memory by Violetta.

Like all of Zeffirelli's work, that *Traviata* is a ghost story. He treats his singers as revenants from the irretrievable other world. His *Cavalleria Rusticana* at the Met in 1970 was a homage to Eleonora Duse, who had played Santuzza onstage. Grace Bumbry was here her reincarnation, cyclonically hurtling across the piazza and up the cliff of steps to the church, groveling in misery before Mamma Lucia and stabbing Turiddu with her bony, angular hands. His *Carmen* in Vienna in 1978 dressed Elena Obraztsova in the image of Galli-Marié; his *Tosca* at Covent Garden in 1965 envisaged Callas, he has said, as a reborn Lina Cavalieri, the singer on whom Puccini had modeled his heroine—the daughter of a poor Roman artisan and mistress of numerous European monarchs, a simple soul for all her flamboyance who remained true to her roots and often abandoned her jewels and her elaborate gowns to go shopping in the Roman streets.

Returning to *Tosca* at the Met in 1985, Zeffirelli hoped to find in

Hildegard Behrens the resurrection of Callas. The motive of that *Tosca* was a pervasive nostalgia, regretting a dead singer and a disappeared city: Zeffirelli loves *Tosca* because it's redolent of a lost Rome, which never actually gets onstage. He imagines Tosca before her first entrance buying flowers to present to the Madonna and greeting her admirers in the market; explaining why Puccini introduces the shepherd in the third act, he remembers the long-gone farms and vineyards near the Castel Sant'Angelo. The Met's stage machinery enabled him to do his time and space traveling hydraulically, when the castle battlements rose in the air to unearth the dungeon of moldered Corinthian pillars where Cavaradossi waited to die. The production became, at this moment, an instantaneous and effortless archaeological dig.

At his most reverential, Zeffirelli has restored to opera the sacredness which, throughout its history, it has questioned and even derided. His courtesan in the 1982 *Traviata* film is more than an expert on carnal passion. She proceeds through the stages of a sacrificial religious Passion. The film begins with a view of Notre Dame. Violetta's vacated apartment—the emptied house of life—is itself a murky, desolated cathedral, where a portrait of her presides on the wall like a religious icon; she lies in state in a candlelit boudoir like a chapel. Revisiting the lost planet of her own past after the prelude, Violetta has arisen from the tomb. Zeffirelli stages the crises of the opera's action as altarpieces, or tableaux of mortified spirit. As Germont pleads with her, the Violetta of Teresa Stratas twists herself, hand on breast, into the semblance of a lachrymose Magdalen, gazing skyward. Alfredo's virginal sister, merely invoked in the opera, is a character in the film, so she and Violetta can be aligned as the two Marys, the one immaculate, the other fallen but upraised by Christ. At Flora's party, Violetta as she sits alone staring into the fire first crosses herself, then on her repetitions of "Pietà gran Dio" joins her hands in prayer. The final scene happens during Carnival. Zeffirelli's staging indicates that this is the preamble to Lent, which leads inexorably to Violetta's crucifixion. Her death, consequently, is a Pietà with the sexes reversed. Cradling her in his arms, Domingo's Alfredo is now the forgiving father Germont had claimed to be in the second scene, when he told Violetta that God spoke through her; then he lays his head on her chest, like a son imploring a mother's pardon, and she collapses into the arms of the almighty patriarch Germont.

Ponnelle doesn't share this sacramentalism, and sees opera as the bequest of a secular rationality. However, for him as for Zeffirelli it's the relic of a world beautiful because extinct. Ponnelle is impatient with attempts to find signs of revolution in *Le Nozze di Figaro*. In his production for Salzburg in the 1970s, Almaviva's castle was a lucid temple of the age of reason, its white open spaces dazzling with sunny clarity. An enlightened ruler in spite of his sexual bullying, Almaviva even had a court of law on the premises. No upsetting of the stable hierarchy was to be tolerated, and when Ponnelle directed the work in Chicago, Geraint Evans withdrew because his Figaro was not permitted to menace the Count and threaten a proletarian showdown. In Salzburg, Ponnelle's setting resembled a rococo solarium, all blazing white walls and wrought iron, close to the sunny Seville of Rossini's opera. By the time he directed *Figaro* at the Met in 1985, the mood had turned somberly baroque. The castle of Aguasfrescas was a gray concrete tomb like the Escurial, its plaster cracked, its pillars chipped. Its inhabitants are trapped in a mausoleum of outdated neoclassical attitudes. The Countess recoils from the light in her cavernous bedchamber, extending her arm in protest like a heroine from Racine, and prays before her bedside altar after "Porgi amor"; the Count when accusing her of adultery brandishes his sword. The feudal lord is refashioned as the Augustan jurist: when the Count in this production dons his legal wig and ermine robes to arbitrate Marcellina's case, he is Ponnelle's wisely impartial emperor from *La Clemenza di Tito*. This *Figaro* concludes not with the storming of the Bastille but with a retroactive dawn of enlightenment. As the confusions are cleared up in the garden, black drapes pulled away from the set create an instant illumination, and Sarastro's bright, reasonable sun arises.

The operatic lost world of Ponnelle is an ideal eighteenth century, a culture of closed and equilibrated musical forms and of philosophical composure: "for me," he said in 1984, "*Figaro* is the best example of a pre-revolutionary time—this time of Beaumarchais, this time of Diderot, this time of Rousseau, and of Voltaire." (These, presumably, are the authors whose vellum-bound books stand in for the fourth leg of Figaro's bed in the Met staging.) He says, "I am happy in this world," but the happiness is retrospective, and Mozart's first and last exercises in neoclassical opera interest Ponnelle because they helplessly predict an end to this temperate, musically regulated classical culture, destroyed by romantic revolution.

His *Idomeneo* at the Met in 1982 revealed that classical society in a state of romantic dilapidation. Mozart's characters, dressed as eighteenth-century grandees, wander among its rubble. One of them romantically relishes the decay of the classical: while Ilia sings "Zeffiretti lusinghieri," Idamante sprawls upstage among the architectural wreckage, basking in the sun like Goethe on his Italian journey lolling on a truncated column in the Campagna. Though Ponnelle's conservatism would no doubt like to arrest history, he finds in *Idomeneo* a formula for permitting change so long as it is genial, mild and kind. The revolution happens here without bloodshed.

The production's votive icon was a hollow, emptily authoritarian god: a huge mask of Neptune, with vacant eye-sockets and a gaping mouth. The mask is the monster, an unjust power in human society. Idomeneo is the jealous guardian of that power, so during the chorus of panic the crowd encircles him rather than the unseen Kraken. He resigns in obedience to a nature which he enrages (in "Fuor del mar") but which the other characters propitiate and tame. The chorus declares that the sea is placid, and Ilia entrusts her hopes to those gentle breezes. Idomeneo saves a classical world by acquiring a romantic wisdom.

Ponnelle's direction elicits a gradual liberation of instinct. Ilia sings her first aria shackled. "Padre, germani" is a muted mad scene, and she is driven near to collapse by Idamante's pleading, which leaves her bent, broken-backed. Classicism can't permit the self-division she feels. Romanticism does tolerate the contrariety of emotions persecuting Ilia, and once unbound she lapses into acquiescence with its energies. This is why Ponnelle staged "Zeffiretti lusinghieri" pantheistically. As she describes those airs, Ilia sways in harmony with them and agitates her hands to create a wind of her own, diffusing her emotion. Only Elettra remains unreconciled. She, for Ponnelle, is romanticism's bad conscience. Rather than consenting to the tranquil natural order, her agitated final aria describes a mental hell, and Ponnelle choreographs that scene as a gibbering breakdown, at the end of which the epileptic Elettra is carried off insensible. She will return soon enough, in the romantic decadence, as the Elektra of Strauss. Nilsson sang Mozart's Elettra at Glyndebourne in 1951, graduating later to Strauss's version of the character; at the Met, encouraged by Ponnelle, Hildegard Behrens played Elettra as one of Nietzsche's Dionysian Greeks, a wiry fury in a henna wig, spitting out volleys of vituperative staccati.

Ponnelle describes *La Clemenza di Tito* as the dying Mozart's Chekhovian lament for an intellectually clement century. Tito, he suggests, is less Suetonius's Titus than the moderate and judicious philosopher-king Joseph II. In the 1984 Met production, Kenneth Riegel wore the white wig of an eighteenth-century lawgiver; in Ponnelle's earlier film of the opera, Tito during the overture remembered and reenacted his forswearing of Berenice, which establishes him as classical man, preferring public duty to private and romantic emotional longings. Yet this serenity is troubled, and can be maintained only by an effort of will. The opera's emotional weather is autumnal, and Ponnelle set the film in the ruins of the Roman forum, lurid with the flames of arson. Sesto's prison is a Piranesian labyrinth: classical architecture has moldered into romantic fantasy, a catacomb of incarceration. And despite Tito's pardon, Ponnelle adds a skeptical postscript to the fortified order. In his *Idomeneo*, Elettra fumes and froths; here a dissident insanity is wished upon Vitellia. Her rondo, "Non più di fiori," is usually considered to be a self-administered sedative, a lesson in moral resignation. At the Met, Ponnelle staged it as a demented bridal night, with Renata Scotto like a premature Lucia running in frenzied circuits before collapsing—as her voice squalled into hysterics—to caress the prompt box. After the revolution, in Ponnelle's view, music will be the sound of madness.

SEVEN

Beating Time

OPERATIC performance acknowledges a conflict of interest between drama and music, the stage and the pit, but even within the musical department there are differences of emphasis. Conductors and singers have antagonistic notions of the art. Birgit Nilsson used to define opera as singing with orchestral accompaniment, not the other way round; Carlo Maria Giulini, conducting *Falstaff* at Covent Garden in 1982, jokingly proposed that the ideal account of this opera would be one without the singers.

Conductors tend to disparage what Boulez sarcastically calls "solo prowess," or "the battle between throat and the volume of orchestral sound." Some of them, resenting their invisibility in the pit, compensate by upstaging the singers. Bernstein, conducting *Fidelio* when the Vienna company visited Washington in 1979, used the podium as a springboard from which he could leap into the air with flailing arms; during the interpolated *Leonore* overture he danced about like the cheerleader for his own subsequent ovation. When Karajan conducted his own production of *Die Walküre* at the Met in 1967, he had the level of the pit raised to hoist himself into prominence. At the same time he dimmed the lights onstage, and Nilsson snarled that she could have gone out for a coffee during the opera without anyone noticing.

Though Giulini loyally supported the singers in *Falstaff*, his conducting made clear what he meant by wishing he could play the opera without them. He rid *Falstaff* of brassy bumptiousness: a work often vulgarized as opera buffa was treated as a Mozartean tragicomedy, poised like *Don Giovanni* between festivity and decay; the orchestra expounded the drama. Under Falstaff's monologues, a discreet, quietly nervous chamber music confided the old man's mortal fears. When Quickly told Falstaff of Alice's love for him and called her a "povera donna," the strings wept in commiseration. The twelve strokes of the clock in the forest at midnight, quakingly enumerated by Falstaff, were an auditory reckoning. The singers attuned their characters to the sounds Giulini made. Renato Bruson's Falstaff was delicate not gross. Describing his youthful leanness, Bruson squeezed the word "sottile" (which denotes his slenderness), emaciating it as he voiced it until he earned the right to rhyme it with "gentile"; planning his conquest of Alice in the inn or serenading her as she played the lute, he sang with the sly softness of a hand attempting a preliminary, tentative caress.

In the theater Karajan gloomily obscures the singers; in recent recordings he has sought to hush them as well. His *Nozze di Figaro* keeps the singing for the most part below a whisper. Figaro's instruction "Susanna pian-pian" is the rule of the performance. The recitative before Figaro's "Si vuol ballare" is muttered tersely. Karajan has no interest in the work's political conflicts—nor does Ponnelle, from whose Salzburg production the recording derives—so the aria itself speeds by nimbly, with no edge of menace. In the Countess's bedroom, Figaro breathes his plans insinuatingly rather than cheerily chortling over them, and even Marcellina's "Ecco tuo padre" isn't a farcical crow of triumph but a secret shamefully stealing out. There is a dramatic logic to this throttling of the voices. The opera is about people guarding information from each other and scheming under their breaths. But the enforced muting stifles character.

In Verdi, Karajan alternates between orchestral might and vocal understatement. By the time he recorded his Salzburg *Don Carlo*, the dynamic imbalance had become extreme. A battering ram of sound obliterates the first entry of Carlo, and the auto-da-fé is a din of relentless brass. The dominance of the orchestra symbolizes the megalomania of the state. The opera's individuals are allowed small havens of instrumental solitude—the sorrowing winds when Posa pleads with Elisabetta, the stabbing strings which transcribe Carlo's panic and the distracted rhapsody of the harp when he faints—but because they are alone in their private griefs there can be no theatrical collision between them: Karajan dampens and decelerates the trio in the garden to turn a shouting match into a triple soliloquy.

Again in *Salome*, recorded before the 1977 performances at Salzburg, the drama is virtually silenced. Salome and Narraboth whisper surreptitiously about the rhetorician Jokanaan, an alien who has the temerity, among these softened voices, to rail and rant. Herod mutters about the ill omen of the spilled blood, and the guard informs him of Narraboth's suicide in a confidential aside. Herodias, no hectoring shrew, contradicts her husband by lowering her voice at him. Salome sullenly hisses her refusal to eat or drink, and is reduced to toneless panting as she awaits the execution. The expression denied to the voices is claimed by the orchestra, which is Salome's thought-stream. So intent was Karajan on dissevering music from drama that at Salzburg he forbade the Salome of Hildegard Behrens to dance, and engaged a look-alike to do so for her. In the final scene, dramatic decadence is replaced by musical transfiguration: Karajan plays the conclusion as a wistful threnody, with Salome's voice bodilessly fluting; like Daphne vocalizing as she changes into a laurel, or like the voice in Strauss's *Four Last Songs* giving way to the instruments which represent the dreamy soaring of the lark or the free flight of the soul, death is her incorporation into the orchestra. When Behrens sang Salome at Covent Garden in 1979, this time with Zubin Mehta conducting, she was able to dramatize the character in ways Karajan had prohibited. Now she was haggard and distraught; presented with the head, she sobbed in dismay. Doing Salome's dance for the first time, she made striptease an obscene and painful self-exposure: the body she bared was already old.

Karajan doubles as director so he can reproduce musical motives onstage. The horizontal scope of his stage in the Grosses Festspielhaus at Salzburg corresponds aboveground to the way space is organized in the pit. The elongated disc Günther Schneider-Siemssen designed for Karajan's *Ring* looped the vast area inside a lasso, and by inclining the platform anchored it in the orchestra. The circle started out from Karajan and returned to him; standing at the point of control, he could tighten or slacken the composition and alter the layout on the disc by the slightest application of musical pressure.

His sets have always been orchestrations of the drama. The third act of his *Carmen* at Salzburg in 1966 happened beside the sea, rather than in the mountains as Bizet expected: the set was a mile-long stretch of beach, strewn with hulks. Carmen and José have escaped from the city to a life above the law in the mountains. But since Salzburg is itself carved out of mountains, that landscape couldn't represent liberty. In landlocked Austria, Karajan reasoned, geographical freedom must mean the seashore.

This, at least, was the official explanation. It's more likely that the scenery was dictated by the score—by the desire to open up a terrain as limitless as Carmen's independence, and as all-embracing as Karajan's orchestra. The solution was a horizontal infinitude, unraveling the loop of Schneider-Siemssen's ring. The beach retreated into distance like music, echoing without ever quite dying away. The design for Karajan's *Lohengrin* at Salzburg in 1976 was another graphic tribute to the musical score. The horizontal composition this time copied that of a medieval missal, yet in silhouette the trellises of straight lines and the niches on upper tiers occupied by the chorus made the stage resemble a page of printed music ruled in separate clefs, across which the characters processed like notes in a precise and regulated order.

In any Karajan production, the orchestra is the dramatic protagonist; and just as the conductor is every instrument in that orchestra, so the director must be every character in the drama. Karajan in rehearsal plays all the parts. Photographs show him in preparation for a Vienna *Tannhäuser* in 1963, drawing the hero's sword or training his eagle eye on a falcon perched on his wrist. Stiff, taut, bristling with a will which electrifies his quiff of silver hair, he grips Wotan's spear and terrifies the Nibelungen during the filming of *Rheingold* in 1979, or swings Donner's hammer, his sweater round his neck and his arms stretched wide, in the 1968 staged production; he truculently sets his jaw and sneers to show Fafner and Fasolt how to do it, brandishing a playback machine which is his instrument of command—a tiny, autocratic giant. Film allows him to be both in the pit and onstage, and he makes Hitchcockian appearances in his filmed *Carmen* as a dozing citizen of Seville under a sombrero, and in *Otello* as an onlooker during the riot.

The primacy of the conductor, in Peter Brook's view, kills opera as theater. In drama, as Brook says, the human action comes first; the orchestral comment follows later. This is the order of events Karajan disputes: the conductor gives the singers musical cues which are then translated into dramatic motivations. His own activity as a director is the enforcement of his control as a conductor.

Nevertheless, conductors ought to be natural allies for the directors whose interpretative mission is the renewal of opera. The director's gift is foresight. He must see beyond the work's location in time, help it to travel the distance between the eighteenth or nineteenth centuries and the present. The conductor's technique involves the mastery of exactly this temporal anticipation: as Antal Dorati has said, he "conducts what is not being heard but will be in the flash of a second"; he is always fractionally ahead of the players. The question of tempo therefore connects with that debate on the progressiveness of opera in which the directors are engaged. The conductor doesn't slavishly beat time as it ticks away; he beats time in the sense of overcoming it, perhaps by hastening it, perhaps by slowing it down. He too is implicated in the revolutionary business of adjusting the clock.

Tempo is history, a speedometer under our control. This awareness pervades the reflections of Pierre Boulez on the operas he has conducted—the *Ring* at Bayreuth in 1976, *Pelléas* at Covent Garden in 1969, *Lulu* in Paris in 1979. For him, the challenge of the *Ring* was its reexploration of time. He sought to remove the work from its chronology, refusing to treat it as a monument fixed in the last century. The question he asks of Wagner's music is "Can we not . . . disregard time so as to rediscover it later?" Conducting, he did just that: disregarding the customary time-values, almost hustling the orchestra with his impatient beat. Boulez urged the music forward into the future by hurrying it; Bernstein, conducting *Tristan* and leaving pauses which last for eternities between the phrases of the first prelude, pushes Wagner backward into timelessness by slowing the music down to a virtual halt.

For Boulez, the *Ring* needs to be saved from time. Its drama, he thinks, is archaically romantic, lost in the past; only its music looks ahead. The themes live independently, more malleable and complex than the characters they tag. The drama is "fossilized," the music "proliferous." Brook's preference for drama over music is here reversed: music consumes the drama, which is merely its pretext; as Boulez puts it, using the scenic imagery of the *Ring* with its zealous flames, "the music's fire purifies the bric-a-brac of the words." Through the cycle the motifs grow and change, and this obsession with time's passing links Wagner with Proust. The novelist, according to Boulez, recovers lost time by the training of memory; the musician reorganizes time so as to reexplore it. The *Ring* incites a revolution not in society (as Shaw believed) but in our mental categories. The music is an associative, indefinitely modulating system of thought: a consciousness, like the polyphonic punning language Joyce invented for *Finnegans Wake*. Boulez criticizes Wagner's lumpish alliterative texts for lacking the Joycean liquidity of the music, and adds that since the music is endless, incrementally repeating itself forever, the dramatic conclusions foisted on the operas always seem overemphatic and fraudulent.

Wagner upsets our sense of chronology and continuity. The music technically gropes ahead, while psychologically it slides in the opposite direction, arousing ancient fears and fantasies; it relativistically advances and recedes at once. Boulez rewrites musical history to reveal Wagner as the progenitor of Berg—or of Boulez himself. *Parsifal*, he says, exchanges "theme as statement" for "theme as gestalt," by which (borrowing a theory from Jung) he means formal pattern or configuration: the music is abstracted from drama, no longer obliged to illustrate things or happenings. Wagner effected a revolution in the musical substance of opera; Berg extended it into the dramatic scheme. Wagner rejected the constraint of separate numbers and closed musical forms; Berg restored them, constructing *Wozzeck* and *Lulu* as hierarchies of distinct units—march, rondo, fugue, symphonic suite—yet managing to make those units flexible and mobile, dramatically propulsive. Wagner must therefore be played as a prophecy of what comes after him. This musical program was carried out by the productions Boulez conducted: Wieland Wagner's *Parsifal* at Bayreuth, which owed more to modern anthropological studies of folklore than to romantic Christianity, or Chéreau's *Ring*, which looked back from the twentieth century at the palatial factories and sublime wreckage of industrialism.

Boulez supported Chéreau's updating of their Paris *Lulu* to the 1930s, in settings of bleak fascist neoclassicism, because "here we are faced with the intrusion of opera into the modern world." That entry into modernity is impelled by Boulez's conducting. Hence the urgency of his *Pelléas*, rid of all misty impressionistic indistinctness. To Boulez this work has the clarity of Cézanne not the vagueness of Monet; it belongs in the twentieth century, and is placed there by Boulez's management of rubato—that variability of tempo which is the conductor's area of self-expression. Performances of *Pelléas* tend to dreamy monotony, allowing the opera to drift into a dim, remote antiquity. Boulez startled it into the present by quickening it, and emphasized the jarring contrasts of tempo as the drama became more violent. The maddened Golaud, pulling Mélisande's hair, swings her back and forth—"A droite et plus à gauche! . . . En avant! en arrière!" That lashing dominance, and the abrupt changes of pace it decrees, defined the character of Boulez's conducting here: his was a *Pelléas* modernized by force.

Rubato is crucial too, as Boulez sees it, to the understanding of *Lulu* and its precarious situation in musical history. The opera was composed, he says, "at the very last moment when 'modern' opera could be a valid quest within a form taken directly from tradition." The dramatic nightmare of *Lulu* is its slowing-down of musical time. This at first seems to prolong Lulu's life. In fact it traps her, holding her hostage until the moment comes for retribution. Boulez notices this rhythmic fatigue in two scenes which correspond in Berg's symmetrical plan. When Schön goads the Painter to suicide, the insistent pulse set by Schön's spelling-out of terms gradually winds down, halting only when appeased by a death. In the London attic, the hasty arrival of the Professor prompts a flurry which also ebbs and falters, so that Lulu's death, with ghastly deliberateness, happens in slow motion. This "handling of time," Boulez says, turns music into drama, propounding Berg's reaction to incidents. The interpreter needs the same imperiousness. Playing with time, Boulez shows *Lulu* to be the end of romantic opera and—in its revival of those mercilessly strict classical shapes—the beginning of something modern, unachieved by Berg who didn't live to complete the orchestration. For both composer and conductor, the imperative is actuality. Berg brought Wedekind forward from the early years of the century into the decade during which he worked on the opera. The anachronistic snatches of jazz and ragtime in the music announce its "openness to the present," and it must be opened once more to the present in which it is performed.

The conductor should play the music as if the composer were a contemporary. This, by chance, was Claudio Abbado's only option with Rossini's *Il Viaggio a Reims*, unperformed since its premiere and restored to the repertory at Pesaro in 1984. The work had no performing tradition; Abbado relied, he has said, on his experience of preparing premieres of works by Berio and Nono. In another tribute to the modernity of *Il Viaggio*, he has likened it to *Waiting for Godot*. Both are set in a theater of absurdity or futility—Godot will never arrive, and the travelers will never get to Rheims. The same understanding made Ken Russell compare Rossini with Gertrude Stein. Referring to his Geneva production of *L'Italiana in Algeri* in 1984 (with Isabella as a flight attendant on a downed Alitalia jet), Russell said, "I couldn't get over the craziness of the rhythm and the meaninglessness of the lyrics—like Dada, like surrealism."

Abbado's Rossini, purged of belly laughs and vocal mugging, has the streamlined modernity of Stravinsky: fanatically precise in its metrics and its dynamic control. A similar dramatic force and rhythmic compulsiveness are trained on Bellini by Riccardo Muti. Bel canto for him licenses no sleepy slackness, and the orchestra doesn't content itself with strumming under the voices. Muti's *Capuleti e i Montecchi* at Covent Garden in 1984 was hard-driven, almost furious in its energy; bel canto here meant a school of demanding technical rigor. Muti insists on returning to original editions of works corrupted by theatrical custom—he performs a *Rigoletto* without supernumerary high notes—but this scholarly accuracy aims always to produce something new. His recording of *Pagliacci* dispenses with sweaty verismo, and reveals an opera painfully conscious of its own modernity. Leoncavallo's clown, like Picasso's saltimbanques or Schönberg's Pierrot, is the artist driven to the social margins, his skill disparaged and his sanity askew. Muti finds sonorities for *Pagliacci* which are eerie, grotesque, unsettlingly distorted: the dissonant babble which announces the wagon, the scuttling accompaniment to the birdsong, the rhythmic sagging when Canio morosely lumbers into the play. The interpreter's achievement is to persuade us that we're hearing a routine-staled work for the first time.

Giuseppe Sinopoli has done the same for the overexposed scores of Puccini. At the Met in 1985, Sinopoli played *Tosca* as a vocal symphony whose romantic orchestral language was turning sick, about to drop out of tonality. In the long prelude before Mario's entrance in the third act, he separated the instruments and made them converse as sourly and astringently as in the chamber music of the concurrent Vienna school. The winds shrilled expressionistically under Tosca's climactic agonies in the second act, and the church bells in the Roman dawn were as ironic in their emotional triviality as tinkling sleigh-chimes in Mahler. Even more disturbingly Mahlerian was the discordant little march to the scaffold, keeping up its jaunty step despite the ululation of the winds and stifled clashes from the drums. This exploded in brazen delight after Mario fell, then had its volume cut, rhythmically staggered and ran off the rails; it stopped altogether with Tosca's cries (which likewise lunged from song into untuned speech), only to start up again in a hugger-mugger crescendo as she rushed to the parapet. The confused end of a melodrama became a tone poem of breakdown, introducing, like Mahler's sixth symphony, the political terrors of the twentieth century.

The enemy in opera is habit, which time hardens into tradition. The repertory is so small that the works in it are soon dulled by familiarity; operagoers settle down into the nostalgic custody of their memories. The conductor's duty is more than the imposition of personality: it is the discovery in a work of qualities no one has attended to before. Interpretation is a re-creation. At its most convinced, it experiences a fusion with the first creation. Bernstein, conducting *Tristan*, feels he is composing the work as he goes along. The extreme slowness with which he conducted the love duet at Carnegie Hall in 1979 seemed to register the creator's self-immersion, playing for time as he pondered the way ahead.

The conductor who brings the work forward from the past into his own present is also removing it from his forebears and contradicting their practice. Bernstein takes a rowdy, flag-waving pleasure in *Fidelio* as the unofficial American national anthem, devoted to individual liberty. Nothing could be further from Klemperer's philosophically pondered *Fidelio* or, alternatively, from Karajan's treatment of the work as a fleet, lightweight singspiel, a postscript to Mozart. Wagner has passed through a sequence of musical revisions to match the changes in dramatic interpretation since Bayreuth reopened after the war. The traditional Wagner was monumental, measured out with the deliberation of Knappertsbusch; in the 1960s, this grave mythological pageant was interrupted by Solti, obstreperous and sometimes crassly vivid, or by Böhm, who conducted *Tristan* and the *Ring* at Bayreuth as if Wagner were Strauss—fluent, energetic, lively. Rehearsing the first scene of the third act in an appendix to his 1966 recording of *Tristan*, Böhm's instructions were the opposite of those which might have been expected from Knappertsbusch: not too slow, not too long, don't hold back, don't drag.

This newly brisk, upbeat, extroverted Wagner was in turn altered, subdued by Karajan's antiheroic lyricism. The conductor's rethinking dictated a new style of singing: compare the war cries of Böhm's Brünnhilde with those of Karajan's. Nilsson for Böhm truly is the cavalry maiden Wotan calls her, and the militaristic orchestra charges into action with her at a positive gallop. Theo Adam's Wotan thunders at Nilsson, who replies with a vocal display of forked lightning. Her repetitions of "Heiaha!" are ejected with the force and exactness of rockets; the whole paragraph dazzles like a fire storm in the sky. Karajan recorded Régine Crespin—a tender Sieglinde persuaded for the occasion to attempt Brünnhilde—in an echoing acoustic high above the orchestra, to blur the voice into the air and soften the staccato brilliance of Nilsson. The last "Heiaha!" here reveals the voice to be warm not metallically burnished. This Brünnhilde is frolicsome but never valiant. The "hei!" announcing Fricka is a sly wink, and when Brünnhilde scampers off leaving Wotan to his domestic tribulations ("Ich Lustige lass dich im Stich!") a smile playfully shines in the tone. Böhm's characters are elements: a storm cloud and a meteor at play. Karajan's are a father and daughter privately conversing.

The refining continues. Carlos Kleiber's recorded *Tristan* eliminates all vocal knockouts. In Isolde's narration, Nilsson used to drive a sword straight through the high note on "Mir lacht das Abenteuer," sarcastically describing Tristan's wooing of a bride for Marke. Sustaining the tone, she made it the clarion of a deadly, trumpeting contempt. Kleiber's Margaret Price flicks the word with her tongue, scarcely sounding it at all: adroit vocal avoidance perhaps, but also an interpretative novelty. Revenge is unimportant for this passive, emotionally discreet Isolde, no relative of Brünnhilde. The most significant words in the text are those Kleiber's singers hardly dare to utter: the problematic "und" in the duet, superstitiously breathed by Price; Tristan's eagerness to die, announced by René Kollo in "Sturb ich nun ihr der so gern ich sterbe" with that "gern" pronounced sotto voce, as a wish so precious and fragile and insecure that he can't risk putting pressure on it. Nilsson and Windgassen, in the Böhm performance, peal when crying each other's names after they drink the potion; Price and Kollo murmur, drowsily or druggedly as if asleep.

Kleiber almost answers Giulini's prescription for opera without the singers. The voices are there, but their dramatic occupation consists of listening to the music. The conversation between Isolde and Brangäne in the second act is about the orchestra, which they both hear but which they interpret differently. Isolde asks if the horns have faded; Brangäne, whose ears are sharper than Isolde's, says they are still near. Isolde argues—almost inaudibly in Kleiber's performance—that fear misleads Brangäne, and when those horns menacingly return she trains a hyperrefined attention on the landscape and hears the water gurgling under them and washing them away. Brangäne who accuses her of blindness also considers that she is deaf, but Isolde is auditing sounds in her head and in the unseen orchestra. The faintest or most distant tremors can be registered as nervous spasms or quickenings of pulse: the wriggling of a single string under Isolde's soft, untroubled voice as she calls Melot Tristan's truest friend, or the ominous slur of brass in her peripheral vision as she mentions the nocturnal hunt. When Nilsson invoked Frau Minne (the Germanic Venus), one goddess proclaimed another. But in Kleiber's orchestra, minutely alive to the agitations of the musical scenery, the worship of Frau Minne begets a shivering, enchanted Mendelssohnian fairy music. Nor do Isolde and Brangäne wrestle and strive to convince each other; in their sisterly intimacy, they are the two halves of the same voice, or the same character.

The climax of the scene is not Isolde's vocal victory. For Kleiber, it happens in the orchestra after she finishes singing, and is at once quietened by expectancy before Tristan appears. The singers, peering down into that mystic gulf, comment with fearful wonder on a drama which has taken up residence in the pit.

EIGHT

A Black Goddess

LIKE everyone else, I was converted to opera by Callas. I was won over at first by speech not song, specifically by her reading of two letters: Lady Macbeth's of her husband's augury from the battlefield, Violetta's of Germont's note with its facile and ineffectual reassurance. In both scenes, she brought to realization what Verdi, their composer, called "la parola scenica"—the word which becomes musical when it becomes dramatic, when it turns into the emotion it had previously merely named. Maria Callas symbolized what opera might ideally be.

Her perusal of Macbeth's letter, in the 1952 La Scala production which Victor de Sabata conducted, was painstakingly rehearsed, yet it sounds improvised, muffled by shock and strained by half-understood consequences. Her voice swoops onto and claws into the crucial words—"vittoria" or Macbeth's new title of "sir" or "serto," the predicted crown, which in her delivery lets off a small exclamatory explosion. Color flames into the tone, and she seems to envenom the words with meanings they're as yet innocent of. The rhythm stumbles: in her eagerness to outrun the message, Lady Macbeth trips herself up. In the aria which follows, the voice unfurls into effulgent song like a bird of night spreading its wings. It is baleful yet alight with malevolence, exactly matching the blade which glints through the murk of which Lady Macbeth speaks. In the sleepwalking scene, this volatile, fiery song has faltered into halting speech again. The words are now accusatory—"una macchia" or "maledetta"—and

Callas makes them tremble as she utters them. Her recollection of Duncan and the quantities of blood he contained wilts with sorrow and pity; recalling the Thane of Fife who had a wife, she drags behind the orchestra, swirling and swooning as if confounded by sleep or fever. She even manages to vindicate that extraneous D-flat on which Lady Macbeth wanders dreamily off. It is eerie and unearthly, a lunar music: we are listening, as Lady Macbeth disappears, to the precise moment of her death, when the voice soars upward through the head and out into space, attaining peace.

For Violetta's letter, in the 1955 Scala staging conducted by Giulini, she finds another voice entirely—the thready, breathless sound of a consumptive, trapped inside a moldering organism and with none of Lady Macbeth's vaulting energy in enunciation. Lady Macbeth forces the words to do her will, extorting from them the implication she desires; Violetta can't even inflect them, and in her asides to Annina she gasps initial syllables without the wind to float the rest, while with the doctor her tone, morbidly depressed, sags beneath pitch. The dying body has been made into a musical instrument, perfectly attuned to Giulini's strings which, accompanying her, scratch an almost sickly sweetness from abrasion. Her high notes are frail, and abruptly ended; every sentence of the letter is a whispered dying fall, its accents suppressed sighs. The signature, "Giorgio Germont," droops toward the grave. Her small aria of farewell ebbs on "Tutto è fini" because she has no strength left to sustain the line.

Callas is admired for her willingness to let vocal beauty suffer in the interest of verbal meaning. But she was more than a great actress with an unreliable voice. She herself insisted on the authority of bel canto, and remembering her early performances as Kundry in *Parsifal* said, "I hated the screams—but I suppose I did them well"; she was capable of creating a dramatic character, psychologically true and detailed, using strictly musical resources and never marring an absolute beauty of tone.

Perhaps the finest case is her Lucia in Karajan's production for La Scala, which visited (and was taped in) Berlin during 1955. She discovers a musical language for Lucia's distraction. At the fountain, her command of "Ascolta" before the aria, quietly fanatical, casts a spell on Alisa. For "Regnava nel silenzio" there's a moonstruck pallor to the tone. The trills are shivers, making the flesh creep; on the word "rossegio," describing the bloodied waters, they dart in fascination around a sight whose horror they perversely beautify. Fearing abandonment by Edgardo, Callas's tone thins to an undefended wisp: a fined-down voice corresponding to a frayed, defenseless mind. In their duet, singing of her sighs and echoing laments, she is already a drifting, ethereal ghost, crying to him on the breezes. The romantic pantheism of song—the sound of Shelley's west wind—is translated by Callas into a human affliction. At every point, the acrobatics are glossed as mental reactions. During her "Quando rapita" monologue, Lucia ornaments the words "eterna fe." The gesture isn't showy; it's reflective and internal: Callas is studying and treasuring the memory of that troth, secretly honoring it.

The character's disorientation is revealed by her musical habits. She cowers behind diminuendi for instance, like that on "quella fonte!" in her first scene. The reduction of volume swallows up and introverts the word and the idea. Her decline can be charted through a series of exhalations of breath—an "Ah" during Edgardo's "Sulla tomba" which is piercing, cold and mortal, like the sound of a soul taking flight; another when Enrico shows her the forged letter, faintingly diminished as if the breath has been startled out of her; a third during the sextet, bolder but more resentfully neurotic, because Lucia is shrinking from reality into the private solace of song. Her mad scene is an episode of recondite sonic research, dramatically appalling because so musically imperturbable. Singing of a "dolce suono" in a voice which is girlishly pure, Callas lyrically retreats to a mad second childhood. When a high note on the word for altar oscillates out of control, it does so because it has taken off from the rational human register and is echoing through the vast vacancy within Lucia's mind. Lucia chases echoes until, in the glassy, unphysical sound Callas makes during her concert with the flute, she herself becomes one: an acoustic specter; Orpheus insane but in tune.

This was the musical Callas, the notes her reverie. In other roles she was less serenely melodic, more intent on scavenging drama from the words. As Cherubini's Medea, she virtually tormented the text into meaning. She bit on words, she chewed them, she spat them. Uttered by her, they had power to kill. In the 1958 Dallas performances, her voice keens and shrills, then plummets into chesty, growling menace. It is a wounded sound, always in pain, and it fastens on words in order to irritate them or make them fester. When she denounces Giasone, the tone curdles on "crudel"; every time she repeats this, or her pealing "Pietà!", she is picking at a scab. In the third act, her invocation is acid and shrewish: "Nume, venite a me, eterni Dei!" This is a witch mimicking a priestess, and the cry "m'assista!" curls out of her chest like darting poison. She rolls the r's in "rovina orrenda!" with a venomous pleasure, as if sending boulders hurtling down into that gulf of perdition. Then on "mi soffocate!" the voice itself is strangled, battling to get out. At "Son vinta già!" the slanging triumph begins to droop, and the tone grows almost weepy. The mania sustaining her has abated, to return when she reveals the plan to kill Glauce with the diadem: "La uccida, o Numi!" is a searing razor of sound, the wobble a result of the ricocheting impetus she presses into the words. When she addresses the "implacabile Dei," the vowels go dark, the voice turns to stone. As the next mood supplants that resignation in "O vile mio cor," the adamantine sound turns combustible again and she castigates her own weakness. Cherubini's temperate neoclassical idiom is shredded; Callas herself seems to be torn apart by her expressive violence.

As Jon Vickers (the Giasone of these performances) remarked, she drove her talent to the point of masochism. Hence her fondness for punning conversions of the stage into a pillory, where she put herself on trial. Hissed during *Medea* at La Scala in 1961, she aimed her lashing "Crudel!" at the hostile audience. In *Anna Bolena* she upbraided the public as her persecutor, scorning its right to judge her: "Giudici? Ad Anna? Giudici?"

By the time of her last concerts in 1973, this accusation had softened into the victim's gentle compliance. Once more appropriating the music she sang as autobiography, she reminded the public that she had destroyed herself to please it. At the end of the London concert on November 26, she announced from the stage, touchingly apologetic, "I must say this evening there was a little more emotion than usual, and when the public loves me that much, I have to give that much more, and there's no end to it." She had placed herself in the predicament of Tosca and all her heroines: oppressed and exhausted by being loved or desired too much; made to suffer for art's sake. "I'll try a little more," she resolved sacrificially, transferring the blame to those who demanded it of her, and offered an encore—Lauretta's "O mio babbino caro" from *Gianni Schicchi*, addressed to her "public caro." If the dedication sounded too ingratiating, her singing at once belied it. Lauretta in the opera simperingly pretends that she'll kill herself if her father denies Rinuccio to her. Callas took this piece of adolescent winsomeness and made a tragic study in emotional blackmail from it, replacing Schicchi's hostility with the possessive love of her own authoritarian master, the audience. When this Lauretta sang of the torments which tugged at her, she sounded truly distraught; when she vowed to kill herself, it wasn't a manipulative bluff, because Callas, at our behest, was then and there doing so.

Her self-excruciation was physical as well as emotional. Most singers pamper the body, since it's the protective casing for their precious instrument. Pavarotti, with what he calls his "calorie problem," has never been more dramatically credible than when swigging the Bordeaux and tucking into a piece of fruit in the Met's 1981 performances of *L'Elisir d'Amore*. Callas, however, two decades before emaciation became fashionable, wasted herself. She starved in order to sculpt the physique she needed for her characters—for expressiveness not elegance. A fat face, she thought, couldn't register tension or cruelty or rage. For those emotions, she needed a chin; and since the source of musical drama lay in the contractions and vibrations of the throat, she needed in addition a lean and accentuated neck. Wiseacres claimed that the drastic diet had weakened her voice. If so, it was one among the many deathly risks she ran, and she didn't regret it: "I have to take chances, even if it means disaster and the end of my career," she once said.

With the delight in suffering suspected by Vickers, Callas saw her art as a servitude. She was an aggressor toward her audiences, assuming that her voice would be disliked when first heard and schoolmarmishly remarking "the public has to be taught"; she was even more brutally unsparing toward herself. During the 1967–68 broadcast season at the Met, she gave a radio interview in which she recurs to the idea of punishing the voice into obedience. "You must serve music," she says, or "the first person we serve must be the composer"; then she reiterates "we are just servants of art." She acknowledges that the voice will be recalcitrant, maybe incapable: it must acquire the virtuosity of an instrument, she says, "whether we like it or not—or whether we can." With disciplinary sadism, she castigates a voice which is self-indulgent, interested only in being beautiful. The image she uses is revealingly destructive: "it isn't enough that you have a beautiful voice; you must take this voice and break it up into a thousand pieces, so she will serve you." The sudden appearance of the personal pronoun tells all: Callas masculinely mistreats a voice which is feminine (and therefore menial, subordinate). Later she looks back, with the same tyrannical conviction, on her "years and years of dominating the voice to do what an instrument does." The interviewer asks whether this is a triumph of will. Callas at once refuses the imputation of male power, and declares the secret to be an abject female submissiveness: what's needed is "love, . . . to serve what we adore." Soon after, the flagellant self-discontent which powered Callas—making her at once the domineering taskmaster and the humbled mistress—is startlingly confessed by the words she chooses. Speaking of the demands she made of herself, she says,

"You set yourself a standard which is always a whip. You're whipping yourself always, like a soldier." Hence her inability to forgive herself when the voice failed her, and her contempt for the easy way out. She couldn't skim through the music, slurring over difficulties; for her there had to be the self-inflicted punishment of an outright disaster—a last, voiceless *Norma* in Paris in 1965.

Callas bestowed her own unsparing integrity on the characters she played: they were versions of herself, sacrificial victims or (failing that) apostates. Paolina in Donizetti's *Poliuto*, which she sang at La Scala in 1960, volunteers for martyrdom with the Christians; Tosca too complains that she's a martyr to her career. In later years, Callas became Violetta, the woman tolerated as a bauble (Callas called all her poodles Toy) by the society which acclaimed and accused her. Elsa Maxwell might have been her Flora. Onassis treated her as a hireling like Violetta, ordering her from the room during negotiations about a film she was due to make by telling her she knew nothing, and was just a nightclub entertainer. Ken Russell believes she was Butterfly, trusting the fickle sailor Onassis who married a haughty American instead.

Perhaps her closest identification was with Norma the perjured priestess, a traitor to the religion which is her art. Lilli Lehmann said that Norma was a role deserving consecration. But opera's first impulse is to profane the sacred, to change Mass into orgy; condemning herself for a passionate treason against her high calling, Callas's Norma is exorcising a private guilt as well as working through a conflict which goes back to the origins of the form. It was an atavistic performance, psychologically as well as historically. This Norma—heard in the broadcast from La Scala in 1955—is stretched between her prophetic duty and her truant personal emotions; between the need to vanquish, which Giulini thought Callas flaunted in the mocking way she bowed during curtain calls, and the need to be loved. As the oracle of the Druids, Callas is mystically drowsy, mesmerized by the moon. As their chieftainess, upbraiding Pollione or calling for the destruction of the Romans, she is arrogant, militant, harpylike. But she lacks the strength and resolve to remain devout, or to espouse vendetta. Severe with herself, she is tolerant of weakness in others, and can't accomplish the deaths she plans for Pollione, Adalgisa or her children; she's a Medea conquered—and therefore deconsecrated—by pity and affection.

In the last scene she is maddened by contradictory motives. She pleads with Pollione, then threatens; she recalls in disgust her plan to slay the children, but goes on to plot execution for Pollione and Adalgisa; she speaks of an offense to the gods, yet must acknowledge that she herself is the source of contamination. Throughout she has been searching for a scapegoat. Now she finds one—herself. On her declaration "son io" her tone lightens and brightens to express the relieved joy she feels in self-criticism and self-destruction. Her death completes the rite, and adheres to the heretical logic of opera by fusing altar, pyre and bridal bed.

This sacerdotal frenzy in Callas explains Jon Vickers's perceptive link between her and Wieland Wagner. Between them, Vickers has said, they revolutionized opera after the war. Callas dispensed with a grandly sema-phoric style of acting, and Wieland Wagner at the new Bayreuth got rid of flimsy picturesque scenery. Though Vickers left it at that, his comment extends further, for Callas and Wieland were engaged in the same revolu-tion—or rather in a restoration of opera to its source in rite.

Wieland emphasized a primitive barbarity in the works he directed: a *Carmen* for Hamburg in 1958 drenched in blood, an *Aida* for Berlin in 1961 transferred from antiquarian Egypt to a darker Africa of phallic totems. Callas too took an art enfeebled by sophistication and demon-strated the savagery in it. She and Wieland even agreed in tracing opera back to classical Greece and its tragedies. Disinfecting Wagner of Teu-tonic propaganda, Wieland tried to discern in him a migrated Greek. The mythology of his works, he claimed, was Mediterranean not Nordic: Lo-hengrin and Elsa are Jove and Semele in another guise, or else (as he sug-gested in a program note for his 1953 production of Gluck's opera in Munich) they are Orfeo and Euridice; Wotan and Brünnhilde are Creon and Antigone. Avoiding the embarrassment of German nationalism, Wie-land was able to argue in 1965 that the *Ring* constituted "a return to mythical sources" and "a revival of Greek tragedy." Richard Wagner had already paid the same compliment to the Italian opera which was so cen-tral to Callas's career: "the poetry of *Norma*," he said, "reaches the heights of Greek tragedy." Wieland modeled his Bayreuth scenic designs on the ancient amphitheaters, treating the crowds beside the river in *Lo-hengrin* or in the meadow in *Die Meistersinger* as a formal, ranked Greek chorus. Callas actually performed in one of those amphitheaters. She sang Norma at Epidaurus in 1960 and Medea there the next year; she slept in the museum at Epidaurus the night before her *Medea*, and in the stone circle gave an account of the heroine closer to Euripides than to Cherubini.

The holy dread with which Callas undertook the ritual of performance was written into her characterization of Medea by Pasolini. In their film, she grows distraught during her journey to Thessaly with Jason because she believes that the necessary rites have been maimed. "You do not mark the center!" she screams, crisscrossing the centerless landscape like a dervish. One woman seemed to have taken upon herself the stress and anguish of us all, and used opera to cast out this evil. Inevitably, there was a cost. Filmed excerpts from Callas's performances attest to the desperate intensity with which she sought to justify opera, regardless of her own vocal or mental survival; she represents song as a nervous crisis, not the canary's blithe caroling. Interestingly, this is what detaches her from Carmen, which she recorded but wouldn't sing onstage. The habanera in a 1962 concert for television gives a demonstration of what it's like not to be Callas. She smirks and sneers, nonchalant and indifferent; she can understand Carmen but couldn't ever be her, because she can't so easily skip out of life's problems. The creed of the habanera is actually anathema to Callas, and a single physical detail betrays her skepticism about what she's singing. Despite her cool swagger, she crosses her arms before her. The body language of defensiveness is Callas's, not Carmen's.

Another character she never attempted onstage enables her, however, to make a rendingly personal statement. This is Eboli in *Don Carlo*, whose "O don fatale" she included in the 1962 concert. Eboli rails against her own beauty, which has corrupted her; in Callas's case, the fatal gift is the voice, and for once the aria is truly and clinically masochistic. Callas begins frowning, her hands clenched, scarcely daring to look up. She sings at first mostly with her eyes closed or grimacing in self-hatred. Her hands clutch her throat and cross there, to identify the source of the problem, and her eyes widen in terror as the trumpets sound their sentence of doom. For Eboli's prayer to Elisabetta, she has a tormented plaintiveness—head bowed, eyes closed, her thin arms and bony hands extended in longing. The thought of the cloister causes her face to uncloud and her eyes to open in innocent wonder: this is her deluded dream of liberation, of a peace to be gained from the renunciation of her gift. It is a fiction, of course. A nunnery is no place for Eboli, and Callas in retirement found no domestic calm. Vowing to save Carlo, she returns therefore to the fray, and ends the aria in a spasm of frenetic, excessive glee.

Tosca at Covent Garden in 1964 was her last will and testament: a study of a woman excruciated by being made to perform. Again a film exists, of her final struggle with the Scarpia of Tito Gobbi. In it, Callas is no flamboyant diva but a stricken beast. Gobbi hauls her from the floor telling her she is too beautiful to resist, and for a moment she looks at him with guileless happiness, trusting him. But when it's made clear to her that he won't spare her, she panics again, biting her lip, gulping for breath, her eyes darting back and forth in search of a way out. She wets her mouth but can't speak (let alone sing), and when he demands an answer nods as if with a broken neck. Demanding the passport, her tone briefly shines and softens on the words "con lui," but there is more nervous lip-biting as she stands over Gobbi, watching him write and—by her shuddering expectation—willing him to continue. She tries every self-administered therapy for nerves: she tightens her hands into locked security, then rubs them together as if, like Lady Macbeth, laving moral stains; she grips her brow to steady her thoughts, and when she swallows some water she tilts her head to make sure—choked as she is—that it will go down. At that instant, she sees the knife, and is transfixed, literally frozen. The glass returns automatically to the table in a hand which appears to have died, or at least to have been cut off from her volition. Gobbi strides toward her embrace, and the look of a trapped animal, sickened by fear, twists her face. Only then does she decide to kill, yet the knife at once emboldens her and she's a gloating fury, smiling through her rage. That exhilarated mood lasts until the moment when, sure that Scarpia is dead, she pardons him. Then she recoils from the knife, imagining perhaps, like Macbeth, that some other agent put it into her hand and that, if she released it, it would hang in air; it clatters to the floor.

The dumb show in which she hunts for the paper Scarpia has signed is almost too distressingly real to be watched. Most Toscas proceed through the motions with a stately precision, doing everything—the cross, the candles, the start of fear at the drum roll—within the musical measure; Callas appears to invent it as she goes, to live it, because for her, as for Tosca in this scene, the stage was a torture chamber from which she could find no exit. She conducts her search with those agitated hands clasped together at her waist, forcing herself to remember and to concentrate. Advancing on the corpse, she moves one leg at a time, each pace requiring a separate discharge of will, as if she were propelling two prostheses. She sobs in guilty revulsion as she puts down the candles, and when she bends—since her body in its drained and aerated state is weightless—she almost falls over. Kissing the cross, she can't unglue it from her lips. Her escape is messy, confused. She grabs her belongings at random, and for no good reason except parsimonious habit snuffs out the remaining candles, veering wildly like a bird in a room. Even after she reaches the door and tugs it open, you can hear her pant, gasp and softly moan, in a monologue more expressive than song. The drums are her death rattle. The spirit has been dyingly exhaled; Callas, having fought her way out of her theatrical imprisonment, is free.

Callas was a muse, but a misused one, overtaken by the fantasies of directors who, through her, were at once renewing opera and criticizing it; and the masochist in her—unsure of her own power and longing for protective guidance—consented to the exploitation. Thus for Visconti and later for Zeffirelli she became a black goddess: the spirit of music and of the sensuality which rages from the romantic orchestra.

Visconti called her "a monstrous phenomenon. Almost a sickness." He was fascinated by the assault of sensual obsession on aristocratic or intellectual self-possession, and he heard music as a symptom of that encroaching malady. In *Senso* it is Verdi's music. Livia's passion for the enemy Austrian officer corresponds to Leonora's for the outlawed troubadour, and the film begins during a performance of *Il Trovatore* at La Fenice. In *The Damned* (which he wanted to call *La Caduta degli Dei*) the music is Wagner's, corroding the industrial bourgeoisie of Nazi Germany as it maddens the king who was Wagner's patron in Visconti's *Ludwig*. In *Death in Venice* the music is Mahler's, confessing the hero's susceptibility to the boy Tadzio and thus to the plague.

The opera productions Visconti directed for Callas at La Scala between 1954 and 1957 cast her as this musical demon, a fatal and decadent creature—the unworthy vestal Giulia in Spontini's *La Vestale*; a monarch's guilty sexual secret in Donizetti's *Anna Bolena*. He placed her in settings of grandeur which the characters she played had defiled. For *La Vestale* the style was that of Napoleonic neoclassicism, and for *Anna Bolena* he copied Callas's dresses from Holbein's portraits of Anne Boleyn and loaded her with jewels. In their production of *La Sonnambula*, Callas saw Amina as a simple rustic. He demanded that she remain the sacred monster—"Maria Callas *playing* a village girl"—and, teaching her tippytoe steps, made her resemble the romantic ballerina Taglioni. Callas longed to be innocently natural; but for Visconti, she summed up the artifice of art. They had a similar disagreement over *Iphigénie en Tauride*. Callas wanted to be wildly Greek, a priestess and prophetess. Visconti instead presented her as a revenant from the Venetian rococo, in costumes drawn after Tiepolo and sets modeled on those of the Bibienas. Their *Traviata* was his definitive effort to mythologize Callas. He advanced the action to the 1880s, making Violetta a courtesan like those frequented by the

French decadents. Zeffirelli called the production Zolaesque: Violetta was sluttish, kicking off her shoes when she gets rid of her guests, exotic and overripe like the tropical growths which defied nature in the winter gardens of Flora's establishment.

This was in 1955; three years later, Zeffirelli directed the same work in Dallas, and designed it for his own imagined Callas, breezier and blowsier, abandoned rather than (as for Visconti) deadly. Zeffirelli found an endearing childish avidity in Callas. In their 1955 production of Rossini's *Il Turco in Italia*, he encouraged her to covet the Turk's jewels and to take inventory of his rings. The role which analyzed her best, he thought, was Tosca, whom he described as "warmhearted, rather sloppy, casual"—a rampant Roman, like Anna Magnani with a voice. The woman whom Visconti considered a monster was for Zeffirelli, more simply and more exuberantly, a star, greedy, ambitious, passionate, sometimes enjoyably ill-behaved. Visconti staged macabre and corruptly beautiful apotheoses for Callas. She attended Flora's party in red satin, manacled with rubies. Zeffirelli staged extravagant and bustling spectacles for her. In their Paris *Norma*, she fluttered through the moonlight on a cloud of white chiffon, and in her forest retreat lolled on a couch of carved oak; as Tosca, she erupted into the church, ready—as Zeffirelli suggested—to "have it right there" with Cavaradossi.

Callas was psychologically co-opted a third time by Pasolini, enrolled in his heterodox theology along with the revolutionary Christ of his *Gospel According to St. Matthew* or the deranging bisexual angel played by Terence Stamp in his *Teorema*. In Pasolini's film, Callas's Medea performs the sacrifice by which Norma is tempted. The heroine of Soumet's play *Norma, ou L'Infanticide*, on which Bellini's libretto drew, slays her children. For Bellini's lyrically gentler character, it's bad enough to briefly forget—as she tells Pollione—that she is a mother. However, Pasolini's Medea tenderly bathes her sons, sings them a lullaby, then stabs them. The murder is, according to Pasolini's reading of the legend, an offering of love to them: Medea the mystic slaughters in order to free those caged selves for regeneration. Hers is a scorching carnal charity, like the erotic redemption dispensed by Stamp in *Teorema*. Pasolini implicates Medea in a religious war. Her Asiatic faith in a rebirth guaranteed by violent death clashes with the new, official, European religion of Jason; the locations repatriate her to Turkey and Syria. The film pays tribute to Callas's maenadic quality when she gyrates entranced across a landscape of mudflats. Pasolini commented that while Callas might appear the modern celebrity, at home in Maxim's or on Onassis's yacht, she was in truth an ancient woman, riven by violent conflicts. Song was the voice of that primeval rage in her.

Even without music, Pasolini's *Medea* acknowledges that for Callas opera was a cult, and entailed a shedding of blood. Self-sacrifice became Callas's creed, so she could turn her vocal tragedy to expressive account. This was the distressing moral of her last concerts with Giuseppe di Stefano. The voice Callas superstitiously described as "odd" or "funny" and which she set herself to break and dominate had an intimate acquaintance with pain: as used by her, it was perpetually on the wrack. It therefore suited the abused, ravaged creatures Callas portrayed in the extracts she sang—Elisabetta besieged by the bellowing Don Carlo of di Stefano, her voice worn down and elderly with worry or depressed (in the prayer which ends their duet) by a hopeless resignation; Carmen in the final duet, whose bravery and bravura, when she declares "Mais je suis brave, et n'ai pas voulu fuir!", consist in her submitting to this last trial of her strength, and whose tone swells briefly into opulence when she asks José to end her misery in "Frappe-moi donc." Another of her faithful women who have been spurned, Santuzza, protested with a cry from the singer's own heart. She remembered Turiddu's vow, and the word "giurato" veered off course, flapping about; but how else could Santuzza's ululation properly have been delivered? Her mournful "Io piango" rumbled from some well of grief within, and in the duet with Turiddu "l'angoscia mia" was a gash ripped in sound. The character, and the singer, gloried in this humiliation. Santuzza proudly begs Turiddu to abase her further: "Battimi, insultami, t'amo e perdono." Callas's self-punishment made these scenes genuine tragedy, not the mere imperfect performance of one.

In the valedictory concerts, the most plaintive performance was that of Gioconda's "Suicidio!" A few years before, Callas had remarked that Ponchielli's opera was at the outer limits of "decent singing," before it declined into verismo; her own singing was no longer decent, yet her wrecked voice authenticated Gioconda's wretchedness. Callas made the word "suicidio" quiver with tension like a taut string. Imagining "le tenebre," the shades of extinction, she found a cavernous chesty resonance for the words which lodged them in a mortuary. Gioconda's desire, she says, is to sleep quietly in the tomb. Meanwhile, the singer must scream in the upper register, or moan in the lower. Only death could silence that indwelling, imperative, complaining demon, the voice; and Callas was already beseeching it to do so.

NINE

Archetypes

NOT EVEN Callas owned or exhausted the roles she sang. A voice is unique: dramatic performance is an art of self-imposition. Every bold interpretation makes the words and music new, and since they are archetypes, the great operatic characters not only tolerate but invite their own renewal.

Callas's way with Tosca was distinct, but couldn't be definitive; the Toscas who followed had to be denials of her. Callas argued that "Vissi d'arte" should be cut because it delayed the action. The aria, perhaps too painfully, summed up her career, as one who lived for an art which killed her. When a later Tosca like Leontyne Price extracted the aria from the drama and delivered it as a concert encore, there was no longer any question of sacrifice: this luxurious voice belonged to a woman who wouldn't consider parting with her jewels to decorate the Madonna, and who (in contrast to Tosca's questioning of God) had been well remunerated by the world.

While Callas's Tosca was frantic, Montserrat Caballé's was comfortable, reposed on a cushioning stream of sound or settled on a sofa where she waited for Scarpia to rape her. Her fussiest concern, as befits the glamorous singer, was for her expensive accouterments. She brought with her to the Covent Garden production a pair of pendulous earrings, one of which—in a performance on tour with the company in Japan in 1979—detached itself and disappeared into the crevasse of her cleavage; its partner she very properly removed just before the dirty work of murdering Scarpia. Preparing her exit from the room, she ritually collected the female impedimenta she'd brought in with her: jewels, gloves, a glittery bag and a brocaded wrap several yards long.

There have been more agitated Toscas, of course. Galina Vishnevskaya sang the role at Covent Garden in 1977, with a Slavic keening in the voice and a desperate rapture onstage. This vulturelike creature wore a pleated Empire gown to the church, and when she raised her arms to embrace Cavaradossi its folds unfurled beneath her arms, giving her—as she encircled and contained him—the wingspan of some volatile predator. Her denunciations of Scarpia were acid with hate, and her glee at Cavaradossi's execution had the fanatic's joy in destruction.

In 1984, Vishnevskaya's autobiography disclosed her psychic sources. She was living through the events which had only recently driven her from Russia. Her operatic heroines were liberators—Aida yearning for her enslaved country, Leonore unbarring the prison and waving an imaginary banner, Shostakovich's Katerina Ismailova killing her way to freedom. Among them all, Tosca is closest to her self-image. Tosca reluctantly consents to sing at government festivities. So was Vishnevskaya, commandeered to serenade the vodka-sozzled bosses of the Communist party at their banquets. Tosca is the functionary of what Vishnevskaya, referring to the Bolshoi, calls a "serf-theater." In the opera of her own life, Scarpia might have been the venal police chief Beria, rapist of young girls; the role turned out to belong to the besotted Bulganin, who laid amorous siege to the young singer. She didn't need to kill him, but could comically outwit him by taking her husband along as chaperon when she had to answer her admirer's late-night summonses. On one occasion, she seems to be singing in prose the battle cry with which Cavaradossi taunts Scarpia: "Mother Russia, how much longer will you grieve for your hangmen? Fight back! Avenge your ravaged, tortured children!" She also has a fine sense of political guile, defending Shostakovich's compromises with the regime by arguing that he was merely playacting: the same tactic Tosca teaches to Cavaradossi.

Vishnevskaya spared Prime Minister Bulganin, but rendered less clemency to the surrogate Scarpias she encountered onstage. She warned luckless baritones not to touch her, and said she couldn't be responsible if they did. One of them she slashed (inadvertently) with her knife; on another occasion, in Vienna, the divine spark literally ignited her in the abandon of this scene. Her nylon costume caught fire from the candles on the dining table, and the Scarpia of the evening—whom she had just killed—had to come back to life to save her. *Tosca* was actually the cue for her departure from Russia: she and Rostropovich left after a recording of the work the Central Committee had permitted them to make was insultingly canceled, to punish them for political disaffection. It's as Tosca that she appears on the cover of her book, her arms crossed in stubborn resistance, deadly devotion glowering from her eyes.

Hildegard Behrens at the Met in 1985 looked for less vindictive political motives in Tosca. As with her Leonore and her Brünnhilde, Behrens quotes as Tosca's motto the moral imperative of Kant: she has the starry heavens above her, and a moral force within her—though it's less into the enlightened firmament than into a reddening dawn that Tosca leaps from the battlements. That jump was the key to Behrens's performance. Whereas Caballé strolled off the parapet, possibly expecting to float, Behrens leaped upward, and was briefly outlined with arms extended, poised in midair. The takeoff suited an interpretation based on the idea of vertiginous choice. Behrens saw a moral vertigo in Tosca when trapped by Scarpia's offer: "she's paralyzed, like standing on the edge of a cliff." The Kantian conscience changes the murder from bloody melodrama. Standing over Scarpia, Behrens raged at him in a croaky chest voice, shaking with disgust and impatience at the need to deal with him so brutally. "Muori!" was her sobbed plea that he should die, and so relieve her. To kill him was necessity, not pleasure. When he did expire, the dagger dropped, her hunched posture straightened, and her growling voice cleared for "or gli perdono." He died as a sacrifice to her "moralische Gesetz," which at once recovered its composure and did the right thing by him, setting down the candles.

This view of the character entailed a friendly dispute with the Cavaradossi of the production, Domingo. He described Tosca's recitation of the murder in the third act as an operatic performance, already embellished with florid gestures and supplied with a hammy vocal climax. Behrens disagreed, insisting that this was the purgative retraversal of a trauma, untainted by exaggeration. Domingo's thesis covered an interpretative innovation of his own. He wanted Tosca to be merely grandstanding so that Cavaradossi could take over from her as the work's tragic character. For Domingo, Mario knows he is going to die, and agrees to the pretense only to spare the less tough-minded Tosca.

Every action of Tosca's has a volume of precedents. When Nilsson at the Met in 1968 sang "Vissi d'arte" prone on the floor, the novelty was written down as a footnote to Maria Jeritza's Tosca, who had done the same. The difficulty is to make the habitual business seem impromptu. No Tosca has done so with as much theatrical courage as Leonie Rysanek. Her interpretation (seen in the Berlin production when it visited Washington in 1975) shuttled between momentary mood-changes. In the church, she was playful, scarcely able to contain herself; she rushed into the prison waving the permit at the guard, and dashed past him as if running for a bus; she rehearsed Cavaradossi for his death with little gestures of encouragement and winks of support from the wings, even blowing him a kiss of congratulation as he fell. Her genius was for delaying the anticipated action, in order to make it, when the music at last decreed it, shocking and startling. Thus she didn't handle the knife expectantly but simply watched it until Scarpia pounced, then threw aside her glass and smashed it, grabbed the blade and plunged it directly into his chest. The deed, like everything Tosca does, was an impulse. She gloated until "or gli perdono," then lost her nerve in revulsion and dismay (just at the point when Behrens morally recuperated) and knelt beside him in an abject heap, apparently as dead as he was. The dumb show with the candles was omitted, because it's expected and formulaic: Tosca's first instinct is to rush away, and Rysanek hurtled to the door only to turn back, shuddering, for the permit; she raced off at the very last moment, when the drums shook her. The same urgency brought new inflections to the text. Her betrayal of the secret—"Nel pozzo del giardino"—was stammered out, choked by her fear and self-loathing. The answer to Scarpia's inquiry about the route of escape, "la più breve," was another panicking aside. And "avanti a lui tremava tutta Roma" was wondering and incredulous, no chesty registration of triumph: this Tosca was amazed at what she had done while the theatrical fit was upon her.

Carmen is another such character, archetypal and therefore teasingly abstract, all things to all the men who desire her, capable of infinite incarnations. The first Carmen of the Met's new production in 1972 was Marilyn Horne, who played the character—very plausibly—as a brash and bouncy American farm girl, her ebullience tightly restrained by her stays. Her successors in 1978 were Elena Obraztsova and Régine Crespin. Obraztsova's Carmen was a Tartar savage. Wielded by her, the castanets looked and sounded like weapons. She writhed and squirmed, hands planted on hips, but her sexuality was largely dental. Her grins were mean and menacing. She gnawed and gnashed as if intent on biting José to death. The voice issuing from behind that ivory portcullis was harshly vibrant and barbaric, sounding across the steppes of central Asia. Crespin did without this chomping omnivorousness. Her voice was silvery not brazen like Obraztsova's, her Carmen no gypsy wanton but a corseted courtesan, as archly sophisticated as the Marschallin. Crespin's presence could turn a bordello into a salon. She auditioned candidates for her affections with choosy connoisseurship, and manipulated José with the cunning of an older, more experienced woman.

The difference between this pair of Carmens was as apparent in their footwork as in their singing. Obraztsova bared legs as well as teeth, and employed her naked foot to stimulate the polish on Zuniga's military boot. Crespin wore black stockings and teetered in natty little shoes; too indirect and ironic for Obraztsova's shameless fondling of a boot, she contented herself with administering a sly kick to Zuniga as she sidled past. This Carmen retained her poise to the end. Most singers hurl back José's ring with a screeched "Tiens!" That word is Carmen's last, and with it she abandons song for screaming. Crespin disdained such verismo effects. She daintily removed the ring and nonchalantly let it drop. Her "Tiens!" was itself thrown away, delivered quietly and indifferently, with a shrug. Then, her affairs in order, Crespin's Carmen elegantly committed suicide on José's knife.

Crespin reclaimed the archetype for France. Yet Christa Ludwig's Carmen at Covent Garden in 1976 suffered from a German romantic weltschmerz, not Crespin's disdainful ennui. Ludwig was roused from her melancholy only when the cards prompted her to experiment with death. Like Isolde, this Carmen was in love with annihilation, and welcomed José as its unwitting agent. Wieland Wagner had already in his 1958 Hamburg production made the connection with a northern fatalism which, as he said, couples Eros and Thanatos. Seville, he thought, could have no claim on Carmen. Frothy and ornate, the city was an appropriate setting for Rossini's frivolous creatures. But Carmen demanded blood and darkness, in which Wieland's sets were drenched.

A Carmen modeled on Isolde has spiritualized her lust. Agnes Baltsa, singing the role at Covent Garden in 1983, was altogether earthier, a cynical and cunning peasant who despised her José because of his craven emotional hunger. With her suitors outside the factory or among the smugglers, Baltsa's Carmen was one of the boys. Teamwork didn't impinge on her freedom of self; José enraged her because he claimed a monopoly. The look of despair on her face as he began the flower song told all: she is doomed, since this castoff won't accept relegation. As Carreras blustered into the inn, throwing his saber on the table with a clatter as he fired off the last note of "Dragon d'Alcala," she sneered "Voilà." He was already a burden to her, and everything she did thereafter was calculated to destroy him before he could destroy her. Her abuse of him in the third act was maniacal; in the fourth act, his plaintive "Tu ne m'aimes donc plus" drove her to a vicious hatred.

Baltsa returned to the role at Covent Garden in 1986, having thought out a newly tragic course for Carmen. The throwing of the flower was no joke: it marked her destruction of José, for which she must pay in the parallel murder of the fourth act. She drew the bloom from her cleavage as abruptly as a switchblade knife, then stabbed José (again Carreras) in the forehead with it. At once she shuddered, aware that she had done something fatal and irrevocable. He discarded the flower; under arrest, her hands tied behind her, she bent to pick it up with her teeth and spat it at him, as she was later to do with his ring. Frightened by his emotion in the flower song, she resolved to frighten him off. That hard-voiced implacable "Non, tu ne m'aimes pas" ordered him to stop loving her, just as she later demanded—to deter him—that he must become a bandit. The card game was an agonizing temptation to her. Before joining in, she paced back and forth, wondering with nervous glances whether she dared to play; she already foreknew the result. If she killed him with the flower by inciting desire, he killed her in the third act with a kiss. Before he left with Micaëla, he tugged on her hair and thrust her to the floor, then forced the breath out of her in savagely kissing her. She was scarcely able to drag herself to her feet again when she heard Escamillo's refrain. Baltsa's Carmen was a witch terrified by her own spells, as much in their power as her victim.

Carmen can tolerate these inconsistent accounts of herself because her secret is her nonentity. Other people, targeted by her, become characters, helplessly compulsive; she never does. In Piero Faggioni's production at Edinburgh in 1977, she was observed throughout by the imprisoned José, who studied her in retrospect but couldn't understand her. Faggioni's Carmen, Teresa Berganza, tantalized by her diffidence. Far from rolling her hips and chewing on roses, she ridiculed her sexuality, as if disowning it. Her languorous intervention after Escamillo's song was a joke not an invitation: she crooned "L'amour," and fell about in giggles. Like Don Giovanni, this Carmen was a comic character who accidentally ended in tragedy when someone called her bluff. The statue arrives at the dinner party; José clumsily stabs Carmen when she dares him to do so. The source of Berganza's portrayal was her wonderful Cherubino, and the connection though unexpected is apt: Kierkegaard called the page an adolescent avatar of Don Giovanni. Her Carmen was as agile, ubiquitous and polymorphous as Cherubino. She specialized in tomboyish disguise (dressing up in Escamillo's cape, as Cherubino, already in travesty, wears a girl's bonnet) and also in evasion, hopping over José's body as she escaped, picking Zuniga's pocket, and poking her tongue out at detractors.

At Glyndebourne, directed by Peter Hall, Maria Ewing was an enigma, perhaps a zero. In every act, her Carmen was the materialization of a mystery. As a nothingness, she appeared from nowhere. Outside the factory, she was already in place when the men asked for her. No one saw her, because they were waiting for the conventional entrance from upstage, and Carmen was meanwhile lounging against the proscenium. When visible, her face was averted. She delivered the habanera with her back turned to the men, disappearing in and out of the crowd; she selected José at random, since he had his back to her. At Pastia's again, she faced away before the gypsy song. When she wheeled round she looked bored, vacant-faced. She soon retreated to lean over the half-door, watching for José; when he arrived she pretended not to notice him. In the mountains, she crouched on the floor, unrecognizable in a boy's clothes. Micaëla's entreaties were greeted by another aloof avoidance: she turned away, her sombrero obliterating her face. And whereas outside the bullring Carmen usually has a grand entrance, here too she was missing from the procession. Searched for, she could be found watching from a balcony in her mantilla.

The archetype fits all sizes and ages. The role is neutral, borrowing character from each performer in turn. The same is true of Carmen's male counterpart, the unknowable Giovanni. Tito Gobbi in Lisbon in 1971 played him as an overripe and overweight Italian Falstaff, his phallic decline signified by the drooping ramp on which he attempted his conquests; Roger Soyer at Edinburgh in 1974 was a cool French gallant; Cesare Siepi at Covent Garden in 1973 presented a professionally suave international roué. In 1970 in Zeffirelli's Covent Garden production, Gabriel Bacquier was an aristocrat with rational appetites, pursuing pleasure in a Watteauesque garden. In 1973 in another Zeffirelli production, for Vienna, Theo Adam made Giovanni a demon-ridden German, a Faust operating in the sensual arena: anguished and harsh-voiced, no mere philanderer but a Wotan ambitious for power. Raimondi, who was a joyless, stricken satyr for Losey and a sadistic motorcyclist zipped into a uniform of leather in a staging by Maurice Béjart, could equally well play a rollicking, ribald Errol Flynn in scarlet thigh-boots for Peter Wood's new production at Covent

Garden in 1981. Thomas Allen's Giovanni at Glyndebourne offered an English gloss on the character: he might have been the burned-out, bleary narrator of Byron's *Don Juan*. Sherrill Milnes at the Met in 1978 delivered an inimitably American Giovanni. This man was a public relations expert, a careerist as intent on being popular as the salesman Willy Loman, and his comeuppance took the form of the overachiever's premature coronary.

Boris Godunov, who dominates the opera though he's in it intermittently, is another all-purpose, archetypal protagonist. He is whatever bogey you imagine the patriarchal principle to be. Boris Christoff, the Tsar's namesake and himself the protégé of a Bulgarian monarch, became the character he played, with a voice rumbling volcanically and an eye which cowed opponents in flashes of fire. Christoff's Boris was a man-god, Dostoyevskyan in his mad sublimity. He shut out the expanses of Mussorgsky's history, which he narrowed to a series of monologues. Recording the work, Christoff coped with the other people in it by annexing them, and sang—in addition to Boris—the chronicler Pimen and the roisterer Varlaam (here as macabre as Death in Mussorgsky's song cycle). The triple act made the opera an authentic nightmare: in virtually every scene the ogre pounced, wearing a new body but still with the same terrifying voice. Another Bulgarian, Nicolai Ghiaurov, followed Christoff at Covent Garden in 1974, and ignored his precedent. Ghiaurov's voice, honeyed not craggy, was schooled in Italy, and lent to Boris a Verdian humanity; Ghiaurov was indeed at his truest as a domestic character, singing with worried love to his children. The Met's new Boris in 1974 was Martti Talvela—haunted too, but without Christoff's tyrannical histrionics; his voice founded in a black despair, he was lonely, yet lacked Christoff's autocratic self-sufficiency. He shuffled brokenly through the crowd, and in his delirium childishly doubled up his looming, vulnerable body and tried to crawl under an overturned table. For once, the soliloquies were just that: the overheard misery of a neurotic introvert. Tarkovsky's production at Covent Garden assigned the role to Robert Lloyd, who didn't retire into a private tragedy but represented a Tsar as himself one of history's indiscriminate victims. For the scene of Boris's delirium, a huge floor-cloth—at once carpet, wedding train and shroud—was unfurled, with a map of the Tsarevich's Russia embroidered on it. Shuisky silkily handled it with a haberdasher's professional touch; Lloyd's Boris, raving, wrapped himself in it like bedclothes. This Boris didn't presume to be the state. Instead, the state was the giant's cloak in which he huddled, like Macbeth, to conceal his dwarfishness.

A character in operatic performance is defined by the texture of a voice. The two great dramatic sopranos of the postwar period, Nilsson and Rysanek, divided Wagner and Strauss between them, but interpreted the same roles in contradictory ways. Though their voices were comparable in power and brilliance, they expressed quite different emotions. Nilsson's was the sound of will triumphant, Rysanek's of love transcendent. The one was missile- or laserlike, precise and pointed; the other was radiant, rapturous, swelling like an ocean or opening like a flower. Nilsson's voice suggested a weapon: Brünnhilde's spear or Leonore's pistol or Turandot's pincerlike fingernails. Rather than this ballistic aggression, Rysanek's singing was the gift of herself, sensual and also sacrificial. Theatrical performance was, for her, like the lives and deaths of Wagner's women, an unrepentant self-expenditure. Nilsson seized the notes from the sky. Hers was the voice of hubris, as superhumanly proud as the chaste Brünnhilde on top of her mountain or the frigid Turandot on top of her staircase; Rysanek's singing was the spontaneous overflow of powerful human feelings. Hence the screams she often interpolated—an expressionism of sound. Her anniversary concert at the Met in 1984 began with one of these and ended with another: her Kundry was announced by the groaning screech she emitted when roused by Klingsor, and her Sieglinde let out a coital shriek of pleasure as Siegmund tugged the sword from the tree.

Nilsson and Rysanek sang three operas together. In *Die Walküre,* Nilsson was the armor-plated goddess, surprised and offended by Siegmund's earthly loyalty, while Rysanek was the beleaguered woman, her voice and body throbbing with joy or quaking with fear. In *Elektra,* Nilsson's divinity suffered a fall. When she sarcastically asked Klytämnestra if she too was not a goddess, the fragile pianissimo utterance of "Göttin" remembered her own loss of heroic immunity. The buried ax served, in her debasement, as the Valkyrie's armament. Rysanek's Chrysothemis—a role rescued by her from insipidity—was an equal and an antagonist, her unsatisfied love set against Elektra's unappeased hate. Rysanek matched Nilsson's measured, angular dance of death with a show of hysterical frustration, pounding the floor and sobbing after her first aria. In their final duet, the voices were synonyms for two incompatible victories: Nilsson's was cruelly arrogant and unforgiving, while Rysanek's swelled with gratitude and gratification.

Their most complex collaboration (seen in San Francisco in 1980) was in *Die Frau ohne Schatten,* whose two heroines are opposed accounts of the eternal woman. Here, Rysanek's Empress was the goddess eager and

338

desperate to acquire humanity. Her vocal acting followed the Empress from fluting ethereality—the disembodied bird calls in her first monologue—through the torments which are her induction into the world. The sound Rysanek made at first was of immaterial softness and delicacy, ideal and emotionless. Her desperation urged a series of startling changes: her wild greeting of the dawn, the cries of terror in her dream, the plunge of two octaves on "Zur Schwelle des Todes!" (musically paraphrasing her lapse from crystalline grace to guilt and pity), and the strained, wracked reascent on another phrase, "Mein Richter, hervor!" This was a performance of vocal vertigo.

Nilsson's role was the Dyer's Wife. This was the part assigned to Rysanek in Munich in 1953; but on a first perusal of the score she found that the Empress had more high notes, and demanded to be recast. Nilsson's initial response was the same. Asked to learn the Dyer's Wife for the Met's new production in 1966 she refused, saying she preferred the Empress; the part was already reserved for Rysanek. Ten years later she relented, commenting that after decades of operatic spear-wielding, head-severing and mother-murdering it would be interesting to take on, as her last role, a woman whose problems are exclusively domestic. But humanity didn't altogether suit her. She played and sang the part in San Francisco as a diminished epilogue to Wagner. The Dyer's Wife is a demotic, drudging Brünnhilde, her vocal heroism reduced to shrewish vituperation. In place of Brünnhilde's battle cry, the Wife begins with a curse on a slangy B-flat, as she douses her in-laws with the household slops. Heroic aloofness (no god, Brünnhilde tells Siegfried, ever dared approach her) is leveled to a defense of her meager privileges: she expels her husband from her bed, grabs jewels, bosses the servants. The parody was sharpened by Nilsson's recollections of those nobler predecessors. The Wife's tantrums were low-life versions of Brünnhilde's cosmic rage in the Gibichung hall, and inside her hovel she prowled and paced like a caged Elektra. As the Empress, Rysanek's voice drew a trajectory through air, bridging earth and heaven across its extended range; Nilsson's voice, denied such sublimation, had to encompass spiky heights, guttural depths, and the treacherous intervals between them.

Nilsson and Rysanek both sang Salome and, eventually, Elektra. Rysanek's version, heard in Washington in 1979 with the Vienna company, was a tribute to the sensual irresistibility of music. Wagner's "art of transition" is in Salome the impatience of desire, which speeds up and shortens her life. Rysanek began as a romping, curious child, crawling and leaping all over the stage, retreating from Jokanaan to curl up fetally in a corner. She bloomed when aroused by Jokanaan; after the dance she was slow, weary, moribund, and in the final scene the discarded veils were her shroud. She wound them round herself and invisibly addressed the head from inside that winding-sheet, only emerging on the very last phrase to reveal a pallid ghostly face and to keel over before the soldiers could kill her. The voice changed from a shy girl's to a hungry woman's to a hollow specter's. Rysanek's Salome attained consummation in song, or in a cry, when she abruptly screamed as the sword fell in the cistern and rolled away, sated, across the floor. Also in November 1979, Nilsson sang Salome's final scene in a concert at the Met, and made it virulent not ardent. The steely voice cleft through the orchestral din like the executioner's blade. The delight of this Salome lay in a biological self-congratulation, as with terrifying vehemence she cried to Jokanaan, "Ich lebe noch, und du bist tot," and in a gloating crescendo reiterated "mich, mich, mich hast du nie gesehn."

Nilsson's early Elektras—particularly those at Covent Garden with Solti—depicted another disinherited Valkyrie. Her first word, "Allein," emerging from her to engulf the theater, was no lament but a statement of uncompromising principle. She brushed away the maids like insects, was casually scornful of Chrysothemis, and absently fingered a strand of her hair to while away the time during Klytämnestra's narration. Her curtsies to Aegisth were lethally mocking. The performance exhibited an effortless supremacy. At Edinburgh in 1974, asked how she had adjusted the role to the tiny King's Theatre, Nilsson bragged, "Oh, I just sang with one vocal cord." At Covent Garden in 1977, conducted this time by Carlos Kleiber, she inserted an acrobatic stunt, audacious as the vaulting antics of a gymnast. When Chrysothemis ran off in alarm, Nilsson swung after her, shaking her fists in the air, and hurled out her curse—"Sei verflücht!"—with her back to the audience; then without a break she completed the circle and wheeled to the front to deliver the baleful next phrase, another personal pledge: "Nun denn, allein!" The gyration and its propulsive force took away everyone's breath but hers.

Gradually, though, the emphasis changed. August Everding's production in Paris, which Böhm conducted in 1974, interpreted Elektra ironically, as a weakling who broods on a vengeance which others must accomplish for her. Musically, the character may be invincible, but dramatically she is shy, ineffectual, even autistic. In Paris, Nilsson's Elektra lurked fidgeting at the edge of the stage, clutching herself as she shrank from the maids; she scuttled away from Orest as if into a hole. She executed Klytämnestra in fantasy only, since her mother's call for light brought on a retinue of torch-bearing vassals to belittle the bemused, groveling Elektra. Orest's tutor scared her off by rebuking her for making so much noise. Though she has kept the ax for Orest, she forgets it: Everding underlined her irrelevance by having the tutor hand Orest a knife before they entered the house.

Everding's analysis provoked a new self-exploration in Nilsson. She began to inflect the text with a ghastly playfulness, and after the shaft of sound which greets "Orest!" her elegy for her spoiled beauty was sung as faint, astringent chamber music. Following from Böhm, Kleiber convinced Nilsson that the score needn't be cataclysmic. Those 1977 performances in London were dizzily fast and lyrically agile. Elektra could whisper rather than having to shout. The killer became a plangent, grief-stricken mourner. The very physique of the role changed. When the Chrysothemis of Gwyneth Jones announced Orest's death, Nilsson exerted herself to suppress the truth in a sequence of denials, "Es ist nicht wahr!", each one louder and more aggressive until, her body shaking with the desperation of the utterance, she simply caved in and collapsed to the floor. Back at the Met for Elektra in 1980, her huge blanched face was haggard with pain, contorted into a classical mask; her arms hung like weary dead weights in her depression. Acquiring vulnerability, her once indomitable Elektra had become tragic.

The same evolution occurred in her Isolde. The narrative in the first act used to be vitriolic. Listening to a tape of the Met's 1960 broadcast, Nilsson remembers that she had stormed onto the stage after a fight with Bing to sing the curse scaldingly against him, not Tristan. In 1983 she returned to this passage in the Met's centennial gala, but no longer used it to prosecute private grudges. The narrative on this occasion wasn't acid. It ached with remorse for lost emotional chances, and the curse was a confused plea for reciprocation, bringing tears to her eyes as she sang it. Isolde's spiteful farewell to life had become Nilsson's elegiac farewell to her career.

In 1981, Rysanek was promoted to Elektra, for a film conducted by Böhm and directed by Götz Friedrich. Hers was the Elektra of a Chrysothemis—loving, even maternal. Interpreted this way, the opera became a study of the female principle. An African fertility goddess with naked bouncing breasts joined Klytämnestra's procession, and bathed in the blood which spurted from the sacrificial ram. Rysanek's Elektra had a psychic intimacy Nilsson's didn't possess, because film made her fantasies visible. In her first monologue, she saw her mother murder her father, then couple with Aegisth: this was the forbidden knowledge which had deranged her. Klytämnestra's monstrous births were the children who killed her to punish her for her sexuality. But as voyeurs they were wishful participants in the carnality of their parents. In Friedrich's production, Agamemnon and Orest were equated as Elektra's fantasy lover; she was at once wife, mother, daughter and sister.

Rysanek's dance in her first scene, supposedly around a funeral pyre, was done squatting, with the head of a statue (dug up to be used in conjuring Agamemnon and Orest) under her skirt. The ungainly movements of her legs looked as if she were giving birth. In the next scene, Chrysothemis writhed in the labor pains of an imaginary pregnancy. Before sending her off, Rysanek for a moment gazed at her with tender solicitude—again the succoring mother. Then when she suborned Chrysothemis to assist in the murder, her hand ran up her sister's leg under the dress, and her face was cradled in the girl's crotch. There followed a soothing Pietà, with Chrysothemis's head on Elektra's chest; that love crossed another barrier of taboo as she stroked Chrysothemis's breasts and imagined a wedding night, with herself as her sister's bridegroom. Grieving for "das Kind," this Elektra was psychologically closer to Klytämnestra than the proud Nilsson ever permitted. She crept timidly into the presence of the mother whose lovemaking she had spied on. But her mother had come to her to be maternally comforted. They joined in another inverse Pietà, with Klytämnestra cuddled, as if being suckled, on Elektra's bosom. Once more a prohibition was defied: Elektra straddled her mother as she foretold her death, forcing a knee between her legs as Klytämnestra shivered, prone, beneath her. This was the rape of her mother, a prelude to the seduction of her sister. *Elektra* here dramatized the kinds of love which are debarred and anathematized (according to Freud) in myth.

Rysanek dared a self-abasement impossible in Nilsson's notion of the character, so insolently solitary. Her address to Orest was a mad scene, in which she twined straw in her hair like Lear on the heath. Orest closed his eyes in dismay, anxious to get away from her. She extended her arms to him in an embrace which he refused. Rysanek's Elektra ended as the rejected mother, and during her last dance Orest and the tutor looked down into the courtyard, sickened, before closing the window on her.

Nilsson and Rysanek were colleagues and contemporaries in this debate over the roles they shared; more often, interpretations alter as one generation yields to the next. The dramatic tenor's repertory passes, for instance, from Jon Vickers to Plácido Domingo, who is duty-bound to make the parts his own. The Enée of Vickers in the Met's *Les Troyens* in 1973 was tragically conscious of his own treachery: he must either betray his mission or destroy the woman who loves him. The character's self-analysis was "Inutiles regrets," sung with that wrenching anguish unique to Vickers. Ten years later, Domingo's Enée, with a voice more at home in balmy Carthaginian nights than on the ringing plains of windy Troy, was the son of a goddess (as Didon admiringly calls him), a lover rather than an agent of the march of mind. In Covent Garden's 1981 *Samson et Dalila,* Vickers portrayed a Samson who was, in his view, "the supreme judge of Israel," sternly upholding the tablets of the law. His body was a monolith in the desert, his voice as granitic as the mountains to which he looked for deliverance. Capitulating to Dalila, he used, for the repetitions of "Je t'aime," an almost feminine croon: when Samson broke faith, he was unmanned. Domingo appeared in the same production in 1985. Without the missionary zeal of Vickers, his performance had an infectious extroversion. Rabble-rouser rather than sermonizer, this Samson enjoyed his coercive vocal power when exhorting the crowd. After he worked them up, he moved among them to press the flesh, a sensual demagogue dressed not in the Mosaic robe Vickers wore but in a shorty tunic, his famous locks in a pigtail. The character Domingo played was an exponent of that "personality cult" which Vickers, denouncing singers who delight overmuch in their "vocal capacity," deplores. Isn't Samson, after all, the victim of his own publicity?

They distributed the accents differently in *Otello* too, Vickers truer to the Shakespearean poetic tragedy, Domingo to the Verdian music drama. The flinty voice of Vickers worried the musical line in its examination of the text—eruptive in rage, yet articulating the lament for Otello's lost glory on a wisp of sound. Instead of Verdi's doting lover, Vickers played a perjured savior and fallen leader. He once cited, as a contemporary case of an Otello's destruction by Iago, Willy Brandt's trust in a traitorous aide.

Domingo's Otello pretended to no grand generality. This was Verdi's character, defined by his exultancy in song, humiliated when reduced to moans, regaining the voice to die upon a kiss in a reprise of the love duet. Domingo's acting delineated the collapse of a particular, cuckolded man, not a symbolic scapegoat. In the second act he anatomized his own symptoms, which began by attacking the sovereign voice. He clutched his throat as if it were dry (in the Met's 1985 performances), gulped and rubbed his face as Iago sang of jealousy. Desdemona's scene with the chorus gave him time for a dumb show of degeneration: restless, unable to concentrate, he prowled the stage in bewilderment and, eventually, panic. He staggered in a faint, and—in a reference to negritude never made by Vickers—fingered his skin in disgust during the quartet as he blamed that visage for alienating Desdemona. In the court scene with Lodovico, he was left with only the remnant of authority—his gold-embroidered, fur-collared robe which, as he stumbled in confusion and disgrace, fell off one shoulder; he grabbed it, gathered it around him and slumped on his throne, using the garment as his comfort and shield. By the opera's end, this uniform of state had gone, and the adopted Venetian reassumed an ancestral identity he had forsworn. In a Moor's white shift, Domingo salaamed before Allah just as the condemned Desdemona prayed to her own chosen deity.

The difference between the two performances was one of dimension. Domingo, who at Covent Garden in 1980 soared in from his ship, cloak swirling, breastplate glinting, had a hectic physical intensity; Vickers strained toward a metaphysical understanding of the character, since tragedy is about free will and determinism—Otello's austere control against his violent impulsiveness. Domingo's references were local, to North Africa and the Mediterranean: he belonged in the vivid picturesqueness of Zeffirelli's production at the Met (which Vickers criticized as outsize) with its Cypriot harbor, its golden fortress and its bristling armory. Vickers, however, universalized the character.

He did so with Britten's Peter Grimes as well. Vickers has spoken of interpretation as a "search for truth"; in this case the truth he discovered amended the meaning intended by the composer and by the first Grimes, Peter Pears. But the new interpreter has right of way. Vickers enlarged the work by his audacious revision of it.

Britten read the George Crabbe poems on which *Peter Grimes* is based while in California in 1941. He said that Crabbe's account of the East Anglian landscape reminded him of what, in his exile, he lacked; he at once set about returning home. Grimes the solitary, who pines for "a whiten'd doorstep, and a woman's care," is the homesick Britten. The longing for reconcilement with the censorious community also imparts an emotional secret: Grimes the boy-killer is the homosexual outcast, looking to Ellen Orford to effect his redemption, even his cure. Crabbe's *Borough* condemns the provincial life which Britten nostalgically envied. His Ellen gives birth to a cretinous child, and Grimes is worn down into sullen despair by the tedium of his life as a fisherman. Crabbe's Grimes at least has the courage of his obduracy and of his gloomy reclusiveness; the operatic Grimes yearns for anchorage and respectable cohabitation. When the deputation invades his hut, the Rector commends his bachelorly housekeeping—"here's order, here's skill." Montagu Slater's libretto creates a community for Grimes to belong to. None exists in the poem, whose characters occupy the solitary confinement of their own short stories. Crabbe's Ellen, Grimes, Swallow, Keene and Auntie never meet. His moral indeed is that they shouldn't: they should practice a stoic claustration. Writing about social clubs and the disaffection they foment in the borough, he advises, "Let's learn to live, for we must die, alone." Slater unites these people, invents Balstrode as arbiter and weather-beaten conscience, and rewrites the shabby, disgraced, blinded Ellen as a Victorian domestic angel, occupied with her embroidery.

Tenderly appealing to the pity of his fellows, the Grimes of Peter Pears was an ineffectual dreamer: a misfit but no menace. That fragile, white, androgynous voice didn't belong in a homespun jersey and sou'wester. Vickers, appropriating the character (most forcefully in his Covent Garden performances with Colin Davis after 1975), seceded from the cozy local color of the work's "familiar fields" and "ordinary streets," and turned Pears's threnodies—"alone, alone, alone" as the apprentice dies, or "I live alone"—into declarations of defiance. As Vickers uttered it, Grimes's recital of the oath at the inquest was an attestation of faith, inordinate in its vocal power and universal in its application. He didn't address himself apologetically to the society which surrounded him; like Florestan in the dark of the dungeon, he called directly upon God. Vickers played Grimes as a barnacled prophet, a martyr extending his arms in the crucified postures of Parsifal as he volunteered for suffering and rejection. The society in which Britten's hero hoped to attain the salvation of anonymity was now—with Davis urging orchestra and chorus to cries of homicidal fury—a lynch mob.

Britten, hearing Vickers sing an excerpt from the role at a concert, was apparently disconcerted, even resentful. Nor was Vickers surreptitious in his takeover. After working with Tyrone Guthrie on the Met's production in 1966, he insisted on verbal changes to toughen up Slater's sometimes telltale, effeminate diction: he reworded his rebukes to John (and commented that he played the scene as an angry father, recalling his chastisements of his own sons, not with the more dubious motives of Britten's

Grimes); he eliminated some asides about the earlier apprentice; and in the mad scene changed "breast" to "heart." Britten, coming home in *Grimes*, hadn't the courage to outface the storms which assail his hero. Vickers invited the blasts of the tempest, and when Balstrode entreated him to shelter indoors, said "Here I will stay." He invested the character with a virile strength of will which alarmed the composer.

That, however, is the fate of dramatic art: if it is to continue living, it must outlive its possessive creators, and entrust itself to the care of the interpreters who will—as in all the cases remembered here—re-create it.

TEN

The Ecstasy and Agony of Song

SINGING opera is more than the production of a voice. What makes it so exciting—ecstatic sometimes, agonized at others—is the voice's pervasion of a body which itself seems to sing. The instrument is the entire organism. With air resonating from the diaphragm up to the head, the performer becomes a pillar of sound, taken over by opera's inbreathing, inspiring god.

When this happens, music reaches that body's extremities—Christa Ludwig's hands, or Geraint Evans's feet. Ludwig's Klytämnestra in *Elektra* at the Met in 1984 inscribed the woman's life history on her tottering, unsteady body. She staggered on tipsily, sustained by her sticks and the attendants who prompted her. At length she cast off these supports and stood alone, only to be felled by Elektra; reviving, she commuted tragedy to comedy in her glee at the death of Orest. Ludwig's hands, tentatively reaching out to Elektra, vouched for her desperate solicitude, even for her wisdom. This was a menopausal Marschallin, still sleepless and now more dependent on cosmetics, as flirtatiously confidential and (when Elektra seems to be cooperating) as nimbly delighted by intrigue, showing off her jewels to another woman. When she talked of how, growing older, we dream, those hands flapped in a gesture of deprecation and acceptance still used by Viennese women in cafés; when she couldn't speak, the hands did so for her, clutching air, fingers twitching to secure a safety which eluded her. To the plangency of the hands, Ludwig added the precariousness of the body, tall but rickety when deprived of those poles; above this scaffolding, her face remained cherubic, despite the fever spots of rouge.

A three-volume biography of this woman was realized physically by Ludwig within the twenty-five minutes of life Strauss allows her. As much as the dancing Salome's, her body thought. Geraint Evans had the same physiognomic intelligence. His characterizations were built from the shoes up—his Claggart in *Billy Budd* minced; his Wozzeck plodded; his Beckmesser scurried like an officious beetle; his Falstaff had a pigeon-toed waddle, the man's center of gravity lowered by the belly he carried before him. Asked why he never sang Don Giovanni, Evans explained by reference to these nether regions: his legs were too short, his bottom too near the ground.

Hildegard Behrens has spoken of making her bare feet, for her Salzburg Ariadne, seem by force of spirit to be the slim, cool pediment of a marble statue; cradling Tristan's head in a Munich production, she narrowed her hands to the tapered digits of a medieval wood carving. Actually her hands and feet are broad, solid, practical. The change in them happened thanks to the music. Such attenuation wouldn't have suited Leonie Rysanek. Once, rehearsing a *Tannhäuser* which Wieland Wagner had staged like a stiff scene from a missal, Rysanek reminded him that she was a baroque not a Gothic figure—made to swoop and soar, not for occupation of a niche. Behrens erosively chiseled the body into form; Rysanek abandoned it to open-armed flight.

Singing is kinetic energy. It takes its pace from the restless liveliness of the music. As Elisabeth in Otto Schenk's *Tannhäuser* at the Met, Rysanek rushed headlong into the hall of song, caressing its furniture, sensuously celebrating its (and her own) return to life. She quivered with an elation half fearful, shuddering in Tannhäuser's presence. Sentenced to stillness during the song contest, she internalized this motion, changing from admiration to bewilderment and thence to nausea at Tannhäuser's blasphemy. She rose with difficulty from her chair, the gladness exhausted in her, to make a last effort of mediation. Her reappearance in the third act was a postmortem visitation. She slumped before the wayside cross like a corpse; painfully erecting herself to sing, she crept away with an infinite stumbling slowness, walking out of life. The baroque figure had succumbed to a Gothic paralysis.

There are singers who don't dithyrambically move with the music, but hold their power in reserve. Janet Baker learned from oratorio a reflective stillness which, in opera, manifested stoical strength. Steadfastness made a moral icon of her Penelope in Glyndebourne's *Ritorno d'Ulisse:* patience implacably growing into a monument. As Alceste at Covent Garden in 1981, she stood on a plinth before a massive idol of Apollon, whose solemn imperturbability she hoped—facing death—she would share. The same statuesqueness suited Jessye Norman's Cassandre, a rampart for the city she tried to save. On the occasion in 1984 when she sang both heroines in *Les Troyens* at the Met, Norman demonstrated the distance between classical equipoise and romantic velocity with a balefully still and resigned Cassandre followed by a Didon provoked to panic when Enée deserts her, circling the room like a stricken animal and prostrating herself, breast heaving, to call down vengeance on him as if in a voodoo ritual.

Hearkening to the oratorio-like stasis in *Samson et Dalila,* Domingo and Baltsa played it at Covent Garden in 1985 as an exercise in suspended animation—tightly restrained in his case, predatory in hers. Baltsa's Dalila raced on in the first scene; seeing Samson, she froze. Thereafter she advanced with cautious stealth, or backed off into a slow-motion, spell-casting dance. Domingo's Samson, not reacting, remained inside the charmed circle of his immunity. Again and again she arrived at its border and found she couldn't cross it, since she couldn't elicit a response from him. Her strategy therefore shifted into reverse. She resolved to will him to her, magnetizing him. She unsettled him by ignoring him (as he had done with her), facing away to sing "Printemps qui commence." He began gradually to edge toward her, impelled despite himself; she, to prosecute her advantage, tripped away. The physical plot—irresistible force encountering immovable object—was repeated in the second act. Coming to her, Domingo found himself helpless within her force field. At the feast, Domingo and Baltsa were both immobilized, gathering inside themselves a power they refused as yet to expend. He was tethered; though she was free, her only movements during the orgy were the beckoning encouragement of motion in others, inciting the revelers by remote control. Samson and Dalila were here the twin pillars of a foundering temple.

Such concentration is hypnotic—a mesmerism emitted in waves by an unmoving body, dramatically invisible (since drama is supposed to consist of character in action) but musically audible. José van Dam's Jokanaan, seen at Covent Garden in 1986, achieved this self-projection, his eyes fixed on some distant horizon, his body rigidly repulsing Salome; Rysanek's Ortrud, in the Met's *Lohengrin* during 1985, was sinister in her inertia. During the first act, Ortrud doesn't sing, except for some mutterings in ensemble. But though relegated to the margin of the stage, Rysanek commanded it by her glaring vigilance. She could propel Telramund with a glance; on Elsa's arrival, she turned away to focus an inner look which could kill. Because Ortrud is so literally manipulative, Rysanek kept her hands concealed beneath her gown. When one of them darted out to prod or prompt Telramund, it was as if she brandished a weapon. The character's apathy conserves strength: the voice is being saved for the execrations of the second act—Rysanek's wild atheistic laughter, derisively tearing apart the word "Gott!"; her cry of Elsa's name, which distended through the dark to make the air quake; the appeal to her demons, spurting from her body like vomit.

A great singer's silence can be as eloquent as the voice in full flood. Gwyneth Jones has often quoted Gibran's declaration that work is "love made visible." That, she says, is why she sings; and it is how she sings—embodying emotion, not just articulating it. She is expert at showing how a mood modulates into its opposite: revulsion calming to determined hatred after Brünnhilde in *Götterdämmerung* is dragged into the Gibichung hall; reproach of the gods reconciled to pity during the immolation. In Götz Friedrich's *Siegfried* at Covent Garden in 1978, her awakening was a reluctant revivification. She recoiled aghast from the sun; Siegfried's departure in *Götterdämmerung* caused her to despair suddenly. Every gesture exemplified the orchestra's stream of consciousness, even though she wasn't singing. In Chéreau's Bayreuth *Ring*, the same musical sequences were invested with a quite different succession of feelings, since here Brünnhilde was not the terrified victim Friedrich made her but a spirit of nature. Stirring in her sleep at the end of *Siegfried*, Gwyneth Jones stretched out an arm, her fingers twitching like a baby's, groping a reality which was still dark; she blinked, grimacing, beating back the light with her lids; finally the face relaxed, and she smiled in joy and wonder—a physiognomic sunburst. Only then did she sing her words of greeting. In Chéreau's *Götterdämmerung*, Jones accompanied Waltraute's narration with a silent monologue of her own. A tear formed in her eye just as Waltraute, prompting the orchestra to resurrect long-buried motifs, said that Wotan still thought only of her. Sorrow changed at once to shifty guilt. Her eyes darting sideways, Jones's Brünnhilde began to calculate ways of resisting her sister's demands. She had been kneeling; to cast off her remorse, she struggled to her feet. Waltraute grabbed her, and her posture at once straightened into defiance.

Gwyneth Jones even dares to place the emotional climax of a role after the last notes have been sung. This occurred with her Brünnhilde in the Met's *Walküre* in 1983. The orchestra spoke through her as—her hands stretched out, her lips soundlessly babbling to translate the grief and regret in the music—she lunged across the vast distance of the stage into Wotan's arms. Blinded by weeping, part of her welcomed the death to which he drew her, part of her wrenched away.

Wagner's characters develop and change while listening to others ✳ sing, or to the orchestra. At the Met in 1979 and 1985, Jon Vickers made Parsifal's collapse into moral conscience evident in his deportment. He swaggered on, having shot the swan. Silent during Gurnemanz's reproof, the brute weakened, and bent in wonder and regret when made to touch the dead bird. The physical change was then registered vocally: the hunter's bluffness was fined down to a choirboy's unearthly pianissimo as Parsifal asked the first abstract question of his life—"Wer ist gut?" The scene in the temple is equally crucial for Parsifal, though he doesn't participate in it. Vickers strained forward to comprehend; waved back by Gurnemanz during the communion, he retreated with awed modesty, and venturing into the emptied circle at the end of the scene he almost tiptoed. His new knowledge, inscribed on his body, is guarded in silence. When Gurnemanz demanded if he understood, Vickers could only mournfully nod.

The Kundry of the 1985 performances was Rysanek. Her character grovels in shadow during the first act, with only a few vocal interjections; in the third act, she must arrive at her salvation with the aid of two words and some preliminary moans. Rysanek, however, enacted the music between and beneath the words, and by doing so could incarnate the progress from savage to seductress to penitent.

She began with an unkempt mane concealing her face. Curled up like a sleeping dog or sprawled at the feet of Amfortas, she existed beneath the level of human consciousness or identity. In Klingsor's den she also groveled, though here the posture meant moral enslavement not (as in the forest) indigence and brutishness. His invocation roused her; her arms flung wide, she rocked in seasick nausea like a marionette the magician operates from above. Her first scream was shrill with terror, the second more gaspingly hollow, her laughter a witchy shrieking. This was a music to suit Kundry's moral state: intemperate, distempered sound. "Weihle," her summons to Parsifal, introduced a new voice—sensuously alluring, delivered (thanks to James Levine's tempo) with an insinuating languor—and with it a new body. The beast had grown into an erotic demon, who slowly stalked Parsifal, then fell on him for the kiss with an abrupt, alarming violence, like an insect biting. Her sting convulsed him, and that response induced an instant metamorphosis in her. The victim had shown himself to be a savior, and Rysanek's seductive guile turned into desperate need. Formerly she taunted him; now she begged him for mercy with clenched hands. Her octave drop on the word "lachte" toppled into a pit of misery without a bottom, and she exposed the face she had earlier kept hidden: a staring skull, constricted in remorse and dread. After this physical and vocal dementia, Rysanek made the character's stillness and silence in the third act seem logical. At peace now, Kundry can gratefully relapse into nonbeing. Rysanek subsided into a different kind of horizontal woman—not the crawling animal but the reverently kneeling worshiper, at last permitted to pray and to die.

Rysanek has called Kundry "*the* woman, the total woman." Her characterization compiles and compresses all female types, mutating from one to the other in obedience to the behests of music. Possessed by the role, she in turn possesses it, and can—because her performance has explained Kundry and thus pardoned her—create it anew, in defiance of its first creator: "I don't like the idea that Christ cursed her," Rysanek says. "Wagner was wrong here." The composer condemns the woman; the singing actress, experiencing her lust for absolution, has redeemed her.

Rysanek waives the curse because, for her, song is ecstatic. For Vickers, however, performance is an agony. If opera is oratorio defamed, the singer must be a spoiled priest. Moral qualms vexed the Wagnerian characterizations of Vickers. He believed the music to be malign, justifying incest in *Die Walküre* and adultery in *Tristan*. He undertook *Parsifal* warily, vetoing interpretations like Wieland Wagner's which enthroned the hero as a messiah; he refused *Tannhäuser* because he couldn't bring himself to blaspheme by asking holy Elisabeth to pray for him.

His Tristan derived a unique intensity from this disapproval—from his presumption, as he told Roberta Knie when they performed the opera in Dallas in 1975, that "Isolde is a bad girl." There and in successive Covent Garden revivals, Vickers sang and acted in opposition to the work. Refusing to dash about with the ardor the music urges, he paced in meditative slow motion, or held himself on guard against the orchestra's insinuations. Refusing to emote, he sang with a softness which chastened the heat of the music and the avidity of Isolde. In the love duet his voice belied its own virility in an abstinent, sexless falsetto. This Tristan was confused and disabled by his sexual vulnerability. But the lesion taught him shame, then a suicidal wisdom which Isolde, blithely consummating their marriage after his death, could never share.

Vocally, this critique of the character and the score was conveyed by Vickers's extreme dynamic contrasts, and his barbed enunciation of the text. He could dwindle in a single utterance of Isolde's name from heroic force to a faltering hush: the throttling of the sound marked Tristan's disorientation and his guilty doubts. His diction pointedly defended words against their overwhelming by music. In the love duet he dealt with the text as delicately as if it were infectious (which it is). Here, words steadied the mind against musical instinct; later, during Tristan's delirium, Vickers fractured the text to match the music's dissolution of tonality, yet even in derangement he remained linguistically exact and lucid, elongating "schön"—as he recalled Isolde's beauty—into an unbroken arc of keening self-castigation.

Dramatically, Vickers resisted the music's sensuality by treating Isolde with gentle, distant condescension. A daughter rather than a mistress, Knie snuggled her head on his chest after they drank the potion in the 1978 London performances; nor did he bound to her in the garden, but edged forward unfolding paternal arms.

According to romantic tradition, the woman in *Tristan und Isolde* consumes the man. The musical bliss of Isolde in her liebestod swamps the tormented verbal intellect of Tristan. Like a ravenous mantis, Nilsson exhausted a trio of Tristans during a single performance at the Met in 1960; when the Covent Garden production was new in 1971, she objected to—and later banned—Tristan's resurrection for a posthumous clinch, which Peter Hall had devised for the last reconciliatory bars. Tristan, she declared, had become part of her.

The Tristan of Vickers entailed a reversal of roles, and a denial of Isolde's erotic supremacy. The opera for him describes the woman's incomprehension of the suffering man. In a concert performance of the duet at the Met in 1981, Vickers extended an arm to enfold Nilsson in an incongruously fatherly, forgiving embrace; she edged away, determined not to be subdued. At the Orange Festival in 1973, with Böhm conducting, they spent much of the duet sitting on a bench. But as the music surged to its climax, Nilsson suddenly stood and advanced to the front of the huge open stage. No longer content to be the partner in a sedentary conversation, she needed to unleash her voice into the night. Vickers followed, and grasped her shoulders as if to detain her. At this moment Tristan is dissuading Isolde from the satisfaction of love, coaxing her toward a suicide pact. The disagreement between the characters suited the singers: Nilsson's proud exhibition of the voice, against Vickers's introverted muting. However, just as he gripped her to caution her against the sexual crisis in the orchestra, a gust of wind flapped the nightdress she was wearing and enveloped him in its folds. He briefly disappeared; the eternal woman had once more won.

Vickers starchily insists that the stage must be a "moral institution," and sees operatic history as a long decline. Art's mission and the artist's calling have given way, he believes, to vocal self-advertisement. Hence his advocacy of Handel's *Samson*. The composer had renounced opera because of egomaniac singers; oratorio—for Handel, for his Samson who censures the pagan shows, and for Vickers—testifies to the rectitude of spirit, determined not to engage in the flummery of operatic performance. The searing rage with which Vickers sang and acted the clown in *I Pagliacci* dramatized his quarrel with his own vocation. Canio's shame is symbolized by the grease and powder with which he has to smear and sprinkle himself. Vickers too has said that his worst trial when singing Otello was having to black up. How can what he calls a "search for truth" be conducted by a false face, or expressed by simulated emotions? Instead of cuckoldry, Vickers's Canio lamented the indignity of his theatrical trade. The character assumed the singer's puritanical mistrust of art. "Even the great Picasso," according to Vickers, "made a devastating confession of his own charlatanism, confessing himself to be nothing more than a mountebank."

For other singers, the risks of opera are physical not ethical. Teresa Stratas performed as an experiment in self-destruction. In Covent Garden's *Pagliacci*, she gleefully invited the knife wielded by Vickers. Song for Stratas was a neurotic, even a necrophiliac symptom. The voice is a spirit perturbing the body, trying to find an escape from that worn, exhausted physique; the actor, bleaching his face like a dancing savage or a modern sidewalk mime, has symbolically quit the living to join the dead. Rubbing white goo on her cheeks before the play in Zeffirelli's *Pagliacci* film, Stratas stared at herself in a tarnished hand mirror until the blanched skin became that of a cadaver, and she seemed to be looking through it to the skeleton beneath. A similar ghostliness informed her other roles—a gaunt Salome in Götz Friedrich's film, truly intimate with Jokanaan only when he too is dead; a tubercular wraith in the moonlit garret of Zeffirelli's *Bohème*; whorish as Jenny in the Met's *Mahagonny* when she fondlingly chalked the tip of a billiard cue, yet also, in the white shift she wore for her lover's execution, starved, spiritual, nunlike.

Outside the ranks of human normality, the great performer is an ambiguous creature. Stratas seemed in her wise childishness to bestraddle the sexes: her singing voice was brightly feminine, her speaking register almost baritonally husky. The descent from one to the other measures the decline of her Violetta in Zeffirelli's *Traviata* film. Her coloratura in the first act is glaring and shrill; for the last act, she lunges from song to speech, reading Germont's letter in the gruff, rasping voice of the consumptive. The disease of the lungs suffered by Violetta or Mimi was—as Stratas played those parts—a case history of the singer's fatal illness.

Stratas's Lulu, in Paris in 1979 and New York the following year, was theatrical danger in person: less the earthy woman of Wedekind's plays than a ruthlessly honest, unconditioned being, whose every motion is a gratuitous act—truly, as Lulu herself says when questioned about her parentage, "ein Wunderkind," a wide-eyed Alice on the loose from wonderland. Stratas refused to treat Lulu as a vamp. The character's specialty is exposure, of herself (under her flimsy dancer's veils) and others. This moral terrorist doesn't edit or censor her thoughts. She confides the truth of her feelings—casually advising Alwa that she poisoned his mother—and her candor can kill. It also kills her, because though Stratas's Lulu was a hostage of phony morality, distressed by the Painter's catechism, she possessed a private moral code to which she was austerely true.

Thus Stratas welcomed Jack the Ripper as her cruel, surgical savior. They are natural allies: with his knife he cauterizes a foul world, just as she purges the men who try to own her by contradicting their professions of love. At the Met, Stratas knelt and begged him to stay, tenderly petting and bribing him until he consented to operate on her. Lulu, who envies her defunct husbands, rationalizes a fascination with death which is both personal to Stratas and general among performers. Returning from prison, wasted, gray-faced, her hair shorn, Stratas spoke with the detachment and divination of those whom illness has acquainted with the end.

In Paris and New York, the Schön she tortured and the Ripper who exacted medical and moral vengeance were played by Franz Mazura, a performer who, like Stratas, teetered on a precipice. Music drove Mazura's Schön from glowering propriety to gibbering mania. His face was a grimly set mask, his head bald and helmetlike. Yet he maintained his uprightness at the cost of nervous anguish, and when provoked by Lulu he paced, twitched, wrung his hands. His voice gave him away—blackly commanding though raw and ravaged, sharpened to a knife edge of attuned screaming. Blackmailed backstage by Lulu the dancer, he began with his hands rigidly clasped behind him. These then reached out stiffly to plead with her—or to strike her dead. He reeled about the room, paralyzed by his grimace in the mirror, then tumbled into a chair, the ramrod composure gone. The Prussian habits remained to incriminate him. Before writing the letter to his fiancée, he fastidiously adjusted his pince-nez. Lulu here dictated his death sentence, and transcribing it he bent ever closer to the table, as if his back had been broken by the task. At home, Mazura's Schön looked snug, only to succumb within minutes to restless paranoia, poking into corners, brandishing a revolver, retreating haunted up the stairs. Though he had turned away, he was visibly unmanned by the lied in which Lulu asserts her freedom, and he staggered off under its impact, his mouth sagging open but deprived of speech. Death restored to him a terrifying strength: invigorated by the bullets, he began hurling the furniture about.

At his end, he shared the percipience of Stratas's Lulu, prophesying that Alwa would be her next victim. Mazura's voice often sounded like a relay from the cavernous, echoing beyond. "Jetzt kommt die Hinrichtung," he remarked of the reckoning as Lulu directed him to write the letter, and a gulf of despair gaped open in the first syllable of the final word. "Sie ist ihr verliebte," he said of his wife's connection to Geschwitz, and the central vowel of the word for love stretched into a wail of agony and disgust. The Ripper, before slaughtering Lulu, notes that "Der Mond scheint." In Mazura's enunciation, that shining became the sound of a baying wolf. This was not the lapse of song into speech, but the extreme extension of speech into a song of pain. Words could no longer match the ferocity of feeling; notes must take over.

Opera is a song of love and death, of conditions which bypass rational understanding. This linked it to those ancient mysteries which the Renaissance revived; its practitioners remain devotees of the mysterious transformations probed by religion. Stratas flirted with death, and sacrificed herself to enacting in life one of her last theatrical roles. When Lotte Lenya, near death, remembered Stratas as the redheaded Jenny from *Mahagonny*, Stratas tinted her hair to resume the performance and moved in with Lenya to watch over her last days. Gwyneth Jones says that she learned what Isolde's liebestod meant by tending her terminally ill father, and sensing without fear the presence of death in the room. Elisabeth Söderström sees singing opera as a rehearsal for death. The music is a welcome extinction: having died onstage, Söderström's whole body repudiates its return to life for a curtain call—"it seems so false and wrong that I feel physically ill."

Söderström relishes the occasions when opera permits her a death and resurrection on her own terms, for instance the fermata when Jenůfa loses consciousness in the second act, and all is silent. Unhustled by the orchestra, the singer can lie there for as long as she is able to compel the audience to wait with her; then when she decides to continue, singing is her resumption of life. Like Orpheus, she has come back from the grave. Opera is often mocked for its voluntary and instantaneous expiries. Elsa in Nestroy's parody of *Lohengrin* spurns the offer of a dagger, boasting in Viennese dialect "I can die on me own." Söderström believes that opera tells the truth about this last passage, comparing her own father's death to the discreet exit of Mélisande and her mother's to the exalted ascent of Violetta.

Performance is a venture beyond the limits of life. This was the fascination of Söderström's Marty in *The Makropulos Case*. Marty like Tosca is an opera singer, the medium's self-image, but she lacks the confidence of Puccini's diva. Rather than glorifying her, song is a debilitation. An alchemist's formula has prolonged existence. Alchemists studied elemental changes, turning earth into air by means of the intermediary element, fire; singing for Marty is another elemental transaction, changing body into spirit by the exhalation of breath. Dying at last, she burns the parchment with the recipe for her immortality, and consigns herself to the judgment of flame. She can't forgive herself for cheating nature. If song doesn't challenge death, it can have neither heroism nor beauty.

Söderström's Marty captured the sadness of the singer, who relies on a physiological genius which is depleted whenever it's used. Singers fear the inevitable day when the organism will betray them, and they fend off that retribution by muffling their throats, whispering in rehearsal, or trusting in charms: Caruso wore an amulet of anchovy round his neck, Pavarotti grubs for bent nails backstage. They all know their high Cs are numbered. When one is let out, it's gone forever, and must be deducted from the total.

Dying as she intoned a prayer, Söderström's Marty—in the 1978 Welsh National Opera production—seemed to decompose, crumbling into a pile of clothes which no longer contained a body. No other operatic character has a career so penitentially extended, but the 337-year-old Marty is in her way exemplary. Operatic performance usurps life, both elongating and abbreviating it. Sherrill Milnes comments that when he finishes an evening as Simon Boccanegra, he feels he has been singing for a lifetime, not three hours; and across the hiatus of twenty-five years within the action, his Boccanegra did age from a debonair buccaneer to a careworn Doge, withdrawn and uncertain. Renato Bruson in the same role charted time's musical passing by clinically anatomizing Boccanegra's symptoms. Bruson studied the way poison infiltrates the body, and at Covent Garden in 1986 appeared ashen and enfeebled in the final scene, alternating between spasms of feverish energy and a breathless lethargy—another Orphic report on the secrets of the grave.

The steep, sudden degeneration is an operatic destiny. Domingo's Don Carlos at the Met in 1983 arrived at Fontainebleau as an ardent youth, his face aglow with an impromptu dream; he reappeared in the cloister as a limping epileptic. In Covent Garden's *Les Contes d'Hoffmann*, comedy allowed him to reverse this inexorable law. He entered the tavern as a seedy and unshaven drunk, only to be magically rejuvenated. His song of Kleinzach was acted with an ugly fervor. Inside a back-to-front greatcoat, with a stick poked up behind him to erect his hump, Domingo's Hoffmann turned into the deformed creature he sang about. But when the music diverged into reminiscence of Stella, his snarling tone lightened, and the monster straightened into the enraptured poet Hoffmann once was. At Spalanzani's party, that youth was born again: within a few bars, the morbid rake shed his years and his decadent disillusion, springy in his step again and mellifluous of voice.

Operatic character advances through the ages of man, fatally hastened by music. As Puccini's Manon Lescaut at the Met in 1984, Mirella Freni telescoped the heroine's existence: a shy virgin at Amiens, a supercilious courtesan in Paris, a bedraggled sinner at Le Havre, a craving animal in the Louisiana waste. Terrified of time, the Marschallin is condemned by the music which is her medium, and Gwyneth Jones, in the Munich *Rosenkavalier* conducted by Carlos Kleiber, frisked in her bed like a young girl, only to change—as the shadows thickened at the end of the act—into the old woman she elegiacally peered at in her mirror. When Agnes Baltsa plays Oktavian, as at Covent Garden in 1984, the Marschallin's warnings startle the boy into adulthood and the understanding of his own mortality. Baltsa listened stunned and bewildered to the Marschallin's account of stopping the clocks; in Faninal's house, Oktavian was already older, more soberly self-aware. Opera's overheated lives are burned out in a day, or an evening.

Since the drama of singing speeds toward destruction, some performers resist it—most often those with the finest voices, who have the most to lose. Montserrat Caballé employed her voice to soothe, even to extinguish drama. Her pianissimi, applied like an electronic control, changed dramatic agitation to suave musical reverie. Adriana Lecouvreur's calming breeze of breath—"un soffio alla mia voce"—served as Caballé's testament; everything she sang was a lullaby. Leontyne Price also stood aside from the exertions of opera, explaining that she gave up the role of Butterfly because of the hard work it entailed: the character had to lift children, clean the house, get dressed and undressed, stay up all night, and Price's voice was too precious for such heavy duty. Asked what the voice meant to her, Price once replied "My voice is God." It was a remark of genuine modesty not outrageous conceit, but her conviction that the sound she made came directly from heaven set her apart. Onstage she assumed a priestly dignity, as the vessel through whom the voice passed directly to earth.

Singers have always claimed or been credited with divinity. George Sand, after seeing Maria Malibran as Rossini's Desdemona in 1831, likened her to one of Raphael's Virgins. During the 1780s, Joshua Reynolds painted Elizabeth Billington (whose later roles included Vitellia in *La Clemenza di Tito*) as St. Cecilia: the musician as the patron saint of music, performing in a sublime sky among a cherubic chorus. Haydn thought that Reynolds had slighted Mrs. Billington by allowing the chubby angels to join in, when they should have been listening and learning. Opera encourages this robbery of godliness. Elektra assures Chrysothemis that they belong with the gods because of their proficiency in killing. A rapture which the Greeks called oracular sustains these characters and those who play them: this is the lunacy of Norma singing "Casta diva" to the moon, or the insanity of Donizetti's Lucia, an Orphic priestess, endowed with a visionary aura by murder and madness.

Since 1959, Joan Sutherland's Lucia has been synonymous with opera, and its conversion of dramatic agony into musical ecstasy. Her performance (given again at Covent Garden in 1985) is the more amazing because Sutherland, jolly and matronly, is so unlike Lucia. The voice with its crazed, giddy ease at free association in the upper atmosphere is under control yet beyond understanding. How does a human being acquire such uncanny skills? Where do those E-flats *come* from?

Lucia's folly is instrumental—a competition first with a harp, later with a flute. The harp, across which the wind seems to stray during the scene at the fountain, records the vagrancy of her mind. The flute, which she overhears and imitates during her playacted wedding, is the sound of her high-pitched distraction. She is maddened by music. At the fountain, Sutherland stared into the pool and gravely mimed the beckoning of the phantom. She buried her head in the flowers, and gazed at the ring Edgardo had given her, kissing it rather than him; her voice sketched false fires in the dusk. Its coloratura was a spectrum of coloration, refracting the light of that soprano sound through a prism of shattered facets. Arriving to sign the marriage contract, veiled in a white dress, Lucia had become the ghost who welcomed her at the fountain. Sutherland's voice quavered behind that veil as from within the tomb.

Her madness was a maenad's wedding—Salome fondling the severed head, Agave singing to the mutilated Pentheus in *The Bassarids*. In her bloodied nightdress, Sutherland crept down the winding stairs and clung to the wall like a spider. She took a posy from a bystander, distributed some of the flowers, then curtly dropped the rest. Like the Medusa in Shelley's poem, she personified the romantic notion of beauty, obscene yet alluring—dramatically guilty yet musically impeccable, even celestial (in her description of the heavenly harmonies which accompany her vows). Salome sings of a "geheimnisvolle Musik" or mysterious music, Isolde in her liebestod of a wondrous melody which no one else can hear. Lucia too carries the flute inside her head, and Sutherland chased the echo of it across the stage, searching for it in corners of the drafty hall. As the mingled reproaches and sympathy of the courtiers crowded upon her, she vocalized wordlessly, singing to keep reality at bay.

Before she fell down in a faint, there was a moment of strung-out bravery when the voice seemed to leap across empty space. Though planted on the ground, Sutherland sang as if on a trapeze. In the repeat of "Spargi d'amaro pianto" she took off from the diving board of a trill, testing a note by making it ricochet up and down until it became a projectile. Then she launched it through air to perch exactly on another higher note before skipping to a lower one—and all in the same breath. It was a feat of lyrical gymnastics, carried out with no visible means of support; a vocal defiance of mortality, like an acrobat's gyrations in the absence of a net. Yet this arabesque also, like a melodic brain scan, registered the ungrounded, veering thought of Lucia. Here was opera's own dizzy high style: a negotiation of rarefied mental heights.

Opera is a sport, a display of physical and technical prowess. At the same time it is a form of almost religious aspiration, reaching for the sky from which music first poured down like Apollo's sunlight. Dancers leap into that lost altitude; singers send out their top notes on exploratory forays, and use their scales as Jacob's ladders. One word defines its visceral effect and its lofty ambition, and that is the first word uttered by Verdi's Otello as he whirls out of the storm. Opera's business is exultation.

IV

AFTERWORD

Afterword to the 1996 Edition

OPERA-LOVERS, as I suppose the book you have just read goes to show, tend to be mythmakers. It is an art which specialises in the supernatural. Song comes more naturally to deities, especially those of the pagan persuasion, than to tongue-tied, out-of-tune earthlings. It's not surprising that the singers who perform these roles, if they do so well enough, should be nick-named divinities. But all myths describe and attempt to atone for a rup-ture: the gods are no longer among us. Opera-goers tend to be gullible believers in golden ages, which mostly—can this be an accident?—coin-cide with their own lost youth. So my first question to myself, in returning to this book ten years later, is to check whether I now spend less time going to the opera than in keeping my collection of memories polished.

Looking back, I admit that it has been something of a doleful decade, with my favourites—the singers whose praises I attempted to sing in the last chapter—trooping one after another into the wings, like the orchestral players deserting their posts in Haydn's "Farewell" Symphony.

Joan Sutherland, with whom my book ends, retired in 1990, and has since auctioned off Lucia's bloodstained nightdress, along with a ware-house full of fans, tiaras and outsize ball gowns. To formalise her renunci-ation of glamour and lyrical lunacy, she has even played the role of a farmer's wife—with scrubbed cheeks and chapped hands—in an Aus-tralian film comedy.

Jon Vickers at about the same time gave up attempting to reconcile the passionate madness of opera with his Christian piety, and after some preachy lectures in the Canadian backblocks he now only exercises his hefty, anguished voice when singing hymns on Sunday in his local church in Bermuda.

Birgit Nilsson unfussily announced in 1984 that the time had arrived to lock her voice in the bathroom. She reappeared occasionally for master classes in New York, scrutinising scores through professorial spectacles and wondering aloud at the variety of musical worlds she had hitherto ignored. "I don't know this piece at all," she mused when a young baritone at the Manhattan School of Music offered to sing her an aria from Rossini's *Guillaume Tell*. Once I watched her expertly coach a soubrette through Blondchen's coloratura tirade from *Die Entführung aus dem Serail*, amazed at the incongruity of the scene: a spear-carrying goddess giving lessons in flirtatiousness to a chambermaid. Illustrating some technicality about the diaphragm in one of these sessions, she accidentally released one of those Nilsson notes, a galaxy of which—pointed, precise, white-hot, and surely beyond normal human reach—hang suspended in my memory. She laughed at the audience's shock, and said, "It's only because I'm wearing a microphone." But the joke hardly explained the mystery. How did such a voice come to inhabit her body in the first place? Nor could her good humour cover the pathos of the situation. Voices die long before their owners.

More recently and more heart-rendingly, I seem to have spent an entire year listening to Christa Ludwig's long and regretful goodbye, at concerts in New York, London, and Salzburg. At her last London recital in 1993, she gave a single encore—Strauss's "Morgen," in which the singer lapses into an elliptical stillness while the piano continues to paraphrase emotions inaccessible to words. After the final notes, no one dared to applaud. The length of the pause, and the gratitude it mimed, amazed even Ludwig, whose tears ruled out further encores. She was right, of course. The silence of a world without such voices is hard to bear.

Of the singers who converted me to opera and summed up its excitements, the longest lasting has been Leonie Rysanek. Over the decade since I completed this book, while her colleagues and contemporaries were retreating to tax havens or classrooms, she enjoyed what could almost be called a new career, as Wagner's Ortrud, Strauss's Klytämnestra and Herodias, and the Kostelnička and Kabanicha of Janáček. Her Ortrud was a demon, her imprecations drawing on those reserves of buried energy which are available to the greatest theatrical performers: this adherent to an old, violent, instinctual religion kept faith with opera itself, as its fury and aggression erupted from within her. Her Kostelnička—a woman torn apart and then painfully reconstructed, demented and finally exalted—revealed to me what Aristotle meant by the cathartic force of tragedy. Pitiable and awesome, searing and healing, this was a reckless exploration of how human nature responds to extreme pressure, conducted in the emotional area which belongs uniquely to opera: love, death, and the likeness between them. It also, in its range from soprano to contralto, from wild cries to guttural whispers, redefined the possibilities of song. Her performance as Klytämnestra concluded, offstage, with two of those inimitable Rysanek screams which (despite the disapproval of purists) explain why music is more eloquent than any words—a shriek of self-consciousness and moral recognition, as she identifies the son who will kill her and acknowledges the crime for which she will die; next an almost voluptuous moan, as she welcomes deliverance and sleep.

The last of Rysanek's roles, the Countess in Tchaikovsky's *Queen of Spades*, was anything but an epilogue. Wigless, undressed, ghoulishly corpselike before her death, she sang the Grétry aria in which the Countess recalls her distant youth with a faint, fragile beauty and brilliance of tone. "The voice of the young Rysanek," as she herself likes to refer to it when listening to her early records, made audible the strange psychological miracle of memory. The Met's new production late in 1995 allowed her a postmortem apotheosis, a demonstration of the subliminal, ardent, impulsive power that was Rysanek's alone. Rejuvenated in Herman's imagination after she dies of fright, the Countess—now wearing her nubile, youthful body once more, and also the red dress which was the uniform of her erotic career—bursts through the floor of his room like a geyser, heaving aside the floorboards. Then she crawls across the floor and into his bed, singing the secret of the cards into his ear as she seductively grapples with him.

Frighteningly vivid, this scene revealed that the theatre, which transcends or transgresses all the limiting conditions of life, is the proper province of immortality. But only for as long as the curtain is up and the lights in the auditorium are off. In the week during which I write this afterword, Rysanek is due to give her final performance at the Met. I expect it to be a traumatic night.

The silence, as Christa Ludwig realised after listening to it for a few minutes in the Wigmore Hall, is oppressive. None of these singers can be replaced: their value lay in their individual uniqueness. Those who come later must do things differently. I would not want to say that Edita

Gruberová sings Lucia or Elvira in *I Puritani* better than Sutherland did. At their level of accomplishment, such judgments are pointless. What's significant is that Gruberová sings the roles in her own way, so as to debar comparison. Hers are more abstract, instrumental performances. She conjures clouds of sound out of nowhere, holds them afloat, then disperses them; the way she uses her voice seems to take anachronistic account of Chopin's love for Bellini. This does not mean that her mad scenes are mere technical demonstrations of how to swell from pianissimo to forte and back again. Their fiendish expertise gives them a chilling clinical accuracy, since lunacy and romantic virtuosity are so closely allied. Gruberová recites Donna Anna's account of the attempted—perhaps successful, perhaps not resisted—rape in *Don Giovanni*, with the same sleep-walking langour and mesmerised fascination. Her haunted, morbid introspectiveness can convince you that you are overhearing a confession which the character is making only to herself: song as the underground stream of illicit consciousness.

I would never have thought it possible, but in 1994 when I heard Cheryl Studer's cadenza in the triumph scene from *Aida*, the memory of Leontyne Price was temporarily erased. Price sang the passage bluesily, blurring the notes and taking jazzy liberties: she was of course entitled to do so since, in this plea for the liberation of Ethiopian slaves, she campaigned on behalf of African America. Studer, with no obligation to send messages about racial politics, played a different character and produced a different sound, bright and crystalline rather than burnished. Her long, slow descent through the scale turned this brief, wordless soliloquy—surely not voiced out loud, for who in the belligerent uproar of the triumph would be able to hear it?—into a touching, tearful elegy, not a protest. On record, no Salome ever asked for the head of Jokanaan more naughtily or more irresistibly than Studer. Nilsson used to demand the gruesome plaything savagely enough to make Herod shudder; Studer inflects her request with a wickedly frivolous, girlish giggle. Opera, which has a relatively immutable repertory, must be saved from repetition by such acts of renewal.

So long as you don't look for substitutes, there are still great voices, and distinctive vocal personalities to go with them—for instance, among the men, Roberto Alagna, a bumptiously healthy tenor to shame the elderly bleating and cheating of Pavarotti, Domingo, and Carreras as they wearily traipse around the commercial circuit; Yuri Marusin, maniacally intense as Tchaikovsky's Herman, and the Nordically implacable Sergei

Leiferkus, superb as Onegin; Thomas Hampson, who learned from Elisabeth Schwarzkopf how to make his voice say anything it wishes, translating words into tonal colour, and Bryn Terfel, who as the Baptist in *Salome* truly sounds like a prophet, transmitting his curses on a homemade whirlwind.

In 1993 I heard two stunning performances of the spurned Ottavia in *L'Incoronazione di Poppea*, which made me stray from my loyalty to the memory of Christa Ludwig in a Paris production. Marjana Lipovsek in Salzburg delivered Ottavia's farewell to Rome with an almost emetic anger and disgust, choking on the repetitions: Monteverdian declamation approached by way of expressionistic Sprechstimme. Anne Sofie von Otter in London raged and railed with as much vehemence, but inside the strict constraints of the character's classical demeanour, like a Racine heroine straitjacketed by her alexandrines. The Poppea on both occasions was Sylvia McNair, whose breathy insinuations—as she toyed with a male Nerone in Salzburg and a female one in London, while dismissing the fatuous serenades of two counter-tenors—seemed to me the most erotic singing I had ever heard.

Nor have I mentioned Galina Gorchakova, predestined to take over all the Verdi and Puccini parts which opera companies say they cannot cast. I first encountered her at a rehearsal in St. Petersburg in 1991. I did not know her name, but learned it very quickly when I heard her rehearsing, immaculately and in full, tireless voice, some of the most tortuous music ever written: the visionary rhapsodies of Renata in Prokofiev's *The Fiery Angel*. It had not occurred to her, she told me later, that she was doing anything particularly difficult. If the next great Aida or Butterfly can wander in from the Siberian hinterland, what other surprising annunciations may be in store? Any period is likely to become a golden age, once it is safely over.

So much for the vocal prospects. With regard to the staging of opera, the state of things is more complicated and contentious than it seemed ten years ago.

One of my proposed titles for this book was *The Rebirth of Opera*. I liked the allusion to Nietzsche, but my editor Elaine Pfefferblit had a succinct objection. "Whenever," she asked, "did it die?" Unable to think of an answer, I succumbed. Ten years on, I think I would reply that in the theatre rebirth precedes and prevents demise, rather than following from it. The rebirth I had in mind was of opera as drama. Maybe there were better singers in the past, when operas were concerts in costume, performed by plush, plump sofas and double-decker buses; never have there been so many who could act as there are now. Stage directors—whose initial concern was to elicit cogent performances from the singers, but who have gone on to claim rights of their own as interpreters—simply did not exist before the 1950s, when Wieland Wagner reopened Bayreuth and Visconti worked with Callas at La Scala. One responsibility of the contemporary stocktaker is to ask whether the revolution Wieland Wagner and Visconti incited has not gone, as revolutions are apt to do, too far.

A backlash has certainly begun, headquartered at the Met: hence the nasty slurs against Graham Vick's production of *Lady Macbeth of Mtsensk* there in 1994. Shostakovich's opera is meant to be shocking, and its cynical violence and flagrant sexuality affronted Stalin. Vick was condemned for emphasising the work's satire on consumerism, which he deftly aimed both at profiteering, post-communist Russia and at the greedy luxury of the New York suburbs. One xenophobic critic called the production a specimen of "Eurotrash." The insult measured the gap, as wide as the ocean, between a lively, risky, quizzical approach to opera and the Met's self-proclaimed role as a museum.

The continents have exchanged their ancient identities. In opera, the Old World is the place of innovation and permanent revolution, while the New World has assumed the duty of conserving the past. Europe, suffering from too much onerous history, periodically breaks free by acts of desecration. Modernism in opera announced itself in 1929 when the cuckolded hero of Hindemith's journalistic satire *Neues vom Tage* ran amok in a museum, smashing a classical statue of Venus. He is dragged off to gaol, but his crime makes little difference to the dutiful, sedated visitors to the gallery, who continue reading their guide books and sagely nodding as if the statue were still there.

Harry Kupfer's opera productions have more than once playfully destroyed the opera houses in which they are set. His *Orfeo ed Euridice* at the Komische Oper in Berlin starts at a performance of Gluck's opera, with an excited, intimidated young couple in attendance: mirrors enlist the rest of us as an onstage audience. The girl leaves the theatre, and is senselessly killed in a traffic accident. The boy hopelessly tracks her through a blitzed urban underworld: out-of-order phone boxes, streets piled with debris, finally (when the Furies assail him) a psychiatric ward. The production demands whether opera, with its gilt trimmings and red velvet upholstery and miraculous resurrections, has any right to exist in a desperate, decaying modern city. Unable to justify daydreams, disbelieving in the resurrection of Euridice, Kupfer in his *La Damnation de Faust* announces the damnation of opera. When Faust is hurled into hell, the dusty tiers of the theatre crack apart and crash to the floor. Yet among the wreckage there is still the false and irritating sound of romantic uplift: an angelic chorus, dispensed by a record on the turntable of a tinny antique gramophone.

Even when the theatre is not demolished, the European ideal is that of a throwaway production, which makes its telling, timely point and never pretends to classical status: a *Macbeth* directed by David Pountney for English National Opera soon after the revolution in Romania, in which the tyrannical couple were frighteningly like the Ceausescus, fantasists who imprisoned a country in their crazed, concerted dream; a *Turandot* directed by Christopher Alden for Welsh National Opera which played the crowd scenes as an exercise in mass hysteria, a psychological preliminary to fascism. Such are the seismic jolts which Europe periodically administers to itself. Audiences too are regularly castigated. The theatre holds up a mirror, as in Kupfer's *Orfeo*, to accuse us of crimes which include being able to afford opera tickets. Gerard Mortier's new regime at Salzburg has lost no opportunity to jibe at the plutocrats who patronised Karajan's festivals. As the lights dimmed before Jürgen Flimm's production of *Poppea*, a bustling socialite in a silver dress jangled into the theatre, noisily searching for her seat. Having found it, to the annoyance of all around, she then caused extra consternation by beginning to sing: she was the goddess Fortuna, sponsor of the gold-digging Poppea and one of the disputants in Monteverdi's prologue.

It's hard to imagine a director getting away with such a sardonic practical joke at the Met. In America, opera counts as an imported luxury, like French champagne or impressionist paintings. Its expense confers prestige; it must be taken seriously. The opera house, like the museum, is a location for good works, munificent donations, sartorial display. It is also the ultimate shop window: a place for the display of cultural icons, which must be preserved from the depredations of an icon-breaker like Kupfer. Museums are quiet places, very like cemeteries.

Met productions nowadays serve as showcases for a dwindling parade of stars. This retreat into stodge and glitz is recent. When I wrote my book, John Dexter seemed intent on renewing the company's repertory, with stark, scaled-down versions of *Lulu, Mahagonny, Dialogues des Carmélites, Billy Budd,* and two triple bills designed by David Hockney— Satie's fairground ballet *Parade* teamed with *Les Mamelles de Tirésias* and *L'Enfant et les Sortilèges,* then three Stravinsky one-acters: *Le Sacre du*

Printemps, Oedipus Rex, and *Le Rossignol.* Later, after the easing-out of Dexter, Göran Järvefelt brilliantly coupled *Erwartung* and *Bluebeard's Castle.* But the Reagan decade belonged to Zeffirelli, who supplied the Met with productions of elephantine lavishness, trips back through time to a golden age of excess and guiltless expense—a *Turandot* which rivalled the Christmas pageant at Radio City Music Hall for spangled vulgarity; a *Traviata* in which the stage never stopped giddily revolving in order to show off more and more overfurnished rooms; a pompously baroque *Don Giovanni.* Designers were required to serve up pretty pictures. When Günther Schneider-Siemssen submitted his plans for the *Ring,* James Levine allegedly doodled in a few more trees. The extra conifers in due course sprouted onstage. The *Parsifal* designed by Schneider-Siemssen concluded in an Easter meadow fitted with spring flowers on metal stalks, which ricocheted alarmingly when Jessye Norman—prior to her diet— capered between them.

Having found directors who understood the large, lush style of the house, the Met engaged them for everything, despite the predictability of the results. Wagner and Strauss (Johann II as well as Richard) were automatically assigned to Otto Schenk. When Zeffirelli overreached himself, the Italian staples were given to Giancarlo del Monaco, who outfitted Butterfly with a proper house and garden, allowed Puccini's Minnie free run of a livery stable, and crammed most of Genoa on stage in *Simon Boccanegra.* Glitter rains down from the ceiling in the current *Queen of Spades,* and royalty even has a walk-on when a super uncharismatically impersonating Catherine the Great totters into a ball. Who cares that the Empress's non-appearance is one of Tchaikovsky's most studied anticlimaxes? The chorus noisily hails her arrival, but the curtain falls just before the door opens: there are, as Elektra wails in Strauss's opera, no gods in heaven. At the Met, however, drama must be sacrificed to the choreographing of an ostentatious, otiose tableau.

The Schenk *Ring* depressingly summed up the company's new priorities. Finely sung and played, it was all the same deadly. Schenk's brief was to execute Wagner's stage directions literally while not bothering his head over the ideas in the piece. Siegfried at least had a proper forge in which to smelt his sword, and the Gibichung hall collapsed impressively, at one performance concussing Hildegard Behrens. But it all meant nothing, which is precisely what Levine wanted. This great account of how we separate ourselves from nature and begin to despoil it, of how we invent gods and must learn to destroy them, of how we construct society—our man-made alternative to nature—and allow it to corrupt us, became a techno-cratic fairy tale. It's sad that the Met missed its chance to create a *Ring* which addressed America, even though the designs sometimes acclima-tised the myth to a new landscape: Valhalla looked like Manhattan perched on the New Jersey palisades, the Gibichung hall was a Hudson Valley mansion, and Brünnhilde went to sleep on the rim of the Grand Canyon. These resemblances remained accidental. Determined to avoid ideology, Levine and his compliant production team chose mindlessness instead.

Of course there is more to the *Ring* than an inquest on the embar-rassments of German history over the last century, which is what the pro-ductions of Götz Friedrich in Berlin and Harry Kupfer at Bayreuth—set respectively in a bunker and on an autobahn—emphasise. Germany may be obliged to confront the historical plot, which turned Wagner's liberat-ing superman into a totalitarian ogre; such conscience-stricken agonies are not mandatory elsewhere. Perhaps it is time to look at the *Ring* as an exercise in theatrical mythmaking, and a model of the way in which we ex-perimentally construct worlds and then, in the same spirit of ludic sedi-tion, pull them apart.

This is how the work appeared in the most suggestive staging of it I have seen, directed by Richard Jones and designed by Nigel Lowery at Covent Garden in 1994 and 1995. It was a parable about what can be imag-ined in the theatre, and about why we need the theatre as a dark, danger-ous place in which to do our imagining. A certain cut-rate, improvised disposability was part of its purpose. The Gibichung hall consisted of card-board boxes, and Brünnhilde was dragged in wearing a paper bag, not a winged helmet, on her head. Before her immolation, she tossed Siegried's sword and his leftover relics into a garbage can. Jones teasingly reminds us that the gadgetry of the *Ring*—the gadgetry which enabled the Rhine maidens to swim and the Valkyries to fly at Bayreuth in 1876, the creakily articulated dragon—is metaphorical. Its inventions were one way of telling a story which we must now tell by other means, because the story it-self has changed since Wagner told it. Hence the vapour trail of the aero-plane which crosses the poisoned, exhausted sky above the Rhine; the shared syringe with which Gunther and Siegfried celebrate their blood brotherhood; the transvestite rampages of Mime, who dysfunctionally pre-tends to be Siegfried's mother; and the drop curtain scribbled all over with graffiti and catchphrases from television programmes—the clutter and lit-ter of history, which invades and chokes our heads—in front of which the

371

Norns brood. None of these solutions purports to be authoritative. The theatre is opportunistic, rejoicing in the short life of its fantasies. As Wagner told his collaborators at the end of one Bayreuth festival, "Next year we'll do it differently." That is why the tradition which the Met seeks to restore is at best an illusion, at worst an error.

This conservatism has had doubly invidious consequences: boring in itself, it has also provoked the wrong kind of rebellion. Operas, if they are worth performing, must inform us about ourselves. Does this imply that they should take up residence in some postindustrial city in the late twentieth century? In the last decade, Peter Sellars has transferred Don Giovanni to Spanish Harlem, Figaro and Susanna to the Trump Tower, and made Despina the proprietrix of a diner somewhere across town. These were decent enough jokes, but they raised more problems than they resolved. Is *Le Nozze di Figaro* merely a television sitcom? Forced into relevance, opera is equated with yesterday's yellowing news headlines—the source for John Adams's *Nixon in China* and *The Death of Klinghoffer*, and for a Handel production which Sellars ought really to have entitled *Reagan in Egypt*. Are there no worlds elsewhere?

Sellars and some of his colleagues—at least as flat-mindedly literal, in this respect, as the directors favoured by the Met—assume that any work which has the misfortune to be set outside the United States should be hustled onto the next flight and rushed through immigration. At an Opera America conference in Houston in 1988, I was startled to hear Stephen Wadsworth complain about the irrelevance of *La Traviata*. "What does it mean to me?" he moaned. "In America? In 1988?" (1988 was then the last word in trendy modernity.) I wondered, listening to him, whether love, sacrifice, forgiveness, moral hypocrisy, the connection between money and family, and the disconnection between pleasure and procreation were all so un-American and old-fashioned. Perhaps New York City Opera's production of *Traviata* answered Wadsworth's objection by infecting Violetta with AIDS, not tuberculosis. Wadsworth himself, staging *Il Ritorno d'Ulisse in Patria* in Milwaukee, made the homecoming hero a Vietnam veteran. Shouldn't he, like Sellars with Adams, have found someone to compose a new and more topical opera for him, rather than using Monteverdi's as a pretext? At large in Europe, Sellars insists on expatriating the operas he directs to Los Angeles. His *Die Zauberflöte* at Glyndebourne was set under the Ventura freeway, his *Pelléas et Mélisande* in Amsterdam took place in the Santa Monica slide area. Is he so terribly homesick? Or so utterly unimaginative?

This glib, cosmetic contemporariness goes against the nature of the art. Opera has its origins in myth, as I argue throughout this book; its songs of love and death keep alive primordial memories. This is why there has never been an easy accommodation between opera and realism. After a long, fraught attempt to verify opera, to prove its verisimilitude, Puccini ended his career with the mythological (and mythic) *Turandot*. There are other, more economical and instantaneous ways to check on where we are today: the season's most pertinent new play, for instance. Opera tells less timely and more fatalistic truths about who we are, and why—so long as our aboriginal emotions direct us—we will never change. In an amnesiac world, its fables keep the past alive.

There have been efforts to administer a lobotomy. In 1995 the playwright Michael Frayn rewrote the text of *La Belle Hélène* for an English National Opera production. It seemed to him self-evident that no one knew or wanted to know about the Trojan war; it didn't matter that it was the story of how a world expired, which Offenbach, satirising his self-indulgent, lustful deities, took to be a warning of moral calamity in the French Second Empire. Frayn preferred a somewhat less significant anecdote about the backstage intrigues involved in putting on a show, and called his version *La Belle Vivette*. Why bother keeping Offenbach's score, if you dispense with the drama he chose to set?

Meanwhile Sellars was vandalising Hindemith's *Mathis der Maler* in a production for the Royal Opera. While Frayn assumed that we have all forgotten the Trojan war and are none the worse for it, Sellars drew a blank on the relatively recent past. Hindemith composed *Mathis der Maler* during the Third Reich, and through the figure of the Gothic painter Grünewald he made a coded assault on the complicity between art and power in the 1930s. Like the persecuted Hindemith later in the decade, Mathis chooses internal exile when his hope for reform is disappointed. The tormented altarpiece he paints is a cryptic autobiography: he can contribute to the struggle without shouldering arms, because art finds a way of atoning for the distresses of life. *Mathis der Maler*, one of the noblest works of our century, struggles to comprehend Germany's political catastrophe and to rationalise Hindemith's personal tragedy.

Sellars acknowledged none of this. Inevitably the opera underwent relocation to California. The set was a cantilevered house in the Hollywood hills, unmoored by the latest earthquake. Hindemith's text was slangily vulgarised to make it feel more at home. When Hindemith's marauding peasants molest the Gräfin Helfenstein, Sellars—in scorching red surtitles, duplicated by a dot matrix board which sent the same message scuttling along the portico of the subsiding house—had them promise to "give her a good fuck." The book-burning fascists became the LAPD; for Hitler's massacre of European civilisation, Sellars substituted Jesse Helms, Newt Gingrich, and their threat to the National Endowment for the Arts. This facile liberal pique trivialised the work, which is about people losing their lives, not performance artists having their grants revoked. Sellars saw to it, however, that all ended happily, manoeuvring a final clinch between Mathis and Ursula. Never mind that Hindemith, who meant the opera to end with the artist's choice of inconsolable solitude, had omitted the heroine from this scene. Suffering through the performance, I forgave Schenk for much of his dogged literalness. At the Met, we would at least have been shown Grünewald's Isenheim altarpiece, without which the psychodrama of Mathis is unintelligible. I assume that the Mathis of Sellars had abandoned fuddy-duddy painting to make those looped, dopey videos which flickered throughout on half a dozen television monitors.

At stake are the competing rights of creator and interpreter. Sellars the self-advertising auteur had blithely replaced the work's concerns with an agenda of his own. Hindemith's response to this streetsmart customising is easy to imagine. In fact he wrote an opera, *Cardillac*, about the creator's jealous guarding of his copyright: the jeweller, reluctant to part with his precious creations, kills his clients to retrieve them.

I realise that I should be wary about laying down principles, since in this book I have defended Vickers against Britten, who disapproved of his Grimes—and Vickers even made some deft emendations to the opera's text, though his purpose was to suppress any hint of sexual misconduct rather than, like Sellars, to naughtily titillate us with four-letter words. In the theatre, everything depends on how well an interpretation "plays." Performance is provisional; nothing is sacred. At the end of his Met *Don Giovanni*, Zeffirelli has Leporello place his list of Giovanni's conquests on a memorial tablet inscribed with Mozart's name and the dates of his birth and death. He does so reverently, as if laying a wreath. The scurrilous trickbook has somehow become the hallowed text of the opera, returned to its rightful owner. This, I guess, was Zeffirelli's reproof to his irresponsible successors. But fidelity is no virtue in the theatre, and the dutiful communion with the creator which Zeffirelli claims for himself by the gesture—a new master-servant relationship, renegotiating that between Giovanni and Leporello—is the sanctimonious cover for a lack of fresh insights. Judgments can only be practical. The Grimes of Vickers happened to be more plausible than that of Pears. Sellars, with his vapid gripes about the cops and the Republican right, enfeebled Hindemith rather than improving on him.

It helps, when a director is intent on superseding the creator, if the work in question was only half an opera to begin with. In 1995 David Pountney—whose auteurist misdemeanours include a *Carmen* set among wrecked cars in a sleazy junkyard and a *Pelléas* in which Mélisande was Baby Doll, lolling in her cot and salaciously sucking her thumb—directed Purcell's *The Fairy Queen* for English National Opera. *The Fairy Queen* is a so-called "semi-opera": Purcell composed musical interludes to be performed between the spoken acts of *A Midsummer Night's Dream*. These episodic diversions have no innate connection with each other or with Shakespeare's play. At Covent Garden earlier in 1995, Graham Vick solved the problem of "semi-opera" by performing *King Arthur* in its arduous entirety, both Purcell's music and Dryden's oratorical pageant. That worked, because the play—impudently reinventing the myth of heroic Britain, with much imperial bluster and some mellifluous propaganda for the wool trade—was unfamiliar yet also ironically timely, now that Britain's proud insularity has been breached by the Channel tunnel and the kingdom is being merged into the United States of Europe. But why should an audience which knew *A Midsummer Night's Dream* sit through another performance of it just to hear Purcell's interludes?

Pountney therefore jettisoned the text altogether and composed his own plot to join up the musical passages. In Pountney's version, Purcell's songs and dances reinterpreted the play, conducting a quartet of lovers through a midnight wood on a quest for their sundered other halves, superintended by fairies who were true erotic demons. The music is great, so why not take it seriously? Purcell composed a comic duet for a lusty bass and a shrinking counter-tenor, who plays a shepherdess. Pountney, refusing to consider this a mere skit, developed its suggestion into a sub-plot about male sexual unions. Elsewhere the music had to be saved from a retrograde dramatic situation. The interlude to the fourth act celebrates Oberon's birthday. Royal anniversaries no longer incite much popular joy in a Britain which has doubts about its own greatness. Pountney turned over the festivities to a raggle-taggle band of ambitious amateurs, including two counter-tenors who sang "Let the fifes and the clarions" dressed as Elvis impersonators, while the grumpy monarch, disgusted by the sycophancy of his court, abdicated to his coffin. The last interlude, set by Purcell in a Chinese garden, became a rally of Red Guards brandishing their books of Maoist proverbs. Since they are singing about daybreak and the irradiation of the gloomy world, made bright by the sun's rebirth, what more logical location for their sentiments than a society undergoing a social and sexual revolution? Questionable in theory it may have been, but it was wittily and fancifully executed, which is what matters; and it made an ungainly, unorthodox masterpiece work once more in the theatre.

Still, it was odd to hear a sparse orchestra of authentic instruments accompanying a production which was so riotously, freakishly inauthentic: one of the witchy crones stored her veils in a derelict washing machine, also used for whipping up spells. This is a puzzling contradiction in contemporary opera, widened over the last decade by the enthusiasm for period bands.

At Drottningholm they close the gap between past and present. The conductor swelters in a wig, and stage directors are restricted to a facsimile of eighteenth-century practice, employing flimsy all-purpose scenic flats, wheezing wind machines and rotating waves on rollers. Only the audience in its mufti is excluded from the charade, and allowed the benefit of modern plumbing during intermissions. But at Glyndebourne in 1991 I heard a *Così fan tutte* played (by the Orchestra of the Age of Enlightenment) with astringent tonalities Mozart would have recognised but set on an Art Deco ocean liner which might have mystified him; and at the Opéra-Comique in 1993 I heard Les Arts Florissants perform Rameau's *Les Indes Galantes* with transverse flutes, Basque drums and clarino trumpets while onstage the jiving Indians smoked marijuana and Howard Crook exactly mimicked the slurred vocalism and shimmying gait of Elvis.

Though verbal texts can be revised or even erased, no liberties—according to the current fashion—may be taken with musical texts. Is this because librettists are held to be the poor relations of composers? Or does it, more interestingly, recognise a disparity between the different senses which opera engages? We are expected to have eighteenth-century ears, but are permitted to keep our twentieth-century eyes. Sight is fickle, impatient, always on the lookout for novelties; perhaps hearing is a more retentive, conservative sense. The ears are intent on remembering: we learn things (melodies, for instance) by having them repeated to us. The structure of music—with its recurrent motifs and echoes, its invisible architecture based on gradations of tempo—depends on the training of memory, which is why so much of Proust's personal history can be compressed into the phrase from Vinteuil's sonata. It's the same strange disparity you become aware of in the Roman amphitheatre at Orange or, several city blocks from the stage, in the top of the Family Circle at the Met. Visually you may be distant, but aurally you seem improbably close, thanks to a quirk of the acoustics. Sound, unlike sight, can travel, so it's attractive to think when listening to a period orchestra that its sounds are making their way to us from out of the past. The eyes gaze ahead; but our ears have been placed behind us.

Opera, uniting opposed arts, also brings together senses with different aptitudes. Wagner, theorising about the Gesamtkunstwerk, assumed that the constituent arts and senses would be fused in the overloaded ecstasy which the romantics called synaesthesia: sound was translated into colour, as in Baudelaire's account of the prelude to *Lohengrin*, and light, as Tristan cries out in his delirium, became audible. But there is another view of opera, prevalent before Wagner and after him, which keeps the contributing arts separate. Stravinsky disliked the narcotic effect of romanticism, and disassembled Wagner's merger of the arts. He relegated the singers in *Le Rossignol* to the orchestra pit, with dancers as their onstage deputies. In his *Oedipus Rex* the characters of the tragedy sing as if from behind hieratic masks. These are their public faces; private agonies can only be revealed when they are out of our sight. Brecht in his essay on *Mahagonny* also insisted that music must stand apart from drama, critically analysing it. In the *Sieben Todsünden* of Weill and Brecht, one Anna dances through life while the other snarls a vocal commentary. These reconstructions of the form returned to the baroque habit of alternating speech and song or music and dance, rather than compounding them.

So did Mark Morris when in 1995 he filmed his production of *Dido and Aeneas*, in league with the Canadian period band Tafelmusik. The voices are marginalised or reduced to noises off, while dancers enact the drama. Morris himself plays both a vampy, man-eating Dido and a strung out, sarcastic Sorceress. Not needing to bother about vocal production, which rigidly cramps your deportment, the dancers abandon themselves to music's emotional narrative. *Dido and Aeneas* can be mournfully static: dying, Dido becomes a monument to herself. Reconceiving the work as a ballet, Morris releases the fury and frenzy in it. Though he may not be a singer, Morris is certainly an operatic performer: his body is so eloquent that he does not need a voice. Perhaps this is what Edward Gordon Craig meant by the über-marionette, the transparent being who would, he hoped, supersede the actor and make his imitative tricks redundant. "Its ideal," Craig said in 1911 of the über-marionette, "will not be the flesh and blood but rather the body in trance—it will aim to clothe itself with a deathlike beauty while exhaling a living spirit." That state of trance, exhaling the spirit in song, is another way of describing the transfigurations I wrote about in the last pages of this book.

After romanticism, too profuse with flesh and blood, the only way ahead was to go backwards. Strauss exchanged Wagner's influence for that of Mozart; Weill and Hindemith chose to derive their styles from the polyphony of Bach. Hence the revival of commedia dell'arte or the puppet play, theatrical forms which expose the determinism of our desires: we are hapless bodies, governed by gravity and our appetites. Zerbinetta and her troupe in *Ariadne auf Naxos* or the Italian comedians in Stravinsky's *Pulcinella* deride the willfulness of characters in romantic opera. Brecht's Anna II is a marionette whose strings are pulled by the mercenary Anna I; and Hindemith composed his scabrous farce *Das Nusch-Nuschi* for performance, allegedly, by Burmese marionettes.

The operatic repertory also grows backward. It may not matter so very much if recently commissioned works about Harvey Milk or Malcolm X do not earn a second hearing. There have been many additions to the canon since I wrote this book, although none of them were written during the past decade. Occasionally an anniversary prompts companies with a conscience to perform works they might otherwise neglect. Purcell died in 1695, Hindemith was born in 1895. Therefore 1995 marked their particular rebirth, which is why—although neither of them featured in my book, except for a glance at *Dido and Aeneas* as a footnote to *Les Troyens*—they figure so prominently in my second thoughts.

In opera, the new is usually the old, rediscovered. This was the case during the 1970s with the rediscovery of the bel canto composers, or of early Verdi. It's now apparent that the church is even broader and more ecumenical, not so narrowly synchronised with the development and decline of romanticism. My section on the repertory assumes that, for practical purposes, opera begins with Mozart and ends with Berg. Today I would pay more attention to Handel, who has been revealed—thanks to Nicholas Hytner's *Xerxes* in London, Harry Kupfer's *Giustino* in Berlin, and Richard Jones's *Giulio Cesare* in Munich—as one of the great musical dramatists. Those productions made clear the rich variety of Handel's achievement: Hytner concentrated on social comedy, Kupfer emphasised political satire, and Jones characteristically stressed the freakish malevolence of characters who are, he pointed out, not very different from the leisured elite of gods in *Das Rheingold*.

Further back, groups like Les Arts Florissants or Les Musiciens du

Louvre have investigated the alliance between opera and French neoclassical tragedy. Romantic composers made sure that tragic misery was softened and sublimated by music. Verdi's Desdemona has her "Ave Maria," and the Elektra of Strauss and Hofmannsthal declares before she collapses that rapture streams from her body like a fountain of jubilant sound. Neoclassical tragedy appeals to our antiromantic century because of its harshness. The son accused of incest may be spared in Rameau's *Hippolyte et Aricie*, but his father Thésée, who believed the calumnies of Phèdre, will never see him again. André Campra's *Idomenée* presses the conflict between generations to a cruel outcome fortuitously and overfondly evaded by Mozart in *Idomeneo*. The Daphne of Strauss escapes ravishment by changing into a tree, and the metamorphosis is accomplished by the soprano's voice, blissfully merging with nature. But in Lully's *Atys* the jealous goddess Cybèle turns the hero, whom she loves, into a tree; she may save him from suicide by doing so, but what use is he to her in this uningratiating form? She remains inconsolable.

These characters, persecuted by deities who symbolise their own irrational instincts, lack the proud antisocial autonomy which romanticism bestows on its holy sinners: Rameau's Phèdre makes her shaming confession to a dismayed chorus. Nor do they delight in dramatising their anguish, tearing passions to tatters. Lully and Rameau demonstrate that music need not take words by storm. Their art of declamation or recitation has gained belatedly in truthfulness: Lulu, after all, speaks her most heartfelt appeal to Schön, rather than singing it. The sparseness and severity of the accompaniment in Charpentier's *Médée* leaves the character nowhere to hide. Grand gestures and maenadic hysteria, permitted to the sorceress in Cherubini's *Medea*, are not possible here. Charpentier's character—stunningly performed by Lorraine Hunt in 1993 with Les Arts Florissants—twists and turns through a succession of moods, trying out a variety of tactics as she pleads, negotiates and threatens. Her revenge when it comes is more psychologically credible and, in the treacherous court where she has been stigmatised as an outsider, more justifiable. Jean-Marie Villégier's production did away with the flying machines of baroque theatre, denying Médée the escape route through the air of which she boasts in her last taunting words to Jason. These are people who must operate, like the rest of us, on level ground, scheming and perhaps killing in order to defend themselves.

Modernism, with its mockeries of Wagner, seceded from the recent past, but made remoter pasts available. Composers in the late twentieth century collaborate happily with the founder of opera, treating him as a contemporary. Henze, in his reorchestration of Monteverdi's *Ritorno d'Ulisse* at Salzburg in 1987, sent the itinerant hero off on a tour of exotic, anachronistic musical worlds. Alexander Goehr at Covent Garden in 1995 volunteered to compose all over again Monteverdi's lost opera *Arianna*, using the extant libretto.

In future, with this augmented repertory, opera may seem a less obsessively romantic form. Surely the dual dominion of Italy and Germany will be weakened. Russian opera, as a result of political changes during the last decade, is no longer represented in the West by two works each of Mussorgsky and Tchaikovsky. The national repertory has been released from political conscription, and from the dreary pomp of those Bolshoi stagings, laid on to entertain dozing dignitaries. In 1990 the conductor Valery Gergiev borrowed the Royal Opera production of *Boris Godunov*, directed by the exiled Tarkovsky, and performed it at the Kirov in St. Petersburg with an English bass, Robert Lloyd, as Boris: a calculated challenge to xenophobia and official blacklisting. For me this discovery began, in the declining days of the Soviet Union and its fractious empire, with Andrei Serban's production of *Prince Igor* at Covent Garden. Borodin's opera about the folly and fallacy of empire may be unfinished, but so is history. There was, as he remarked, "no definite victory over the Polovtsian Tartars." Like Mussorgsky, he deals with peoples not persons, attempting to answer the question over which Tolstoy broods in the epilogue to *War and Peace*: "What force moves the nations?"

Gergiev's troupe, forced by penury to proselytise abroad, has been responsible for a series of restitutions: *The Fiery Angel* with Gorchakova and Leiferkus at the Kirov in 1991, Tchaikovsky's *Iolanthe* at the Royal Albert Hall in 1993. And there are many more masterpieces where these came from! In 1994 the company began touring Rimsky-Korsakov's *Sadko* and his *Legend of the Invisible City of Kitezh*. The first is an innocently fantastic celebration of maritime trade. The adventurer Sadko weds the daughter of the King of the Sea; for Rimsky-Korsakov, man commandeers the elements without suffering the guilt which afflicts the characters of the *Ring*. *Kitezh*, known as the Russian *Parsifal*, is about the recourse to mysticism at times of political disaster. The menaced city simply disappears, instantly promoting itself to paradise. These are operas of ideas: as in the *Ring* or *Parsifal*, scenic marvels—the underwater court in *Sadko*, the transubstantiating mist in *Kitezh*—act out the relations between man, nature and supernature. Opera, from Rameau's *Les Boréades*, with its exploration of windy outer space, to Hindemith's opera about the astronomer Kepler, *Die Harmonie der Welt*, has always been what baroque theorists called a "theatre of the world," a spectacle able to contain the cosmos.

Often since 1986, when asked by editors to write something about opera, my excuse for refusing was that I had no new ideas. It is good to realise, returning to this book, that I have not said all I have to say on the subject, and even better to discover that I have not heard all there is to hear. The time has not yet come to retire with my memories.

Index

Abbado, Claudio, 302, 314
Abduction from the Seraglio, The, see Entführung aus dem Serail, Die
Academy of Music (New York), 246
Adam, Theo, 316, 336
Adriana Lecouvreur (Cilea), 194, 195, 197, 201, 358–59
Aeneid (Virgil), 136
Aeschylus, 208, 282, 283
Africaine, L' (Meyerbeer), 131–32, 137
Age of Innocence, The (Wharton), 247, 250
Ägyptische Helena, Die (Strauss), 62–63, 210
Aida (Verdi):
   music of, 45, 135, 157–58, 159
   performances of, 281–82, 286, 301, 302–3, 324, 331
   text of, 66, 72, 135, 147, 148, 153, 156–58, 159, 161, 279
Akhnaten (Glass), 45, 66, 232, 235, 275
Albert Herring (Britten), 40–41, 223, 235, 262–63
Alceste (Gluck), 19, 22, 89, 91, 127, 152, 208, 349
Alcina (Handel), 88
Alfano, Franco, 201
allegro, 123
Allen, Thomas, 337
Amour des Trois Oranges, L' (Prokofiev), 261, 294
Andrea Chénier (Giordano), 90, 197–99, 257, 279, 284
Anna Bolena (Donizetti):
   performances of, 321, 327
   text of, 39, 40, 110, 118, 119
Apollo:
   Dionysus vs., 16, 23, 24, 31, 76,
213, 230–32
   in modern opera, 28–29
   as Monteverdian sun-god, 15, 21, 81, 213, 231
   Nietzsche on, 31, 32
   as opera's patron, 82, 232
Arabella (Strauss), 181
Ariadne auf Naxos (Strauss), 30–31, 194, 211, 212–14, 260, 348
Armida (Rossini), 88
Armide (Gluck), 88, 249
Armide (Haydn), 88
Armide et Renaud (Lully), 88
Aroldo (Verdi), 72
Auber, Daniel, 82
Auchincloss, Louis, 249, 257
Auden, W. H., 30, 108, 229, 230, 263
Aufstieg und Fall der Stadt-Mahagonny, Der (Brecht and Weill):
   performances of, 254, 354, 356
   text of, 27, 38, 42, 212, 216, 225–26, 228
Auvray, Jean-Claude, 299, 301
"Ave Maria" (*Otello*), 149, 164, 173

Bacchus, *see* Dionysus
Bach, Johann Sebastian, 78
Bacquier, Gabriel, 336
Baker, Janet, 89, 263, 348–49
ballets, 52, 60, 62, 64, 73, 88
Ballo in Maschera, Un (Verdi), 51–52, 148, 153, 155–56, 159, 160, 180
Baltsa, Agnes, 334–35, 349, 358
Barbiere di Siviglia, Il (Rossini), 14, 36, 51, 77, 110–11, 113, 119, 177, 196, 281, 300, 305
Bartered Bride, The (Smetana), 216, 266, 284
Bartók, Bela, 215–16

Bassarids, The (Henze), 30, 31, 230, 231, 360
Baudelaire, Charles-Pierre, 38, 171, 243
Bayreuth Festival:
   design of, 31, 170, 184–85, 324
   discomfort of, 260
   performances at, 185, 202, 259, 260, 286–87, 298, 299, 312, 313, 316, 324, 350
   Wagner at, 29, 31, 72, 167, 168, 170, 272
Beardsley, Aubrey, 171, 172, 294
Beaumarchais, Pierre Augustin Caron de, 100, 110, 209, 300, 305
Beckmesser (*Meistersinger*), 348
Beecham, Thomas, 76
Beethoven, Ludwig van:
   Cosima Wagner on, 179–80
   Fidelio, 13, 15, 84, 106, 123–29, 130, 166, 179, 260, 261, 284, 297–98, 308, 316
   humanism of, 128–29, 132
   non-operatic music by, 95, 97, 129, 245, 291
Behrens, Hildegard, 304, 306, 310, 332, 333, 348
Béjart, Maurice, 336
bel canto:
   Callas and, 319–20
   comedy of, 118–19, 127
   madness in, 40, 112–13, 118, 359–60
   romantic music of, 109–12, 117, 119–22, 150, 220
   technical perfection of, 21, 122, 314–15
Belle Hélène, La (Offenbach), 62
Bellini, Vincenzo:
   Capuleti, 117–18, 314–15
   Norma, 30, 31, 66, 84, 90, 109, 117–18, 120, 122, 131, 180, 236, 237, 303, 323–24, 328, 359
   Puritani, 39, 120–21, 131, 236
   Sonnambula, 117, 120, 121, 122, 327
Belmont, Mrs. August, 248, 249, 254–55
Berg, Alban:
   Lulu, 37–38, 42, 52, 85, 216, 219,

226, 227–28, 229, 312, 313–14, 355–56
   Wagner as progenitor of, 313
   "Wein," 38
   Wozzeck, 15, 26, 216, 217–19, 313, 238
Berganza, Teresa, 276, 335–36
Bergman, Ingmar, 271–72, 280
Beria, Lavrenty Pavlovich, 331
Berlin Opéra, 78, 333
Berlioz, Hector:
   Damnation, 57–58, 59, 161
   Harold en Italie, 57
   historical perspective in, 137, 139, 140, 142
   Requiem, 161
   Roméo et Juliette, 118, 239
   Troyens, 42, 58, 91, 95, 124, 132, 133, 135–37, 138–39, 140, 142, 161, 178, 254, 343, 349
Bernstein, Leonard, 118, 256, 289, 308, 312, 315–16
Besch, Anthony, 292
Bibiena family, 237, 327
Billington, Elizabeth, 359
Billy Budd (Britten), 223–24, 284, 348
Bing, Rudolf, 247, 254–55, 341
Birtwistle, Harrison, 216, 230, 231–32
Bizet, Georges:
   Pêcheurs, 73
   see also *Carmen*
blasphemy, 11, 60, 75–76, 78, 170, 176, 348, 352
Bluebeard's Castle (Bartók), 215–16
Bohème, La (Puccini):
   performances of, 257, 295–97, 354
   text of, 16, 189, 191, 195–96
Böhm, Karl, 316, 317, 340, 341, 353
Boito, Arrigo, 36, 61–62, 63, 153, 161–65, 283
Boris (*Boris Godunov*), 337
Boris Godunov (Mussorgsky):
   performances of, 252, 274, 297, 337
   text of, 133, 140, 141–43, 144, 146, 239
Borodin, Alexander, 133, 140
Borough, The (Crabbe), 344–45
Bouffes du Nord, 275, 279
Boulez, Pierre, 265, 308, 312–14

Bourgeois Gentilhomme, Le
(Molière), 212
Brecht, Bertolt:
epic theater of, 301
Mahagonny, 27, 38, 42, 212, 216,
225–26, 228, 254, 354, 356
on opera, 190, 227, 274
other works, 27, 52, 225
Bride of Lammermoor, The (Scott),
112–13
brindisi, 36–38
Britten, Benjamin:
Albert Herring, 40–41, 223, 235,
262–63
Billy Budd, 223–24, 284, 348
Death in Venice, 16, 216, 230–31
Midsummer Night's Dream, 15, 16,
218, 224–25, 263
Peter Grimes, 16, 26–27, 39–40,
235, 344–46
Turn of the Screw, 16, 216, 224
Brook, Peter:
Carmen, 275, 280, 283, 288–90,
291
on opera, 274–75, 279, 280, 282
on theater, 274–75, 279, 280, 311,
312
Brooklyn Academy of Music, 247
Brünnhilde (*Ring*), 259, 316, 332,
339, 350–51
Bruson, Renato, 309, 358
Bulganin, Nikolay Aleksandrovich,
331
Bumbry, Grace, 303
Burgess, Anthony, 293
Bury, John, 263
Busoni, Ferruccio, 63–65
Butlin, Roger, 261–62
Butterfly (*Madama Butterfly*), 323,
359
Byron, George Gordon, Lord, 57, 337

cabalettas, 160
Caballé, Montserrat, 257, 330–31,
332, 358–59
Cain, James M., 242–45
Calisto, La (Cavalli), 81, 82, 235,
275–77
Callas, Maria, 318–29
as Amina, 327

as Anna Bolena, 321, 327
as Carmen, 325, 329
directors on, 303–4, 327–29
as Eboli, 325
as Elisabetta, 329
on film, 325, 328–29
as Gioconda, 329
as Giulia, 327
as Iphigénie, 327
as Kundry, 319
as Lady Macbeth, 318–19, 326
as Lauretta, 321
as Lucia, 319–20
as Medea, 320–21, 324–25, 328–29
as Norma, 323–24, 328
as Paolina, 323
as Santuzza, 329
self-flagellation of, 321–23, 324–25,
329
as Tosca, 303, 304, 323, 325–28,
330
Vickers on, 324
as Violetta, 318, 319, 323, 327–28
Camerata, 19, 20, 25, 30, 90, 167, 190
Campanello, Il (Donizetti), 110, 112
Canio (*Pagliacci*), 354
capitalism, 176, 237, 247, 250, 287,
295
Cappuccilli, Piero, 301
Capriccio (Strauss), 213, 260
Capuleti e I Montecchi, I (Bellini),
117–18, 314–15
Career in C Major (Cain), 243
Carmen (Bizet):
adaptations of, 243–45, 267,
269–70, 275, 280, 283
character of heroine, 250, 257, 270,
279, 288–89, 291, 325, 329,
333–36
eroticism in, 42–43, 49, 52, 191,
216
films of, 243–45, 269–71, 291, 312,
325
music of, 12, 43, 45, 46, 48–50, 51,
53, 197, 271
performances of, 250, 270–71, 275,
279, 280, 283, 288–92, 303,
310–11, 324, 325
text of, 11, 13, 36, 37, 38, 47, 50,
51, 55, 64, 191, 193, 214, 226,
227, 236, 301

Carmen Jones, 267, 269–70
Carreras, José, 256, 257, 334–35
Carrière, Jean-Claude, 289
Caruso, Enrico, 236, 250–51, 357
"Casta diva" (*Norma*), 120, 122, 359
Cavalieri, Emilio de, 66
Cavalieri, Lina, 303
Cavalleria Rusticana (Mascagni):
    performances of, 303, 329
    text of, 12, 37, 64, 72, 189, 191,
        195, 244
Cavalli, Pier Francesco, 81, 82,
        275–77
Cendrillon (Massenet), 115
Cenerentola, La (Rossini), 114, 115,
        119, 281
Chagall, Marc, 239, 253–54, 257,
        258, 272
Charles X, King of France, 115, 129
Charlotte (*Werther*), 14
Charpentier, Gustave, 187, 189, 196,
        246
Chéreau, Patrice, 176, 259, 282, 299,
        313, 350
Cherubini, Luigi, 320–21, 324
Cherubino (*Nozze di Figaro*), 335–36
Christianity:
    criticism of, 11, 62, 78, 200, 206,
        207–8, 285
    deified artist and, 168–69, 172–74,
        184, 185
    French opera and, 72–73, 270
    operatic symbolism and, 195, 304
    paganism vs., 19, 38, 172–74, 185
    see also religion
Christoff, Boris, 337
Christ Stopped at Eboli, 269
Cilea, Francesco, 194
classicism:
    formal regulation in, 280–81
    of Gluck, 96, 106, 263
    of Monteverdi, 81, 93, 95, 105, 106
    Mozart's transition from, 94–97,
        305–7
    mythology of, 174, 200
    revivals of, 25, 188, 314
    romanticism vs., 76, 268
    static characters of, 88–89
Clemenza di Tito, La (Mozart),
        93–97, 305–7, 359
Clever, Edith, 273
Cocteau, Jean, 76, 229, 233

Cologne Opera, 279
coloratura, 33, 87, 117, 213, 355, 360
comedy:
    of Dionysus, 35, 155
    in *Falstaff*, 148, 162, 165–66
    of operatic genres, 138, 190–91,
        221, 228
    in romantic opera, 32, 111–13,
        115–16, 118–19, 129
    of Shakespeare, 78, 137, 263
    tragedy vs., 103, 113, 138, 146,
        153–55
Comte Ory,Le (Rossini), 34, 115–16
conductors, 308–17
Constant, Marius, 290
Contes des Hoffmann, Les (Offen-
    bach), 26, 34, 215, 287, 358
Corsaro, Frank, 292, 294
Così Fan Tutte (Mozart):
    music of, 92, 93, 95, 97, 102, 103,
        179
    performances of, 278, 284
    text of, 97, 98, 102–5, 106
Covent Garden:
    Aida, 281–82, 286
    Alceste, 349
    Andrea Chénier, 279
    Boris Godunov, 274, 294, 337
    Capuleti, 314–15
    Carmen, 334–35
    Contes d'Hoffmann, 287, 358
    design of, 239
    Don Giovanni, 303, 336–37
    Donnerstag, 29
    Elektra, 340, 341
    Falstaff, 303, 308–9
    Götterdämmerung, 298–99
    Lucia, 359
    Otello, 344
    Pagliacci, 354
    Pelléas, 312
    Peter Grimes, 345
    Rosenkavalier, 274, 287, 358
    Salome, 279, 310, 349
    Samson, 88, 343, 349
    Siegfried, 350
    Simon Boccanegra, 358
    Tosca, 303, 325–27, 330–331
    Traviata, 294
    Tristan, 352, 353
Cox, John, 261–62
Crabbe, George, 40, 344–45

Crawford, Joan, 243
Crespin, Régine, 257, 316, 333–34
"Critic, The" (Weegee), 252
"culinary" opera, 44, 190, 212, 226
Culshaw, John, 265–66
Cunning Little Vixen, The (Janáček),
  14, 145, 216, 220–21
curtain calls, 108, 356

Dafne (Peri), 213
Dagon, 16, 66, 69
d'Albert, Eugen, 188–89
Dali, Salvador, 279
Dalila (*Samson et Dalila*), 257, 349
Dallas Opera, 320, 328, 352
Damiani, Luciana, 302
Damnation de Faust, La (Berlioz),
  57–58, 59, 161
Damned, The, 327
D'Annunzio, Gabriele, 75, 155, 187
Dante Alighieri, 71, 187, 199, 200
Daphne (Strauss), 14, 82, 213
da Ponte, Lorenzo, 100, 102
Darwin, Charles, 142, 189
Davies, Peter Maxwell, 275
Davis, Colin, 345
death:
  musical mysticism of, 52–54
  onstage, 356–58
  opera singers on, 329, 355, 356–57
  suicide, 86
Death in Venice (Britten), 16, 216,
  230–31
Death in Venice, Visconti, 327
Debussy, (Achille) Claude, 75, 203–4,
  239, 312, 313, 357
Delibes, Léo, 66, 73
della Mirandola, Pico, 19, 23
de Molina, Tirso, 43
de Sabata, Victor, 318
Desdemona (*Otello*), 359
Devils of Loudon, The (Penderecki),
  56
Dexter, John, 254, 284
diabolism, 24, 30, 55, 62, 65, 105,
  239–41, 243, 300
Dialogues des Carmelites (Poulenc),
  14, 216, 222–23, 284
Dickinson, G. Lowes, 108
Dido and Aeneas (Purcell), 133–34
Didon (*Troyens*), 349
Dionysus:

Apollo vs., 16, 23, 24, 31, 76, 213,
  230–32
comedy of, 35, 155
disruptive force of, 45, 78, 232
drink and, 33–38, 40–41, 219, 228
madness and, 30, 39–40
modern Teutonic myth and,
  230–31
Nietzchean tragedy and, 30–34, 67,
  191; 230, 306
rituals of, 151, 209, 213
Wagner's heroes and, 76, 167, 184
directors:
  on Callas, 303–4, 327–29
  conductors and, 310–12
  of filmed opera, 266–74
  historical interpretations by,
    292–307
  on Mozart, 279, 281
  on theater vs. opera, 280, 283–84,
    288
  as theatrical innovators, 274–91
di Stefano, Giuseppe, 329
dithyrambs, 31, 33, 45, 228
Doktor Faust (Busoni), 63–65
Domingo, Plácido, 270–71, 304, 332,
  343–44, 349, 358
Don Alvaro (Rivas), 139
Don Carlos (Verdi):
  performances of, 247, 285, 301–2,
    303, 309, 325, 329, 358
  text of, 72, 135, 147, 148, 156–57,
    159, 180
Don Giovanni: (Mozart):
  character of hero, 269, 336–37,
    348
  erotic imperative in, 42–44, 49,
    51–52, 64, 97, 106, 171, 193,
    216
  film of, 267–69, 270, 299
  influence of, 154, 156, 229, 241
  music of, 14, 43–44, 45, 46–48, 50,
    53, 56, 94, 99, 111
  performances of, 193, 242, 260,
    269, 293–94, 303, 336–37, 348
  text of, 11, 12–13, 15, 16, 31–32,
    34, 36, 38, 45–47, 50, 66–67, 88,
    94, 97, 101–3, 109, 110, 114,
    146, 226, 309, 335
Donizetti, Gaetano:
  Anna Bolena, 39, 40, 110, 118,
    119, 321, 327

Donizetti, Gaetano, *continued*
  Campanello, 110, 112
  Don Pasquale, 12, 112, 119
  Elisir d'Amore, 11–12, 117, 119, 322
  Fille du Régiment, 118
  Lucia, 12, 14, 39, 40, 112–13, 117, 120, 257, 319–20, 259–60
  Lucrezia Borgia, 35–36, 110
  Maria Stuarda, 118, 119
  Poliuto, 323
  Roberto Devereux, 118
Don Juan (Byron), 337
Donna del Lago, La (Rossini), 12, 119, 120
Donnerstag (Stockhausen), 28–29, 235
Don Pasquale (Donizetti), 12, 112, 119
Dorati, Antol, 311–12
Dostoyevsky, Fyodor, 145, 337
drama:
  active individualism of, 125, 151
  music vs., 104, 108, 151, 163–64, 213–14, 224, 273, 278–91, 311, 312, 313, 340
  realism in, 169, 192
dreams, 56, 120, 142–43, 174–75, 285–86, 300
Dreigroschenoper, Die (Brecht and Weill), 27, 225
Drexel, Mrs. John, 250
Dudley, William, 261
Duke (*Rigoletto*), 299, 300
Dumas, Alexandre, 13, 147, 294
Duse, Eleanora, 303

Edinburgh Festival, 270–71, 335, 340
Edward VII, King of England, 239
Eight Songs for a Mad King (Davies), 275
Ein Heldenleben (Strauss), 178
Einstein on the Beach (Glass), 232, 235
Either/Or (Kierkegaard), 43–45
Elektra (Strauss):
  performances of, 92, 338–42
  text of, 14, 30, 32, 39, 90, 208–9, 306, 359
Elisir d'Amore, L' (Donizetti), 111–12, 117, 119, 322

Enfant et les Sortilèges, L' (Ravel), 14–15, 216, 220–21
English National Opera:
  Butterfly, 275
  Fidelio, 297
  Mazeppa, 285
  Mosè, 293
  Orfeo, 276
  Rienzi, 292
  Rigoletto, 299
  Trovatore, 292
ensemble opera, 103–4, 130
Entführung aus dem Serail, Die (Mozart), 33–34, 93, 97–99, 260–61
Epidaurus, 324
Ernani (Verdi), 148–49, 161, 180, 301, 302
Eros, 16, 42–54, 231
Erwartung (Schönberg), 206, 211
Esclarmonde (Massenet), 73
Escurial, 302, 303, 305
Esterháza, 261
Eugene Onegin (Tchaikovsky), 144, 191–92
Euridice (Peri), 276
Euripides, 324
Evans, Geraint, 305, 347, 348
Everding, August, 340–41
Ewing, Maria, 288, 289, 336
expressionism, 206, 222, 315, 338

Faggioni, Piero, 270–71, 335–36
Falstaff (Verdi):
  music of, 15, 103, 162, 166, 223
  performances of, 262, 303, 308–9, 348
  text of, 35, 36, 51, 67, 114, 140, 147, 148, 156, 162, 165–66, 175, 226
Fanciulla del West, La (Puccini), 186–87
Fauré, Gabriel, 204–5
Faust (Goethe), 11, 56–57, 58, 61, 63, 64
Faust (Gounod):
  ballet in, 60, 62, 64
  influence of, 229, 240–41
  performances of, 58, 78, 247–48, 278, 279
  text of, 11, 55, 57, 58–61, 215, 239
Favola d'Orfeo, La (Monteverdi):

influence of, 24, 25, 28, 105, 166, 229, 236, 240
music of, 22, 28, 171, 216
performances of, 19, 276
text of, 13, 15, 19–23, 24, 27, 30, 31, 55, 81–82, 105, 126, 175, 240
Fedeltà Premiata, La (Haydn), 261
Felsenstein, Walter, 279
Feuersnot (Strauss), 207, 246
Fidelio (Beethoven):
  alternate overtures for, 123, 127–28, 308
  music of, 13, 123–29, 130, 179
  performances of, 127–28, 260, 261, 284, 297–98, 308, 316, 331, 332
  text of, 15, 84, 106, 123–29, 166
Fille du Régiment, La (Donizetti), 118
film:
  of *Bartered Bride*, 266–67
  of *Butterfly*, 273, 295
  of *Carmen*, 243–45, 267, 269–71, 291, 312, 325
  of *Cenerentola*, 281
  of *Clemenza*, 306–7
  of *Don Giovanni*, 267–69, 270, 299, 336
  of *Elektra*, 341–42
  of *Figaro*, 281
  of *Medea*, 325, 328–29
  non-operatic, 236, 243–45, 266, 269, 271, 291, 327
  of *Otello*, 311
  of *Pagliacci*, 354
  in presentation of *Lulu*, 219
  of *Rigoletto*, 281, 299–300
  of *Salome*, 354
  of *Tosca*, 325–26
  of *Traviata*, 273–74, 303, 304, 355
  Wagner and, 272–73, 282, 290, 311
  of *Zauberflöte*, 271–72, 280
Finnegans Wake (Joyce), 312
Fiery Angel, The (Prokofiev), 56
Firebird, The (Stravinsky), 239
Fischer-Dieskau, Dietrich, 265
Fitzcarraldo, 236
Flagstad, Kirsten, 248, 251
Flaubert, Gustave, 81, 113
Fledermaus, Die (Strauss), 34, 38, 211
Fliegende Holländer, Der (Wagner):

music of, 167, 169–70
performances of, 285–86, 299
text of, 56, 205, 286–87
Flying Dutchman, The, see *Fliegende Holländer, Der*
Fortuny, 249
Forza del Destino, La (Verdi), 139–40, 147, 148, 156, 159, 173
Four Last Songs (Strauss), 310
Francesca da Rimini (Zandonai), 187–88
Frau ohne Schatten, Die (Strauss), 83, 88, 211–12, 215, 338–39
Freeman, David, 275–76, 277
Freischütz, Der (Weber), 13, 55–56, 120, 216, 225, 238
French opera, 14, 52, 60, 72–73
French Revolution, 197–98, 294, 298
Freni, Mirella, 295, 358
Freud, Sigmund, 56, 176, 209, 342
Freyer, Achim, 78
Friedrich, Götz, 298–99, 341–42, 350, 354
From the House of the Dead (Janáček), 145–46

Galli Marié, Célestine, 291, 303
Garnier, Jean-Louis-Charles, 238–40, 241
Gatti-Casazza, Giulio, 248, 252, 255
Gautier, Théophile, 120, 239–40
Gay, John, 225
Gazza Ladra, La (Rossini), 129
George III, King of England, 275
Germany, psychological history of, 272, 273, 297, 327, 334
Gershwin, George, 27–28, 66, 215, 267
Gespensterbuch (Apel and Laun), 56
Ghiaurov, Nicolai, 337
Gianni Schicchi (Puccini), 199, 200, 321
Gioconda, La (Ponchielli), 12, 162, 329
Giordano, Umberto, 90, 197–99, 257, 279, 284
Giulini, Carlo Maria, 308–9, 317, 319, 323
Giulio Cesare in Egitto (Handel), 86–87, 89, 293

Glass, Philip, 232, 235
Glinka, Mikhail, 143
Gluck, Christoph Willibald von:
    Alceste, 19, 22, 89, 91, 127, 152,
        208, 349
    Armide, 88
    classicism of, 96, 106, 263
    Greek tragedy in, 208
    Iphigénie en Aulide, 30, 90–92,
        208
    Iphigénie en Tauride, 30, 90–92,
        208, 327
    Orfeo, 15, 20–23, 24, 26, 90–91,
        127, 171, 231, 263–64, 276, 324
    romantic revisions of, 91–92
    sacrificial rites in, 90–91, 94
Glyndebourne Festival, 259–64
    Albert Herring, 262–63
    Ariadne, 260
    Calisto, 276–77
    Capriccio, 260
    Carmen, 288, 289, 336
    Così, 284
    Don Giovanni, 260, 293–94, 337
    Entführung, 260–61
    Falstaff, 262
    Fedeltà, 261
    Fidelio, 260, 261, 284
    history of, 260
    Idomeneo, 261–62, 306
    Midsummer, 263
    Orfeo, 263–64
    Ritorno, 89, 349
    Three Oranges, 261, 294
    Zauberflöte, 262
Gobbi, Tito, 325–26, 336
Godard, Jean-Luc, 291
Goelet, Mrs. Ogden, 249
Goethe, Johann Wolfgang von:
    Faust, 11, 56–58, 61, 63, 64
    Italian journey of, 306
    on Mozart, 56, 107, 211
    Werther, 191, 192
Gogol, Nikolai, 220
Götterdämmerung (Wagner):
    music of, 177, 179, 181
    performances of, 298–99, 350
    recordings of, 265–66
    text of, 13, 31, 32, 36, 84, 132,
        138, 139, 167, 168, 180–81, 187,
        202, 205, 208, 209, 212, 230

Gould family, 246, 256
Gounod, Charles:
    Faust, 11, 55, 57–62, 64, 215, 229,
        239–41, 247–48, 278, 279
    personal background of, 60
    Roméo et Juliette, 117–18, 179
Gozzi, Carlo, 294
Greek tragedy:
    Italian opera and, 63
    Nietzsche on, 30–32, 67, 208–9,
        282
    opera performances and, 282–83
    Renaissance resurrection of, 20, 25,
        167
    sacrificial rites of, 90, 209
    satyr plays performed after, 173
    vulgarization of, 195
    Wagnerian opera and, 324
    see also tragedy
Gregor, Hans, 238
Grétry, André, 193
Grisi, Giuditta, 117
Gruberová, Edita, 300, 301
Guillaume Tell (Rossini), 129–30,
    131
Guiraud, Ernest, 288, 289
Gunther, John, 263
Gurre-Lieder (Schönberg), 205–6
Guthrie, Tyrone, 345

Hall, Peter:
    Albert Herring, 262
    Calisto, 276–77
    Carmen, 288, 336
    Don Giovanni, 260, 293
    Fidelio, 260, 284
    Midsummer Night's Dream, 263
    Oresteia, 283
    Orfeo, 263–64, 276
    Ring, 299
    Ritorno, 89
    on theater vs. opera, 280, 283–84,
        288
    Tristan, 353
Hamburg Opera, 285, 334
Hamersley, Lily, 247
Hamlet (Shakespeare), 33, 39, 47, 131
Hamlet (Thomas), 33, 39
Hammerstein, Oscar, II, 267
Hampe, Michael, 279, 284

Handel, George Frederick:
  Alcina, 88
  classic heroes of, 95, 215, 225
  Giulio Cesare, 86–87, 89, 293
  Messiah, 66, 78
  Orlando, 278
  Rinaldo, 86, 88
  Rodelinda, 87–88
  Samson, 66, 67–70, 76, 88, 354
  Saul, 278
  Semele, 45, 67, 68–69, 89
  Serse, 12, 86, 87, 118
  Tamerlano, 86, 88–89
  theater renounced by, 67, 77, 78,
    354
Hänsel und Gretel (Humperdinck),
  202, 258
Hanslick, Eduard, 241, 260
Harold en Italie (Berlioz), 57
Haugland, Auge, 273
Haussman, Georges-Eugène, 296
Haydn, (Franz) Joseph:
  Armide, 88
  on Billington portrait, 359
  Dionysian women in, 231
  Fedeltà Premiata, 261
  Orfeo ed Euridice, 23, 24
hedonism, 43, 51, 69, 85, 109, 115,
  129, 239, 303
Heine, Heinrich, 129, 131, 175
Helen of Troy, 60, 61, 62–63, 64
Henry, O. (William Sidney Porter),
  257
Henry IV (Shakespeare), 140
Henze, Hans Werner:
  Bassarids, 30, 31, 230, 231, 360
  Tristan, 207
  We Come to the River, 235
heroes:
  of Handel, 95, 215, 225
  rejection of, 186–88, 190, 192, 197,
    228
  in Wagner, 167, 168, 216
Herz, Joachim, 295, 297, 298
Herzog, Werner, 236
Heure Espagnole, L' (Ravel), 226
Heyward, Du Bose, 27, 28
historical opera:
  as accidental destiny, 139–40
  epic dramatizations of, 133
  as episodic charade, 140–43

political despair in, 145–46
  as recurrent fate, 133–39
  rhythmic momentum in, 123–27
  Russian patriotism in, 143–45
history:
  in Berlioz, 137, 139, 140, 142
  chronicling of, 142–43
  directorial interpretations of,
    292–307
  geography vs., 142
  of Germany, 272, 273, 297, 327,
    334
  individual persecuted by, 135, 139
  mythology vs., 298, 299
  of opera, 30, 128–29, 212, 214,
    225, 226, 230, 238
  in Russian opera, 140–45
  in Verdi, 139–40
  Wagnerian opera and, 138, 139,
    168, 175–76, 185
Hitler, Adolf, 133, 296, 301
Hockney, David, 262
Hoffmann, E. T. A., 15, 51, 102, 103,
  242, 358
Hofmannsthal, Hugo von:
  Ägyptische Helena, 62–63, 210
  Ariadne auf Naxos, 212–14
  Elektra, 90, 92, 208–9
  Frau ohne Schatten, 211–12
  on Goethe, 57
  Rosenkavalier, 209–10
Hogarth, William, 210, 229
Holbein, Hans, 327
Holst, Gustav, 15
Homer, 83, 204
Horne, Marilyn, 86, 256, 257, 289,
  333
Hour of the Wolf, 271
Hugo, Victor, 13, 35, 239, 240, 299
Huguenots, Les (Meyerbeer), 71, 130,
  131
humanism, 128–29, 132
Humperdinck, Engelbert, 202
Hunt, Leigh, 109–10, 112
Hytner, Nicholas, 292

Idomeneo (Mozart):
  performances of, 261–62, 305–6,
    307
  text of, 84, 91–92, 93–95, 152, 283

Idomeneo (Mozart), *continued*
impressionism, 203–4, 313
Incoronazione de Poppea, L' (Monteverdi):
  influence of, 215, 219, 225
  music of, 32, 82, 84
  text of, 12, 16, 33, 42, 66, 81,
    84–86, 118, 215
individuality:
  Apollo as god of, 32
  of drama, 151
  immersion of, 135, 139, 183–84
  romantic tragedy of, 103, 191
Iphigénie en Aulide (Gluck), 30,
  90–91, 208
  Wagner's revision of, 91, 92
Iphigénie en Tauride (Gluck), 30,
  90–91, 92, 208, 327
  Strauss's revision of, 91, 92
Iris (Mascagni), 190
Isaiah, 145
Isis, 45
Isolde (*Tristan*), 316–17, 341, 348
Italiana in Algeri, L' (Rossini):
  performances of, 281–82, 314
  text of, 16, 32, 38, 114–15, 119,
    130
Italian opera, 14, 52, 63, 72
  see also bel canto; realism; verismo

James, Henry, 224, 242, 247, 250, 255
Janáček, Leoš:
  Cunning Little Vixen, 14, 145,
    216, 220–21
  House of the Dead, 145–46
  Jenůfa, 145, 216–17, 218, 238, 357
  Kátya Kabanová, 146, 221
  Makropulos Case, 221, 226–27,
    228, 357
Jenny (*Mahagonny*), 354, 356
Jenůfa (Janáček), 145, 216–17, 218,
  238, 357
Jeritza, Maria, 333
John of Leyden, 71
Jones, Gwyneth, 341, 350–51, 356,
  358
Jongleur de Notre-Dame, Le (Massenet), 38
Jonson, Ben, 221
Jordan, Armin, 273
Joyce, James, 182, 312

Jung, Carl, 52, 298, 313

Kabale und Liebe (Schiller), 151–52
Kahn, Otto, 247
Kallman, Chester, 30, 230
Kant, Immanuel, 332
Karajan, Herbert von, 308, 309–11,
  316
Kátya Kabanová (Janáček), 146, 221
Kavanaugh, Mrs. George Washington,
  252
Keats, John, 109, 115, 120
Kempe, Rudolf, 259
Khovanshchina (Mussorgsky), 133,
  140–41, 143–44, 145
Kierkegaard, Søren, 43–46, 52, 102,
  231, 336
King Lear (Shakespeare), 142, 301,
  342
Kleiber, Carlos, 316–17, 340, 341,
  358
Klemperer, Otto, 316
Knappertsbusch, Hans, 316
Knie, Roberta, 352, 353
Knight, Richard, 251
Knot Garden, The (Tippett), 275
Kollo, René, 317
Komische Oper (East Berlin), 279
Kupfer, Harry, 286–87, 297–98

"La donna è mobile" (*Rigoletto*), 34,
  154
Lady Macbeth of Mtsensk (Shostakovitch), 219–20
La Guardia, Fiorello, 253
Lakmé (Delibes), 66, 73
Lalo, Edouard, 74, 203
language:
  music and, 20, 25–27, 57, 61–63,
    145–46, 214, 224, 239, 273, 356
  rationality of, 57, 61, 224
  sacred vs. secular, 76
Lanza, Mario, 243
La Scala (Teatro alla Scala):
  Aida, 301, 302–3
  Anna Bolena, 327
  Don Carlos, 301–3
  Ernani, 301, 302
  history of, 236, 237–38

Iphigénie en Tauride, 327
Lucia, 319–20
Macbeth, 318–19
Medea, 321
Nerone, 237
Norma, 322–23
Otello, 238
Poliuto, 323
Requiem (Verdi), 160
Simon Boccanegra, 238
Sonnambula, 327
Traviata, 319, 327–28
Vestale, 327
Lawrence, D. H., 182
Lazaridis, Stefanos, 301
Lehmann, Lilli, 323
Lehnhoff, Nikolaus, 259
Lenya, Lotte, 356
Leoncavallo, Ruggero, 189, 194
Leonora (Paër), 127
Leonore 40/50 (Liebermann), 127
Leonore no. 3 (Beethoven), 128
Leonore overtures, 123, 127–28, 308
Leppard, Raymond, 277
Leroux, Gaston, 240–42
Levi, Carlo, 269
Levine, James, 255, 351
Licht (Stockhausen), 28
Liebermann, Rolf, 127
liebestod:
  Isolde's music of, 53, 54, 150, 221,
    353, 360
  of Juliette, 118
  operatic mystery and, 20, 150
  performance of, 285, 356
Lied von der Erde, Das (Mahler),
  129, 205
Life for the Tsar, A (Glinka), 143
Lincoln Center, 239, 253–58
Lind, Jenny, 254
Lloyd, Robert, 273, 282, 337
Lohengrin (Wagner):
  music of, 15, 168, 170–71
  performances of, 242, 248, 311,
    324, 349–50
  text of, 67, 84, 170–71, 187, 215
Lohengrin parody (Nestroy), 357
Losey, Joseph, 267–69, 273, 299, 336
Louise (Charpentier), 187, 189, 196,
  246
Louvre (Paris), 246

love-death, 152, 228
  see also liebestod
love potions, 35, 40
Lucia (*Lucia di Lammermoor*), 257,
  319–20, 359–60
Lucia de Lammermoor (Donizetti):
  performances of, 257, 319–20,
    359–60
  text of, 12, 14, 39, 40, 112–13, 117,
    120, 359–60
Lucrezia Borgia (Donizetti), 35–36,
  110
Ludwig, Christa, 334, 347–48
Ludwig II, King of Bavaria, 242, 327
Luisa Miller (Verdi), 147, 151–52,
  196
Lully, Jean-Baptiste, 88, 212
Lulu (Berg):
  performances of, 312, 313–14,
    355–56
  text of, 37–38, 42, 52, 85, 216, 219,
    226, 227–28, 229
Lyubimov, Yuri, 78, 300–301

Macbeth (Shakespeare), 33, 142,
  149–50
Macbeth (Verdi), 33, 147, 149–50,
  160
McCracken, James, 257
Madama Butterfly (Puccini):
  performances of, 273, 275, 295
  text of, 37, 196–97, 201, 216
madness:
  bel canto scenes of, 40, 112–13,
    118, 359–60
  Dionysus and, 30, 39–40
  revolutionary music and, 307
  tragedy reborn in, 92
Maeterlinck, Maurice, 203
Magic Flute, The, see Zauberflöte,
  Die
Magnani, Anna, 328
Mahagonny, see Aufstieg und Fall der
  Stadt-Mahagonny
Mahler, Gustav:
  Fidelio produced by, 127–28
  in film score, 327
  Lied von der Erde, 129, 205
  on opera performances, 238
  Peter Hall on, 293
  symphonies of, 56, 315

Makropulos Case, The (Janáček), 221, 226–27, 228, 357
Man and Superman (Shaw), 53
Mann, Thomas, 31, 36, 272
Manon (Massenet), 14, 52, 189–90, 197
Manon Lescaut (Puccini), 52, 84, 189–90, 197, 358
Manzoni, Alessandro, 161
Mapleson, James Henry, 247
Marat, Jean-Paul, 198
marches, 58, 124, 138–39, 144, 145
Maria Stuarda (Donizetti), 118, 119
Maria Theresa, Archduchess of Austria, 209, 211
marriage, 44, 106
Marriage of Figaro, The (Beaumarchais), 100, 110
Marriage of Figaro, The (Mozart), *see Nozze di Figaro, Le* (Mozart)
Martyre de Saint Sébastien (Debussy), 75
Mascagni, Pietro:
    Cavalleria, 12, 37, 64, 72, 189, 191, 195, 244, 303, 329
    Iris, 190
    Nerone, 237
Mask of Orpheus, The (Birtwhistle), 216, 230, 231–32
Massenet, Jules:
    Cendrillon, 115
    Esclarmonde, 73
    Jongleur de Notre-Dame, 38
    Manon, 14, 52, 189–90, 197
    Roi de Lahore, 73, 242
    Thaïs, 42, 62
    Thérèse, 197
    Werther, 14, 34, 72, 191, 192, 215
Matrimonio Segreto, Il (Cimarosa), 279
Maxwell, Elsa, 323
Mazeppa (Tchaikovsky), 140, 285
Mazura, Franz, 355–56
Mazzolà, Caterino, 96
Medea (Cherubini), 320–21, 324, 325, 328–29
Medea (film), 325, 328–29
Mefistofele (Boito), 61–62, 63, 162, 250
Mehta, Zubin, 310
Meistersinger von Nürnberg, Die (Wagner):

music of, 126, 168, 173, 174, 202
    performances of, 324
    text of, 23, 173–75, 215, 246
Melba, Nellie, 249, 257
Melchior, Lauritz, 248, 251
memory, 122, 228
Mendelssohn, Felix, 131, 317
Mephistopheles, 16, 55–64, 78
Merchant of Venice, The (Shakespeare), 137
Mère Coupable, La (Beaumarchais), 209
Meredith, George, 165–66
Mérimée, Prosper, 43, 45, 51, 243, 269, 271, 289
Merry Wives of Windsor, The (Shakespeare), 36, 165
Mesmer, Franz, 105
Messel, Oliver, 261
Messiah (Handel), 66, 78
Metropolis, The (Sinclair), 248
Metropolitan Museum (New York), 247, 262
Metropolitan Opera, 246–58
    Armide, 24
    Bartered Bride, 284
    Billy Budd, 284
    Bohème, 257
    Boris Godunov, 252, 337
    Carmélites, 284
    Carmen, 250, 257, 288, 289, 333–34
    Cavalleria, 303
    centenary gala for, 257–58, 341
    Chagall murals at, 239
    Clemenza, 306–7
    concerts at, 338, 340
    design of, 247, 248–49, 254
    Don Carlos, 247, 358
    Don Giovanni, 337
    Elektra, 341, 347
    Elisir, 322
    Faust, 247–48, 249, 279
    Figaro, 305
    Fliegende Holländer, 285–86
    Frau ohne Schatten, 339
    history of, 236, 242, 246–52
    Idomeneo, 305, 307
    Italiana, 281–82
    at Lincoln Center, 239, 253–58
    Lohengrin, 248, 349–50
    Lucia, 257

Lulu, 355–56
Mahagonny, 254, 354
Manon Lescaut, 358
Mefistofele, 250
Otello, 257, 344
Parsifal, 351–52
Peter Grimes, 345–46
Prophète, 284
Rinaldo, 86
Salome, 76, 250
Samson, 257, 258
Semiramide, 257
social elitism and, 236, 242, 246–258
Tannhäuser, 348
Tosca, 303–4, 315
Tristan, 249, 251, 341, 353
Troyens, 254, 343, 349
Walküre, 308, 351
Metropolitan Opera Association, 248
Metropolitan Opera Ball, 249–50
Metropolitan Opera Club, 248
Meyerbeer, Giacomo:
    Huguenots, 71, 130, 131
    Prophète, 71–72, 131, 284
    Robert le Diable, 60, 131
    social breadth of, 131, 133, 175
    Wagner on, 136, 178
Midsummer Night's Dream, A (Britten), 15, 16, 218, 224–25, 263
Midsummer Night's Dream, A (Shakespeare), 275
Migenes-Johnson, Julia, 270
Mignon (Thomas), 189
Milanov, Zinka, 255
Miller, Jonathan, 299, 301
Milnes, Sherrill, 243, 337, 357–58
Milton, John, 67
Minton, Yvonne, 273
Moïse et Pharaon (Rossini), 293
Molière (Jean-Baptist Poquelin), 43, 212
monarchy, opera houses designed for, 238–39, 242
Monteverdi, Claudio:
    on Apollo, 15, 21, 213, 231
    classicism of, 81, 93, 95, 105, 106
    paganism in, 84, 235, 236
    Poppea, 12, 16, 32 33, 42, 66,

81–82, 84–86, 118, 215, 219, 225
    on recitative vs. lyric, 22, 223
    Ritorno, 82–84, 87, 89, 204, 349
    see also Favola D'Orfo, La
Moore, Grace, 249, 251
Mosè in Egitto (Rossini), 77, 293
Moses, Robert, 253
Moses und Aron (Schönberg), 70, 76–78, 221
Moshinsky, Elijah, 88
Mozart, Wolfgang Amadeus:
    classical-romantic transition in, 94–97, 305–7
    Clemenza, 93, 94, 95–97, 305, 306–7, 359
    Così Fan Tutte, 92, 93, 95, 97, 98, 102–5, 106, 179, 278, 284
    Cosima Wagner on, 179
    directors on, 279, 281
    Entführung, 33–34, 93, 97–99, 260–61
    Goethe on, 56, 107, 211
    Idomeneo, 84, 91–92, 93–95, 152, 261–62, 283, 305–6, 307
    influence of, 209–12, 228, 316
    on love, 87–106, 235, 239
    musical clemency in, 92, 93–94, 106–8, 123
    Rossini on, 114
    see also Don Giovanni; Nozze di Figaro, Le; Zauberflöte, Die
Muette de Portici, La (Auber), 82
Munich opera, 286, 324, 339, 348, 358
Mürger, Henri, 189, 296–97
museum, opera as, 301, 303
music:
    of bel canto opera, 109–22
    classical-romantic transition in, 96–97
    of comic opera, 111–12, 113
    as Dionysian force, 23, 24, 214
    drama vs., 104, 108, 151, 163–64, 213–14, 224, 273, 278–91, 311–13, 340
    emotional expression in, 11–12, 14–15, 16–17
    erotic impulse and, 43–47, 48–50, 52–54, 55
    as fallible human art, 21–26

music, *continued*
French vs. Italian, 52
language and, 20, 25–27, 57,
61–63, 145–46, 214, 224, 239,
273, 356
liberation through, 65
magical properties of, 111–12
modern directors and, 278–91
Nietzschean dithyramb and, 31
Orpheus as divine symbol of,
19–24, 81
realism and, 64
restitution through, 217–18
rhythm in, 115–17, 141, 216–19
in twentieth century opera, 26–29,
216–17
Mussolini, Benito, 237, 292
Mussorgsky, Modest:
Boris Godunov, 133, 140, 141–43,
144, 146, 239, 252, 274, 297,
337
historical perspective of, 141–43,
144
Khovanshchina, 133, 140–41,
143–44, 145
Mozart vs., 239
song cycle by, 337
Muti, Riccardo, 314–15
mystery, 11, 15–20, 184
mythology, 104, 106
consumerism and, 277
Grecian and German, 212, 213
political themes and, 81, 84,
95, 106, 298, 299
realistic adaptation of, 186, 187,
188
Teutonic, 230
in Wagner, 64, 167, 174, 175–76,
185, 186, 202, 207, 212, 316

Nabucco (Verdi), 147, 158
Naked City (Weegee), 251–52
Napoleon I, Emperor of France, 75,
129, 133, 301
Napoleon II, Duc de Reichstadt, 129,
131
Napoleon III, Emperor of France,
238, 246
nature:
cycles of, 83, 172–74, 195, 216, 266
fickleness of, 225

in filmed opera, 266
gods as forces of, 82
hostility of, 23, 138
industrial economy and, 168, 180
love bond and, 106
in modern opera, 220, 225
musical depiction of, 14, 15, 87–88,
119
onomatopoeia of, 200
orchestral song-cycles on, 205–6
production techniques and, 241–42
as romantic wisdom, 306
women and, 137
Nazis, 296, 327
neoclassicism, 313, 327
Nero, 81
Nerone (Mascagni), 237
Nestroy, Johann Nepomuk, 357
Newman, Ernest, 265
New York City Opera, 292
Nietzsche, Friedrich:
on Bizet, 290
Brecht's rejection of, 226
on Dionysian element in opera,
30–34, 67, 78, 136, 212, 214,
230, 306
on operatic origins in Greek tragedy, 67, 208, 209, 282
on Wagner, 25, 185, 209
Nilsson, Birgit:
as Brünnhilde, 259, 316, 338
as Dyer's Wife, 339
as Elektra, 338, 339, 340–41, 342
as Elettra, 306
as Isolde, 341, 353–54
opera defined by, 308
recordings of, 266, 316–17
as Salome, 339, 340
as Tosca, 332–33
as Turandot, 338
vocal texture of, 338
Nilsson, Christine, 247, 249–50
noise:
electronic synthesis and, 207
music condemned as, 221, 223
realistic music as, 199, 216
Nono, Luigi, 314
Norma (Bellini):
music of, 120, 122
performances of, 237, 303, 323–24,
328

text of, 30, 31, 66, 84, 90, 109, 117–18, 122, 131, 180, 236, 324, 328, 359
Norma (Soumet), 328
Norman, Jessye, 349
Nose, The (Gogol), 220
Nose, The (Shostakovitch), 220
Notre Dame cathedral, 239
Nozze de Figaro, Le (Mozart):
  influence of, 51, 96, 110, 209–10, 211
  music of, 15, 97, 99–100, 118–19, 123, 125–26
  performances of, 281, 305, 309
  text of, 42, 44, 93, 94, 97–103, 105, 106, 123, 177, 226

Oberon (Weber), 292–93
Obraztsova, Elena, 303, 333–34
Oedipus complex, 193, 209
Oedipus Rex (Stravinsky), 76, 226, 228–29
Offenbach, Jacques:
  Belle Hélène, 62
  Contes d'Hoffmann, 26, 34, 215, 287, 358
  hedonism in, 239
  Orphée, 24–26, 231, 241
  Périchole, 34
Onassis, Aristotle, 323, 329
onomatopoeia, 46, 200
opera:
  comedy in, 32, 35, 78, 103, 111–13, 115–16, 118–19, 129, 137–38, 146, 148, 153–55, 162, 165–66, 221, 228, 263
  divine vs. human in, 81–86
  effeminacy vs. virility in, 243–44, 352
  French, 14, 52, 60, 72–73
  German, 13–14, 52, 72
  gods of, 16, 25, 66
  human potentialities embodied in, 32
  Italian, 14, 52, 63, 72
  language vs. music, 20, 25–27, 57, 61–63, 145–46, 214, 224, 239, 273, 356
  material splendor of, 59, 168, 180, 181, 196, 277, 236, 237, 239, 274, 277, 303

modern directors' doubts on, 278–80, 282, 283
  musical force celebrated in, 13–14, 26
  mystery in, 11, 19–20, 184
  oratorio vs., 66–71, 72, 75, 76–77, 78, 221, 225, 348–49, 354
  origins of, 19, 30, 67, 82, 136, 173, 194, 208, 216, 230, 240, 282
  religion in, 66, 71–76, 81, 128–29, 131, 152, 236–37, 360
  ritual in, 30, 68, 69, 90–91, 94, 95, 153–55, 209, 218
  Russian, 133, 140–45
  social values opposed by, 12–13, 31–32, 235–45
  static characters in, 88–89
  in twentieth century, 26–29, 207, 216, 222, 226, 315
  Viennese, 78, 128, 238, 246, 303, 308, 312, 331, 339–40
  see also performance; political themes; specific movements in opera
Opéra, Paris:
  design of, 238–42, 246
  performances at, 60, 171, 172, 303, 312, 323, 328, 340–41
opera buffa, 309
Opéra Comique, 279
Opera Factory, 277
opera houses, 235–42, 265
  design of, 31, 170, 238–42, 247–49, 254, 260, 324
  social elitism and, 235–39, 242
operetta, 24–26, 34
Ophuls, Max, 266–67
Orange Festival, 259, 353
oratorio:
  devotional aspect of, 66, 69, 70, 72
  Faust as, 56
  Fidelio and, 127, 128–29
  opera vs., 66–71, 72, 75–78, 221, 225, 348–49, 354
  Stravinsky and, 228, 229
orchestra, operatic:
  conductors and, 308, 309, 310, 311, 315, 316, 317
  in modern opera, 220
  Wagner and, 15, 25, 40, 136, 170, 178–79, 203, 205

Oresteia (Aeschylus), 282, 283
Orfeo (Monteverdi), see *Favola d'Orfeo, La*
Orfeo ed Euridice (Gluck):
  performances of, 263–64, 276, 324
  text of, 15, 20–23, 24, 26, 90–91, 127, 171, 231
Orfeo ed Euridice (Haydn), 23, 24
Orlando (Handel), 278
Orphée aux Enfers (Offenbach), 24–26, 231, 240
Orpheus:
  as divine hero, 14, 15, 16, 19–24, 27–29
  as fallible human artist, 21–26
  in modern opera, 28–29
Otello (Rossini), 113–14, 359
Otello (Verdi):
  music of, 32, 45, 149, 162–64, 165
  performances of, 238, 257, 283, 287–88, 311, 343–44, 354
  text of, 33, 113, 139, 147, 148, 161–64, 165, 166, 173, 194, 215, 360
Othello (Shakespeare), 32, 33, 113, 162–64, 283, 287
outdoor performances, 259–64
Ozawa, Seiji, 78

Paër, Ferdinando, 127
paganism:
  Christianity vs., 19, 38, 172–74, 185
  of emotional regression, 190
  Handel's censure of, 354
  human appetites personified by, 38, 42, 84, 235
  in Monteverdi, 84, 235, 236
  opera based on, 20, 165, 239
  in Renaissance, 19, 20, 173–74, 190
  rituals of, 11, 69
Pagano, Mauro, 302–3
Pagliacci, I (Leoncavallo), 189, 194, 195, 315, 354
Palais Garnier, 73, 267–68, 277
Palestrina, Giovanni Pierluigi da, 60
Palestrina (Pfitzner), 222
Palladio, Andrea, 268, 299
pantheism, 66, 95, 205, 306, 320
Parade (Satie), 296
Paris Opéra, see Opéra, Paris
parody:

  in *Così*, 103
  in *Macbeth*, 150
  in *Mahagonny*, 225
  by Offenbach, 34
  of Orpheus, 39
  by Strauss, 207–8, 214
  of Wagner, 40, 172, 339, 357
Parsifal (Wagner):
  film of, 272–73, 282, 290
  influence of, 202, 203, 204, 206, 235
  performances of, 170, 202, 273, 282, 313, 319, 351, 352
  text of, 72, 167, 168, 169, 174, 175, 180, 181, 183–85, 195, 202, 203
Pasolini, Pier Paolo, 325, 328–29
passacaglias, 218, 224
patricide, 94
Pavarotti, Luciano, 299, 300, 322, 357
Pears, Peter, 344, 345
Pêcheurs de Perles, Les (Bizet), 73
Pelléas et Mélisande (Debussy), 203–4, 239, 312, 313, 357
Penderecki, Krzysztof, 56
Pénélope (Fauré), 204–5
Penelope (*Ritorno*), 349
performance:
  aging in, 357–58
  conductors in, 308–17
  generational differences in, 343–46
  historical superimposition in, 292–99, 302
  innovative staging in, 274–78
  physical acting in, 347–60
  resistance to, 324–27, 352–53, 354, 356, 358–59
  singers' interpretations in, 318–46
  tradition in, 313–15, 316
  see also *specific artists, opera houses and operas*
Peri, Jacopo, 213, 276
Périchole, La (Offenbach), 34
Peter Grimes (Britten), 16, 26–27, 39–40, 235, 344–46
Petite Messe Solenelle (Rossini), 71
Petrarch, 153
Pfitzner, Hans, 221
Phantom of the Opera, The (Leroux), 240–42
pianissimi, 338, 351, 358
Picasso, Pablo, 315, 354

Pintilie, Lucian, 290–92
Plato, 19–20, 181, 197
political themes:
  of democratic freedom, 99, 126–32
  directorial interpretations and,
    292–99, 301–7
  mythology replaced by, 81, 84, 95,
    106
  in Verdi's operas, 129, 132, 153,
    156–58
  in Wagnerian opera, 168, 175–76,
    235, 290, 298, 299
  see also historical opera; history;
    revolution
Poliuto (Donizetti), 323
Ponchielli, Amilcare, 12, 162, 329
Ponnelle, Jean-Pierre:
  films of, 281, 299–300
  formalism of, 280–82
  operas staged by, 262, 281–82,
    285–87, 304–7
Pons, Lily, 251
Ponselle, Rosa, 243
Porgy (Heyward), 27, 28
Porgy and Bess (Gershwin), 27–28,
  66, 215, 267
Poulenc, Francis, 14, 216, 222–23,
  284
prehistory, 136, 298, 300
Preminger, Otto, 267
Prénom: Carmen, 291
Prévost d'Exiles, Antoine-François,
  189
Price, Leontyne, 330, 359
Price, Margaret, 317
Prima Donna, The (Crawford), 248
Prince Igor (Borodin), 133, 140
"Procurer's Song" (Wedekind), 228
Prokofiev, Sergey, 56, 133, 144–45,
  261, 294
Prophète, Le (Meyerbeer), 71–72,
  131, 284
Proust, Marcel, 312
Prowse, Philip, 88–89
psychodrama, 285–86, 300–301
Puccini, Giacomo:
  Bohème, 16, 189, 191, 195–96,
    257, 295–97, 354
  Butterfly, 37, 196–97, 201, 216,
    273, 275, 295
  Fanciulla, 186–87
  Gianni Schicchi, 199, 200, 321

late operas of, 199–201
Manon Lescaut, 52, 84, 189–90,
  197, 358
music vs. drama in, 186
realistic opera of, 186, 189–90, 194,
  195–97, 199–200
Suor Angelica, 199, 200
Tabarro, 37, 189, 199–200
Tosca, 31, 37, 74–75, 82, 194–95,
  201, 237, 292, 303–4, 315,
  325–28, 330–33
Trittico, 37, 189, 199–200
Turandot, 13, 197, 200–201,
  338
Purcell, Henry, 133–34
Puritani di Scozia, I (Bellini), 39,
  120–21, 131, 236
Pushkin, Aleksandr, 191

Queen of Spades, The (Tchaikovsky),
  144, 191, 193

Rachmaninov, Sergey, 224
Racine, Jean, 195, 305
Raimondi, Ruggero, 78, 269, 270,
  336–37
Rake's Progress, The (Stravinsky):
  performances of, 28, 278, 297
  text of, 28, 39, 42, 210, 216, 226,
    228–30, 231
Ramey, Samuel, 243
Rank, Otto, 193
Rappresentatione di Anima, e di
  Corpo, La (Cavalieri), 66
Ravel, Maurice, 14–15, 216, 220–21,
  226
realism:
  artistic protagonists and, 194–97
  criticism of, 64
  of drama, 169, 172
  heroism rejected in, 186–87, 188,
    190, 197
  pleasure repressed by, 191–93
  political revolution and, 197–98
  Puccini and, 186, 189–90, 194,
    195–97, 199–200
  religion and, 192, 194, 195, 200
recordings, 257, 265–66, 309, 310,
  315, 316–17, 325, 332

religion:
  deified artist and, 168–69, 172–74,
    184, 185
  in opera vs. oratorio, 66–78, 128–29
  in realistic opera, 182, 194, 195,
    200
  in Verdi, 158–61, 164, 168–69
  see also Christianity; paganism
Renaissance:
  cultural rebirth in, 200, 221
  Greek tragedy resurrected in, 20,
    25, 167
  Hugo's vision of, 299
  music of, 15, 224
  paganism revived in, 19, 20,
    173–74, 190
Requiem (Berlioz), 161
Requiem (Verdi), 147–48, 150,
  158–65, 168–69
revolution:
  directorial technique and, 292–94,
    297–98, 302, 305–7
  failure of, 207
  French, 197–98, 294, 298
  music of, 216, 222
  opera as means of, 168, 176, 197,
    199, 312–13
  performance tempo and, 312
  realism and, 197–98
Reynolds, Joshua, 359
Rheingold, Das (Wagner):
  music of, 12, 13, 92, 170, 176, 179
  performances of, 311, 312
  text of, 20, 82, 138, 168, 175–77,
    180
rhythm, 115–17, 141, 216–19
Richard III (Shakespeare), 141–42
Riegel, Kenneth, 306
Rienzi (Wagner), 292
Rigoletto (Verdi):
  music of, 147, 154, 243
  performances of, 281, 299–301, 315
  text of, 13, 34, 51, 90, 147, 153–54,
    155, 156
Rimbaud, Arthur, 171
Rinaldo (Handel), 86, 88
Ring des Nibelungen, Der (Wagner):
  performances of, 176, 282, 298,
    299, 310, 312, 313, 316
  text of, 82, 108, 138, 168, 175–76,
    202, 208, 211–13, 324
  Wagner's rehearsals for, 31

see also Götterdämmerung; Rhein-
  gold; Siegfried; Walküre
Ringstrasse, 238, 246
Ritorno d'Ulisse in Patria, Il
  (Monteverdi), 82–84, 87, 89, 204,
    349
Robert le Diable (Meyerbeer), 60, 131
Roberto Devereux (Donizetti), 118
Rockefeller, John D., III, 253
Rodelinda (Handel), 87–88
Roi de Lahore, Le (Massenet), 73,
    242
Roi d'Ys, Le (Lalo), 74, 203
Roi s'Amuse, Le (Hugo), 299
roles, archetypal, 330–46
Romani, Felice, 118
romanticism:
  bel canto and, 109–22
  bohemianism and, 295–96
  classicism and, 76, 138, 268, 269,
    314
  Dionysus and, 30, 39
  on genius, 122
  Gluck revisions and, 91–92
  heroes of, 229
  modern opera and, 30, 285, 312
  Mozart's transition to, 94–97,
    305–7
  reconversions to, 198–99
  religion and, 30, 294
  rhythms in, 115, 116–17
  sensuality in, 43–44, 51, 191–93
  violence of nature in, 23
Romeo and Juliet (Shakespeare),
  117–18
Roméo et Juliette (Berlioz), 118, 239
Roméo et Juliette (Gounod), 117–18,
  179
Ronconi, Luca, 301–3
Ronde, La, 266
Roosevelt, Theodore, 295
Rosenkavalier, Der (Strauss), 209–11,
  246, 274, 284, 358
Rosi, Francesco, 269–71, 273
Rossini, Gioacchino:
  Armida, 88
  Barbiere di Siviglia, 14, 36, 51, 77,
    110–11, 113, 119, 177, 196, 281,
    300, 305
  Beethoven vs., 245
  Cenerentola, 114, 115, 119, 281
  Comte Ory, 34, 115–16

directors on, 279, 281
Donna del Lago, 12, 119, 120
Gazza Ladra, 129
Guillaume Tell, 129–30, 131
Italiana en Algeri, 16, 32, 38,
    114–15, 119, 130, 281–82, 314
Mosè in Egitto, 77, 293
on Mozart, 114
Otello, 113–14, 359
Petite Messe Solenelle, 71
rhythmic vocal line of, 115, 116–17
Semiramide, 71, 116–17, 257
Tancredi, 116
Turco in Italia, 328
Viaggio, 115–16, 129, 314
rubato, 313–14
Russell, Ken, 78, 278, 279, 295–97,
    314, 323
Russian opera, 133, 140–45
Ryan, Mrs. Nin, 247
Rysanek, Leonie:
    roles of, 259, 333, 338–42, 348–52
    vocal texture of, 338

sacrificial rites, 30, 68–69, 90–91,
    94–95, 141, 154–55, 209
St. Matthew Passion (Bach), 78
Saint-Saëns, Camille, 66, 69–71, 76,
    78, 257, 258, 343, 349
Salome (Strauss):
    music of, 284, 310, 360
    performances of, 207–8, 250, 279,
        310, 339–40, 349, 354
    text of, 13, 16, 31, 37, 52, 75–76,
        84, 85, 184, 200, 207–8, 283,
        310
Salzburg Festival, 305, 309, 310–11,
    348
Samson (Handel), 66–70, 76, 88, 354
Samson Agonistes (Milton), 67
Samson et Dalila (Saint-Saëns), 66,
    69–71, 76, 78, 257, 258, 343,
    349
Sand, George, 359
San Francisco Opera, 259, 285–86,
    339
Santuzza (Cavalleria Rusticana), 303,
    329
São Carlos theater (Lisbon), 237
Satie, Erik, 296
Satyagraha (Glass), 232
satyrs, 30, 82, 165, 173

Saul (Handel), 278
scene design, 88–89, 131, 249,
    260–63, 310–11, 324, 334
Scènes de la vie de Bohème (Murger),
    296–97
Schaubühne Theater Company (West
    Berlin), 282
Schenk, Otto, 348
Schiller, Friedrich, 140, 151–52, 301
Schlesinger, John, 274, 279–80, 287
Schneider-Siemssen, Günther, 310,
    311
Schönberg, Arnold:
    atonal music of, 230
    Erwartung, 206, 211
    Gurre-Lieder, 205–6
    Moses und Aron, 70, 76–78, 221
    on musical limitation, 217, 219
    on revolution, 222
Schopenhauer, Arthur, 188, 229
Schuman, William, 253
Schumann, Robert, 56
Schweigsame Frau, Die (Strauss), 221
Scott, Walter, 112–13
Scottish Opera, 292, 293
Scotto, Renata, 307
Segreto di Susanna, Il (Wolf-Ferrari),
    191
Sellars, Peter, 278, 279, 293
Semele (Handel), 45, 67, 68–69, 89
Semiramide (Rossini), 71, 116–17,
    257
Sendak, Maurice, 261
Senso, 327
Serban, Andrei, 292
Serenade (Cain), 243–45
Serse (Handel), 12, 86, 87, 118
Shakespeare, William:
    comedy of, 78, 137, 263
    Hamlet, 33, 39, 47, 131
    Henry IV, 140
    history plays of, 140, 141
    Lear, 142, 301, 342
    Macbeth, 33, 142, 149–50
    Merchant of Venice, 137
    Merry Wives, 36, 165
    Midsummer Night's Dream, 275
    Othello, 32, 33, 113, 162–64, 283,
        287
    Richard III, 141–42
    Romeo and Juliet, 117–18
    speaking techniques for, 283, 284

Shakespeare, William, *continued*
  in translation, 284
  Verdi vs., 147, 154
  Winter's Tale, 137
Shaw, George Bernard, 53, 78, 107–8,
  149, 312
Shelley, Percy Bysshe, 320, 360
Shostakovitch, Dmitri, 219–20, 321
*sieben Todsünden der Kleinbürger,
  Die* (Weill and Brecht), 52
Siegfried (Wagner):
  music of, 14, 178–79
  performances of, 249, 350
  text of, 167, 168, 175, 178–80, 208,
    212, 215
Siepi, Cesare, 336
silence, 158, 216, 221, 349–52, 357
Simon Boccanegra (Verdi):
  performances of, 238, 357–58
  text of, 152–53, 158–59, 162, 246
Sinclair, Upton, 248, 250
Sinopoli, Giuseppe, 301, 315
Slater, Montagu, 345
Sloan, George, 255
Smetana, Bedřich, 216, 266, 284
Söderström, Elisabeth, 356–57
Solti, Georg, 265, 316, 340
Sonnambula, La (Bellini), 117, 120,
  121, 122, 327
Sophocles, 30, 76, 90, 92, 208
Sorrows of Young Werther, The
  (Goethe), 191, 192
Sources of Music, The (Chagall), 253
Soyer, Roger, 336
Spontini, Gasparo, 327
Stalin, Joseph, 297, 301
standees, 256–57
Stanford, Charles, 260
Stassov, Vladimir, 143–44
Stein, Gertrude, 314
Stein, Peter, 282–84, 287–88, 290
Stendhal (Marie-Henri Beyle), 38, 129
Stiffelio (Verdi), 72
Stockhausen, Karlheinz, 28–29, 232,
  235
Stratas, Teresa, 304, 354–56
Strauss, Johann, 34, 38, 211
Strauss, Richard:
  Ägyptische Helena, 62–63, 210
  Arabella, 181
  Ariadne auf Naxos, 30–31, 194,
    211, 212–14, 301

Capriccio, 213, 260
Daphne, 14, 82, 213
Elektra, 14, 30, 32, 39, 90, 92,
  208–9, 306, 338–42, 359
Feuersnot, 207, 246
Four Last Songs, 310
Frau ohne Schatten, 83, 88,
  211–12, 215, 338–39
Heldenleben, 178
  on history of opera, 212, 214, 215
  Iphigénie en Tauride revised by, 91,
    92
  modern Wagnerian performance
    and, 316
  Mozart's influence on, 209–12
  on musical realism, 64
  as parodist, 207–8, 214
  Rosenkavalier, 209–11, 246, 274,
    284, 358
  Salome, 13, 16, 31, 37, 52, 75–76,
    84, 85, 184, 200, 207–8, 250,
    279, 283–84, 310, 339–40, 354,
    360
  Schlagobers, 212
  Schweigsame Frau, 221
  Wagner and, 182, 207–14
  waltzes by, 211
Stravinsky, Igor:
  Firebird, 239
  modernity of, 314
  Oedipus, 76, 226, 228–29
  Rake's Progress, 28, 39, 42, 210,
    216, 226, 228–30, 231, 278, 297
Strehler, Giorgio, 238
Suetonius, 306
Suor Angelica (Puccini), 199, 200
Sutherland, Joan, 88, 118, 257,
  359–60
Syberberg, Hans Jürgen, 272–73, 282,
  287, 290
Symons, Arthur, 184–85
symphonies, 56, 95, 97, 129, 218–19,
  244–45, 315

Tabarro, Il (Puccini), 37, 189,
  199–200
Talvela, Martti, 337
Tamerlano (Handel), 86, 88–89
Tancredi (Rossini), 116
Tanglewood, Berkshire Festival at, 78
Tannhäuser und der Sängerkrieg auf

Wartburg (Wagner):
music of, 15, 167–68, 173
performances of, 60, 171, 311, 348
text of, 23, 42, 91, 167–68, 171–76, 243, 352
Tarkovsky, Andrei, 274, 297, 337
Tchaikovsky, Modest, 191
Tchaikovsky, Peter Ilyich, 140, 144, 191–93, 285
Te Kanawa, Kiri, 256
tempo, 46–50, 142, 311–13, 315–16, 351
tenors, 160, 343–46
Teorema, 328
Teutonism, 61, 144, 168, 230–31, 290, 298, 324
Thaïs (France), 62
Thaïs (Massenet), 42, 62
Thérèse (Massenet), 197
Thomas, Ambroise, 33, 39, 189
Tiefland (d'Albert), 188–89
Tiepolo, Giovanni Battista, 327
time:
history and, 123–24
modern conductors on, 311–12, 314, 316
musical measurement of, 226–27
reversal of, 228–29
Wagner's suspension of, 185
Tippett, Michael, 275
Tolstoy, Leo, 144, 145
Tone, Franchot, 243
Tosca (Puccini):
performances of, 292, 303–4, 315, 325–27, 328, 330–33
text of, 31, 37, 74–75, 82, 194, 195, 201, 237, 323
Toscanini, Arturo, 238
traditional performance, 313–16
tragedy, 92, 192
comedy vs., 103, 113, 138, 146, 153–55
irreversibility of, 108, 149, 218, 229
see also Greek tragedy
Traubel, Helen, 248
Traviata, La (Verdi):
film of, 273–74, 303, 304, 355
music of, 148, 155
performances of, 294, 312, 327–28
text of, 13, 14, 34, 84, 147, 153, 154–55, 156, 165, 196, 236, 301
Tristan (Henze), 207

Tristan und Isolde (Wagner):
Britten's parody of, 40–41
music of, 12, 53–54, 91, 166, 167, 172, 179, 181, 182, 189, 203, 210, 360
other operas vs., 193, 203, 205–8, 210, 225
performances of, 175, 249, 285, 315–17, 341, 348, 352–54
recordings of, 265, 316–17
text of, 11, 13, 20, 31, 36, 42, 52–54, 66, 67, 83, 97, 117, 167–69, 175, 181–83, 187–88, 190, 198, 221, 229, 239
Trittico, Il (Puccini), 37, 189, 199–200
Triumph of Music, The (Chagall), 253–54
Trovatore, Il (Verdi):
music of, 126, 150–51, 283
text of, 23–24, 154, 159, 165, 292
Troyens, Les (Berlioz):
music of, 124, 135–37, 138–39, 178
performances of, 254, 343, 349
text of, 42, 58, 91, 132, 133–38, 140, 142, 161
Truman, Harry S., 295
Turandot (Puccini), 13, 197, 200–201, 338
Turco in Italia, Il (Rossini), 328
Turn of the Screw, The (Britten), 16, 216, 224
twentieth century opera, 26–29, 207, 216, 222, 226, 315

Ubu Roi (Jarry), 275
Under the Hill (Beardsley), 172

van Dam, José, 269, 349
Vanderbilt, Mrs. Frederick, 250
Vanderbilt family, 246, 249, 251, 255, 256
Veblen, Thorstein, 253
Venice Opera, 28, 88
Verdi, Giuseppe:
Aida, 45, 66, 72, 135, 147, 148, 153, 156–58, 159, 161, 279, 218–82, 286, 301, 302–3, 324, 331
Ballo in Maschera, 51–52, 148, 153, 155–56, 159, 160, 180

Verdi, Giuseppe, *continued*
  Don Carlos, 72, 135, 147, 148,
    156–57, 159, 180, 247, 285,
    301–2, 303, 309, 325, 358
  Ernani, 148–49, 161, 180, 301, 302
  Forza del Destino, 139–40, 147,
    148, 156, 159, 173
  historical perspective of, 139–40
  late operas of, 148, 161–66
  Luisa Miller, 147, 151–52, 196
  lyricism in, 197
  Macbeth, 33, 147, 149–50, 160
  Nabucco, 147, 158
  political themes of, 129, 132, 153,
    156–58
  religion in, 158–61, 164, 168–69
  Requiem, 147, 148, 150, 158–61,
    162–65, 168–69
  Rigoletto, 13, 34, 51, 90, 147,
    153–56, 243, 281, 299–300, 301,
    315
  Simon Boccanegra, 152–53,
    158–59, 162, 238, 246, 357–58
  Stiffelio, 72
  Traviata, 13, 14, 34, 84, 147, 148,
    153–56, 165, 196, 236, 273–74,
    294, 301, 303–4, 355
  Trovatore, 23–24, 150–51, 154,
    159, 165, 283, 292
  Vespri Siciliani, 246
  vocal soloists in, 160–62
  see also Falstaff; Otello
verismo:
  agenda of, 186, 198, 201
  in performance, 315, 329
  rougher Dionysian world of, 36–37,
    150, 189, 191
  see also realism
Verlaine, Paul, 171
Vespri Siciliani, I (Verdi), 246
Vestale, La (Spontini), 327
Viaggio a Reims, Il (Rossini), 115–16,
  129, 314
Vick, Graham, 275, 295
Vickers, Jon, 88, 321–22, 324,
  343–46, 351–54
Viennese opera, 78, 128, 238, 246,
  303, 308, 312, 336, 339–40
Vinay, Ramón, 287–88
violence, 23, 150, 209, 215–16, 239
Virgil, 133, 136, 137–38, 142
Visconti, Luchino, 294, 303, 327–28

Vishnevskaya, Galina, 331–32
"Vissi d'arte" (Tosca), 75, 330,
  332–33
Voix Humaine, La (Poulenc), 14,
  223

Wagner, Cosima, 179–80
Wagner, (Wilhelm) Richard:
  art as power in, 168, 170, 176, 180,
    185
  on art of transition, 274, 339
  Bayreuth theater of, 29, 31, 167,
    168, 170, 185
  conductors' tempo in, 312
  deified artist of, 168–69, 171–74,
    184, 185, 204
  filmed opera and, 272–73, 282, 290,
    311
  Fliegende Holländer, 56, 167,
    169–70, 205, 285–87, 299
  on Greek tragedy, 30, 67, 324
  heroic myth in, 167, 168, 186, 216
  heroines in, 138, 186, 206, 352
  historical perspective of, 138, 139,
    168, 175–76, 185
  Iphigénie en Aulide revised by, 91,
    92
  on Italian music vs. French music,
    52
  Lohengrin, 15, 67, 84, 168, 170–71,
    187, 215, 242, 248, 311, 324,
    349–50, 357
  Mann on, 31
  Meistersinger, 23, 126, 168,
    173–75, 202, 246, 324
  on Meyerbeer, 136, 178
  modern directors on, 44, 176, 282,
    298, 313, 352
  music vs. drama in, 167, 169–71,
    174, 177–78, 179, 180, 181–83
  myth in, 64, 167, 174–76, 185–86,
    202, 207, 212, 316
  Nietzsche on, 25
  orchestra in, 15, 25, 40, 170,
    178–79, 203, 205
  political themes in, 168, 175–76,
    235, 290, 298, 299
  revolutionary music of, 312–13
  Rheingold, 12, 13, 20, 82, 92, 168,
    170, 175–77, 179–80, 311, 312
  Rienzi, 292
  Ring, 31, 82, 108, 138, 168,

175–76, 202, 208, 211–13, 282, 298–99, 310, 312–13, 316, 324
Schopenhauer's negation and, 188, 229
Siegfried, 14, 167–68, 175, 178–80, 208, 212, 215, 249, 350
on singing, 287
Stravinsky on, 76
successors influenced by, 202–14, 224, 230, 313
Tannhäuser, 15, 23, 42, 60, 91, 167–68, 171–76, 243, 311, 348, 352
theatrical lighting and, 241
Vickers's disapproval of, 352
Walküre, 32, 168, 173–74, 177–78, 180, 186, 259, 308, 338, 351
on waltzes, 211
see also *Götterdämmerung*; *Parsifal*; *Tristan und Isolde*
Wagner, Siegfried, 202
Wagner, Wieland:
on *Parsifal*, 313, 352
on *Ring*, 176, 298
scenic designs of, 324, 334
on *Tristan*, 44
Waiting for Godot (Becket), 314
Waldsmann, Maria, 160
Walesa, Lech, 297
Walküre, Die (Wagner):
music of, 177–78, 179, 181
performances of, 259, 308, 338, 351
text of, 32, 168, 173–74, 177–78, 180, 186, 208, 352
Wallenstein's Camp (Schiller), 140
waltzes, 211
War and Peace (Prokofiev), 133, 144–45
Watteau, Antoine, 261, 303, 336
Weber, Carl Maria
Freischütz, 13, 55–56, 120, 216, 225, 238
Oberon, 292–93
We Come to the River (Henze), 235
Wedekind, 228, 314, 355
Weegee, 251–52
Weill, Kurt:
Dreigroschenoper, 27, 225
Mahagonny, 27, 38, 42, 212, 216, 225–26, 228, 254, 354, 356
sieben Todsünden, 52

"Wein, Das" (Berg), 38
Welsh National Opera:
Butterfly, 295
Carmen, 290
Fidelio, 297–98
Makropolous Case, 357
Otello, 283, 288
Tamerlano, 88–89
Wernicke, Herbert, 286
Werther (Massenet), 14, 34, 72, 191, 192, 215
West Side Story (Bernstein), 118, 256
Wharton, Edith, 247, 250
Whitman, Walt, 254
Wilde, Oscar, 171, 207
Wilson, Robert, 235
Winckelmann, Johann Joachim, 91
Windgassen, Wolfgang, 265, 317
Winston, Harry, 258
Winter's Tale, The (Shakespeare), 137
Wixell, Ingvar, 281, 288–300
Wolf-Ferrari, Ermanno, 191
Wood, Peter, 261, 336–37
Wozzeck (Berg), 15, 26, 216, 217–19, 313, 348

Zandonai, Riccardo, 187–88
Zauberflöte, Die (Mozart):
music of, 12, 44, 45, 56, 106–7, 225, 288
performances of, 108, 262, 271–72, 280
revisions of, 107–8, 235
text of, 14, 66, 93, 98, 105–8, 166, 179, 211, 230, 237, 239
Zeffirelli, Franco:
Alcina, 88
Bohème, 257, 296, 354
Callas and, 327, 328
Cavalleria Rusticana, 303
Don Giovanni, 303, 336
films of, 273–74, 303–4, 354–55
Falstaff, 303
on Lyubimov's *Rigoletto*, 301
Norma, 303
Otello, 238, 344
Tosca, 303–4
Zinovieff, Peter, 231–32
Zola, Émile, 187